A FIELD
GUIDE
TO GRAD
SCHOOL

Jessica McCrory Calarco

A FIELD GUIDE TO GRAD SCHOOL

Uncovering the Hidden Curriculum

PRINCETON UNIVERSITY PRESS

PRINCETON AND OXFORD

Requests for permission to reproduce material from this work should be sent to permissions@press.princeton.edu

Published by Princeton University Press
41 William Street, Princeton, New Jersey 08540
6 Oxford Street, Woodstock, Oxfordshire OX20 1TR

press.princeton.edu

ISBN (pbk.) 978-0-691-20109-2
ISBN (e-book) 978-0-691-20110-8

British Library Cataloging-in-Publication Data is available

Editorial: Meagan Levinson and Jacqueline Delaney
Production Editorial: Jenny Wolkowicki
Cover design: Chris Ferrante
Production: Erin Suydam
Publicity: Kathryn Stevens and Maria Whelan
Copyeditor: Joseph Dahm

This book has been composed in Arno

Printed on acid-free paper. ∞

Printed in the United States of America

10 9 8 7 6 5 4 3 2 1

To all the mentors
who have helped me uncover
the hidden curriculum of grad school
and academia as a whole

CONTENTS

ACKNOWLEDGMENTS

I didn't have a field guide to get me through grad school, but I did have a team of mentors who helped me uncover the hidden curriculum and who have continued to help me navigate academia as a whole. This book, like my academic career more generally, would not have been possible without their advice and support. And this book is my effort to pay it forward—to share with you the insights they've shared with me.

As an undergrad at Brown University, I stumbled into sociology, not knowing what it was but enamored with the first two courses I took (Sociology of Education and American Society) my freshman year. The professors I met in those courses, John Modell and Michael White, were critical mentors for me in so many ways. In their courses, I learned the concept of the "hidden curriculum" and about the inequalities that exist and persist in schools. I learned to see social problems as structural problems and to recognize how research can inform good policies. Those professors also encouraged me to consider a PhD for grad school—before that, I thought I'd maybe be headed to law school instead. Outside of the classroom, Professor Carl Kaestle gave me a chance to see faculty life from the inside. As his research assistant, I got to help with editing manuscripts, collecting data, and juggling the demands of teaching, research, and service. Without that kind of "insider" experience, I don't think I would have ever considered an academic career.

As a grad student at the University of Pennsylvania, I knew where I wanted to get (a job as a professor), but not exactly how to get there or what to do along the way. Thankfully, I found a terrific team of mentors who told me things I didn't know to ask and helped me keep the imposter syndrome at bay. Annette Lareau has opened so many doors for me and helped me choose which ones to go through when the options left me feeling overwhelmed.

Annette's thoughtful feedback on manuscripts, her patience in talking through ideas, and her tireless advocacy and encouragement have been a tremendous source of support in my career. Grace Kao has never been shy about sharing her knowledge of academia and its downsides, and her frank advice to "publish or perish" guided me from day one at Penn. Working with Grace and other students in the "Grace Space" helped me develop my research skills in a hands-on, interactive way. I learned that I could turn not only to my professors for support but also to other grad students as well. That includes my coauthor Sebastian Cherng, my office mates Ruth Burke, Monica Grant, Caroline Sten Hartnett, Radha Modi, Kristin Turney, and Junhow Wei, and my writing group buddies Liz Lee, Keri Monteleone, and Laura Napolitano. Melissa Wilde, in turn, taught me to appreciate the importance of clarity and brevity and consistency in academic writing and to approach the writing process systematically and with careful attention to the logic and structure of the argument. Along those lines, the courses I took as a grad student taught me so much about what it means to do good research, how to think theoretically rather than just empirically, and what to expect in an academic career. That included ethnography with Annette Lareau, David Grazian, and Stanton Wortham, statistics with Paul Allison and Bill Bielby, research design with Melissa Wilde, theory with Randall Collins, paper writing with Robin Leidner, and a proseminar on academic publishing with Jerry Jacobs.

As a faculty member at Indiana University, I've been lucky to find so many great mentors to help me navigate this phase of my career. The department chairs I've worked under (Jane McLeod, Eliza Pavalko, and Brian Powell) guided me to and through the tenure process and continue to share knowledge of academia, constructive feedback on my work, and regular encouragement to keep going on the difficult days. Jane, Eliza, and Brian have also advocated for me and my career in so many ways, writing letters of support for grants and awards, connecting me with other scholars and opportunities outside my department, and helping me think through challenges I wasn't sure how to tackle on my own. My other department colleagues have also been so much more than colleagues, commiserating about the challenges of balancing academia and parenthood, offering feedback on manuscripts, strategizing about research projects and teaching-related challenges, and helping me understand the inner workings of the university as an organization with its own priorities and goals.

As a teacher and a mentor, I have also learned so much from my students. Having taught well over a thousand students at IU, I can't list them all here, but I'm especially grateful to the students who've collaborated with me on manuscripts, worked with me on my own projects, and assisted me in the classroom. In the context of this book, I am also deeply indebted to Indiana University grad student Katie Beardall, University of Pennsylvania grad student Marcus Wright, and former Penn State grad student Duane McCrory for reading drafts of this book and for offering such insightful feedback on those drafts.

As a writer, I recognize the value that good editing brings to any project, and I am so grateful for the support I've received from Meagan Levinson, Jacqueline Delaney, and the rest of the editorial team at Princeton University Press. After seeing my tweets about the hidden curriculum of grad school, Meagan reached out to me with the idea for this book, and she has supported, encouraged, and guided me in every step of writing it. Meagan's feedback (and the feedback from the anonymous reviewers) helped me clarify the audience and the argument for the book, incorporate more effective examples, and hone the writing to be as efficient and compelling as possible.

While credit for idea of this book goes to Meagan Levinson, it was inspired by the many scholars who shared their own hidden curriculum stories on Twitter. The stories shared in those posts resonated with me and with so many current and former grad students. It was incredibly challenging to choose which tweets to include here, and I am tremendously grateful to all the scholars who so graciously allowed me to share what they wrote.

As we will talk about in the book, going to grad school and pursuing an academic career can strain even the strongest of friendships, partnerships, and family ties. Despite those challenges, Dan Calarco has stuck by me on this journey, never wavering in his support, and reeling me back to reality when I find myself getting pulled into the petty politics of academia. Our kids, in turn, are my constant reminder to be more careful in balancing work and nonwork life. At the same time, our kids are also my reminder of why it's important to make academia the kind of equitable, inclusive place I want it to be. At least for the moment, my daughter wants to be "a teacher and a scientist." That sounds pretty close to "professor" to me. And if she sticks with that goal, then having me as a parent will almost certainly give her a leg up in pursuing her dreams. To me, as someone who studies inequalities in school and the role privileged parents play in maintaining those inequalities, that leg up doesn't seem fair. And so, in the interest of leveling the playing field, I want to do what I can to help other future scholars get that same support along the way.

A FIELD
GUIDE
TO GRAD
SCHOOL

INTRODUCTION

What does it mean to write a literature review? Who should you choose for your dissertation committee, and how should you ask for their help? How big should a conference poster be? If a journal tells you to revise and resubmit, should you celebrate or cry?

These are the kinds of things you'll need to know to be successful in grad school, but they probably won't be covered in class. Instead, they're part of the hidden curriculum—the things you're expected to know or do but won't be explicitly taught.[1]

Of course, that begs questions—If the knowledge and skills and strategies in the hidden curriculum matter for success, why are they hidden at all? Why not just make them part of the formal (i.e., explicitly taught) curriculum, instead?

The hidden curriculum of grad school stays hidden, in part, because it's taken for granted. Unlike the formal curriculum, which tends to focus on ways of thinking, the hidden curriculum tends to involve ways of doing: how to do, write about, and talk about research, how to navigate complex bureaucracies, and how to ask others for help when you feel lost. Those ways of doing are easy to take for granted because once scholars learn them, they enact them in subconscious ways. And once those ways of doing are taken for granted, they become a lot harder to teach.

Think, for example, about your grandma's blueberry pie (or whatever favorite dish you have that a friend or relative makes). Your grandma probably doesn't follow a recipe, and if she tried to tell you the recipe, there's a good chance she couldn't easily tell you exactly what she does. Essentially, the taken-for-grantedness of your grandma's pie-baking knowledge can make it hard for her to share that knowledge with you, which makes it hard for you to re-create her pie for yourself.

That same taken-for-grantedness works to keep the hidden knowledge of academia hidden as well. Like your grandma with her pie, your professors are experts in the kind of work they do.

After doing that work for many years (or decades), your professors can do it almost without thinking. As a result, they might forget that the hidden curriculum is hidden. They might forget there was a time when they didn't know how to do what they do. They might forget that you don't know what they've spent a career learning. They might struggle to explain what they know in a way that makes it easy to understand.

Taken-for-grantedness, however, isn't the only reason the hidden curriculum of academia stays hidden. Rather, the hidden curriculum also stays hidden because professors have little incentive to uncover that knowledge for their students. In academia, and especially in departments with graduate programs, the big rewards—grants, publications, jobs, tenure, promotions, and awards—go to scholars who do prolific, prestigious research. Doing that kind of research takes a tremendous amount of time and energy. Meanwhile, being a good teacher and a good mentor— the kind of teacher and mentor who systematically uncovers the hidden curriculum of grad school for their students—also takes a tremendous amount of time and energy. But exerting that time and energy doesn't come with external rewards.

Because of that incentive structure, professors have a tough choice to make. Professors can focus on research—chase the big rewards—but they probably won't have the time or energy left over to give you hands-on support. Professors can also focus on teaching and mentoring—provide a high level of hands-on support—but they probably won't have the time to do the research they need to be successful in their careers. And, of course, professors can try to be great at all these things, but that probably means working themselves to exhaustion—putting their health and their career and their relationships at risk.

* * *

Ultimately, then, the hidden curriculum tends to stay hidden, and that hiddenness perpetuates inequalities in grad school and in academia as a whole. Grad students from more privileged groups—e.g., those who are white, affluent, male, cis-gender, heterosexual, native-born, and able-bodied—tend to reap more of the big rewards in academia. They're more likely to get into "top" programs, get chosen for "top" fellowships and "top" grants, get their research published in "top" journals, get hired for "top" jobs, and get tenured to keep those "top" jobs. Of course, grad students from privileged groups don't get those big rewards because they're smarter or work harder. They get them because of how they are perceived by key gatekeepers, because they typically have access to more resources, and because they have an advantage in learning the hidden knowledge they need to succeed.[2]

Privileged students' advantage in learning the hidden curriculum is, in part, a network advantage. If you're from a more privileged background, you probably have friends or family members who've been to grad school. Those friends and family members can be your guides to grad school—they can help you uncover the hidden curriculum for yourself. Meanwhile, if you're not from a privileged background, then you probably can't rely on your close friends and family members to help you navigate the hidden curriculum of grad school. You might even face criticism from friends and family about the demands of grad school or the type of person you've become.[3] That lack of support, in turn, can make it harder to succeed.

Privileged students' advantage in learning the hidden curriculum is also an entitlement advantage. If you're from a more privileged group, you're probably pretty comfortable talking with your professors and asking them for help.[4] When you've asked for things in the past, your teachers and professors have probably said yes. And those yesses have probably made it easy to feel entitled to support. Of course, you might've encountered one or two professors who were too intimidating to approach for help. Or you might've had a professor who denied your request. But if you're a student from a more privileged background, you probably didn't have to worry about whether your professor said no because of who you are. Meanwhile, if you're not from a privileged background, you might find it more difficult to ask professors for help. Professors—like all people—are prone to subconscious biases.[5] Given that possibility of bias, you might worry about how your professors will judge you for needing help.[6] You might worry that if a professor sees you as "difficult" or "demanding," they won't want to invest in you or your career.

Essentially, students from privileged groups have an advantage in learning the hidden curriculum, and that advantage helps those students to be more successful in their careers.[7]

If you're a student from a less privileged group, you probably think those advantages are deeply unfair. And you're probably not alone. In the United States, the "average" grad student is still a white male student from an affluent, highly educated family, but the face of that average student is changing. Between 2000 and 2016, the number of graduate students in the United States increased from 2.2 million to 3 million,[8] and those increases were concentrated almost entirely among students from systematically marginalized groups.[9] That includes low-income students, first-generation college students, students of color, LGBTQ students, women students (especially in STEM fields), and international students.

If you're a student from one of those groups, you might need a little extra help navigating the hidden curriculum of grad school. And that's okay because you deserve success as much as those students who came in knowing the hidden curriculum of grad school or who have more resources to figure it out on their own.

At the same time, it's important to consider who you ask for help. In most schools, departments, and disciplines, the people who work hardest to help grad students succeed are professors from systematically marginalized groups and especially women faculty of color.[10] Because of their commitment to making academia a more diverse, inclusive, and equitable space, professors from systematically marginalized groups often take it upon themselves to provide the kind of hands-on guidance students need.[11]

In doing so, however, they often put their own careers—and even their own health—at risk. And those are the professors academia needs the most.

12

Nina M. Flores, PhD @bellhookedme · Jul 23, 2018

#HiddenCurriculum around #gradschool is real, especially for 1st gen students. First year in college I had no clue about grad school. I remember the embarrassment of trying to figure out if I was an undergrad or grad. All I knew is I wanted to graduate, so I selected "graduate".

Nina M. Flores, PhD @bellhookedme · Jul 23, 2018
Replying to @bellhookedme
I can still feel the shame of not knowing the difference between graduate & undergraduate status as a freshman in college. But with no one who had this basic "inside knowledge" about #highered in my life, how would I have known this intuitively? I wouldn't have. And I didn't.

If we want to avoid overburdening professors from marginalized groups, we have to find another way to help students uncover the hidden curriculum and get the guidance they need to succeed. Arguably, the best solution would be to make the hidden curriculum part of the formal curriculum. Graduate programs could explicitly teach students—all students—everything they need to succeed. That's certainly something I'm working toward in my own department. Maybe someday it'll be something you can work toward in yours. Those changes are important, but they also take time.

In the short term, my hope—as a sociologist who studies inequalities in education, as a professor who cares deeply about quality teaching and mentoring, and as someone who struggled (and sometimes still struggles) to understand academia—is that this book will be your field guide to grad school. In it, I uncover key parts of the hidden curriculum. I also offer strategies to help you build the confidence you'll need to uncover the rest for yourself.

Along those lines, it's important to note up front that some aspects of the hidden curriculum vary across disciplines, across departments, and across degrees. Essentially, what you need to know to be successful in a doctoral program in sociology at Stanford is going to be somewhat different from what you need to know if you're getting a master's degree in computer science at Oklahoma State.

Given those variations, a book like this one is not easy to write. I'm coming at this as a social scientist, and that's the part of academia I know best. While this book also includes material relevant to the humanities and lab sciences,[13] there will inevitably be things I forget to mention and things I don't discuss in the level of detail you need. That said, I do my best to uncover as much of the hidden curriculum as I can, given the limits of my own knowledge and the limits imposed by the publishing process—more on that in chapter 8. To do that, I focus on the parts of the hidden curriculum that apply widely across disciplines, departments, and degrees. At the same time, I also point out key sources of variation in the hidden curriculum and offer suggestions on how to look for, ask for, and ultimately get help with uncovering the parts of the hidden curriculum that are unique to your discipline, your department, and your degree.

Specifically, we'll talk about the hidden curriculum as it relates to:

- Applying to and choosing a program
- Building your team
- Deciphering academic jargon
- Reading and writing about other people's research
- Staying on track in your program
- Doing research and finding funding
- Writing about research
- Publishing and promoting your work
- Talking about your research (and surviving the Q&A)
- Going to conferences (without breaking the bank)

- Navigating the job market
- Balancing teaching, research, service, and life

In these chapters, I share my own (sometimes embarrassing) stories from grad school (and post–grad school). And I share stories that others (including current grad students, former grad students, and other professors) have shared on Twitter as part of a larger discussion of the #HiddenCurriculum of grad school. Essentially, we'll uncover the hidden curriculum of grad school by talking openly and honestly about the things we didn't know.

I also share resources—like email templates, writing outlines, and checklists—that can help make grad school feel less like getting locked out when everyone else has the key. This includes resources I've created to help my own students navigate the hidden curriculum of grad school and resources that other scholars and organizations have created to support their students and scholars as well.

14

Jess Calarco @JessicaCalarco · Jul 21, 2018

The #hiddencurriculum of academia isn't just hidden from undergrads. It's hidden from grad students, too.

I'm sure we all had things we were embarrassed we didn't know in grad school. So let's tell those stories. I'll go first. (1/many)

Kristin K. Smith @kksmith312 · Jul 20, 2018

Just told an undergrad about graduate assistantships, stipends, & tuition waivers. Her mind was blown. We need to do a better job educating students about #gradstudent opportunities - esp for rural, low-income, non-traditional students #highered

---

* * *

My hope is that this field guide to grad school will take some of the stress out of navigating the hidden curriculum. That it will leave you with more time and energy to pursue the passions that brought you to grad school. That it will help you feel confident in yourself and your worth as a scholar.

In grad school, feeling confident is critical because the hidden curriculum is a perfect catalyst for self-doubt. When you're struggling to navigate the hidden curriculum, it can feel as though everyone else solved the puzzle while you're still finding the pieces. Essentially, the hidden curriculum contributes to "impostor syndrome"—that feeling that you're not good enough or smart enough to be in your program, that maybe you got into grad school by mistake.[15]

[16]

Jess Calarco @JessicaCalarco • Sep 4, 2018

This is such an important conversation! Acknowledging the #hiddencurriculum seems like the first step in combating imposter syndrome. Helping students recognize that there are things that matter for success that aren't always explicitly taught (and then making those explicit).

Liana Sayer @LCHSayer • Sep 4, 2018

Discussing #HiddenCurriculum in prosem & curious about strategies to quell #impostersyndrome mine of staying silent isn't effective @JessicaCalarco @sarahburgard @SarahDamaske @familyunequal @tristanbphd

If you've struggled with impostor syndrome, you know the toll it can take on your physical and mental health. Research has found that grad students experience "strikingly high" rates of depression and anxiety, much higher than among the general population.[17] Those health problems also appear to be closely linked to grad students' feelings of inadequacy—the kind of inadequacy you might feel when you can't see the hidden curriculum and you feel like you're being tested on things you never learned.

As a field guide to grad school, this book can help you fight off those self-doubts. As you read, you'll see you're not the only one who's felt confused or inadequate or alone in grad school—far from it. You'll learn key parts of the hidden knowledge you need to succeed. And you'll learn strategies that can help you be more confident in asking for the help you need to figure out the rest.

Chapter 1

CHOOSING A PROGRAM

 Devon Cantwell @devon_cantwell · Dec 8, 2018

I was talking to some folks I knew from high school tonight and they were really surprised to learn that there was even such a thing as a fully funded Ph.D. program. We are all from low-income backgrounds and knew very few people who ever went to grad school. #hiddencurriculum

You think you might want to go to grad school. But how do you decide? And even if you know you want to go to grad school, how do you decide which program to choose?

Some people go to grad school because they're not sure what else to do, but I don't think that's the best approach. Given the time, effort, costs, and trade-offs involved, you should go to grad school only if it'll help you achieve your career goals and only if it won't break the bank—or your spirit—in the process.

Essentially, it's important not to treat grad school as an end in itself. Instead, going to grad school is more like packing for a trip, where the destination is the job you want to do with your degree. If your ideal trip is a month in Paris, you might want to learn some French and you might need a passport and visa before you go. If instead you want to spend a week hiking in the Appalachian Mountains, taking French classes would be a waste of time and money. Meanwhile, if you don't have a solid pair of boots, a fully stocked backpack, and key survival skills, there's a good chance you won't last the whole week or, worse, that you'll get hurt along the way.

Like different destinations, different careers require different tools, knowledge, and credentials. You want to choose a program that can get you where you want to go. To put these decisions in context, let me tell you a bit about my own path to grad school. As an undergrad, I worked as a research assistant for an education historian. I got to help edit a book manuscript, and I even got to do research in the National Archives in Washington, DC. That taste of real academic research, plus my love for college classes more generally, had me hooked—I didn't just want to work for a college professor, I wanted to be one myself. At the time, though, I had no idea how to actually become a college professor—no one in my family, or even my extended family, had ever gotten a doctoral degree. I was lucky, though, in that my undergrad professors noticed my passion for research and encouraged me to consider grad school.

At first, I was hesitant—I didn't know anything about doctoral programs, and my dad really wanted me to go law school instead. He saw law school as a clear path to a stable, well-paid career. But I wanted to do research. And I wanted to teach. So eventually, after a number of incredibly helpful conversations with my undergraduate professors, and lots of research online, I decided to take the GRE (a standardized admissions test for grad school) and apply to doctoral programs.

At the time, I was double majoring in sociology and education studies, and I was interested in researching inequalities in schools. Given those interests, I initially looked into doctoral programs in education. However, when I mentioned this to my undergrad professors (including one in sociology and two in education studies), they all urged me to consider a doctoral degree in sociology, instead. With a doctoral degree in education, my job prospects (at least in academia) would be limited to schools of education. With a doctoral degree in sociology, I'd have more options—including both sociology departments and education schools. That's because disciplinary departments (e.g., sociology, history, biology) typically hire only scholars trained in those disciplines. For identity and status reasons, those disciplinary departments tend to view scholars trained in interdisciplinary programs as lacking the expertise to teach in a disciplinary program. Meanwhile, interdisciplinary schools and programs (e.g., education, public health, public policy/administration) hire a bigger mix of scholars, including some trained in disciplinary departments and others with interdisciplinary degrees.

Those conversations helped me navigate the complexities of academic culture—they helped me figure out what I couldn't have figured out on my own.

That's what I hope to do in this chapter—help you identify key factors to consider when deciding whether to go to grad school, what kind of degree to pursue, and which program to choose. We'll talk about matching your degree to your career goals. Distinguishing different degrees and programs. And choosing a program that meets your short-term and long-term needs. Finally, we'll talk about how to apply. How to boost your GRE scores and how to cope if your grades and scores aren't as high as you want them to be. How to write a strong personal statement and how to tailor it for each program on your list. How to ask for letters and how to respond if you get asked to write them yourself.

Matching Your Degree to Your Career Goals

When one of my undergraduate students tells me they're interested in grad school, the first question I ask is "What do you want to do after grad school?" The answer to that question will determine what kind of degree you should get and whether you should go to grad school at all. As we'll talk about more in the next section, different degrees (and nondegree certificates) serve as credentials for different types of careers. If you want to teach chemistry at a school like the University of Chicago, you will al-most certainly need a doctoral degree. If you want to be a public policy analyst at a think tank, or if you want to be a school social worker, a master's degree is probably all you'll need. And if you want a high-paying job in computer and information systems management, an internship during college might open more doors than a graduate degree.

So, how do you figure out which kind of degree you'll need for the career you want? If you've already graduated and started working, you may have reached the limits of what you can achieve with just a bachelor's degree, and you might be looking to grad school to help you move up the ladder in your field. If that's the case, then I'd recommend talking with some of the higher-ups in your organization about their experiences in grad school and what degrees and programs they'd recommend you try to pursue.

If you're still an undergrad, or if you're working but interested in switching fields, then I'd suggest starting your grad search process by thinking about your career role models—people whose careers you'd love to have yourself. It might be someone you know, like a favorite college professor, or the director of the nonprofit you volunteered with in college. Or it might be someone you know of, like an economist you saw interviewed on TV.

Once you have the names of a few potential role models, you can start doing some research. It might feel a bit like stalking, but that's why websites like LinkedIn exist. So don't feel weird. Aca-demics (people who teach and/or do research in college or uni-versity settings) Google each other's research and websites and CVs all the time (CV stands for *curriculum vitae*, which is basically the academic version of a résumé—more on academic jargon in chapter 3). Look up where your role models went to school, what degrees they earned, and what jobs they had before they got to where they are today. Then, ideally, do a little triangulation. Find other people working in similar positions, and look up their career trajectories as well. That'll give you a sense of whether you need a degree and, if so, what kind of degree you need, to get where you want to be.

Now, you might not have a specific career role model in mind. Instead, you might have a sense of the kind of career you want. Maybe one involving research, or writing, or marketing, or product design. Maybe you want a career where you're working directly with people and making a difference in their lives. Maybe you're worried about the environment and climate change. Maybe you like working with numbers. Or maybe you love listening to podcasts about politics and policy. A visit or an email to the career services office at your undergraduate college or university can help you link those interests to potential careers and possibly put you in touch with alumni who work in those fields. Even if you have already graduated, they'll be able to help you think through various career options that match your interests and possibly connect you with alumni who can tell you more. Remember, the career services people have an interest in helping you because if you get a good job, the university can brag about you in its stats, and you'll probably be more likely to donate money to the university someday too.

Along those lines, there are *lots* of careers that require (or at least increasingly require)[2] graduate degrees. There are the obvious grad-school-linked careers, like college professor and research scientist. Beyond that, though, you might also need (or at least benefit from having) a graduate degree if you want a high-level career in a field like:

- Public policy
- Market research
- Pharmaceutical development and testing
- Nonprofit management
- Computer science and engineering
- Marriage and family therapy
- Social work
- Criminology

- Biostatistics
- Financial analysis
- Public relations
- Human resources
- Information science
- Database administration
- And so many more[3]

As you're wading through various career options, trying to make sense of people's résumés and CVs, you'll probably encounter lots of acronyms—things like MSW and MBA and PhD. In the next section, we'll talk about what all those letters mean. We'll also talk about why it's not just the letters that matter but also (at least for many careers) the school that granted the degree.

Essentially, once you figure out what degree you'll need for the job you want, it's time to find a program that offers that type of degree (or nondegree) you'll need.

Considering Your Options

Grad school isn't just one thing. There are nondegree programs, master's programs, and doctoral programs, and they differ in important ways. The primary thing to consider in choosing among those programs is what you want to achieve, career-wise, by going to grad school. Beyond that, though, you'll also want to think about the amount of time it'll take you to complete these different programs and the amount of money you'll have to spend (and forgo) in the process.

Nondegree Programs

Some programs and schools offer certificates, badges, and other microcredentials that will, at least in theory, bolster your job-related skills or make you more appealing to potential employers. For example, if you want to learn the business side of publishing and connect to important players in the industry, the Columbia Publishing Course at Columbia University is a six-week summer program that can give you a leg up in your career.[4] Or maybe you've finished an MD degree, and you're interested in doing research, but you don't want to get a PhD, then something like Brown University's Certificate Program in Clinical and Translational Research might be a good fit.[5] Or if you already have a career in research or business, but you need more advanced skills to do the kind of work you want to do, then the University of North Carolina's Data Analytics Boot Camp might be worth considering.[6]

High-quality nondegree programs have the potential to make graduate training more accessible, more affordable, and more diverse, especially since many of these programs are offered online or with night and weekend classes designed for working professionals. In reality, however, few programs achieve that goal.[7] And some "predatory" programs are intentionally designed to take your money without doing anything for your career.[8]

Given the problems with many nondegree programs, this book focuses on master's and doctoral degree programs instead. That said, if you decide that a nondegree program is the best option for you, please proceed with caution. Ask lots of questions. Talk to people who've completed the program. Opt for public and nonprofit options over for-profit schools.

Master's Degrees

Master's degree programs generally involve an extra one or two years of education beyond a bachelor's degree. In some fields, that extra training can help you get out of an entry-level job and give you a shot at getting the corner office someday. In other fields, those extra one or two years might mean the difference between a job and no job at all.

Master's degrees also come in lots of "flavors." If you're interested in the social sciences or humanities (e.g., English, history, political science, Middle Eastern studies), then you'll probably get a master of arts (MA) degree. If instead you're interested in the lab sciences and related fields (e.g., physics, chemistry, computer science, mathematics), then you'll probably want to look into master of science (MS) degrees.[9] Some fields also have their own specialized master's degrees, like an MPH in public health, an MFA in fine art, an MSW in social work, or an MBA in business.

Whatever field you're pursuing, it's important to distinguish 4 + 1 programs and stand-alone (or "terminal") master's programs from those that build into a doctoral degree.

- 4 + 1 Programs: If you're still an undergraduate student, you might be able to get your master's degree through a 4 + 1 program at your current school. These programs typically involve completing an additional year of coursework beyond your bachelor's degree and also completing a master's project. In most cases that extra year of training has to be completed in the same field where you're getting your bachelor's degree.
- Terminal Master's: The idea of a "terminal" master's sounds kind of ominous, but basically this just means that you're getting a master's degree without the immediate intention of getting a doctoral degree (more on doctoral degrees in a minute). The 4 + 1 programs just described are one way to get a terminal master's, but if you're out of undergrad, or you want to switch schools or fields of study, you can apply to terminal master's programs at other schools or in other departments, instead. This might be the option for you if you're interested in jobs that require just a master's.[10] Or if a stand-alone master's will give you a better shot at getting into the your top-choice doctoral program.[11]
- Nonterminal Master's: A nonterminal master's is a stepping stone on the path to a doctoral degree. In some fields and programs, it's possible to get a doctoral degree without first finishing a master's. In other fields and programs, you

will earn a master's degree as part of the doctoral program. That kind of master's degree is considered nonterminal in that you continue in the same field at the same university after finishing your master's degree.

Doctoral Degrees

If you want a career in academia, or a career in research more generally, a doctoral degree might be the degree for you. Not all doctoral degree recipients go on to careers in academia, though, as we'll talk about in chapter 11, and not all scholars who teach or do research in academia have doctoral degrees.[12]

As with master's degrees, doctoral degrees come in many "flavors." One of the most common is the PhD, or doctor of philosophy degree. Like the master of arts degree, the name here is a bit misleading—philosophy isn't the only field in which you can get a PhD. Rather, there are PhD programs in mathematics, art history, education, physics, even nursing. There are also non-PhD doctoral programs, such as the EdD in education, the JD in law, and the DoS, or doctor of science, degree.

Depending on your discipline, you might spend three or four years getting a doctoral degree, or you might spend nine or ten. The length varies across disciplines.[13] The physical sciences, life sciences, earth sciences, engineering, and mathematics tend to have the shortest time-to-degree (six years on average). The social sciences are a little longer (eight years on average), and the arts and humanities are the longest (nine years on average).

Given those differences, you might assume arts and humanities students just aren't as motivated or as focused on getting their dissertation done. But those time differences are really a function of differences in how grad programs are structured.[14] If you're in an arts, humanities, or social science program, for example, you'll probably have more required coursework than you would in a lab science program, which can add an extra year or more. And you'll probably also have to develop an independent dissertation project, which can take a considerable amount of time, especially since you'll probably have to wait to start your dissertation research until after you've done your coursework and qualifying exams. If you're in a lab science discipline, on the other hand, there's generally less required coursework, which can shorten the time-to-degree. In many lab science disciplines, your dissertation will most likely stem from your work on one of your advisor's projects, rather than a project you develop and carry out yourself. And you'll typically be able to get started on that dissertation research fairly early in your program, rather than having to wait until after you've done your coursework and exams. All those factors together can lead to a much shorter time-to-degree.

Distinguishing Degrees and Programs: Money and Status

Once you figure out what degree you'll need for the job you want, you'll need to find a program that offers that type of degree. There will likely be hundreds of programs that fit the bill. So how do you narrow the list and decide where to apply? First look at the price tag. Then look at whether the potential value of the degree is worth the cost.

Funding Considerations

The cost of grad school can feel especially daunting for students who left college with substantial student debt. If you're one of those students, you're definitely not alone.[15] And you might be worried about taking on even more debt to pay for grad school. That's why it's important to consider the financial costs (and the short-term and long-term financial benefits) associated with different degrees.

Master's Funding: Professional master's programs (e.g., MBA, MSW, MPH) and other terminal master's programs typically are not funded. This means you'll be responsible for paying the full cost of tuition, fees, and living expenses. And those costs can add up quickly, even over one or two years.

Those costs are particularly high at private universities. The one-year Master of Arts Program in the Social Sciences at the University of Chicago, for example, requires that students take nine courses—at a cost of more than $60,000.[16] And that's not including living expenses, books, laptops, and other basic needs.

Public universities and online master's programs can be a more affordable option, especially if you're an in-state student (i.e., a resident of the state where the school is located). Tuition and fees for the sixteen-month master of social work (MSW) degree at the University of Michigan, for example, costs about $48,000 for Michigan residents who have already completed a bachelor's degree in social work. For an out-of-state student with a bachelor's degree in social work, that same degree will cost more than $72,000.[17]

If you're looking to cut costs further, you might look for programs that offer scholarships for master's students. That said, scholarships for master's students are relatively rare and seldom cover the full cost of tuition and fees. That's because, in the context of limited taxpayer funding for higher education,[18] many universities and departments use their terminal master's programs to help make ends meet. In those programs, students pay the full cost of getting their degree.

Of course you might not be able to afford $60,000 or $72,000 for a degree, and you might not be able to rely on your family to help.[19] If that's the case, then getting a terminal master's degree will probably mean finding your own scholarship (more on this in a minute), taking out loans, or possibly asking your employer to help you fund some of the costs.[20]

Doctoral Funding: Unlike terminal master's programs, many doctoral programs provide some level of funding for students. In many PhD programs, for example, you'll pay only a portion of the total tuition and fees, and you might even get a stipend from the university—a small salary to live on while you're getting your degree. That's because PhD programs are usually designed to train future university professors. Given the income that professors typically earn,[21] most would struggle to pay off the loans from an unfunded doctoral degree. Doctoral students (and especially PhD students) also provide a source of low-cost labor for departments and universities.[22] If you go that route, you'll probably be expected to work as a teaching or research assistant, or even teach your own classes, in exchange for financial support in getting your degree. This also explains why professional doctoral programs (like a JD in law or an MD in medicine) are funded more like terminal master's degrees—if you're a student in one of those programs, you don't typically do any service for the university, so you pay the full cost of your degree.

That said, while most doctoral programs do provide some level of funding support for students, there are also huge variations in how much funding you'll get and what you'll have to do to get it. There are variations across universities, across different degrees and disciplines, and sometimes even across different students in the same program.

Some of those variations relate to the number of years of funding you'll get and whether that funding comes with any guarantees. In some programs, for example, and especially programs in the lab sciences, your training is probably funded through grants your advisor got from outside agencies. That means that if your advisor's funding dries up, yours does too. And that's why, as we'll talk more about in chapter 6, it's important to ask lots of questions up front about how long your advisor's funding will last and what happens if that funding runs out before you finish your degree. In other programs, and especially programs in the arts, sciences, and humanities, your training is paid for by the department, rather than through grants to individual faculty members. In those programs, you'll typically be offered a funding package that includes a set number of years of guaranteed funding. You might, for example, be offered "full funding" for four or five or six years. This means the department will pay some portion of your tuition and fees and sometimes provide a stipend for living expenses during those years. If you don't finish your doctoral degree within the funded years, you'll probably stop getting a stipend (if you got one in the first place), and you might have to pay for (or find grant funding to pay for) any additional years of tuition and fees.[23]

There are also variations in the size of the stipend you might get in grad school (if you get one at all). Prestigious private universities, for example, generally offer bigger stipends than public universities and smaller private colleges because they have larger endowments and charge higher tuition at the undergraduate and master's level, and because they use some of that money to fund doctoral training programs.[24] Programs in science and technology generally offer larger stipends than do programs in the social sciences, arts, and humanities because they bring in more external grant funding and also because students in those fields often face higher opportunity costs in terms of forgone salary in pursuing their degrees.[25] Some students, in turn, may also receive higher stipends than other members of their cohorts, either as part of a "recruitment bonus" or because their advisors have more grant funding to use for graduate stipends.[26]

A third source of variation in doctoral funding relates to the work you'll have to do to earn your stipend. Your funding package might come with non-service years—years where you get funding without doing any research or teaching-related service for the department. Or you might have to work—as a research assistant, a teaching assistant, or an instructor—every year, unless you get outside funding to cover your costs (we'll talk more about teaching and research assistantships in chapters 5 and 6).

Even "fully funded" graduate programs won't necessarily provide the level of financial support you'll need to make ends meet. If you have a high level of financial responsibility—young children or siblings or parents to support—you might find yourself looking for supplemental income while you're getting your degree. As we'll talk about in chapter 5, some programs will let you do hourly work for professors to earn extra money. But that's not the case everywhere. Your program might have rules against extra work. And if you're an international student, you might be legally prohibited from doing any paid work on the side.

Grants and Fellowship Programs: Given the limits of grad school funding, you might be interested in looking for programs where you'll have a higher likelihood of getting grants or fellowships to help cover your costs and possibly give you a higher stipend as well.

With a few key exceptions, you can apply for graduate fellowships and grants only after you've been admitted to grad school. When you're considering various programs, however, it can be helpful to look for programs where students have a track record of success in getting supplemental support. Specifically, I'd recommend checking out the web pages of current students (you can usually find links on the program web page) and looking for information about the fellowships, grants, and other financial support they've received. You can also look at the web pages for various government agencies and foundations that fund graduate-level grants and fellowships and see where most of their recipients are getting their degrees.

To get you started in that search, here's a list of a few particularly notable scholarship and fellowship programs that fund students and early career scholars from a wide array of universities and disciplines:

- The National Science Foundation (NSF)
  - NSF Graduate Research Fellowship Program (GRFP)[27]
  - NSF Doctoral Dissertation Research Improvement Grants[28]
  - NSF CAREER Program[29]
- The National Institutes of Health (NIH)
  - NIH Training and Career Development Grants[30]
  - NIH Dissertation Awards[31]
  - NIH Career Development (K) Awards[32]
- The U.S. Department of State's Fulbright Programs[33]

- The Marshall Scholarship[34]
- The Rhodes Scholarship[35]
- The NAEd/Spencer Dissertation Fellowship Program[36]
- The William T. Grant Scholars Program[37]
- The Robert Wood Johnson Foundation Health Policy Fellows Program[38]

Some funding agencies also provide dedicated support for grad students and scholars from systematically marginalized groups.[39] Those include:

- The Ford Foundation Fellowship Programs[40]
- The Alfred P. Sloan Foundation Graduate Scholarship Programs[41]
- American Academy of University Women
  - American Fellowships[42]
  - Career Development Grants[43]
  - International Fellowships[44]
  - Selected Professions Fellowship[45]
  - Research Publication Grant in Engineering, Medicine, and Science[46]
- The U.S. Department of Education's Jacob K. Javits Fellowship Program[47]

When you're looking into various programs and checking out the web pages of current students, you might see some of these "big name" grants and fellowships listed, and you might also see other university or discipline-specific fellowships and grants listed as well. That's because, and as we'll talk more about in chapter 6, there's a huge array of funding sources for graduate students and early career scholars. Some grants and fellowships are internal (funded by the department or the university), while others are external (funded by an outside organization). Some cover the full cost of your graduate education (e.g., stipend, tuition, and fees), while others cover only specific research-related expenses (e.g., equipment, payments to study participants, transcription costs, data access costs, conference and travel costs, or publishing-related expenses like submission fees and page fees). Sometimes that extra money adds on to your existing funding; in other cases, your scholarship or fellowship substitutes for funding you would've gotten from your advisor or department, or it fills gaps in years where you otherwise would've had no funding at all.

Like I said, we'll talk more about finding and applying for these opportunities in chapter 6. At the application stage, though, the key is to get a sense of whether the programs you're considering have been successful in helping students get the financial support they need.

Status Considerations

Money should matter in your decision about whether and where to go to grad school, but it's not the only important thing. It seems crass, but if the end game is to get a good job, and especially if the kind of job you want is an academic job (i.e., teaching and/or doing research in a college or university setting), you'll also want to think about status as well.

Some grad programs, for example, are more highly ranked than others. This idea of program rankings generally refers to the *U.S. News & World Report* rankings. Every year, *U.S. News & World Report* publishes a list of what it considers the best graduate programs in various fields.[48] What counts as best, though, is highly subjective, as the rankings are based on surveys that ask faculty to rate the "academic quality" of other programs in their field.

Of course, even highly subjective rankings can carry real weight. The name of the school on your diploma can affect your chances of getting funding, getting your research published, and even getting a job.[49] In the academic job market, for example, there are far fewer tenure-track positions than applicants who want those jobs. That's because universities pay tenured and tenure-track faculty more than lecturers, adjuncts, and grad students, even when they're teaching the same course. And they typically pay the same amount for teaching that course, whether it enrolls seven students, seventy, or seven hundred. Thus, when budgets are tight, it makes fiscal sense for universities to hire fewer tenure-track faculty members and offer larger classes and more classes taught by non-tenure-track instructors instead. Unfortunately, however, and because the demand for most tenure-track jobs exceeds the supply, universities can be very selective about whom they hire. In that kind of tight job market, employers tend to opt for job candidates with elite pedigrees.[50]

Distinguishing Degrees and Programs: Meeting Your Personal Needs

Figuring out what kind of degree you need for the career you want is the first step in narrowing the list of possible grad programs. The second step in narrowing that list is eliminating the programs that are too costly or not well known enough to make them worth the time and effort you'll spend getting a degree. Even at that point, though, there might still be two or three dozen programs to which you could reasonably apply.

So how do you narrow the list from there? Arguably, you should narrow the list to eliminate those programs that won't meet your personal needs. No amount of money or status is worth being miserable for many years, so you'll want to look for programs that offer both high-quality training and a high quality of life.

People and Programs

People (and the training, mentoring, and support those people can provide) are particularly important to consider in choosing where to get your degree. That includes the people in the program—potential advisors, other professors, staff members, and fellow graduate students. It also includes people in the community—having friends and being part of organizations outside of academia can make grad school feel a bit less isolating and a bit less stifling.[51] We'll talk more about interacting with advisors, professors, and other grad students in chapter 2. For now though, here are a few things to consider, people-wise, in choosing a program.

Advisors: Different disciplines and different departments do advising in different ways. If you're applying for a doctoral program in a lab science field, you'll probably apply to work with (and for) a particular professor, who will then serve as your advisor. If you're instead applying for doctoral programs in the social sciences, arts, and humanities, or if you're applying for a terminal master's program, you'll probably apply to the program as a whole and then either choose or be assigned an advisor once you get there. You can usually figure out which type of program you're applying to by looking at how graduate students are listed on the department website (i.e., whether they are grouped by lab/advisor or listed more generally). If you're not sure, you can also email the professor or staff member in charge of the graduate program (they're usually listed on the department website as the "graduate chair" or "director of graduate studies") to ask.

Regardless of whether you're interested in programs with lab-model advising or those with non-lab-based advisor-student relationships, there are a few key factors to consider in narrowing down the list. First, you'll want to identify potential advisors who are active in teaching and research.[52] Second, you'll want to look for potential advisors whose expertise aligns with your interests. It doesn't have to be a perfect match, but it does have to be close enough that your advisor can reasonably advise you on the kind of work you want to do. Third, you'll want to look for potential advisors who aren't likely to leave before you finish your degree. Some universities, for example, have a track record of not granting tenure to assistant professors and especially those from systematically marginalized groups.[53] If you're applying to one of those schools, you'll want to think carefully about whom you choose as your primary advisor. If your advisor is denied tenure or leaves for other reasons, you might have the option of following your advisor to their new school, but you might have to switch advisors instead. That's not to say, though, that you should avoid assistant professors as potential mentors. Because of their proximity to grad school, assistant professors are often among the most caring mentors for grad students, and they can be tremendous role models, especially if you're considering careers in academia.

So far we've talked about the importance of finding an advisor who's a good professional match for you and the kind of work you want to do. But what makes a good advisor isn't just found on their CV. You'll want to look for advisors who are easy to talk to, who give timely, constructive feedback, who aren't already over-burdened with a huge number of students, and who are willing to invest in your career. And you'll have to do some digging (contacting potential advisors, talking to their current grad students, and asking strategic questions during visit days) to find out which of your potential advisors fits those bills as well.

Other Professors: While you'll probably have one primary advisor in grad school, no one person can be your go-to mentor for every aspect of your career. Instead, you'll want to develop strong relationships with at least four or five faculty members as you work toward your degree. That doesn't mean, however, that you need to find a program with five professors who all do exactly the kind of work you hope to do. That program probably doesn't exist. And if it did, it might leave you feeling a little stifled. Instead, and as we'll talk more about in chapter 5, you should choose a program with a team of faculty members who can collectively (and cooperatively) meet your professional and personal needs.

Other Grad Students: Some programs admit one or two grad students every year. Others admit ten or twenty or more. Having a cohort (i.e., a group of fellow students entering the program at the same time) is really helpful. That's because grad school can be disorienting—you're usually moving to a new place and taking on new responsibilities—and because having people to talk to, especially if those people are in a similar situation, can make it a little bit less so.[54] That said, large cohorts also create competition—for attention and support from faculty, for coveted research and teaching positions, for funding, and for awards.

When considering potential grad programs, take a look at their websites. You'll probably be able to find lists of current grad students with links to their bios or CVs. Calculate (roughly) how many students they admit every year. Calculate the faculty-to-student ratio. Make note of which students are winning awards and getting fellowships and publications (i.e., is it the same handful over and over, or are those rewards more evenly distributed?). Look for evidence of grad students collaborating with faculty members on projects and collaborating with each other as well. Those details can give you a sense of whether the culture among grad students is more collaborative or competitive. As we'll talk more about in chapter 2, you don't need to be best friends with the other students in your program, but it can also be hard if you don't have any peers to turn to for support.

Location

In terms of geographical considerations, it's important to keep in mind that where you live in grad school might not be where you end up long term. For example, if you're getting a doctoral degree and you want an academic career, you'll probably have to change cities when you finish your degree. That's because most universities and departments won't hire their own grad students as faculty members, at least not in the first few years after graduation. To give another example, maybe you're interested in getting a master's in public policy analysis and getting a job at a policy research center. Only one of the top ten ranked master's programs in public policy analysis in the United States is located in Washington, DC.[55] And yet DC is a huge hub for policy research. So if you get an MPP degree elsewhere, you might end up having to move to get the job you want to do with your degree.

If you're probably going to have to relocate after grad school, it can sometimes be worth it to go (quite literally) outside your comfort zone to get your degree. Grad school can be a great opportunity to explore a different city, a different region of the country, or even a different part of the world.

That choice, however, does come with risks. U.S. sociologist Dr. Brooke Harrington, for example, studies tax havens. In 2017, while she was working at a university in Denmark, Harrington was hit with criminal charges. Why? Because she presented her research to the Danish Parliament—something she was invited to do.[56] Now, this might seem ridiculous, but Danish officials were cracking down on immigrants who were engaged in unauthorized work activities. Harrington's work permit allowed her to do work only for the university, and Denmark's officials decided she was breaking the rules. In the United States, meanwhile, and in the wake of President Donald Trump's travel ban on visitors from primarily Muslim countries, some graduate students and scholars were left stranded outside the United States and unable to return, and others were unable to travel home to see their families.[57] Of course, these stories are troubling. But the point is to say that, in the context of systemic racism and anti-immigrant sentiments, it's important to consider the risks that go along with living outside your comfort zone, even if only for a short time.

Those risks, unfortunately, go beyond just the legal and logistical, and include risks to your physical and mental health. On some campuses, for example, you might be more likely to encounter racist or sexist or anti-immigrant or anti-LGBTQ attitudes. In those spaces, you might also be more likely to experience mistreatment because of other people's biases toward people like you. That mistreatment sometimes comes in the form of questions like "Where are you *really* from?" or comments like "You did better than I thought you would on this assignment."[58] In other cases, mistreatment happens when people assume you don't belong, such as when a white student called the police on a Black Yale graduate student who was taking a nap in her dorm's common room.[59] These "microaggressions" might seem inconsequential, but research shows they can have a serious, negative impact on your physical and mental health and overall quality of life.[60]

Of course, microaggressions and other forms of mistreatment can happen anywhere—from big cities to small towns and everywhere in between. And yet, some programs, universities, and local communities have cultures that are more "toxic" than others.[61] Along those lines, and before committing to a grad program, it's important to do your homework and find out as much as you can about what life is like there for people like you. Reach out to current students in the program. Ask about their experiences—how they've been treated by faculty, by fellow students, and by people in the community. Ask whether students like them have a history of leaving before finishing their degree. Getting that information up front can you help you make informed choices about where to apply. Or if you decide to enroll anyway, having that information in hand can help you be better prepared for the challenges you might face and push you to find a network of people and organizations who can support you in being resilient to those challenges (more on this in chapter 2).[62]

Geographical considerations, however, aren't just about local culture. Rather, in deciding where to go to grad school you might have other concerns that limit your options geographically. Maybe you have a spouse or partner whose job tethers them to your current city. Maybe you have young children who don't want to leave their friends or their schools. Maybe you have a medical condition that requires specialized treatment or an elderly family member who needs regular care. In that case, you might have to think strategically about what types of degrees and programs you can consider based on the types of jobs you can get locally after you get your degree.

Location is also closely linked to cost of living, and that might be something you have to consider when choosing a program as well. For me, cost was a big factor. I applied to ten PhD programs in sociology and got admitted to four—NYU, Stanford, the

University of Chicago, and the University of Pennsylvania. All four were ranked in the top fifteen PhD programs in sociology. All four had great professors and great students, and all four offered similar amounts and types of funding. Given those similarities, and after a lot of deliberation, I ended up choosing the program that would cost me the least in the end. Going to Penn meant that I could live with my parents, who live about an hour outside of Philadelphia by train. Those cost savings also meant that I could afford to buy a car, which I needed for my dissertation fieldwork and also made it easier to visit my partner (now spouse), who was living and working in Washington, DC.

Of course, making a choice based on location can also come with trade-offs. Because of where I lived in grad school, I spent a *lot* of time commuting—sometimes twenty hours a week. And while some of that commuting time was productive (I got a lot of writing done on busses and trains), it meant I spent very little non-class time on campus. I didn't go out for drinks with my grad school friends or hang out with them on the weekends. I didn't linger after class to talk about theory or strategize about conference submissions. And once I was in the field full-time doing research for my dissertation, I didn't always make it to department events.

Given how geography matters, and for each program you're considering, you should probably ask yourself:

- Will I have to move after grad school to get the kind of job I want?
- Will I be able to afford to live there for as long as it'll take to get my degree?
- Will I be able to handle being this far from (or close to) key people in my life?
- Will living in this place cause me to face regular threats to my well-being?
- Will I be able to find a community to help me deal with the challenges I face?

Ultimately, you might decide to take some risks or make some trade-offs on location in the short term. But if being in a particular location matters to you, that's okay too. And you shouldn't be ashamed for letting it factor into your choice. Because, as we'll talk more about in the next section, grad school is much more tolerable (and potentially even enjoyable) if it isn't your whole life.

Work/Life Balance

Along those lines, there's this idea that grad students and academics more generally are supposed to love their work. And there is, at least in theory, a lot to like about grad school—the opportunity to spend time reading and learning and thinking and talking about new ideas, the flexibility to work when and where are best for you, and the freedom to do research that matches your own interests and that might make a difference in other people's lives.

But that work-as-passion model also comes with problems. It can make you feel pressured to work all the time. It can make you feel guilty about taking time off or having interests that don't perfectly align with your academic work. A recent article in *Times Higher Education* included quotes from various academics about their "guilty pleasures," which included things like traveling and watching comedy movies.[63] Presumably, the article was intended to show that academics have lives and passions outside of research and teaching. But by framing those hobbies and interests as "guilty pleasures," the article implied that academics should feel guilty about doing anything not connected to their work.

As a grad student, you don't have to accept the work-is-life culture. You don't have to work all the time, and there's a good chance you'll be more productive if you take breaks and if you have hobbies and interests that have nothing to do with work. I run almost every morning. I try to leave work by four or four thirty so I can spend the afternoons with my kids. On the weekends, I rarely get much work done—with two little kids, Saturdays and Sundays are always packed with birthday parties and craft projects and grocery shopping and making dinners for the week. And while I sometimes get my laptop back out in the evenings to answer emails or finish a proposal or give students feedback on their work, I try to spend most of that time with my spouse, or doing laundry, or watching the latest Netflix shows.

Pushing back against the work-is-life culture is harder in some programs than in others. In the department where I teach, it's rare for faculty to be in the office past five or six o'clock. Our department also has softball and indoor soccer teams, along with regular picnics and happy hours and other nonacademic events. Not all programs work that way. And that's why it's important to ask lots of questions up front. Ask current grad students and faculty about how many hours they work. Ask what they do for fun. Look for a program where you'll be able to thrive both intellectually and personally.

Of course, even if you do find a program where grad students and faculty have a good balance between work and nonwork life, it's hard to fully escape the publish-or-perish pressure of an academic career. We'll talk more about managing those pressures in chapter 12, but it's important to say here that if you're worried about adjusting to the intense work pressures of grad school, you're definitely not alone.

Adjusting to the work-is-life culture of academia is challenging, especially if you're not going straight to grad school after finishing your undergrad degree. If you've graduated and started working, you might have a nine-to-five job where you leave work at work, and it might take you a while to get used to the grad school routine. The transition from full-time work to grad school can be financially hard too, particularly if you're taking a big pay cut or self-funding your degree. That's why, as we talked about at the beginning of the chapter, it's important to think strategically about the decision to go to grad school and about whether you really need an extra degree. It's also why it's important to do some number crunching up front. You'll want to figure out whether you'll be able to afford your degree and whether the ultimate payoff will be worth it in the end.

Selectivity

So far we've talked about narrowing the list of programs to which you will apply. But as you probably know from undergrad, applying doesn't guarantee you'll get in. Many programs—and especially prestigious, well-funded doctoral programs—are highly selective. They admit only a small fraction of the students who apply. That means you have to think strategically in choosing your final list. In general, I recommend applying to two or three "there's a slim chance I can get in here" programs, three to five "there's a decent chance I can get in here" programs, and one or two "there's a very good chance I can get in here" programs.

But how do you figure out which programs fall in each category? If you're applying to grad school in the United States, the *U.S. News & World Report* websites can give you a general sense of the "average" student admitted by each school. Some grad program websites will also include information about the students they usually admit. That includes GRE scores (though some programs are moving away from requiring the GRE), GPAs, and information about the kinds of experience or credentials incoming students generally have. You can also do a little digging and check out the CVs of students recently admitted to the program. Look at where they went to college, whether they won awards or wrote honors theses, and whether they got any additional training (like a certificate or terminal master's) or had work experience before pursuing their current graduate degree.

After you finish scouring the web, I'd recommend reaching out to some of your professors from undergrad, and especially those in the field where you're planning to apply. Your professors probably have friends or former grad school colleagues at a range of universities across the country or even around the world, and they can probably give you more inside information about those various programs than you'd ever find online. Ideally, your professors will also know you and your interests and your strengths, and they'll be able to help you figure out where you'll be both happiest and most likely to get in.

So, once you identify two or three professors who might have some good insights, how do you ask them for help? First, I'd recommend making a list of programs you'd be interested in attending. Next, drop your professors an email. Maybe something like this:

Dear Professor [LAST NAME],

I hope all is well with you! Since we last chatted, I've been [BRIEF UPDATE ON WHERE YOU ARE IN SCHOOL (E.G., "WORKING ON MY HONORS THESIS") OR WHAT YOU'VE BEEN DOING, WORK-WISE, POST-DEGREE (E.G., "WORKING IN MARKET RESEARCH")].

I'm writing to see if you would be willing to chat with me about applying to [MASTER'S/DOCTORAL] programs in [FIELD]. I've made a list of programs I'd be interested in attending (see below), and I would be grateful for your help identifying which of these programs would give me the best chances of admission.

For context, my undergraduate major is/was [MAJOR], my GPA is/was [GPA], my GRE scores are [GRE SCORES]. I am interested in studying [BRIEF DESCRIPTION OF THE RESEARCH TOPIC/QUESTION YOU HOPE TO FOCUS ON IN GRAD SCHOOL], and I [DO/DO NOT] have prior research experience [IF YOU HAVE PRIOR RESEARCH EXPERIENCE, BRIEFLY EXPLAIN HERE].

I would appreciate any advice you can provide, and I would be happy to meet in person or talk by email or by phone. That said, I'm sure you are very busy, and I completely understand if you are unable to help at this time.

Best,
[YOUR NAME]

[LIST OF SCHOOLS, RANKED IN ORDER OF YOUR
PREFERENCE]

These conversations with your current or former professors can also give you a chance to ask for letters of recommendation, which you'll ultimately need as part of your grad school applications. And that's where we'll turn next, covering the various components of the application and how to put it all together.

Applying to Grad School

Once you've narrowed down your list of potential programs, start putting together the materials you'll need to apply. The parts of an application vary across disciplines, departments, and degrees, but you'll generally need:

- Completed application forms
- Application fees
- Personal statement
- Writing sample(s)
- GRE scores
- Undergraduate transcript
- Letters of recommendation

A few suggestions about key parts of the application:

Application Fees

Be ready for sticker shock. Each application you submit might cost up to a hundred dollars or sometimes more. Programs use these fees to bolster their budgets and to make sure only "serious" students apply. Even with those application fees, top programs might get hundreds of applications each year. And the graduate admissions committee—which is generally made up of program faculty—has to review all those applications. Those committee members have plenty of other work to do, and having an admission fee can (at least in theory) keep the number of applications from getting out of control.

That said, if you don't have the money to pay those fees, don't feel like you can't apply. Many programs offer fee waivers for students with limited resources. If you don't see information about fee waivers on the graduate admissions website for the departments where you're applying, you can reach out to the graduate program chair or director or members of the admissions committee and ask them if your fees can be waived. You might have to complete a separate application for a fee waiver and provide additional financial documentation, but if your request is granted, it can save you a lot of money in the end.

Personal Statement

This is your chance to make your case for admission. It should be clear, concise, and tailored to each program, giving the admissions committee a clear sense of:

1. Why you're interested in grad school:

Even though this is a "personal statement," you don't have to tell your life story. But you should give the admissions a sense of what brought you to grad school. That could be a specific research question, a specific career goal, or a passion for teaching. You should also give them a sense of what you hope to achieve while you're there (e.g., doing research on a particular topic, acquiring critical skills, building your professional networks, etc.). This part of the personal statement should be roughly a paragraph long.

2. Why you're going to be successful in grad school
   (especially if you've struggled in the past):
For better or for worse, and as sociologist Dr. Julie Posselt
explains in *Inside Graduate Admissions*, grad programs (especially
doctoral programs) like to make sure bets.[64] They want to invest
in students they perceive to have high chances of success, because
when their students are successful, the program looks good.
Unfortunately, that practice of picking students who seem like
sure bets has the effect of increasing inequalities in grad school
and in academia more generally. That's because, despite their
proclaimed interest in supporting diversity in grad school and in
academia, members of graduate admissions committees sometimes
find themselves relying on racist, sexist, and classist notions of
"merit" when deciding whom to admit.[65]

Thankfully, if you know how the system works, you can tailor
your personal statement to clearly show the admissions committee
why you're a good bet, even if that bet is against their skewed sense
of the odds.

One way to do that is by explaining how your past experiences
have prepared you for success in grad school. Maybe you were a
teaching assistant or a research assistant for one of your
undergraduate professors. Maybe you conducted your own
research as part of an honors thesis or a capstone project. Maybe
you have hands-on experience with the people or topics you hope
to study. What did you learn from those experiences? How did
they point you to the work you're hoping to do in grad school?
And how will they help you succeed?

Of course you might not have that kind of experience, but that
doesn't mean you should panic or abandon the idea of grad school
entirely. Instead, that means you'll have to get a little more creative
about selling your likelihood of success. In those cases, show that
you have a clear plan for getting the most out of grad school. That
means identifying a specific project you want to complete, how
you'll complete it, and why it'll be an important contribution to

the field. It's okay if that project doesn't end up being the project you actually complete in grad school. The point is to show the admissions committee you're capable of thinking through a project from beginning to end.

Along those lines, it's also important to use your personal statement to address anything in your record that might raise a red flag about your chances of success. Maybe that's the grades you got as an undergrad. Or gaps in your employment or educational history. Or low scores on your GRE. Acknowledging those parts of your record shows you're not trying to hide anything. Accounting for those parts of your record, to the extent you feel comfortable doing so, can also give the admissions committee confidence that you'll be successful despite (or even because of) your past struggles. For example, you might say something like:

> While my undergraduate GPA (2.9) is lower than that of a typical applicant for this program, it reflects the challenges I experienced during college and which I have worked to overcome. Throughout my time in college, my family has struggled financially, and I have worked long hours to both support myself and help my mother provide for my younger siblings. Those long work hours, plus frequent trips home to help, initially made it difficult to focus on my coursework. During the spring of my junior year, however, I began working as a research assistant for a professor, and the higher pay with that job allowed me to reduce my overall work hours and focus more on my schoolwork while learning important research-related skills. Reflecting that shift, my GPA for my last three semesters of college was substantially higher (3.7).

You don't have get into the full details—you just have to provide enough information to help the admissions committee avoid seeing your past struggles as red flags. Overall, this section of the personal statement should be the longest—usually at least one or two meaty paragraphs that flesh out what you're going to do in grad school and why the committee should trust that you'll be successful in achieving your goals.

3. Why this program is the best fit for you:

For application committees, picking sure bets doesn't just mean picking students who are going to be successful. It also means picking students they're sure will attend. For example, if you apply to a school ranked twenty-fifth but the admissions committee thinks you're good enough for a school ranked fifth, they might reject you if they think their program is your backup. So it's your job to convince the committee you're serious about their school.

Now, you might be wondering—does that kind of rejection really happen? It does, because admissions committees have to worry about "yield." Basically, programs want to admit exactly the number of students they have resources to support. Let's say, for example, that a doctoral program in political science has funding for a maximum of ten students. The admissions committee might admit fifteen students, with the expectation that five or more will end up going elsewhere. The admissions committee might also pick five students to put on a wait list. That way, if six or more of the admitted students go elsewhere, the program can admit students from the wait list to fill the extra slots. The problem, however, is that by the time the grad committee gets to the wait list, all five wait-listed students might have already committed to going elsewhere. If that happens, the admissions committee has to decide whether to stick with a smaller-than-ideal cohort (which could make it hard to fill required grad classes and provide teaching support for faculty) or admit students the committee initially deemed to be either not strong enough for admission or not a good fit. To avoid ending up in that kind of situation, admissions committees look for students who show a strong interest in their program. The assumption is that those students will probably attend if they get in.

As an applicant, then, you want to signal your seriousness about every program to which you apply. That means doing your homework. Make a clear case for why you're applying to each program. Talk about how the department's strengths (research, methods, courses, faculty, etc.) align with your interests. Talk about which professors you want to work with and why (note: even if they're listed on the website, they might be retired/inactive, so check their CVs). Mention (if it's true) why you like the location. Mention other aspects of the program or the university (e.g., specific workshops or research clusters, locations, other adjacent departments and programs, location, etc.) that make it a particularly good fit for your interests and your needs.

Length-wise, this section can usually be one paragraph or maybe two. Style-wise, keep it professional. Being overly gushy about your admiration for a specific professor might lead the committee to worry that you won't be capable of thinking for yourself.

Writing Samples

Good writing samples don't just show how many big words you know. They show that you can think and write clearly. And they show that you can use evidence to support a persuasive and logically structured argument. With those goals in mind, the best writing samples are usually solo authored. That means you're the one who did the work. The best writing samples also include evidence. That could be data you gathered or analyzed yourself (e.g., in an undergraduate thesis). Or that evidence might be the findings from other people's research that you synthesized to make an argument (e.g., in a paper you wrote for an undergraduate course). Possible writing samples include:

- Undergraduate thesis
- Master's paper (if you're applying to doctoral programs and you already have a master's degree)
- Course papers you wrote as an undergrad or in a master's program

- Published journal articles, book chapters, or draft manuscripts (if the manuscripts you're submitting are coauthored, you'll want to explain in your personal statement what role you played in conducting the research and writing the final report)
- Published media articles (e.g., newspaper articles, magazine articles, blog posts)

Don't stress if you don't have all these types of writing samples to include. Submitting a course paper or two is usually fine.

That said, experience with conducting and publishing research can give you a leg up in the admissions process. That's another reason why it can be helpful to start thinking about grad school long before you finish your undergrad degree. While you're still in college, for example, you might ask your advisor about completing an undergraduate or honors thesis in your department. You might also ask your professors if they're looking for undergraduate research assistants to help with their research. Of course, you might have to ask a few different professors before you find one with openings, and being told no, especially repeatedly, can be a frustrating and disappointing process. But if you do find a professor willing to work with you, it can be a great chance to learn about and help with the research and writing process, and you might be able to get independent study credit (or even get paid) for your work.

Grades and Test Scores

There are lots of problems with using grades and standardized test scores to make decisions about who gets admitted to grad school. Standardized test scores, for example, aren't very good at predicting which students will do best in grad school.[66] Those supposedly merit-based measures are also biased against students from systematically marginalized groups.[67] Given those problems, some grad programs in the United States have stopped requiring that students submit GRE scores with their applications.[68] Most programs, however, still require GPAs and college transcripts, and many still require GREs or other standardized test scores (e.g., GRE subject tests, TOEFL).

Thankfully, there are things you can do to reduce the impact those grades and test scores have on your chances of admission. In terms of grades, and as we talked about a few sections back, you can add a few sentences to your personal statement that put those grades in context. If possible, you can also talk about how you've turned things around (even if that isn't reflected in your overall GPA) or you can highlight how you received higher grades in the courses that will matter most for your graduate degree.

If you haven't taken the GREs yet, or if you still have time to take them again, there are also things you can do to help boost your score. One option is to enroll in expensive test-prep courses from companies like Kaplan or Princeton Review. But if you don't have that kind of cash on hand or time for weekly classes, there are also plenty of no-cost, time-flexible ways to improve your scores. When we were in undergrad, for example, my roommate and I Googled "GRE vocab words." We found dozens of lists online, made huge stacks of vocab cards, and quizzed each other every night before bed (nerdy, I know . . .). We also took free practice tests we found on the Educational Testing Service (ETS) website.[69] We spent about three months prepping, and in the end we both got into the programs we wanted, and we both got our degrees—without spending a dime on prep for the tests.

Letters of Recommendation

Grad school applications almost all require letters of recommendation. While I have doubts about the benefits of asking for five letters versus three or even two, I do understand why grad programs ask for letters in the first place. Unlike undergraduate grades and GRE scores, research shows that students with more positive letters of recommendation tend to be more successful in grad school.[70] Letters of recommendation also allow programs to get a sense of how others perceive you as a student and a scholar: how well you cope in the face of setbacks, how self-motivated and self-aware you are, whether you work well with others, and whether you get your work done well and on time.

This is also why programs generally request that applicants waive their right to view letters of recommendation. If you waive that right, then your letter writers will know that their letters are confidential. That means, at least in theory, that your letter writers will have more incentive to be honest in their letters. And that will make the admissions committee more willing to trust that the letters are honest in their assessments of your weaknesses and strengths.

While a "good" letter can help you, bad or even flat letters (those that contain little useful information) can ultimately tank an application. And that's why it's important to choose letter writers who can write about you as glowingly as possible—those who can provide concrete evidence of how great you are and offer a clear (and professionally informed) take on what a promising future you have.

Keep in mind that it will be hard for a professor (or a work supervisor, or anyone else) to write that kind of glowing letter if they don't know you very well. Along those lines, it's important to start building relationships with potential letter writers long before you go to grad school. So how do you do that? If possible, and while you're still an undergrad, take at least a few small seminar-style classes and show the professors in those classes that you can actively participate in class discussions (a key skill for grad school). Also go to your professors' office hours. If the class is on the larger side, talking with the professor outside of class and coming prepared with questions and thoughts about the material can be an effective way to signal your engagement in the class and your interest in scholarly work. In those conversations, and to the extent you feel comfortable doing so, it can also help to be open with your professors about challenges you've faced. If your professors know that your mom died right before finals at the end of sophomore year, or if they know that you've been working twenty hours a week to make ends meet, on top of going to school, then they can use that information to help explain any gaps or deficiencies in your academic performance and also speak to your resilience and motivation.

If you can't make it to office hours, it's also okay to email your professors to ask about meeting at other times, or to just drop them a note with links to materials that made you think of what was talked about in class. I assign podcasts for my students to listen to in my Introduction to Sociology class, and I love when students send me links to new and relevant episodes—it helps me keep the content fresh.

The process of finding letter writers can be more difficult if you're not going straight from an undergrad degree in a particular discipline to a graduate degree in that same field. But that doesn't mean it can't be done. If you don't go straight from undergrad to grad school, for example, you can build your chances for better letters by maintaining ties with the professors you had long ago. Dropping them a note of congratulations when they publish a new paper and emailing them with brief updates on your own career (and how what you learned from them has helped you in that career) are great ways to stay in touch. If you haven't stayed in touch, it's important to provide some context when you do reach out to reconnect. If you can find it, email them a copy of the final paper you wrote for their class. Or mention things you learned in their course and how they've stuck with you over the years. All those bits of information can help your former professors write better letters on your behalf.

If you're in that long-out-of-undergrad group, or even if you're not, you might also ask for letters from people who aren't professors in your field. Maybe you have a work supervisor who can speak to your skills and your strengths on the job. Or maybe you're particularly close with a professor from outside the field where you want a degree. Some departments might weigh those letters less heavily than letters from professors in their discipline. That's because admissions committees tend to put more trust in letter writers who are known quantities—i.e., well-respected scholars in their field. If you have to choose, though, it's generally better to have a really glowing and detailed letter from a lesser-known scholar or a nonacademic mentor than to have a flat letter from a well-known scholar who barely knows who you are.

Once you decide whom to ask, make those requests as a follow-up to the kinds of can-I-get-your-help-deciding-where-to-apply-to-grad-school conversations we talked about. At the end of those conversations (if you're having them in person), or in a separate email, you can thank them for their advice and ask if they'd be willing to write you a letter of recommendation. If you're asking by email, you can use a template like this:

Dear Professor [LAST NAME],

I am in the process of applying to [MASTER'S/DOCTORAL] programs in [FIELD], and I wanted to write to ask if you would be willing to write a letter of recommendation for my application. Given our experience working together [IN CLASS/ON A PROJECT, ETC.], I thought you could speak to my strengths [AS A STUDENT/AS A RESEARCHER/WITH PROJECT MANAGEMENT, ETC.].

I will attach a copy of my personal statement and a list of the programs to which I am considering applying, with the dates those applications are due. Please let me know if there is any additional information I can provide, or if you would like to meet to talk more.

Also, if you are unable to write a letter at this time, I completely understand.

Thank you for your support!

Sincerely,

[YOUR NAME]

Generally, if they're willing to offer advice on the front end of the decision-making process, they'll also be willing to help you out with a letter. Just be sure to leave enough time. Start these conversations at least three months before the applications are due and then ask for letters at least two months before the deadline. If it's getting close to that deadline, and you still haven't gotten notice that the letters are in, it's also okay to check in with reminders (two weeks out, one week out, two days out, day of). You might even offer to send reminders when you ask for the letters up front—I know I appreciate when students can help keep me on track.

When you ask for letters of recommendation, include information and materials that can help your letter writers write strong letters on your behalf. Some letter writers might ask you to put together a list of key points to include. Some letter writers might even ask you to draft the letter for them. This isn't (generally) considered cheating, even though it might feel weird. Treat it as a chance to help your letter writer better convey the skills and strengths you'll bring to grad school (and a chance to avoid gendered or otherwise biased language that might hurt your chances of getting in).[71] Don't feel like you have to be humble or self-deprecating. Write the letter as if you were recommending someone else—someone you like, respect, and want to succeed. If your letter writer feels the letter is too positive, they can always edit it before they click "send."

***

As we've talked about, admissions committees want to pick sure bets—they want to admit students they think are going to succeed. And yet even if you have perfect GRE scores, perfect grades, a carefully crafted application, and a set of stellar recommendations, admission is never guaranteed. That's because graduate programs, and especially highly ranked, fully funded doctoral programs in particularly "desirable" locations, often have hundreds more applicants than they could ever admit. So do your best to put together a solid application, but don't be ashamed if you don't get into your top choice program, or even if you don't get into any program at all.

The Grad School Visit

Now, if you're lucky enough to be accepted into a grad program (and if you're really lucky, accepted to more than one), you might be invited to a "visiting day" or "open house" event. If you can afford it, definitely attend. And if you can't make it (maybe you have an exam or a work commitment or a family commitment that same day, or maybe the costs of travel are too high), definitely ask the graduate program director for help setting up phone or Skype conversations with faculty and current grad students instead.

In terms of those travel costs, some programs will cover travel expenses like airfare and hotels. However, and as the tweet from grad student Roxy Brookshire suggests, you might be expected to pay those costs up front and then wait to be reimbursed. If you don't have a credit card or don't have the money to pay those costs up front, let the program director know. There may be workarounds they can use to get the expenses paid for you. And don't feel ashamed—there are plenty of students in the same boat. If the program is committed to helping you succeed, faculty and staff will help you find a way to get to visiting day.

72

 Roxy Brookshire @RoxyBrookshire · Jul 21, 2018
Replying to @JessicaCalarco

#hiddencurriculum everyone will assume you have a credit card and they can just reimburse you for travel ... possibly.

In most departments and disciplines, visiting days operate as two-way interviews. Technically, if you've already been admitted, and especially if you have other options to choose from, then, at least on some level, the program is probably trying to impress you.

That's because the program has an interest in keeping its yield as high as possible—getting all the admitted students to accept so the committee doesn't have to scramble and fill slots from the wait list.[73]

At the same time, though, and even if you've already been admitted, you still want to be in interviewee mode. As we'll talk about in later chapters, the opportunities available in academia are rarely evenly distributed or openly advertised. So if the other professors and grad students you meet during visit day come away with a good impression of you, they might be more likely to think of you when they're deciding whom to invite to work with them on a paper or whose name to submit for an award.

As frustrating (and often unfair) as it is that first impressions matter, there are things you can do to start your visit days off on the right foot. One trick I use—whenever I visit any campus, whether for an interview or to give a talk—is to make a "cheat sheet" of all the faculty and students I'll be meeting throughout the day. During the visit day, for example, you'll typically have scheduled meetings with a number of professors and students. You can also let the graduate program director know, in advance of the visit day, if there are particular people on campus with whom you'd like to meet. Once you have that list of meetings (and this might not be until the day before your visit), head to the program website and start looking up names. Then make yourself a cheat sheet with key details about each person. My cheat sheets usually have a picture of each person (downloaded from the website, or sometimes from social media), along with information about their primary areas of interest, the methods they use in their work, any recent publications, and any particular questions I want to ask them about their work.

In addition to one-on-one meetings, visit days will also give you a chance to get a feel for the department and the university and the surrounding community. You'll probably get a tour of the campus and maybe the neighborhoods where grad students live. You might even get to sit in on classes or lectures or other department events.

That kind of hands-on, face-to-face interaction will give you far more information about the people and the program than you could ever learn from websites or emails or brochures. Of course the programs you visit will try to put their best foot forward on visiting day. But there are questions you can ask to help chip away at that veneer and get the real story of what life in that department is like.

That includes questions for professors, such as:

- How many grad students are you currently working with?
- What's your approach to working with grad students?
- What graduate courses do you typically teach? (And how often are they offered?)
- What projects are you working on? (And are there ways for grad students to get involved?)
- When you publish with grad students, what does the division of labor typically look like?
- What do you think of this town/university/department overall?
- What would you change about this town/university/department?

In terms of questions for other grad students, you might ask:

- What professors do you work with? (And how did you develop those relationships?)
- Are there any professors you avoid working with? (And, if so, why?)
- How are grad students typically funded during the graduate program (e.g., departmental fellowships, teaching assistantships, faculty grants, external fellowships)?
  - What do grad students do for funding during the summer months?
  - How are grad students supported if their advisors leave or no longer have funding to support them?
  - How much debt (if any) do grad students typically incur while they're in the program?

- What are grad students required to do in order to receive funding (e.g., serving as teaching assistants or research assistants, teaching their own courses)?
  - How much time do these commitments typically involve?
  - Are these commitments year-round, or only during the academic year?
  - Are there limits on the amount or types of work students are allowed to complete?
  - Do faculty typically "follow the rules" when it comes to the demands they make on grad students?
- What does it take to be successful in this program?
- How long does it usually take for students to complete the program?
- What types of career paths do grad students typically pursue after they complete their degrees?
- Where do you turn for help when you're not sure about something grad-school-wise?
- What's the culture like here?
  - Do grad students help each other succeed, or are they more competitive?
  - How do faculty treat grad students?
  - What's it like living in this community?
  - Have there ever been times when someone here made you feel uncomfortable or unwanted?
- What do you think of this town/university/department overall? What are your favorite and least favorite things?
- What would you change about this town/university/ department?
- Where do grad students typically live?
- How do grad students typically get to and from campus, and how much does it cost (e.g., car, public transit, university busses)?
- What options are there for school/child care for young children, and how much do they cost?
- What do grad students do for fun?

In terms of program directors and program staff, you might ask:

- How are grad students typically funded during the graduate program?
  - What's included in the funding (e.g., health insurance, vision and dental coverage, relocation funding, conference travel funding)?
  - How are taxes handled (i.e., are they automatically deducted, or do students have to calculate and submit their own owed amounts)?
  - What do grad students do for funding during the summer months?
  - How are grad students supported if their advisors leave or no longer have funding to support them?
- What are grad students required to do in order to receive funding (e.g., serving as teaching assistants or research assistants, teaching their own courses)?
  - How much time do these commitments typically involve?
  - Are these commitments year-round, or only during the academic year?
  - Are there limits on the amount or types of work grad students are allowed to complete?
- What does it take for students to be successful in this program?
- What's the expected timeline for completion, and what happens if it takes students longer than that to complete?
- What types of career paths do grad students typically pursue after they complete their degrees?
- What happens if students are struggling to stay on track?
- What types of jobs do students typically get when they graduate?
- What kinds of support does the program provide to students in helping them find jobs?

By asking these questions, you can get more insight into the school and the program than you'll ever find online—insights that can be critical for determining which program and which people will best meet your needs. As you might have noticed, some of these questions repeat across different groups. That's intentional. Because, as I teach the students in my qualitative methods classes, it's important to triangulate your evidence. Faculty and staff, for example, might perceive department culture differently than do grad students, and those differences can tell you something about the degree to which faculty and staff are aware of and responsive to students' concerns.

* * *

Along those lines, and as we'll talk about in the next chapter, you want not just a single advisor you can work with but rather a team of people who will support you as you navigate your way through grad school and beyond.

Chapter 2

BUILDING YOUR TEAM

 Justin Zimmerman @JZPhilosophy · Jul 27, 2018
Replying to @JessicaCalarco

It's good to have friends in a program to ask "stupid" questions to. Somebody has to tell you the norms of academia! #phdlife #HiddenCurriculum

---

As an undergrad, a grad student, and a faculty member, I've been lucky to have great mentors. People who've taught me to write well and think clearly and do good research. People who've given me detailed feedback and explained how I could do better. People who aren't afraid to acknowledge the harsh realities of academic competition and who push me to keep going despite the low chances of success.

Of course, even the best mentors aren't perfect, and some are far less than perfect.[2] Maybe your advisor will make you spend months chasing them down for a recommendation letter, which you'll need for an internship, which you'll need in order to graduate. Or maybe the professor you work for will berate you for not getting the "right" results in the lab. My hope is that you won't encounter that kind of toxic treatment in grad school, but there are certainly plenty of grad students and former grad students who have.

Now, it's easy to see that kind of mistreatment as an individual problem—the product of a few "bad apple" professors who interact with their students in less-than-professional ways. In reality, though, the under-mentoring and mis-mentoring of grad students isn't just an individual problem.[3] It stems from and is baked into the structure of grad school and the structure of academia as a whole.

Professors, and especially professors who work in schools or departments with graduate programs, face immense pressure to be as productive as possible with their research. That means getting large amounts of external grant funding, carrying out innovative and important projects, and publishing large numbers of high-impact books and articles based on their research. Essentially, while a professor's job responsibilities might include research, teaching/mentoring, and service, only the research part really "counts" for things like tenure and promotion (more on what these terms mean in chapter 3). As a result, professors have little professional incentive to put time and effort into effective teaching and mentoring. Instead, professors who put themselves first (and treat their students primarily as resources for their own success) often have the best chances of rising to the top.

Meanwhile, professors who do care enough to be good teachers and good mentors are often overburdened with requests.[4] That's particularly true for women scholars of color and scholars from other systematically marginalized groups, who do a disproportionate share of both student mentoring and university service. That unfair burden, in turn, can make it harder for good mentors to be successful in their research and their academic careers.[5]

If we want to lessen that unfair burden, then we need to make mentoring a team sport. The "we" here is mostly referring to faculty, and especially faculty from privileged groups. White faculty, for example, shouldn't shy away from mentoring students of color, just as men shouldn't shy away from mentoring women. Rather, and as sociologist and National Center for Faculty Development and Diversity founder Dr. Kerry Ann Rockquemore has argued, privileged faculty should educate themselves about how to effectively mentor scholars from systematically marginalized groups, and they should look for opportunities to offer effective support (e.g., by offering to serve on committees, read drafts of manuscripts, and write letters of recommendation, as well as by intervening when microaggressions occur).[6] I strongly encourage you take a look at the many mentoring resources Rockquemore has created, and I hope you'll look for ways to be an ally and mentor to others in your own career. In the short term, you can also lessen the unfair burden on faculty from marginalized groups by building a robust team of mentors to help you meet your needs.

As we'll talk about in this chapter, that kind of team-based approach to mentoring is beneficial not only for the professors who act as your mentors but also for you as the student. We'll talk about how to build a team that includes not only your primary advisor but also other professors, grad students, staff members, family, friends, and organizations. We'll also talk about how to manage all those mentor-mentee relationships. And we'll talk about what to do if one of those relationships breaks down. Finally, we'll also talk about the everyday social aspects of grad school and how to navigate those spaces, especially if they're not your scene.

Building Your Team

As a grad student, you'll want to find a whole team of mentors to support you. And you'll want to choose people, or at least some people, who are willing to stick with you long term. That's because you won't need their help just in grad school. As a postdoc, or a professor, or a professional in another field, you'll probably still need to turn to your mentors for recommendation letters, for advice about research and writing and teaching, and for help figuring out what moves to make next in your career.

Ideally, you'll want to build a team that has at least one person who:

- Studies topics related to the kind of research you want to do
- Uses the methods you're most interested in using
- Gives thoughtful advice and can help you with strategic planning

- Writes well
- Gives constructive feedback
- Is well connected and well respected in the field
- Has time to listen and listens supportively, especially when you're feeling blue

You might get lucky enough to find people who can cover more than one of those categories, but it's rare to find someone who can cover them all. Furthermore, even if you have a mentor who can do all these things, relying on that person exclusively can make it hard for them to support other students and be successful in their own career. And that's why it's important to find multiple mentors and think of your mentors as a team.

Meeting Your Needs

Now, not everyone on your mentoring team has to be a professor in your department or a professor in your field or even a professor at all. We'll talk more about strategies for connecting with potential mentors in a minute. For now, though, let's talk through the various types of people you'll want to find.

Your Topic Person: When you're doing research, you'll need help figuring out what to study, how to study it, how to stay on track in getting the work done, and how to write about what you find. Your topic person is your "what to study" person when it comes to research. Ideally, this person should be a professor (and preferably a tenured professor) who is an expert in the subfield or topic you want to study in your research. Now, let's say, for example, that you want to study how the hidden curriculum of grad school impacts students' mental health. You don't need to find an advisor who also studies how the hidden curriculum of grad school impacts students' mental health. If your advisor studies higher education or even high school students' mental health, that's probably a close enough match.

In the arts, humanities, and social sciences, it can actually be better if your advisor's interests aren't a perfect match for yours. In the lab sciences, you're generally expected to write a dissertation based on research you're doing with your advisor. In the arts, humanities, and social sciences, on the other hand, you're generally expected to come up with and carry out a dissertation project on your own. In those fields, if your dissertation research is too similar to your advisor's research, hiring committees and tenure committees might assume that your advisor just "gave" you a topic to study, and they might worry that you won't be able to come up with future research ideas.

That said, and even in fields where being an "independent thinker" is highly valued, it's still important to have a mentor who knows your topic fairly well. Your topic person should be able to help you make sense of key debates in your subfield, and should be able to help you design a dissertation project that speaks to those debates. This person will probably be your dissertation advisor or chair (more on what these terms mean in chapter 3), but that might not always be the case.

Your Methods Person: When it comes to research, your methods person is your "how" person—the person who can help you design a solid research project and help you figure out how to get back on track if things go wrong along the way. Maybe you're trying to figure out why your statistical models keep failing to converge. Maybe you can't get the tensile test machine to work. Maybe you can't get anyone to agree to do an interview or get access to the archive you need. Maybe you're trying to decide whether you need a comparison case. This is the person who can guide you through those challenges. And they'll probably be a professor. But, in some cases, a university staff member or a more advanced grad student might give you better (or more timely) advice. That said, if your primary dissertation advisor/chair uses a different research method than you do, it's generally good to have at least one other professor on your dissertation committee who knows your method well. That way they can back you up (and give you guidance) if your primary advisor questions your methodological approach.

Your Advice Person: When you're doing research, you might need help staying on track and getting the work done. Your advice person is the person who can help you strategize and make a concrete plan. The person who understands the realities of academia—the competition and the inequalities and the culture of overwork. The person who's willing to be frank with you about the strengths and limitations of your own work. The person who believes you can succeed and who is willing to help you work toward achieving the next steps in your career. Given the amount of insider knowledge it takes to really understand academia, this person will probably be a professor, or maybe a former grad student who's already made it out into the real world. But they don't have to be someone in your department. As we'll talk about a bit later in this chapter, there are ways to make connections with scholars at other schools as well.

Your Writing Person: With respect to research, your writing person is one of the people you can turn to for help in learning to write clearly, concisely, and compellingly about what you find. Ideally, this should be someone whose writing you love to read. As we'll talk about in chapters 4 and 7, good writing—i.e., clear, compelling, engaging writing—is sorely undervalued in academia. So when you find someone whose writing you admire, let them be your guide. You don't even have to know them (though it never hurts to drop them an email saying how much you appreciate their work). You can just use the structure and style of their writing as a model for your own. Not in a plagiaristic way, but in an "I see what you're doing here and I'm going to strive for something similar" sort of way.

Your Feedback Person: Your feedback person is another key person to turn to in learning how to write clearly, concisely, and compellingly about what you find in your research. This is the person who takes the time to really engage with your work. The person who doesn't just point out problems to fix but also explains why something you wrote doesn't work. The person who offers edits and suggestions and who explains those edits and suggestions in a way that helps you move forward rather than leaving you feeling stuck. This person might be a professor, but they might also be a grad student, or someone at the university writing center, or even a family member or friend.

Your Networking Person: This is the person who knows how to play the game and who's willing to stake your bets. To do that, this person has to be well connected and well respected in your field and in the field where you want to work post-degree. They can find out who's hiring, and maybe even get you a postdoc, just by making a phone call. They can walk around with you at a conference and introduce you to their friends from other industries or other schools. This person will almost always be a tenured full professor in your field. They might not do exactly the same kind of research you do, but their connections can help you build your own.

Your Listener Person: This is the person you trust to listen when you're dealing with challenges in your program and in your life. As sociologist Dr. Mario Small explains in his research on first-year grad students, grad school "often exhibit[s] a boot-camp quality that heightens stress, undermines mental health, and repeatedly creates the need to talk—not merely about work but also about life goals, marriage, health, finances, and more."[7] At the same time, however, that "boot-camp quality" of grad school can also forge strong bonds between you and the other grad students in your program. Because those other grad students are going through the same things at the same time, they can be a useful source of support, especially if you're willing to help support them in return.[8]

Of course, and especially if your life circumstances are different from those of other students in your program, you might have trouble forming those new and supportive bonds. In that case, and as we'll talk more about in a bit, it's especially important to find other people who will listen and help you work through the tough times. Maybe you can turn to your partner or your parent or a friend from home, but they might not understand the unique structures or stressors of grad school. If that's the case, then you might also look for a mental health professional who has experience working with grad students. Your university will probably have trained counselors who can help in the short term (some universities also offer a set number of free counseling visits each semester), but it can be very much worth the investment to find a long-term therapist you trust.[9]

Assembling Your Team (and Thinking Outside Your Department)

Essentially, you'll want to assemble a whole team of people to help you succeed in grad school and beyond. That includes your advisor, of course, and other professors. But it also includes other grad students, staff members, family and friends, and maybe even a therapist.

For some students, it's easy to find that team of mentors, but if it isn't easy for you, you're definitely not alone. You might have trouble finding professors you can trust, or you might find that you have little in common with other grad students in your program.

Thankfully, if you're looking to fill unmet needs in your network, there are plenty of places you can turn. First, you might consider joining a national organization that facilitates mentor-mentee relationships. These organizations were initially developed to support students and faculty from systematically marginalized groups, but they are open to more privileged students and faculty as well. They include:

- The National Research Mentoring Network (NRMN) is a free online mentoring platform that has connected thousands of mentors and mentees at various career stages. The NRMN was originally created to support the diversity of the biomedical field by providing culturally responsive mentoring for students and faculty from systematically marginalized groups. Over time, however, the NRMN has expanded to connect mentors and mentees from a wide variety of academic disciplines and in both academic and nonacademic careers.

- The National Center for Faculty Development and Diversity (NCFDD) supports academics and higher education administrators at all career stages. As part of its professional development and productivity-related workshops, the NCFDD connects its members with peer coaches and with other scholars at similar stages in their careers. While an NCFDD membership is not cheap, the organization strongly encourages scholars to ask their universities to provide financial support for their memberships, and their website even provides suggestions for "making the ask." I had the opportunity to participate in the NCFDD's Faculty Success Program when I was a new assistant professor, and the skills I learned and connections I made have been invaluable in building a successful career.

In addition to these national networking organizations, joining professional organizations can also help you find mentors to fill your team. Whatever field you're pursuing for your degree, there will almost certainly be a professional organization (or twenty) you can join. Just in sociology, for example, there's the International Sociological Association, the American Sociological Association, the European Sociological Society, the Society for the Study of Social Problems, the Population Association of America, the Association of Black Sociologists, Sociologists for Women in Society, the Sociology of Education Association, the Law and Society Association, the Society for the Scientific Study of Religion, the Eastern Sociological Society, the Pacific Sociological Association, the Southern Sociological Society, and dozens of other geographic or subfield-specific organizations. If you don't know the names of the key organizations in your field, ask your professors or check out their CVs—there might be a list of the organizations to which they belong.

As the list above suggests, some professional organizations are topic specific, while others focus on supporting scholars from systematically marginalized groups. Some of the latter group of organizations serve students and scholars from a wide array of disciplines. I'll list a few key examples of that type of organization below. I'd also recommend looking up scholars in your discipline who share your background and checking to see which organizational memberships they list on their websites or CVs.

- American Association of University Women
- Association for Women in Science
- HERS (Higher Education Resource Services)
- National Association of Women Artists
- National Black Graduate Student Association
- National Black Student Union
- Out in Science, Technology, Engineering and Mathematics (oSTEM)
- Prospanica
- Society for Advancement of Chicanos/Hispanics and Native Americans in Science

Even if academia wasn't designed for people like you, it's important to know that there are people and organizations to support you and help you assemble your mentoring team. That mentoring team, in turn, can help you patch together a grad school experience—and a career—that reflects your whole self and meets all your needs.

Pipeline Programs

You don't have to wait until grad school to start building your network of support. Organizations like the NRMN, for example, are even open to undergrads looking to connect with scholars in their field. If you're still an undergrad, there are also pipeline programs you can apply for to help you learn about grad school and connect with faculty and with other students interested in pursuing graduate degrees.

In addition to providing students with mentoring and training opportunities, some of these programs also support students financially in getting their undergraduate degrees. They include:

- The McNair Scholars Program is a publicly funded program that supports diversity in academia by providing undergraduate scholarships and mentoring for low-income students, first-generation college students, and students from systematically marginalized racial and ethnic groups who are interested in pursuing grad school and academic careers.[10]
- The Mellon Mays Undergraduate Fellowship Program (MMUF) is a privately funded program that supports academic diversity by providing undergraduate scholarships and mentoring for students from underrepresented minority groups who are interested in pursuing PhDs in the arts, sciences, social sciences, and humanities.[11]
- The SSRC-Mellon Mays Graduate Initiatives Program supports MMUF fellows as they transition from undergrad to grad schools and into their post-PhD careers, providing gap funding for the summer between college and grad school, funding for travel and research grants during grad school, funding to complete dissertation projects, and workshops that support professional development at all stages of the academic career.[12]

Other pipeline programs fund students to participate in short-term research or training opportunities, which often occur during the summer months. There are hundreds of these short-term programs, many of which are targeted at students attending particular universities or interested in particular fields. If you're interested in these programs, but you're not sure where to start, ask professors you know from undergrad if they can point you in the right direction. You can also check out the programs below as examples:

- The National Institutes of Health STEP-UP (Short-Term Research Experience for Underrepresented Persons) Program funds high school students and undergraduate students to participate in hands-on summer research experiences. The goal of the program is to support students in pursuing careers in biomedical, behavioral, clinical, and social science research. Participants work alongside mentors at local universities and also have the opportunity to present their research at a conference at the NIH.
- Other examples of short-term and summer programs include:
  - The CUNY Pipeline Program for students pursuing PhDs in any discipline except law, business, and medicine[13]
  - The ICPSR Summer Program in Quantitative Methods of Social Research[14]
  - The Stanford Summer Research Program–Amgen Scholars Program for undergraduate students interested in scientific fields[15]
  - The Stanford Summer Community College Premedical Program[16]
  - The Perry Initiative for Women in Engineering and Medicine[17]
  - The Council on Legal Education Opportunity (CLEO) Pre-Law Summer Institute[18]
  - The Prelaw Undergraduate Scholars (PLUS) Programs[19]

Making Connections Online

While professional organizations and pipeline programs are great channels for making formal connections with scholars outside your program, you might be interested in making more informal connections as well. If that's the case, then social media is a great resource.

On Twitter, for example, and as you've seen in the tweets throughout this book, scholars regularly share their thoughts on academia and offer advice for navigating grad school and academic careers. By following those scholars, you can learn a lot, even without saying anything at all. In fact, if you're new to Twitter or any other online platform, it can be helpful to just observe for a while before joining the conversation. That way you can get a sense of the norms around what to post (and what not to post) in your field. Then, when you're feeling bold enough, it's okay to jump in.

As you're thinking about whom to follow on Twitter or other social media platforms, try to build as diverse a network as possible. Of course you can start by following scholars you know and scholars whose names you know from research or things you've seen online. But don't stop there. Follow grad students and junior scholars. Follow Black scholars, Latinx scholars, Indigenous scholars, Asian scholars, and scholars from other racial and ethnic groups. Follow LGBTQ scholars. Follow women scholars. Follow scholars from other universities, other disciplines, and other countries. If you're not sure where to find those scholars, search for professional organizations and academic journals in your field— check out whom they follow and who follows them. You can also search for academia hashtags, like #AcademicTwitter, #Academic-Chatter, #phdlife, #phdchat, and #gradschool, to find people who are tweeting about those topics, and who have great insights to share, even if their research, backgrounds, and experiences are very different from yours.

This kind of intentionality in network building is especially important if you're from a more privileged background. The more privileged you are, the easier it will be to surround yourself with other scholars who look and think like you. Building a diverse network can help you think beyond your own bubble, and it can help you be a better ally to your students and your colleagues from systematically marginalized groups. But it works that way only if you're willing to listen and learn. Be mindful of your unearned advantages. Be supportive when other scholars share stories about the challenges they've faced. Be open to new information, but don't demand that others do the work of teaching you.

After you've taken the time to listen and learn, it's okay to start sharing your own thoughts. For your first tweets, post a few things to your own timeline rather than commenting on other people's posts. You might find a recent research or news article relevant to your interests, then tweet out a link with a brief description or short take. That way, when you do start commenting on other scholars' posts, they can check out your timeline to get a sense of who you are.

Along those lines, it's helpful to use your posts to show that you're not just in it for yourself. If all you post are links to your own new research, you're missing out on the social part of social media, and your timeline will feel pretty flat. Instead, and once you've added a few posts of your own, look for other interesting posts that you can comment on and retweet to share. Essentially, if you show that you want to be part of the conversation, and especially if you do so constructively, creatively, and with an eye toward promoting other people's ideas, other scholars will be more likely to follow back, comment on your posts, and share what you post with their followers.

That said, it's important not to get angry if you don't get an immediate follow-back or reply, especially from a "big name" scholar in your field. Given how vicious online spaces can sometimes be, many public scholars ignore or turn off their notifications. That way they don't have to see hateful stuff people post to them or about them online. Many public scholars are also wary of interacting with social media users who don't use their real names, who don't have a picture or avatar in their profile, or who don't post much information about themselves.

Along those lines, I'd also encourage you to think carefully about how you respond to other people online. You don't always have to be kind—if you have a tweet that "blows up" and gets a thousand likes and retweets and comments, you don't have to reply to each one. And if someone else posts something hateful about you or in response to one of your posts, feel free to block them and report them without guilt. But please, don't knowingly contribute to academia's already rampant culture of cruelty. If you're going to disagree with someone's take, do it respectfully—don't write anything you wouldn't say to their face. And if you're going to make a joke, be sure that it's not at the expense of someone with less power or privilege than you.

Once you make new online connections, you might be able to use those online conversations as a bridge to start in-person conversations. I'm always honored to hear from students that they follow me on Twitter or that they've appreciated things I post online. In a few cases, I've even had online conversations turn into coauthored papers with scholars I didn't previously know. If there's a scholar online you've connected with and with whom you want to chat more, drop them a message and ask if they would be interested in meeting for coffee at an upcoming conference. We'll talk more about how to frame those requests in chapter 10. More senior scholars often have conference schedules packed with committee meetings, but they might be able to squeeze in a quick chat. Meanwhile, other grad students and junior scholars are often looking to build their own teams of friendly faces, and they'll likely be eager to connect.

Asking for Help

The whole point of having a team of mentors is that you'll have multiple people to turn to for help. And there are plenty of things you might need help with in grad school:

- Understanding course concepts
- Learning the ins and outs of research methods
- Developing research projects
- Finding funding
- Working through setbacks in your research
- Getting feedback on proposals and applications and paper drafts

- Publishing and presenting your work
- Getting letters of recommendation
- Navigating the hidden curriculum in your program and your field

You might be lucky enough to have mentors who will reach out and check in to see how you're doing on all these fronts. Most mentors, though, are busy with their own lives and careers. If you need their help, you'll probably have to ask.

Of course, asking for help can be scary. I get it. I feel nervous every time I have to ask a colleague for a recommendation letter, a teaching assistant to help me with grading, or a staff member to help me fix a problem with my computer. I worry that maybe I don't deserve the position or the grant or the award I'm applying for and that I'll just be wasting someone else's time. I worry that the person I'm asking for help will feel obligated to say yes, even if they're incredibly busy. I worry that they'll resent me for making extra work for them. I worry that the question I'm asking is something I should've been able to figure out on my own.

Despite those risks, though, when I do get up the courage to ask, most people are willing to help. And if someone I ask does say no, it's usually because they've already said yes to as many things as they can manage while still taking care of their own work and well-being. Now you might be thinking—she's a white, privileged professor, of course people say yes when she asks. And there's truth to that. But research has also shown that when students and even students from marginalized groups speak up—and especially if they ask the "right" way (more on this in a minute)—they're more likely to get what they need than if they didn't ask at all.[20]

How to Ask for Help

So what is the "right" way to ask for help?

First, ask respectfully. That means distributing your requests equitably (i.e., not relying on one person to meet all your mer_toring needs, just because they're the most accessible or approachable or reliable). It also means making your requests as clear and concise as possible, avoiding last-minute requests, and acknowledging the other person's right to say no.

Second, ask appreciatively. That means acknowledging the work you're creating for someone when you ask them for help and showing gratitude both for their consideration of the request and (if they say yes) for their help and support. As we'll talk about in a minute, showing gratitude also means being open to feedback—even if that feedback isn't exactly what you want to hear.

Third, ask efficiently. Most professional requests can be made over email, with an offer to follow up with an in-person or phone conversation if needed. That includes things like asking for recommendation letters, asking for feedback on proposals and drafts, and asking questions about assignments and topics discussed in class. For requests that require a conversation, schedule an appointment or stop by during office hours. For example, if you're asking a professor to be on your dissertation committee, they'll probably want to talk with you about the project before deciding. That said, there are some scholars who have very specific preferences regarding in-person versus digital requests. If you're not sure how best to approach a particular professor or staff member for help, ask for advice from a more senior grad student who works with the person you want to ask. And if you decide to go the email route, take a look at the sample emails throughout this book for models of how to be respectful, efficient, and appreciative in making requests.

Of course, even if you ask respectfully, appreciatively, and efficiently, that doesn't mean other people will always say yes to your requests. And while a decline might sting, it might (at least in some cases) be a perfectly reasonable response. The people you ask might be dealing with personal challenges such as health problems or family responsibilities that make it difficult for them to take on extra requests. Or the people you ask might have already agreed to as many things or more things than they can reasonably handle, and declining your request is the only way they can leave time to get everything else done. As we'll talk more about in chapter 12, it's important to find balance in an academic career. And if we want to find balance in our own careers, we have to respect other people's need for balance as well.

How to Pay It Forward

That said, if you're trying to be respectful of your mentors' time, you might feel guilty about asking them for help. You might be asking yourself: "How could I ever pay this person back?"

With faculty mentors, the best way to "pay back" the support you've gotten is to be open to the feedback you get. Beyond that, though, you shouldn't worry about thank-you gifts or trying to do for your faculty mentors what they've done for you. That's not how academia works. Academia works (or at least should work) on a pay-it-forward model. Your faculty mentors help you today. And then when you're successful tomorrow, you help those who come after you.

With peer mentors, on the other hand, it's good to strive for reciprocal relationships of support. You might start a reading group with other grad students studying for the same comprehensive exam. Or you might start a writing group with other grad students where you meet every month to give each other feedback on your work. That kind of peer support is invaluable. And many of those groups last well beyond grad school. I know academics who have been part of the same reading or writing group for more than twenty years, and there will never be a phase of your career where you don't need other people for support.

Accepting Feedback

Asking for help in grad school (and in academic careers more generally) often means asking for feedback—on grant proposals and fellowship applications, research designs and paper drafts, course materials you develop for your classes, and statements you submit when applying for jobs. It's important to be open to that kind of feedback, and it's important to learn how to use the feedback you get. That's because, in grad school, and especially if you're interested in a career in academia, you won't get feedback just from the people you trust. You'll also get feedback (and often anonymous feedback) from other scholars who review your grant proposals, your fellowship applications, and your manuscript drafts. We'll talk more about the peer-review process in chapter 8. For now, though, the key is to know that what happens to those grant proposals and fellowship applications and manuscript drafts will depend, at least in part, on how you respond to the feedback you get.

It can be difficult to take feedback, especially if you disagree with the advice you're given or if that feedback tells you there's a lot more work to do. In general, though, even the harshest feedback usually contains at least some elements of truth, and even the most nitpicky requests can ultimately improve the final project or paper you produce. In writing this book, for example, I got feedback from five anonymous reviewers, along with my editor and a few other students and colleagues and friends. That review process left me with almost twenty pages of advice and suggestions on things to edit, cut, or add. It took months of work to make those changes, but I'm certain that the book is better as a result.

That said, and as we'll talk about in chapter 8, there are times when it makes sense to push back against a reviewer's critique. In general, though, I try to approach the feedback I get by remembering that if one person is concerned or confused by something I wrote, then there's a good chance other people will be too. So I try not to dwell on the idea that I did something wrong and focus instead on how I can fix what I wrote to avoid similar concerns or confusion with future drafts. That doesn't always mean doing exactly what your professor or your best friend or the anonymous reviewer tells you to do, but it does mean using their feedback to figure out what needs to be fixed.

When giving feedback to my own students and colleagues, I opt for a contextualized approach. That means including not only critiques of the work ("here's what's wrong") but also explanations for those critiques ("here's why that's a problem") and tentative suggestions for ways to fix the problems that generated the critique ("here's one thing you might try"). Essentially, I try to start a dialog with the person seeking feedback rather than just pointing out what's wrong or dictating what they should do.

That kind of contextualized approach, however, also takes more time than it would to take a merely critical ("here's what's wrong") or dictatorial ("here's what you have to do") approach. And so there's a good chance that at least some of the feedback you get won't come fully contextualized. You might see margin notes from your advisor that say just "fix this" or "not clear." Or you might see a suggested revision from a reviewer with no explanation to justify why that's what you should do. In those cases it's important to try to fill in the rest of the context yourself—figuring out what the problem is and how you should fix it, or understanding why a particular revision might be necessary beyond just "that's what the reviewer told me to do."

If you get that kind of vague or overly harsh feedback, and you can't work through it on your own, it's definitely okay to ask for help. Show the feedback you've gotten to another professor or a more senior grad student you trust. Ask them for help in contextualizing the feedback, stripping away the harshness, and finding the meat of what's helpful and what can be ignored. It's more work in the short term to ask for help, and you might feel nervous about showing others the negative feedback you got, but it'll give you a better chance of correctly identifying the problems in your work and finding a solution that effectively solves those problems in the end.

Dealing with Conflict

As this discussion of harsh feedback suggests, the people you encounter in grad school won't all be supportive, and the relationships you build won't all be conflict-free. We'll talk in this section about the kinds of problematic relationships you might find in grad school and also about potential strategies for dealing with those conflicts and getting the help you need.

Harassment, Discrimination, and Abuse

Because of grad students' precarious status in academia, and because faculty members have so much power over their careers, grad students are particularly vulnerable to harassment, abuse, and discrimination from faculty members, and they often have little power to speak up or push back.[21] That includes sexual harassment as well as other forms of harassment and discrimination on the basis of gender, race or ethnicity, nationality, sexuality, or physical ability.[22] That kind of treatment, in turn, is not appropriate, and, depending on where you are, it might be against university policy and even against the law.

The National Academies of Sciences, Engineering, and Medicine (2018), for example, recently released a report on the sexual harassment of women in academia. The report documents extremely high rates of sexual harassment of women in academia and especially in medicine, science, and engineering. The report also describes the negative impact that harassment has on women and their careers. The report concludes that sexual harassment is not an individual problem. Rather, whole departments and disciplines are complicit in tolerating a culture of harassment and abuse. Based on those findings, the report concludes that universities, departments, and disciplines need to make it easier for victims to speak up and ensure they are heard when they do.

Those recommendations point to a hard reality of academia (and workplaces more generally). While the harassers and abusers are the ones causing the problem, organizations rely on victims to speak up if they want justice to be done.[23] Without an official report from a victim, there's often very little chance that the organization will take steps to stop or address the abuse.[24]

My hope is that you won't experience any form of harassment or discrimination or abuse in grad school. If you do, I hope you'll consider filing a report. Because you have a right to a healthy work environment, and your fellow grad students do too.[25]

That said, if you experience mistreatment in grad school or at any point in your career and you choose not to speak up, you shouldn't feel as though you are letting anyone down. You might be worried about being judged for speaking up, or about the possibility of retaliation, either from your abuser or from others who might take the abuser's side.[26] If your university or your department or your discipline doesn't provide the kind of supportive environment that the National Academies' report recommends, the risks you're worried about are real.[27] Given those risks, it's important never to blame yourself—or anyone else—for waiting (even years) to speak up or for deciding that it's not worth it to report at all.

Ultimately, though, if you experience harassment or discrimination and you want to file a report, look for faculty and staff members you can trust. That could be your advisor, or the graduate program chair, or another faculty or staff member. Ask to set up a meeting—you don't have to share details up front. You can even ask to meet outside of the department (e.g., at a coffee shop) if that feels like a safer option. In those meetings, the faculty or staff member can help you file a formal report or even file one on your behalf.

If you're worried about possible backlash, though, and if you'd prefer that no one in your department knows that you're filing a report, you can report directly to university officials instead. Universities are supposed to have clear (and confidential) reporting procedures for harassment, discrimination, and abuse. If you're not sure where or how to report, Google your university name plus "report harassment" or "report discrimination" or "report misconduct." Universities, at least in the United States, are also required to have an email account (abuse@[UNIVERSITY].edu) where anyone can submit reports.

If you're on the fence about reporting, and you just want to get a sense of what your options are, you can also frame your report in hypothetical terms. You might, for example, call the university office tasked with handling reports of harassment and discrimination (calling allows more anonymity than email, online, or in-person reporting) and say something like: "I have a question about a hypothetical situation. If, hypothetically, a student experiences [the thing that happened], what would you suggest the student should do? The person you speak with can then talk you through the hypothetical options and put you in touch with other people or offices on campus that can provide support. Some universities also have faculty or staff members who are designated "confidential" advocates and who can speak with you in detail about what you've experienced without triggering an official report.

Overwork and Under-mentoring

Harassment and discrimination are probably the most talked-about forms of mistreatment that students and scholars experience in academia, but unfortunately they're not the only kinds of mistreatment you might face. Your advisors and other professors, for example, might subject you to the kinds of overwork and under-mentoring that make you doubt yourself and your decision to go to grad school and that make it harder for you to succeed in your career.[28] Maybe a professor you work for expects you to do substantially more work than other grad students in the department. Maybe they expect you to do things (like picking up their dry cleaning or buying them coffee) that are outside the bounds of your official teaching or research-related work. Or maybe they repeatedly subject you to harsh criticisms and justify it by saying that they're preparing you for what you'll face in peer review.

In my view, faculty members shouldn't knowingly contribute to academia's culture of overwork or to its culture of cruelty. It's okay for your mentors to prepare you for cruelty ("Here's a harsh peer review I got and how I dealt with it"). It's not okay to inflict cruelty for practice ("I'll be harsh on you, so you'll be ready for peer review"). It's okay for your mentors to prepare you for the intensive demands of an academic career ("Here are all the things I have to do in the next month"). It's not okay to overwork you to avoid the work they're supposed to do themselves ("Do all these things so I can go on vacation next month").

Now, I'm not saying that your professors should give you only positive feedback or that they shouldn't give you any work to do. As we talked about a few sections back, there's value in learning to take constructive criticism from faculty and peers. And as we'll talk about in chapters 5 and 12, there's value in learning to manage academia's heavy workloads and juggle the many hats you'll have to wear. What I'm saying is that your professors should be thoughtful about how they frame the feedback they give you and about the work they give you to do. In terms of feedback, that means showing you how you can do better—helping you build their skills. Not just telling you what you did wrong. And in terms of workloads, that means respecting your rights and your time. Not just giving you work for the sake of work or because they can't do it all themselves.

The problem with overwork and under-mentoring is that they can take a serious toll on students' mental and physical health.[29] There have even been documented cases of graduate students committing suicide because of the hostile environments they encountered while working with professors in their labs.[30]

If you experience that kind of mistreatment in grad school, please know that you don't deserve to be treated that way. And please know that you're not alone.

If you face that kind of mistreatment, and as we'll talk about in a minute, you might decide to change advisors, change programs, drop out of coauthored projects, or even leave academia as a whole. An alternative, however, is to turn to trusted people and organizations that can help you get the support you need to survive and thrive in academia despite the toxic treatment you face. That might include fellow grad students, key faculty and staff members, friends and family members, therapists, or professional organizations like the ones we talked about in the "Building Your Team" section above.

Dealing with Drama

In some cases, the conflicts you encounter in academia won't be your own conflicts but conflicts between other people. There might, for example, be two faculty members in your program who refuse to serve on committees together. Or there might be a professor or grad student who is creating a toxic environment for some of the other students in your class. Conflicts like that happen in all kinds of work environments.[31] But the total institutionness of grad school (i.e., the fact that grad students' work lives and social/personal lives are often deeply intertwined) can make those professional conflicts resonate on a much deeper level.

Because of that blurry line between personal and professional relationships, academic departments often have factions and frenemies and long-standing beefs. Those petty (or sometimes not so petty) debates can create real consequences for students—like having to choose one faculty member or another for your dissertation committee, because having both faculty members on your committee would inevitably turn every meeting into a debate. If you suspect there are conflicts afoot in your department or program, ask other more advanced grad students for insights (e.g., "What do I do if Professor A and Professor B don't get along, but I want them both on my committee?" or "How do you deal with Student C when he's dominating the discussion in class?"). Other students might not know the full backstory behind the conflicts or complicated personalities in the department, but they'll probably have strategies and suggestions for navigating the debates.[32]

Changing Things Up

Even in the absence of abuse or harassment, you might have some academic relationships that just don't work out as planned. Maybe you're working on a coauthored paper with a fellow grad student and you're doing all of the work, but that isn't reflected in the authorship order (i.e., your name is listed in a lower status position than theirs). Or maybe the topic of your dissertation changes and your current advisor is no longer a good fit. That latter scenario is sort of what happened to me. Between my second and third years in grad school, the focus of my dissertation shifted such that I had to choose a new advisor for my work. At first I was super nervous—both about telling my master's paper advisor that I was interested in going in a different direction for my PhD and also about contacting a new professor in our department to ask if she would be interested in working with me instead. Thankfully, both professors were incredibly gracious and understanding. And the shift in advisors was fairly seamless.

Ideally, that's how it should be. Because advisor-student relationships aren't primarily about the advisor (or at least they shouldn't be). Instead, those relationships should be about the student and about finding the match that makes the most sense for the student's career.

At the same time, it's understandable to feel nervous about switching advisors or negotiating authorship or pulling out of projects. These relationships, while essentially professional, can also feel deeply personal. Because of the time invested. Because of the stakes. Because egos are involved.

Given the risks, approach these tough conversations—like mentoring conversations more generally—from a place of openness, appreciation, and respect. That means being open about your needs while also acknowledging the support you have received from the other person and your gratitude for that support. For example, here are a few sample scripts you can use if you need to change things up:

- Changing Advisors: "I am grateful for the work you have done and the support you have given me as my advisor over the past two years. However, my research is moving in a new direction, and I think it would make sense to choose a new primary advisor whose work is more closely aligned with my own. That said, if you are interested and available, I would love to have you continue as a member of my dissertation committee."

- Changing Authorship Order: "When we first discussed this project, we decided you would be the [HIGHEST STATUS] author, because you had the most experience with the topic/method and because you intended to take the lead with data analysis and writing. However, since we began work on the project, I have played the primary role in analyzing the data and writing up the results. Given that work, and given the shift away from our original plans, I think it would be appropriate for me to be the [HIGHEST STATUS] author on this project, instead. Would you be open to that change?"

Renegotiating relationships is never easy. But it's possible to have these conversations and leave the relationship intact. You can still be friends with a fellow grad student, even if you decide not to coauthor a paper together. And you can still have a former advisor on your dissertation committee, even if you decide they're not the best fit to be chair.

Of course there might be situations where your best option (or your only option) is to just cut the cord. And that's okay because you want a team that supports you. And you don't have time for professional relationships that don't meet your needs. Cutting the cord, however, doesn't mean that you'll be able to avoid a particular professor or a fellow grad student for the rest of your grad school career. You might have to take classes with them. Attend the same conferences they attend. See them at department events.

The Social Life of Grad School

Along those lines, most departments have all kinds of formal and academic events. Your department, for example, might have weekly or monthly "brown-bag" (i.e., bring-your-own-lunch) events where a speaker gives a talk about their research. These regularly occurring academic talks are sometimes called a colloquium or seminar series. Whatever the term, the idea is that there's a different speaker every month or every week talking about a different topic and the whole department is invited (or expected) to attend. The speaker might be a grad student or faculty member from your department or a scholar visiting from another department or university. There might also be weekly or monthly workshops where grad students and/or faculty meet to talk about or sometimes hear presentations about research on a particular topic.

In addition to those more formal, academic events, most departments have informal and social events as well. That includes start-of-semester breakfasts or picnics, holiday parties, and happy hours. In my department, we even have department softball and indoor soccer teams, where grad students and faculty play together (or, more often, lose together) in a local recreational sports league.

Those events can sometimes feel awkward. Professors aren't known for being the most socially adept creatures. And if you're new in the department, you might find yourself trapped in a corner making clumsy small talk with a professor you've never met before or a grad student with whom you've had an uncomfortable interaction in the past. Or maybe your department or your grad school cohort has lots of events that revolve around alcohol or coffee and that's just not your scene. (As someone who doesn't drink either alcohol or coffee, I've been in that situation plenty of times.)

Given all that awkwardness, you might be tempted to just skip out on the social stuff entirely—you might go to class, go to required meetings with your advisor, and then disappear to your office or the library or your apartment in between. If that's what you need to do for your own health and well-being, that's okay. But that decision can also have consequences.

For better or for worse, professors and other grad students will use your attendance at department events to gauge your commitment to the department and to academia as a whole. If a professor needs a research assistant for a project, for example, they're probably going to ask a student they see all the time, not someone who's never around, even if that second (less visible) person would technically be a better "fit" for the project. The professor will probably see that first student as harder working and more committed to research, even if that's not actually the case. Given those risks, you might want to push yourself to do the social stuff even if that's not where you want to be.

Pushing yourself to attend department events can also have more direct benefits for your career. Going to weekly seminars or workshops, for example, might feel like a waste of time, especially if the topic isn't directly relevant to your own research. But seeing academic talks can help you learn to give better talks yourself (more on this in chapter 9). Those talks also give you a chance to practice thinking on your feet—by coming up with questions for the speaker, even if you're too shy to ask them. And they can help you practice speaking in front of large groups—by asking your questions during the question-and-answer portion of the talk.

Going to department social events can also give you a chance to practice talking more informally about your research. Almost inevitably, someone will ask "What are you working on?" or "What are you finding in the field?" And being forced to answer those questions can sometimes help you better articulate the answers for yourself.

Those social events, however, are also a place where you might run into your department's resident "peacocks"—the professors and other grad students who look for any opportunity to brag about what they're doing or how much they know. Those peacocks, in turn, tend to throw around a lot of big words and buzzwords that you may have never heard before. And that's where we'll turn in chapter 3. We'll talk about all the jargon and acronyms that you'll encounter in academia—from epistemologies and heuristics to R&Rs and ABD.

Chapter 3

DECIPHERING ACADEMIC JARGON

 James Noonan @_jmnoonan · Jul 22, 2018

For the first two years of grad school, I'd sit & nod my head whenever people used the words "heuristic" & "epistemology." Students in classes I TA'd would ask me what they meant & I'd fumble, embarrassed, through an unsatisfying explanation. #HiddenCurriculum

Academia is full of jargon. There are the abbreviations—R1, R&R, ABD. The ranks and titles—associate professor, doctoral candidate, postdoc, provost, dean. And the names—Foucault, van Leeuwenhoek, Herodotus, Du Bois, Pauli, Bărnuțiu. There are the disciplinary buzzwords—efficiency, heteroscedasticity, superhyperfine. And the big words that just sound smart—heuristic, epistemology, pedagogy, exegesis.

The problem with jargon is that it's everywhere in academia. It's on the department websites you need to navigate in order to apply. It's in the books and articles you read for your exams. It's in the emails you get from department administrators. It's in the conversations you have with your advisor during office hours and with your peers after class.

Living in an age of Google and smartphones make it easier than ever to look up words and their meanings. And yet while Google and smartphones might make it a little easier to manage the jargon problem, they don't solve it completely.

If you come across an unfamiliar word in a book you're reading, you can certainly look it up online. But some words, and especially jargon words, have multiple (and often discipline-specific) meanings. For example, the word "discipline," in an academic context, means "field of study"—biology, sociology, economics, computer science. Meanwhile, some disciplines study discipline—like the consequences of spanking young children or using harsh punishments like suspension or expulsion at school. Essentially, looking up words doesn't guarantee that you'll get the right meaning for the context.

Looking up a word also doesn't guarantee you'll know how to pronounce it when the professor calls on you in class. Certainly, text-to-speech technology is improving rapidly. But a word like Bourdieusian (bore-DOO-zee-uhn—which describes research or ideas related to the work of sociologist Pierre Bourdieu) is bound to trip up even the best artificial intelligence.

Another problem with jargon is that you won't always see it written out. If a professor or a classmate drops a word like heteroscedasticity (a measure of differences across subgroups in the amount of variation in the values observed for a set of variables, and a problem for statistical regression analyses), you might not know how it's spelled. If you can't spell it, it's a lot harder to write it down or look it up. And if you're midconversation, it would be awkward to pull out your smartphone and try to figure it out.

In those awkward moments of confusion, you might feel pressured to fake it—to smile and nod and pretend like you know what's going on. In sociology, we actually study that kind of fake-it-till-you-make-it approach to social interaction. Erving Goffman describes it as a form of "face-work" or "face-saving."[2] Essentially, faking knowledge avoids the embarrassment of admitting that you don't know what everyone thinks you should know.

That fake-it-till-you-make-it approach, though, does have drawbacks. Faking it means you stay confused—you don't get the information you need to understand what's going on. That can make it hard to participate in conversations, leaving you feeling like an outsider, even among your peers. Faking it can also make you feel like a fraud, especially if the people you're talking with figure out that you don't actually know what you implied you know. As we talked about in the introduction, feeling like a fraud is a key part of imposter syndrome, and imposter syndrome can have real and negative consequences for your health and well-being.[3]

This chapter is aimed at helping you avoid that kind of fake-it-till-you-make-it approach. We'll start by covering some common (and commonly misunderstood) academic terms. Next, and because much of the jargon in academia is specific to a discipline (e.g., biology) or subdiscipline (e.g., molecular biology) or even department (e.g., molecular biology at Berkeley), I'll also offer some strategies for making sense of the more context-specific words you'll encounter in your program and your field. We'll talk about why you shouldn't feel embarrassed about not knowing key jargon terms. And we'll talk about how to ask when you encounter one you don't know.

General Jargon: A (Heavily Abridged) Academic Dictionary

Academic jargon falls into a few different categories. That includes the degrees and requirements, the acronyms, the ranks and titles, the names, the buzzwords, and the big words. We'll talk in the next section about the jargon terms specific to particular disciplines or subdisciplines or departments. For now, let's cover a few common (and commonly misunderstood) terms.

The Degrees and Requirements

Master's to Doctorate: We talked in chapter 1 about the different degrees you might pursue in graduate school—including various types of terminal and nonterminal master's degrees, all the way up through the doctoral degree. In the interest of brevity, I won't rehash those distinctions here. But if you're confused about the difference between an MS and an MPH or between "funded" and "unfunded" programs, go check out chapter 1.

Exams: As an undergrad, you probably took plenty of exams. And there are exams in grad school too. Unlike your undergrad exams, though, the exams you'll take in grad school won't require just a bunch of memorization and regurgitation of facts. Instead, when you're taking exams in grad school, you'll have to synthesize and apply the stuff you've learned. As we'll talk about in chapters 4 and 5, that transition from memorization to application can be challenging, and it can take a while to adjust. The point of that transition isn't to make grad school harder than undergrad. It's to get you ready for the kind of mental work you'll have to do when you're doing your own research. Along those lines, the exams you take in grad school don't cover just the material you learn in a single course. Instead, you'll typically also have to take comprehensive exams that involve fusing what you've learned across a whole discipline or subfield of research.

Those exams go by a few different names, and they take different forms in different disciplines and departments. They might be called "preliminary" exams or "comprehensive" exams or "qualifying" exams or even "oral" exams, and you might hear them referred to by shortened names like "prelims," "comps," "quals," and "orals." Depending on your program, you might also have to complete more than one exam from that list. In my doctoral program in sociology, for example, we had a "qualifying" exam after our first year, which tested our knowledge of key theories and topics in sociology as a whole. Then, during our third and fourth years in the program, we had to complete two "comprehensive" exams, each covering a different subfield of sociology (mine were in education and family).

The goal with these types of exams is to make sure you're prepared to (1) teach (especially graduate-level courses) in a particular field or subfield and (2) do research in that field or subfield. In a lot of departments and disciplines, these exams take the form of a timed writing exercise. Typically, you'll develop or be given a reading list of relevant materials. Then, after you have some time to read and digest those materials (usually at least a few months), you'll be given a list of questions. Then you'll have to choose a certain subset of those questions that you want to answer. And then you'll have a limited amount of time (maybe seventy-two hours; maybe six months) to write a series of short essays answering those questions. Finally, a committee of faculty members from your department (and possibly one or two from outside your department) will read your answers and decide whether you "passed" the exam.

In some departments and disciplines, you might also (or instead) complete an "oral" exam. These are usually similar to written exams, with readings done in advance and multiple questions to answer. However, unlike written exams, oral exams are typically conducted as a face-to-face meeting, where the student explains their answers aloud to a committee of faculty members, who may also ask additional follow-up questions during the exam.

Dissertation: A dissertation (sometimes called a doctoral thesis or just a thesis) is the capstone of a doctoral degree. It's a substantial, independent project (usually involving some sort of research) that you use to produce a written report. You'll work with your advisor (sometimes called your dissertation committee chair or just your "chair") and a few other faculty members (who form the rest of your dissertation committee) to develop a project. Then you'll carry out the project and write up the results.

What that final dissertation looks like varies a lot across disciplines, departments, and degrees. In some disciplines your dissertation will probably resemble a book manuscript with five or six chapters. In that case, the idea is usually that you'll try to publish what you've written, either by getting a book contract or by turning your dissertation into a set of articles for academic journals. In other disciplines, your dissertation might take the form of a grant proposal, using preliminary evidence from your research to outline and justify the next project (or set of projects) you hope to complete. In that case, the goal is usually to submit the grant proposal to funding agencies who might be interested in supporting your postgraduate work.

If you want to get a sense of what dissertations typically look like in your program, you can head to your university library—students are usually required to file a hard copy of their dissertation when they finish their degree, and you can ask a university librarian for help in finding examples from recent grads in your field. Another option is to head to proquest.com—it has an online repository that includes millions of dissertations from around the world. If your university has a subscription to ProQuest, you'll even be able to download those dissertations for free (ask your librarian if you can't find it by searching the library website).

Proposals: Before you can write your dissertation, you might have to write a proposal. The proposal lays out what you're going to do for your dissertation (i.e., the research question you're going to answer, or the hypothesis you're going to test), how you're going to do it (i.e., what methods you will use to collect and analyze data), and why your dissertation is important (i.e., what contribution your work will make to the field). In some programs, you'll need to have your proposal approved by your advisor and your committee before you begin the research for your dissertation. In other programs, it's more common to start completing preliminary research for your dissertation, then write your proposal based on those preliminary findings, and then carry out the rest of your research. This approval process sometimes happens as part of a proposal defense meeting with your committee—more on this in a minute.

Protocol: If your research involves human subjects, animal subjects, clinical trials, or data collected in education or health care settings, then approval from your committee isn't enough to give you a green light to start work. Instead, and before you do any work on the project, you'll also need to have a version of your research proposal approved by the offices at your university that oversee compliance with laws governing the conduct of research.[4] This official and often highly standardized version of your proposal is typically called a protocol. It outlines what you will do in your research, what your subjects will be expected to do, and how you will protect your subjects from undue harm in that process.

Defense: A defense can be either a proposal defense or a dissertation defense. In a lot of departments and disciplines, you'll have to do both. The word "defense" might sound kind of scary—like you have to stand up and defend your proposal or your dissertation from the attacks of your committee, but it's not (usually) as adversarial as it sounds. Ideally, you'll have lots of meetings with your dissertation committee chair where you review drafts of your proposal or your dissertation and get the document to a state where you both think it's pretty solid. At that point, your chair should encourage you to schedule a defense (if they don't suggest it, it's okay to ask if you're ready).

The defense itself typically involves a face-to-face meeting with your whole dissertation committee. You'll probably be asked to give a short presentation about your project. Then the committee will ask you questions, and you'll be expected to respond. After the presentation (or sometimes before, or sometimes both), the committee will ask you to leave the room so they can discuss privately. Then they will invite you back in and tell you whether you have "passed" your defense. In some cases, your committee might also give you a list of revisions you have to make to your proposal or your dissertation before you get a "pass."

And passing is a big deal. Once you pass your proposal defense, you're officially approved to start your dissertation research. And once you pass your dissertation defense, you can put your degree on your CV. To do that, however, you first have to know what I mean by CV. And that's where we'll turn next.

The Jargon Terms and Acronyms

Bureaucracies love jargon, abbreviations, and acronyms, and academia is no different. Some of those are discipline- or department-specific. In my current department, for example, we have KSISR, PEC, SHEL, WIM, SRP, and GRC—these acronyms mean nothing (or might mean something completely different) to anyone outside of Indiana University Sociology. That said, there are some academic jargon terms and acronyms that are commonly used across departments and disciplines. Not knowing them can make for some serious confusion.

CV: This stands for curriculum vitae. It's the academic version of a résumé, but they're not exactly the same thing. Résumés tend to be one or two pages long, usually with a brief overview of your academic credentials (i.e., where you went to school, when you graduated, and what degrees you earned), your work history, and the major responsibilities or accomplishments you've had with each job. CVs are much longer and more detailed, with no page limit and more parts. Unlike résumés, which focus on work experience, CVs focus primarily on your research-related accomplishments, with some attention to teaching, service, and nonacademic work as well. While there are some variations across disciplines, a CV typically includes your:

- Academic credentials (i.e., universities, dates, and degrees)
- Academic work history (i.e., universities, dates, and ranks)
- Peer-reviewed publications (those completed and, sometimes, those under review)
- Other publications and reports
- Awards and honors
- Grants and fellowships
- Conference presentations
- Service (to your discipline, your university, your department, and the larger community)
- Teaching experience
- Other relevant work experience (you don't have to include every other job you've had, or even any at all; just those relevant to your academic work)

Appendices A–C have some examples that illustrate how my CV has changed over the course of my career. You can also check out your professors' listings on your program's web page—many academics post online links to their CVs.

Biosketch: This one isn't an acronym, but it's useful to talk about in the context of CVs. Biosketches are typically required as part of grant or fellowship applications, and you'll usually have to enter your information into the biosketch form provided by the organization to which you're applying for support. Along those lines, the point of a biosketch isn't to give an overview of your whole career but rather to make a case for why you're the right person to do the research you've proposed. To do that, you'll generally want to write two or three paragraphs highlighting your relevant expertise and contributions to the field, followed by a short list of pertinent publications and sometimes short lists of relevant educational credentials, awards, honors, and grants/fellowships as well. For sample biosketches and advice on writing your own, I'd recommend checking out the National Institutes of Health website.[5] Dr. Sara Rockwell, the associate dean for scientific affairs at the Yale University School of Medicine, also has some useful tips for preparing a biosketch and editing it for different fellowships and grants.[6] Rockwell notes that, especially for junior scholars, the biosketch is often the part of the application that matters the most. In the biosketch, an applicant "must convey all of the information needed to convince the review committee that the applicant is able to direct the project and that he or she merits support."

TA: Teaching assistants are grad students (or sometimes undergrads) who help professors with the classes they teach. In some departments and universities, TAs go by other names, such as "graduate assistants" or "proctors." As we'll talk more about in chapter 5, the responsibilities associated with being a TA vary across disciplines, departments, and degrees. But most doctoral programs and some master's programs expect students to serve as a TA for at least a portion of their grad school career.

RA: Research assistants are grad students (or sometimes undergrads) who assist professors (or sometimes other graduate students) with their research. Some RA positions don't come with any money attached—they're just an opportunity to work on a research project and sometimes get authorship credit as well. Other RA positions do come with money attached, and those positions can be an important funding mechanism for grad students, as we'll talk more about in chapter 6. That said, those funded RA positions vary in terms of the amount of support they provide and the type of work you'll be expected to do.

Some of that variation has to do with where the money comes from and how much you can get. For example, your advisor might have a grant that provides money for graduate training. In that case, most or all of the money for your tuition, fees, and stipend will come from your advisor's grant. And you'll probably spend most of your non-class time working for that professor on their research projects. In other cases, your advisor or another professor might have a limited amount of research funding that can be used to pay grad students or undergrads for hourly work. Working for that professor, in turn, would allow you to earn extra money on top of whatever stipend (if any) you already receive. That said, if you're already fully funded (through your department, through another professor's grant, or through a grant or fellowship you have received), there will probably be limits on the number of extra hours you can work.

Other variations in RA positions have to do with whether your work as an RA builds into your dissertation research. If you're in a lab science field, and especially if you're funded through a training grant your advisor has received, then your dissertation research will probably stem directly from the work you're doing as an RA. In other cases, and especially if you're in a field where students are expected to complete dissertation projects that are fully independent of their advisors' research, the work you do as an RA might be only loosely related to your own dissertation research, or it might not be related at all, but it can still be valuable as an opportunity to learn new skills, network, and assemble your team.

IRB and IACUC: If you're interested in doing research that involves people (e.g., surveys, interviews, observations, experimental interventions, and clinical trials), you'll probably need approval for your research from the **Institutional Review Board** (IRB). Similarly, if you do research with animals, you'll need approval from the **Institutional Animal Care and Use Committee** (IACUC). If you do research involving clinical trials, research in health care, or research in education, you might need approval from other regulatory and compliance-related offices within your university as well.

Offices like the IRB and the IACUC are tasked with ensuring that universities and their researchers are complying with laws governing the ethical conduct of research.[7] Those laws, in turn, have emerged in response to incidents where university researchers have caused significant harm to the subjects of their work.[8] In an effort to reduce the chances of harm, the IRB and IACUC require researchers to complete relevant trainings and also submit their research protocols for official compliance review.

The IRB, for example, is tasked with protecting the human subjects who participate in research, or at least ensuring that researchers are doing their best to protect the privacy and confidentiality of their research subjects. Thus, if you want to do a project involving human subjects (even if it's something as simple as analyzing survey data that someone else collected), you'll probably need to get approval from the IRB.

That approval process can vary substantially across different countries (which have different laws governing the conduct of research), across different universities, and even within the same university over time. For example, in the seven years that I've been at Indiana University, we've gone from a system where all IRB protocols were written as Word documents and submitted via email to one where completing a protocol involves filling out an ever-changing set of online forms.

Given those variations, it's easy to make mistakes or forget things when you're filling out the forms. But don't fret too much about getting it perfect the first time. That's because once you submit your protocol for approval, it will get carefully reviewed by a staff member who works in research compliance (usually someone tasked with handling proposals specific to your field) and some-times by a committee of faculty members as well. If there are any problems with your protocol, or if something isn't clear, the staff member or the committee of faculty members will return your protocol and request that you make changes before resubmitting it for review. In some cases, you might also have to meet with the IRB or IACUC or other regulatory committee to discuss your pro-posed project and answer questions about how you will handle especially risky parts of your research.

If you're not sure which types of approvals (if any) you'll need for your project, or where to start in terms of putting together a protocol, I'd recommend reaching out to the office of research compliance at your university (a quick web search for [YOUR UNI-VERSITY] + research + compliance should get you to the right contact information). You can email the office a very brief (one or two sentences) description of the type of project you're hoping to complete and ask for help figuring out which type of approvals you'll need, what you'll need to include in your protocol, and where to find any relevant forms. You can also ask your advisor or more advanced grad students to share copies of their research pro-tocols, which you can use as templates in preparing your own.

PI: The **principal investigator** is the scholar responsible for designing and carrying out (or at least overseeing others who are carrying out) a research project. In some disciplines, the PI will also take a lead role in writing IRB protocols and grant applica-tions and in writing manuscripts based on the project. Some uni-versities (and some grant funding agencies) allow grad students to be PIs on their own projects. Others require grad students to find a faculty member to serve as a PI instead.

RFP: Funding agencies—whether private foundations or gov-ernment agencies—rarely just give money to people who ask. Instead, those agencies typically decide on a set of priorities and then put out a **request for proposals** that match those priorities. An RFP will outline a set of topics and/or methods and/or do-mains of research the agency is interested in funding. The RFP will also outline various logistical details, including which types of researchers are eligible, the maximum amount of funding per project, the timeline during which the work must be completed, and the total number of projects that will be funded through the RFP. When you apply for funding through an RFP, you should be sure to follow the guidelines and write a proposal that explains how your project aligns with the agency's stated priorities. You'll also need a detailed budget, along with justification for how you'll use those funds. In some cases you might also need a letter of support from your university or from your department, stating that it has approved your proposed budget and will assist with managing the funds you get as part of the award. In chapter 6, we'll talk about where to find RFPs and get support with putting together your proposals.

LOI: While some RFPs require researchers to submit full proposals for consideration, others request a **letter of interest** first. LOIs are more informal than full proposals. They tend to be fairly short (or at least shorter than full proposals). They typically have rough rather than detailed budgets. And they don't typically need letters of support from university officials. The funding agency uses these LOIs to identify the most promising projects. Then the funder invites those researchers to submit full proposals for consideration for the award.

ABD: This is **all but dissertation**. Essentially, if you say "I'm ABD," this means you've completed all your program requirements except the doctoral dissertation. So you're done with required coursework, done with any qualifying or comprehensive exams, done writing and defending your dissertation proposal. You just have to finish your project and write it all up and then you can get your degree.

R1: R1 doesn't technically mean anything, at least not anymore. But it's still a term that gets thrown around a lot in academia. It refers to universities or departments labeled **Research 1** under the Carnegie Classification of Institutions of Higher Education.[9] The Carnegie system was developed in 1970, in the wake of the rapid expansion of higher education, as a way of categorizing different types of colleges and universities.[10] The initial classification system included five categories of doctoral-granting institutions (ranked by their emphasis on research), two categories of "comprehensive colleges" (i.e., those that offer master's degrees but not doctoral degrees), two categories of liberal arts colleges, one category of two-year colleges and institutions, and nine categories of professional schools and other specialized institutions (theological seminaries, teachers colleges, etc.).

The specific categories have changed over time, but they typically lump together colleges, universities, and sometimes specific schools within a university that operate in similar ways (number of faculty, degrees granted, emphasis on research vs. teaching, etc.). While the R1 designation is no longer officially used for Carnegie categories, it is used colloquially to refer to universities or schools within a particular university where there is a heavy emphasis on research over teaching and where graduate training focuses on preparing doctoral students for careers in academic research. The R1 label is used to distinguish those "elite research" institutions from other universities, colleges, and schools where there is less of an emphasis on research and usually more emphasis on teaching instead.

Peer Review: This isn't an acronym, but it's helpful to discuss here as it's relevant to understanding R&Rs, which we'll talk about next. The whole point of peer review, which we'll consider more fully in chapter 8, is to ensure the rigor of scholarly research. While not all research is peer reviewed, many funding agencies, journal editors, and book publishers rely on a peer-review process to help them evaluate your work. When you submit an application to a funding agency, for example, that funding agency will probably ask other experts in your field to read and assess your proposal. Similarly, if you submit a manuscript (an unpublished draft of an academic paper or book) to a journal or a book publisher, the editor might also send it out for peer review. In general, and whether you're submitting a funding application or a manuscript, you'll eventually get comments back from the reviewers outlining what they liked and didn't like about your work, and the funding agency or editor will use those comments, in part, to make a decision about whether to fund or publish your work. Those comments, in turn, will usually be either single blind or double blind. **Single blind** means the reviewer knows who you are, but you won't be told their name. **Double blind** means the reviewer isn't told who you are and you aren't told who they are.

The point of double-blinded peer review is to decrease the chance of bias against junior scholars, lesser known scholars, and scholars from systematically marginalized groups. That said, less scrupulous reviewers will sometimes try to break the blind and identify the author by Googling information from a manuscript or proposal. In other cases a reviewer might opt to disclose to you (the author) that they were the one who reviewed your work. In some cases you might be able to guess their identity (e.g., because they recommended that you cite all their work). In that case, though, there's a chance you might be wrong. With one of the first pieces I submitted for peer review, one anonymous reviewer recommended that I cite a bunch of work by sociologist Dr. Hugh Mehan, then added, quite insistently, "I am not Hugh Mehan." So that reviewer probably wasn't Hugh Mehan. Or it might've been Hugh Mehan just trying to throw me off track.

R&R: As we'll talk about in chapter 8, there are a few different possible outcomes from the peer-review process. One of the most confusing is the R&R. In this case, you might get an email saying something like "We regret to inform you that we are unable to publish your manuscript in its current form, but we invite you to **revise and resubmit** your manuscript for further review." This might not seem like a great outcome, but it's actually a reason to celebrate (at least if it's the first R&R on that particular paper). It means the journal won't publish your manuscript as is but that the editor is inviting you to revise your manuscript (using the included feedback from the reviewers) and then submit it to that same journal again.

An R&R isn't a guarantee that your manuscript will eventually be published in that journal, but it substantially increases those odds. Many journals, for example, have overall acceptance rates of less than 10 percent (meaning they publish less than 10 percent of the papers submitted). But the ultimate acceptance rate for R&Rs is usually much higher, sometimes higher than 50 percent. The vast majority of manuscripts get rejected (either by "desk reject," where the editors read the manuscript and opt not to send it out for review, or after going through the peer-review process). And almost no manuscripts get accepted as is, with no changes required.

Your invitation to revise and resubmit will probably come with a laundry list of changes the reviewers expect you to make. It's okay to be frustrated with those reviewers (and especially Reviewer 2, who always seems to be the nitpicky mean one), but you should be proud of yourself for making it this far. An R&R is basically the best outcome you can hope for when you submit your manuscript to a journal. Once you revise and resubmit your manuscript, you're hoping for an email letting you know your manuscript has been "accepted for publication." Or, more likely, "conditionally accepted" for publication—this means you have to make a few more changes, but the article won't be sent out for another round of peer review. Instead, the editors will review your changes and then decide whether the manuscript is ready for publication.

Ranks and Titles

Like most big bureaucratic organizations, academia has an org chart—a hierarchical diagram that shows how different members of the organization are structured, by status, authority, and responsibility. And as with most big bureaucracies, there are titles (highly confusing titles) that go along with each different part of that hierarchy. To make things even more confusing, across universities you might find different titles for the same job, or the same title referring to different jobs. Here's a basic primer, with the caveat things might work a little differently at your institution:

Undergraduate Students: These students (undergrads) are pursuing an associate's (two-year) or bachelor's (four-year) degree.

Graduate Students: These students (grad students) have already completed a bachelor's degree and are pursuing master's or doctoral degrees. Some grad students may have other responsibilities besides just taking classes. For example, they might serve as "research assistants" (helping professors with research projects) or as "teaching assistants" (helping professors with classes) or even as "instructors" (teaching their own classes).

Doctoral Candidate: In some departments, grad students who've reached the ABD (all but dissertation) stage get the special title of doctoral candidate. In other departments, the title doctoral candidate applies to anyone pursuing a doctoral degree, regardless of how far along they are in their program.

Postdoctoral Fellows: These not-quite-student-not-quite-faculty scholars (postdocs) have finished their doctoral degrees but aren't yet professors.[11] Some postdocs are funded through formal programs, which are typically associated with universities or foundations and provide short-term (usually one or two years) grant funding for independent research (plus a modest salary). These postdocs typically focus on research, though some programs also involve teaching. Other postdocs are funded by professors. In that case the postdoc typically works for the professor (and is paid to do so) as part of a larger grant-funded project. As we'll talk more about in chapter 11, postdocs are increasingly required as prerequisites to faculty positions in many lab science fields.

Adjunct Professor: In an era of dwindling state and federal funding for higher education, colleges and universities are increasingly relying on part-time instructors (adjuncts) to teach classes.[12] Adjuncts (who may have completed their doctoral degree or may be working toward a degree) are typically paid on a per-class basis and rarely receive other employment benefits (health insurance, retirement contributions, etc.). Adjuncts are not tenure-track professors.

Tenure Track: Universities have a number of different "tracks" for professors. Each track (tenure track, lecturer track, clinical track, etc.) has a different set of requirements for hiring and promotion. The tenure track is typically the highest paid track and generally involves the greatest expectations for research and departmental service. Professors on the tenure track are eligible to get tenure.

Tenure: Tenure is essentially job security, though the amount of job security that tenure provides varies across institutions. Before tenure, tenure-track professors work on short-term contracts (usually a few years), which have to be periodically renewed. The decision about whether to renew is made by other (tenured) professors in the department and by other administrators higher up the academic chain. After a set period of time (usually five to seven years), tenure-track professors will have the opportunity to apply for or "go up" for tenure.

The complexities of the tenure review process could fill a whole book, and we'll talk a bit more about it in chapter 11. The key thing to know though is that applying for tenure generally involves preparing folders of materials documenting your contributions to research, teaching, and service in your discipline. All those materials get reviewed by your departmental colleagues, outside scholars, and university officials, and you get tenure only if you get a vote of yes at each of those levels of review.

Historically, being granted tenure meant lifetime job security. That's still the case at some universities where, as long as you don't violate university policies, you can remain employed until you decide to retire. More recently, though, some universities have created post-tenure review processes aimed at encouraging tenured professors to remain active and effective in their research, teaching, and service. In those places, an unsatisfactory post-tenure review can sometimes mean you're out of a job.[13]

Visiting Assistant Professor: VAPs are kind of like teaching postdocs. They are short-term (usually one to two years), nonrenewable (or at least not usually renewable), non-tenure-track positions where the VAP is paid (usually with benefits) to teach a full load of courses. The specific number of courses varies, but it's usually on par with or slightly higher than the typical teaching load for tenure-track faculty in that department. To be eligible for a VAP position, you typically have to have completed a doctoral degree.

Lecturer: Lecturers are non-tenure-track professors with renewable contracts and, in some cases, opportunities for promotion over time. Lecturers have typically completed their doctoral degrees, but their jobs focus on undergraduate teaching rather than on research and graduate training. As a result, lecturers typically have a higher teaching load (more courses per semester) than tenure-track faculty, but they are often paid substantially less, even when they remain at the same institution for their whole careers.

Assistant Professor: This is the first step on the tenure track. Assistant professors are typically hired as full-time, salaried faculty members with benefits. These contracts are generally renewable for up to six years. At some universities, these timelines can be extended if you take family or medical leave. In my case, for example, I had two babies while I was an assistant professor, so I was eligible to extend my contract timeline (or "clock") by one year.

As the time runs down on your contract, you can apply for promotion to associate professor. In some cases, being promoted to associate professor also comes with tenure. But that's not the case everywhere. At Harvard, for example, associate professors aren't automatically granted tenure. Either way, if you apply for promotion and you don't get it, you'll typically have to find a new job elsewhere.

Associate Professor: This is the second step on the tenure track. Assistant professors who successfully make it through the review process are promoted to associate professor. As we talked about with assistant professors, being promoted to associate professor usually comes with tenure. At some universities, though, tenure and promotion to associate professor are separate steps involving two different review processes. At those universities, there are associate professors with tenure and associate professors without tenure.[14] Either way, the promotion from assistant to associate will likely come with at least a small pay increase. Being promoted to associate professor also comes with a fairly large increase in service responsibilities, including service to your department, your university, and your discipline. Some associate professors remain at the associate level for the remainder of their careers. Others opt to apply for promotion to full professor.

Full Professor: This is basically the last step on the tenure track. Professors with impressive records of research, teaching, and/or service may consider "going up" for full professor. This promotion process closely mirrors the process for promotion to associate professor. However, if you go up for full professor and you don't get it, you can usually stay at the same institution at the associate professor rank, though you'll probably be prohibited from applying for promotions again in the future. Those who are promoted to full professor typically receive an increase in pay and become eligible for higher-level administrative roles (e.g., dean, provost) within the university.

Named Professor: If you're a full professor and you have a particularly distinguished research (or sometimes teaching) record, you might be honored as a named professor. This title bump usually comes with a pay increase, funded by private donations to the university and usually named for the person who donated the money to support the position (or someone they want to honor).[15] So, for example, if I donated a whole bunch of money to the university where you work, you could end up being the Jessica Calarco Professor of Your Field. It's a weird status thing, but hopefully it explains why some of your professors have someone else's name in their title.

Administration: Many universities operate under a system of faculty governance.[16] Essentially, this means faculty members are the ones tasked with deciding how the university (or at least certain parts of the university) will run. Under that system, professors (usually full professors) from various departments or schools within the university are selected to fill administrative roles, including president, provost, and dean as well as lower-level positions (vice presidents, vice provosts, associate deans, etc.) under them.

Dean: Under a faculty governance model, programs and departments are usually clustered into "schools" or "colleges." Departments like English, African American studies, and biology, for example, might all be part of the university's college of arts and sciences. Meanwhile, that same university might have a separate business school, law school, med school, and college of education. Each one of those units within the university will generally have its own dean. The dean, in turn, is tasked with setting policies for their unit and making decisions about how that unit will run. That includes decisions about which departments, divisions, or programs will get to hire new faculty, which ones will get a new building, and which ones will get to offer new degrees. The dean is also tasked with ensuring that their unit is complying with policies and strategic plans put in place by the provost or the president of the university as a whole. Depending on the size of the unit they run, the dean might also rely on a team of associate deans to help with overseeing more specialized areas. Within a college of arts and sciences, for example, there might be an associate dean for the arts and humanities, one for the social and historical sciences, and one for the natural and mathematical sciences. There might also be an associate dean of graduate education and an associate dean of undergraduate education.

Provost: While the dean is in charge of a particular unit within a university, the provost usually has authority at the university or campus level. Unlike the president of the university, though, who oversees everything, the provost typically focuses on the academic aspects of university life, including everything related to research, teaching, and learning as well as the budgets that support academic work. The provost generally works closely with the president of the university to develop policies, priorities, and strategic plans. They also work closely with deans to ensure that what's happening on the ground is consistent with the vision they set.

Jargon: Insider Knowledge by Design

In addition to all the degrees, titles, and acronyms, there are plenty of other big words and buzzwords and jargon terms that get thrown around among grad students and academic faculty. Putting together a cross-disciplinary (and cross-national) list of these terms would be almost impossible. That's because, even if two disciplines use the same buzzword (like "structure" in chemistry, sociology, and architecture, for example), there's a good chance they use it in different ways. So rather than bore you with definitions, I think it'll be more useful to talk about why there's so much jargon in academia and what to do when you encounter words you don't know or aren't sure how to say.

The key thing to remember with jargon is that it's insider knowledge—by design. Jargon terms are developed by and used within a particular domain or subdomain or sub-subdomain or sub-sub-subdomain of social life. They might be terms that are used only in academia, or only in psychology, or only in experimental social psychology, or only in a particular professor's lab. Or they could just be words (like heuristic or exegesis or epistemic) that people use to make themselves sound smart.

As a grad student, you shouldn't be expected to know the jargon going in. But because jargon gets taken for granted, there's a good chance professors and staff and other advanced grad students in your department will assume you already do. Those other people in your department have all been using the jargon terms for so long they forget what it's like to not know them. They may forget that you—the new person—don't yet know those terms as well as they do. And they end up using those jargon terms in conversation, in class, in assigned readings—without ever explaining what those terms mean.

For you, the new person, that casual use of jargon can feel incredibly intimidating. You start wondering, "Am I supposed to know that already? Did I miss that in the readings? Does everyone else know what that means?" And from there you start to feel like

"Maybe I'm not smart enough to be here" or "Maybe I got in by mistake."

In those moments of self-doubt, it's important to remember:

- If you're confused, someone else probably is, too. Just because other grad students are smiling and nodding when the professor drops a term like "maximum likelihood estimate" doesn't mean you missed something. They could be just as confused as you.
- Professors are human. Speaking as a professor, I can say that if I've taught the same class multiple times (and even if I haven't), it's easy to forget what I've covered and what I haven't covered in class. I might *think* we already talked about maximum likelihood estimates this semester, or that I assigned a reading that included that definition, when in fact I'm remembering a discussion or a reading from last semester. Ideally, it should be on the professor to think critically about their instruction, avoid unnecessary jargon, explain key terms, and encourage students to seek help if they're confused. But professors are also human, and they're going to forget sometimes.
- It's okay to ask. Along those lines, it's important to remember that you should be allowed to ask questions when you're confused. Good professors welcome that kind of questioning and don't make students feel stupid for asking. By asking, and especially by asking in class, you can help create an environment where all students feel comfortable acknowledging what they don't know (rather than worrying about having to look like they know everything already).

That said, asking does come with risks. Some professors might judge or chastise you for not knowing some key piece of information, even if there was no reasonable way for you to have known without asking. Some classmates (those "peacocks" we talked about earlier) might also use your question as an opportunity to jump in and show off what they know, even if it was never actually taught. But as we talked about in chapter 2, those people are probably just using their own privileged knowledge of the hidden curriculum to help themselves (or others like them) get ahead.

That's part of why, as we also talked about in chapter 2, it's important to find a team of people you can trust. People—inside or outside your department—who won't judge you for asking questions or getting the help you need. Find those people, bring them your list of unknown terms, and walk through them together (program staff, like the graduate program director, can be especially helpful in this regard). You might even think about creating your own department dictionary, with key terms and definitions and things students should know. And you can ask your department administrators about sharing that dictionary with new students or posting it online for all students to share.

* * *

Over time, you'll start to feel more comfortable with the jargon that gets thrown around in your discipline. Eventually, you might even take those words for granted yourself.

In the short term, though, it's important to be mentally prepared for when you encounter jargon in the research you read. And also to think critically about when and how you include jargon when you're writing about research. So that's where we'll turn in chapter 4.

Chapter 4

READING AND WRITING ABOUT OTHER PEOPLE'S RESEARCH

1

 Jess Calarco @JessicaCalarco · Sep 1, 2018

My first year of #gradschool, I was overwhelmed by the amount and density of the reading. I spent hours slogging through. I had piles of notes. But I felt lost.

Reading and writing are a *big* part of grad school. You'll read for class. For comprehensive exams.[2] For your master's project or doctoral dissertation. To stay on top of new developments in the field.

And you might be thinking—"I already know how to read." But reading in grad school doesn't just mean starting at the beginning, reading to the end, and taking notes along the way. I mean, you could read that way. But you'd never have time to eat or sleep or do any of your own research. Because there's just too much to read.

Unfortunately, the hidden curriculum of academia makes it easy to feel like a slacker for even considering not reading it all. And that "feeling like a slacker" thing is exactly how the hidden curriculum produces impostor syndrome. Because no scholar can read (or has read) everything. Certainly not in full detail.

That said, the solution isn't just to skim haphazardly or skip half the readings on the syllabus or quit reading entirely. The solution is to approach reading like research—with a set of questions to answer and set of strategies to use in the process.

This chapter offers some of those strategies. We'll talk about how to read in grad school and also how to write—clearly and persuasively—about what you read. For your class assignments. For your comprehensive exams. And in the "literature reviews" you write as justification for your own research.

Reading for Meaning in Grad School (and Beyond)

It's easy to walk into a professor's office, look at the shelves and shelves of books on the wall, and think: "Wow! They've read so much. How do they find time to read it all?" The truth is, we haven't read it all. At least not every word. And most of us have stacks of books (and journals and articles) we've aspirationally filed under "to be read." My current stack includes at least fifteen books, plus a digital file with more than two dozen PDFs of journal articles I've downloaded from JSTOR or Google Scholar. And I'll almost certainly add more to both stacks before I finish what's already there.

How to Read in Grad School

When I do sit down to read, I almost never read beginning to end. Instead, I start with the abstract and introduction, then skip around a bit, with a few strategic goals in mind. Here are some suggestions for what that looks like.

First, read as much of each article or book as it takes to identify:

- The central research question
- The data/methods used to answer the research question
- The central argument/answer
- The key patterns that support the central argument/answer
- The evidence that points to those larger patterns (e.g., statistical correlations, examples from field notes or interview transcripts)
- The limitations (i.e., what questions it doesn't answer; what perspectives or possibilities it doesn't consider)

- How you would cite the article/book/chapter in your own work (e.g., as an example or explanation of a particular method, to define a specific concept or term, or to highlight key findings from empirical research)

Second, figure out how each reading relates to other things you've read, especially other things by the same author or in the same subfield/genre. Does this particular study:

- Support, explain, clarify, extend, or challenge what's been said before?
- Develop a new theoretical model?
- Use a new method?
- Add a new case/population?

Third, decide if this is a book, article, or chapter that you'll need to read in full. Some readings are going to be highly relevant to your own research, and those readings deserve a more in-depth read. In that case, you'll want to read carefully, and you'll want to take more detailed notes. In addition to noting the pieces of information outlined above, you'll also want to be able to articulate how these books, articles, and chapters inform your work and also how your work is (or will be) different from the research reported in the studies you've read.

What to Read

While undergrad readings are usually assigned, grad school involves readings you find yourself. Sure, the classes you take will have plenty of assigned readings. But you'll almost certainly have to do additional reading to support the arguments you'll make in your course papers, your master's paper, your qualifying or comprehensive exams, and your dissertation. Depending on the topics you write about, there could be hundreds or even thousands of articles you could potentially read and include. So how do you find those readings? And how do you know when to stop?

The first thing to know is that, as a grad student, you'll have access to your university's physical library and its digital library as well. You should probably just go ahead and bookmark the university library web page in your web browser. It's a site you'll return to over and over again when you're looking for resources.

Once you get to the library web page, I'd recommend looking for annual review articles related to the topics you're studying. Most disciplines have a journal that's dedicated to publishing review-style pieces that summarize and synthesize and often make an argument about the state of research on a given topic within a given field. And that journal is usually called something like *Annual Review of* [YOUR FIELD]. You can find that journal by searching your university library's web page or by using a digital archive like JSTOR or Google Scholar or Web of Science. Also, if you use one of those digital archives, be sure that you search for it and access it through your university library's web page. The public versions of those sites let you search for academic articles and read abstracts, with the option to download the full papers for a fee. The versions of those same sites that you can access through your university library web page will let you download most journal articles, in full, for free.[3] Or at least, free for you. In reality, your university is paying huge sums of money each year—hundreds of thousands or even millions of dollars in the United States—to journal publishers so that faculty, staff, and students can have free access to the articles they publish.[4]

Annual review articles are chock-full of citations to potentially relevant research on the topics you're interested in studying. So, as you're reading them, make note of particularly helpful references, then look up, download, and read those articles as well. Then repeat that same process for especially relevant research you find cited in the new articles you've read. Like the annual review articles, all those articles you find cited should also be available on digital research repositories.

That citation-based approach to finding readings is useful, but it might not capture all the research that's highly relevant to the work you want to do. When you focus on the most-cited research, you're more likely to miss relevant research by women and especially women of color, whose research tends to be under-cited in most fields.[5] You're also more likely to miss new research, research by junior scholars, and research in other disciplines that could inform your work. Essentially, it's important to read and cite responsibly, which means checking that you're not just reading and citing the same white men and the same old studies that everyone has cited before you.

So how do you read and cite responsibly? First, actively seek out work by Black scholars, Indigenous scholars, and other scholars of color, with a particular focus on women scholars from those groups. Follow those scholars on Twitter. Follow the people they follow. Read their work, and read the work of the people they follow. Also, check out the #CiteBlackWomen website and podcast,[6] both of which feature important new research from Black women scholars and work toward increasing the visibility of and respect for Black women in academia as a whole.

Second, and as sociologist Dr. Pam Oliver has recommended in a recent blog post,[7] you can work toward reading and citing more broadly by changing how you search for research online. When conducting key word searches on sites like JSTOR, Google Scholar, and Web of Science, don't just look for the most-cited papers or the papers published in the most highly ranked journals. Instead, look for the newest research, and be sure to include research in specialty journals and journals in other fields. You can also find great new research even before it's published. Many fields have websites where scholars can post working papers and preprints of their work. In the social sciences, for example, you might check out the SSRN's Research Paper Series, the National Bureau of Economic Research's Working Papers repository, and SocArXiv.[8] Another option for expanding your research network is to go to conferences in your field and specifically seek out presentations by junior scholars and other scholars from systematically marginalized groups.

A third way to stay updated with your reading and citations is by signing up to get email notifications about new research related to your work. Most journal websites, for example, allow you to subscribe to table of contents notifications. Each time a new journal issue is released, you'll get an email with a list of the new articles and links to learn more. Online databases like Google Scholar also allow you to sign up for a variety of free notifications. You can get notified when other scholars cite your published work. Or if other scholars publish work that's relevant to the topics you study (i.e., by requesting notifications for research including specific key words). Of course, depending on your key words, you might end up with notifications about a huge volume of research. If you need suggestions for narrowing your search terms, I highly recommend checking out the tips that Pam Oliver includes in her post.

Remembering What You Read

There are lots of ways to take notes on what you read. If you're someone who likes hard-copy reading with bright-colored highlighters and sticky tabs and spiral-bound notebooks to keep things organized, Dr. Raul Pacheco-Vega has great suggestions for that kind of visual/tactile approach on his blog.[9] Personally, I'm horrible with paper. And I've found that a digital approach (to note taking, especially) helps me keep better track of what I've read.

Regardless of whether you opt for hard-copy or digital notes, I do think it's helpful to have a standard note system for all your reading. My basic note system looks like this:

- **Citation**
- **Key background:** two to three short bullet points identifying the theory/prior research on which the authors are building and defining key terms.
- **Data/methods:** one or two short bullet points with information about the source of the data and the method of analysis, with a note if this is a novel or particularly effective example of that method.
- **Research question:** stated as briefly as possible.

- **Argument/contribution:** two to three short bullet points, briefly describing the authors' answer to the central research question and its implications for research, theory, and practice.
- **Key findings:** three to four short bullet points identifying key patterns in the data that support the authors' central argument.
- **Unanswered questions:** two or three short bullet points that identify key limitations of the research and/or questions the research did not answer that could be answered in future research.

I also use a citation manager to store all my articles and notes. Personally, I like Zotero because it integrates fairly seamlessly with both Microsoft Word and Google Scholar. There's a Zotero plug-in for Google Chrome. And that means that when I'm logged into Google Scholar (through my university account), I can click the icon in my browser to automatically upload the citation and even a PDF of the article (or a link to the book) to my Zotero account. It's not perfect—sometimes I have to manually add or edit citations or upload my own PDFs. But using a citation manager saves a ton of time. And if you don't like Zotero, there are plenty of other options, including EndNote and Mendeley.[10]

Now, when you're dutifully uploading notes and PDFs and adding citations to your reference manager, it might not feel like you're saving time. But the time saving comes on the back end—when you're using the citation manager to recall (and especially to write about) what you've read. Because it's easy to think "Oh, I'll totally remember this article." But five months from now, when you're studying for comps, or five years from now, when you're finishing your dissertation, there's a good chance you won't remember it as well as you thought you would.

With a citation manager, it's much easier to find that article you read five months or five years ago. Even if you remember only a tiny bit of what you read. You can use your citation manager to do a key word search of all your notes and even all your attached

PDFs. Or you can use tags and folders and links to organize clusters of relevant work.

Another great thing about citation managers is that they make it incredibly easy to cite the work you've read. Zotero, for example, has a downloadable plug-in for Microsoft Word. So, when I'm writing a paper, or a book manuscript like this one, and I want to add a citation, I just click the Zotero tab at the top of the document, click "add/edit citation," and then search for the citation I want to add. Zotero then automatically adds the (fully formatted) citation to my reference list at the end.

Writing about Other People's Research

That brings me to another set of suggestions—for how to write about what you've read.

In grad school, you'll be expected to write about your own research. But you'll also be expected to write about other people's research. In your papers for class. In your comprehensive exams. In the literature review sections of your own articles and book chapters.

The key with each of these types of writing is to make an argument and to use the research you've read as evidence to support that argument. So, let's talk about what that looks like.

Literature Reviews

Early in grad school, I had a few professors ask us to write "literature reviews" as final papers. What I learned the hard way, and contrary to what the name might imply, a "literature review" is not a summary of all the research that's ever been done on a given topic. And it shouldn't be thirty-four pages double-spaced.

Rather, if a professor asks you for a literature review, they probably want you to use evidence from existing research to make an argument about what we do and don't know about a given topic.

To get to that point, and as Dr. Raul Pacheco-Vega lays out in a very helpful blog post,[11] the first step is to essentially map the research on a given topic, looking for key themes, disagreements, and unanswered questions.

After you map the literature, the next step is to figure out what argument you can use that literature to make. In most cases, that argument will be a justification for your own research. To build that kind of justification, you want to write a literature review that identifies:

- What we know about some issue (or what scholars in a given subfield generally agree on) *(this lays the foundation for your argument)*
- What we don't know about that issue (or what scholars in a given subfield disagree about) *(this points to your research question)*
- Why that unanswered question (or point of disagreement) is important to address *(this points to the potential implications of your study)*
- What existing research tells us about the best way to answer that unanswered question (or resolve that point of disagreement) *(this becomes the justification for your data/methods/analysis)*
- What existing research might predict in terms of the answer to that unanswered question (or the resolution to that point of disagreement) *(this becomes the justification for your hypotheses)*

Once you have your literature review outlined, the next step is to fill in the details with discussions of prior research. When it comes to filling in the details, I'd recommend a synthesis-style approach. That means using the existing research as evidence to support an argument about the literature. And it might look something like this: "Research consistently shows that the sky is blue (Smith 2008; Johnson 2009; Peters 2010). However, the specific hue of blue varies across different locations (Peters 2010). Less clear, however, are the factors that lead to variations in hues across locations."

We can contrast that synthesis-style approach to writing about previous research with a summary-style or chronological approach. That approach would look more like this: "Smith (2008) used an observational approach to determine that the sky is blue. Johnson (2009) then used a magnified observational approach to determine that the sky is cerulean blue. Peters (2010) then applied Johnson's approach across varied locations to determine that the sky is cerulean blue in some locations but periwinkle blue in others." The problem with that summary-style or chronological approach is that it almost always includes more detail than necessary without actually doing enough to guide the reader through the argument. A synthesis-style approach, by contrast, keeps the focus on your argument, using previous research as evidence to clearly explain what is known and what is not.

Comprehensive Exams

Comprehensive exams (or qualifying exams or field exams) often take the form of literature reviews, though the different disciplines and departments run them in different ways. For the exam itself, you might get seventy-two hours to write three essays of ten pages, each answering a different question. Or you might have to spend two hours answering questions aloud from a committee of faculty members. Or both. And in some departments, you might go through that whole process two or three times.

Regardless of what form the exam takes, you'll probably spend a few months getting ready. First, you'll either be given or put together a list of articles, chapters, and books that are especially important in your field. Next, if you create that list yourself, you'll have to get it approved by a committee of faculty members. And finally, you'll read (or at least "read") everything on that list.

The tips above will help you with the reading part. When it comes to the writing part, there are a few things that'll help you with your exam.

First, make an argument. In many disciplines, a single exam question will take the form of a list of three or five or eight questions about a given topic. It'll be tempting to just go through and answer each question one by one in different sections of the response. But that's not the best way to write a strong exam. Rather, by making an argument (and by supporting that argument with evidence that answers the exam questions), you can show your readers that you are truly an expert in your field. An expert isn't just someone who can regurgitate what they've learned but someone who can synthesize what they've learned and use that knowledge to inform others as well.

Second, don't just summarize the research. It's tempting to show you know what you know by describing each study you read. But that makes for a less than compelling read. Again, the key here is to synthesize the literature. That means explaining how the research you read supports your argument (and engaging counterarguments as well). That means citations not at the beginning of each sentence but at the end of the sentence.

Now, the whole spend-six-months-reading-then-spend-three-days-writing model might seem like a cruel form of academic torture. And, arguably, the timed writing part isn't necessary for an effective exam. But having time to read extensively on a subject, write about it, and get feedback from scholars in your field is useful training. It might be the only time in your career when you get to just read and think deeply about a topic. It's also an opportunity to strategize about how you'll teach that topic in your own classes. And it's an opportunity to identify lingering questions you can answer with your own research.

* * *

We'll turn to the topic of writing about your own research in chapter 7, but before that, let's talk a little more about staying on track in your program, so that you can make it to the exam stage and ultimately get your degree.

Chapter 5

STAYING ON TRACK IN YOUR PROGRAM

1

 Taniecea Mallery @tamallery • Jul 22, 2018

I took & barely passed a course in grad school that I
assumed was required. The next semester, I realized that
I could/should have audited the course instead. (Of
course I didn't even know that auditing — taking a
course not for credit — was even a thing.)
#hiddencurriculum

Most graduate programs have a series of requirements you'll need
to fulfill before you can get your degree. But there probably won't
be a checklist that lays out exactly what you're supposed to do and
when. Instead, the path to a master's or doctoral degree looks a lot
like one of those convoluted yes/no flowcharts where the lines
cross and backtrack all over the page. And the official flowchart
might not actually match the one that plays out in practice. You
might be able to take History 507 before you take History 506,
even if the requirements say otherwise. Or you might be able to
start your dissertation research even if you haven't officially de-
fended your dissertation proposal. Knowing how to navigate the
complicated flowchart of program requirements is critical for staying on track in your program—and for making timely progress
toward your degree.

Of course, the specifics of the progress-to-degree flowchart—
everything from which courses you'll need to take to when you
should start applying for jobs—vary across disciplines and departments and degrees. That flowchart might even vary for different

students in your program if they have different advisors or if they're getting an interdisciplinary or joint degree. Thankfully, though, there are some common ways to figure out what your flowchart looks like. And there are some strategies you can use to stay on track in moving from one box to the next.

Finding the Flowchart

Your advisor and your other professors might not always be the people to ask if you're confused about next steps in your flowchart to degree. I've been at Indiana University for more than seven years, and I still have to look up some of our graduate program requirements. I can't seem to remember which courses are always required, which ones are required except when students have a certain type of waiver, and which ones aren't explicitly required but are part of a you-must-take-one-of-these-three-courses list. And I always get mixed up about whether we have "comprehensive" exams or "qualifying" exams (because where I did my degree, we had both). Some of that confusion comes from the fact that requirements change over time, and the rules that apply to one cohort of grad students might be different from the rules for another.

Along those lines, and if you're struggling to figure out your flowchart to degree, I'd highly recommend a chat with the professor who oversees your department's graduate program (sometimes called the graduate chair or the director of graduate studies). That person, who is usually a more senior professor, is responsible for managing admissions and recruitment, reviewing program requirements, and making final decisions about stipends and fellowships and awards. In some departments and programs, the director of graduate studies is also responsible for monitoring students' progress, helping students stay on track, and fielding questions and complaints.

Given the demands, both logistical and social-emotional, involved, director of graduate studies is usually a rotating position. One professor will be director for a few years. Then someone else will rotate in (or, in some cases, be assigned the position despite not wanting the job).

Because of their intimate knowledge of the graduate program, the director of graduate studies (or possibly another faculty member who recently rotated out of the position) is a great person to ask if you're feeling confused. They'll know which courses you need to take. How many drafts students typically submit before getting their master's paper approved. How many hours you'll get to write your comprehensive exam. What it means to be officially ABD.

If the director of graduate studies is busy (and there's a decent chance they might be), you might check in with a staff person instead. Most departments or programs have an administrative staff member who is responsible for helping to oversee the graduate program. This person probably handles a lot of the day-to-day paperwork and logistics of running the program. And they probably know the formal flowchart and requirements better than most of the faculty do.

BUT (and this is a big but) if you do ask a staff person for help (with this or with anything), please be respectful of their time. Department staff people are often responsible for a huge number of logistical tasks. They're rarely paid enough for what they do. And they often work in public or semipublic offices where it's easy for others to barge in and interrupt their work. A little courtesy (like asking if they have a minute rather than immediately launching into a request) and a little gratitude can go a long way.

In some cases (this is more common with doctoral programs than master's programs), you might also be able to ask more advanced students for help with finding and deciphering the flowchart to degree. Other grad students might not know the logic behind the flowchart. And they might not know all the loopholes and alternative pathways. But they'll at least have their own experience to offer as a guide.

Along those lines, I highly recommend asking more advanced students if they would be willing to share their materials with you.

That means course papers. Master's projects. Qualifying exam reading lists (and, if it's allowed, the questions and answers too). Dissertation proposals. Fellowship applications. Job market materials. And various dissertation drafts. The goal in asking other students to share their materials isn't to copy what they've done. Rather, it's to use their work as a model for your own. To get a sense of how much work is required, what format it should be in, and how it should be framed. As we'll talk more about in chapter 6, there's no reason to reinvent the wheel.

Navigating Interdisciplinary Degrees

Of course, if you're in an interdisciplinary program, other grad students' experiences might be less relevant to your own, and there might be more than one flowchart to degree. If you're getting a joint degree, you might even have to work with your advisors to create your own flowchart.

Those complexities can make interdisciplinary and joint degree programs more challenging to navigate and lengthier to complete. You'll almost certainly need help with figuring out which courses will and won't count toward your degree(s), finding and synthesizing literatures across different disciplines, framing your research for audiences in different fields, and understanding which job market doors will be opened by your expanded tool set and which ones will be closed because they'll see you as too "outside of the box." You might also need to complete two sets of qualifying exams, and you might need two advisors.

Thus, if you're considering interdisciplinary or joint degree programs, it's important to make sure you have mentors who can answer those questions and who you know you can trust. And it's especially important to check in regularly with those mentors to make sure you're on the right track.

So now that we know how to find the flowchart in your program or create the one that works for your degree, let's talk a bit more about the kinds of things you'll want to know along the way.

Coursework

Most programs have a set of required courses. Usually that list includes a few methods classes (i.e., how to do research or creative or applied work in your field) and maybe some classes covering key theories and ideas. Those requirements might feel onerous or constraining. But the point is to make sure that all students have a basic understanding of the central ideas, debates, and methods in their field.

And yet even if those courses are designed to make you an expert in your field, that doesn't mean that everyone in your field agrees on what an expert ought to know. Because universities put a high value on academic freedom,[2] professors usually have a great deal of latitude in deciding what materials to cover in the courses they teach. As a result, there's no guarantee your courses will represent the full diversity of your discipline. The syllabi in some classes, for example, might include only books, articles, or chapters by scholars at the most "elite" universities, even though scholars at less prestigious colleges and universities do tremendously important research as well. Or the syllabi might overlook key contributions by scholars from marginalized groups, even if those scholars teach at "elite" schools.

If that's the case, then I highly urge you to educate yourself on your field's diversity. Seek out courses that examine your discipline (or related disciplines) through a critical and intersectional lens. That includes courses on race and ethnicity and immigration, courses on gender and sexuality, and courses on social and economic inequality. If those courses don't exist, look for others that, at the very least, have more diverse syllabi, and maybe ask about creating your own independent study. If you're feeling especially brave, you might also consider sharing some of the research you've found with professors whose syllabi could use more diversity. It doesn't have to be a confrontation. You can just drop the professor a quick email with links to one or two key sources and say something like: "I read this new book/article recently, and I wanted to pass it along in case it might be useful for students in your class." As a teacher, I really appreciate when students help me stay updated on new and relevant research and when they push me to consider new perspectives I didn't think to include.

I also recommend using your coursework as an opportunity to build your methodological tool kit. While some disciplines tend to favor a particular approach to research and scholarship (e.g., econometrics in economics, or experimental research in psychology), that doesn't mean it's the only approach. Learning a variety of methods can help you avoid taking for granted what counts as the "right" kind of question or the "right" kind of answer. Knowing multiple methods and cutting-edge techniques for collecting and analyzing data can also help with your job market prospects, as we'll talk more about in chapter 11.

Grades

Taking courses in grad school is mainly about acquiring the knowledge you need to become an expert in your field. But courses also act as a signal. Despite all the problems and potential biases, your professors and your future employers will almost certainly use the courses you take, and the grades you get in those courses, as indicators of what kind of scholar you are and what your potential might be.[3]

4

 Tim Haney @timhaneyphd · Jul 25, 2018

Grades matter (you should get As), but they also don't matter at all. So many of my undergrad students go on to grad school thinking their courses and grades are the be-all-end-all. It's the mentorship and collaboration that matters, not grades.

Along those lines, and as sociologist Dr. Tim Haney's tweet implies, grades do matter in grad school. Grad students are generally expected to get As in all their classes. A C in grad school is typically viewed as "failing." In some programs, a C won't count toward your degree, and you might be placed on probation or even dismissed from your program if you earn more than one or two Cs. That said, one B+ doesn't make you a failure. And it doesn't mean you don't belong.

Instead, a grade like that is a signal that you need extra help. Schedule a meeting to talk to the professor. Not to ask for a higher grade but to learn what you could've done better and what you can do better in your next class. You can say something like "I didn't do as well as I hoped to in this class / on this assignment, and I was wondering if I could talk to you about what I could do to improve in future classes/assignments."

If the professor doesn't agree to meet, or if you come away from the meeting still feeling unclear, you can find someone else to ask instead. Show your assignment or your final paper to another trusted professor and ask for their feedback. Or ask a friend who did well in the course to see their assignments and learn from what they did.

Ultimately, and whatever grades you get, it's important to remember that grad school isn't easy. As we talked about with exams in chapter 3, the transition from undergrad to grad school (or from undergrad to work to grad school) involves rethinking the way you think about doing work. In grad classes, you're expected to synthesize and apply what you've learned. You're expected to go from being a mere consumer (and regurgitator) of knowledge to becoming someone who produces knowledge through research. That process of adjustment is easier for some students than for others, but with time and patience and effort, most grad students eventually adjust.

So, if you don't get the grades you wanted, don't let those grades define you, and don't let those grades convince you that you don't belong. And if you do get the grades you want, don't judge others who need extra help to learn what may have come easy to you.

Assignments and Deadlines

Coursework in grad school comes with grades, and it also comes with assignments and deadlines. Compared to the work in your college courses, however, assignments and deadlines in grad school tend to be a lot more flexible. Your master's paper, for example, might be something you're supposed to finish by the end of your second year, but, if you're completing your master's as part of a doctoral program, it might be okay if it slides into the first half of your third year, particularly if your research involves a large amount of data collection or analysis or if it took longer than expected to get approval for your work. Or you might be allowed to "double count" a paper, using it as the final assignment for two different courses, as long as you get permission from both professors first.

Along those lines, if you want to take advantage of academia's flexibility, you'll usually have to ask. That might mean emailing your professor or stopping by during office hours to explain what's going on and ask for an extension or an alternate assignment to complete. As we talked about in chapter 2, it's important to approach those requests politely and with a sense of respect for your professors' time. At the same time, and if you're worried about being perceived as disrespectful for just making those flexibility requests, know that there are plenty of other students who wouldn't bat an eye at the idea of asking for extra time or special assignments or even higher grades.[5]

If you get that flexibility you ask for, use it carefully. Especially when it comes to deadlines, flexibility can quickly lead to a backlog of work. Let's say, for example, that you take an "incomplete" in the fall semester because you couldn't finish your project before the grading deadline or because you were dealing with a personal situation that made you miss a few weeks of class. Taking an incomplete might feel helpful in the short term, but once the spring semester starts, you'll suddenly have new courses and new work to do, plus that work you didn't finish before. And that kind of added stress can create a cascade of missed deadlines that puts you even further behind. Along those lines, if you get yourself into a situation where you're considering taking an incomplete, I highly recommend sitting down with your advisor and making a concrete plan for what you will accomplish and when (ideally as soon as possible). You might also be strategic about which courses you take the following semester, choosing ones that involve less work overall or at least less work up front, so you don't get too far behind.

Setting Your Own Schedule

In addition to flexible deadlines, grad school also has a lot of un-structured time. Your classes might fill only ten or fifteen hours a week. Even if you have homework for those classes or other work obligations you have to complete (like grading for a professor or doing research in a professor's lab), you'll probably have at least some control over when and where you do those tasks. You'll probably also have at least some time left over for your own non-class-related work.

Unstructured time can be great for productivity. For example, if you write best first thing in the morning, you can do that and then use the rest of the day for other nonwriting tasks. You can also prioritize time-sensitive projects, projects you're most pas-sionate about, and projects that matter the most for your career. You can even use unstructured time to help manage life-related challenges, like an illness or a death in your family or the birth of a child. The summer after my second year in grad school, for ex-ample, I was hospitalized because of a serious infection—even after getting out of the hospital, it took me weeks to get my strength back and months to feel like myself again. I didn't tell my professors at the time, though I probably should have. Instead, I used the rest of the summer to recover, going to campus only a handful of times. Even when school started again in the fall, the flexibility of my academic schedule made it fairly easy for me to keep up with follow-up medical appointments and work from home one or two days a week.

The Perils of Unstructured Time

At the same time, unstructured time can also create challenges for grad students and for scholars more generally. That's in part because there are so many things you can be doing and so many things you're told you *should* be doing with your time. Reading for class. Planning your master's project or your dissertation. Doing background readings for your projects. Writing grant and fellowship applications. Meeting with your advisor. Doing fieldwork and statistical analyses. Writing paper drafts and research reports. Prepping the courses you're teaching and the conference presentations you're scheduled to give. Going to talks on campus and serving on departmental or university or disciplinary committees. And that's just the academic stuff. It's not counting email or laundry or dishes. It's not counting exercise or sleep. It's not counting volunteer work with local organizations, attending religious services, or spending time with family and friends.

With so many things to do and no clear time when you're supposed to do them, it can be really easy to get distracted and overwhelmed. As a result, you might find yourself spending too much time on some tasks (like email, or laundry, or even analyzing and reanalyzing data) as a way of avoiding other "scarier" or "harder" tasks (like writing). Or you might feel too overwhelmed with the lack of structure to do any tasks at all.

Learning to Manage Your Time

Along those lines, I'd argue that a critical thing to work on learning in grad school is how to manage your time. In grad school, you'll be the one expected to remember your own deadlines. And you'll probably have to remind your advisor of those deadlines. In grad school you'll also be expected to get your work done on time. And while some deadlines might be flexible, letting incompletes and half-finished papers pile up increases the chances that nothing will ever get done.

Thankfully, if you're interested in learning to better manage your time, there are lots of great resources and approaches to consider. The National Center for Faculty Development and Diversity (NCFDD) recommends starting with a semester plan that outlines your big goals, then breaking those goals down into concrete tasks, and finally putting each task on your calendar during a weekly planning meeting. If you have the opportunity to participate in an NCFDD workshop, I highly recommend it. My own approach to time management, which I'll describe in detail in chapter 12, is based in part on what I learned from the NCFDD's Faculty Success Program.

Even if you don't have the opportunity to participate in an NCFDD workshop, there are lots of free online resources that can help you set goals, plan your tasks, and schedule your time more effectively. On their blogs, for example, sociologists Dr. Whitney Pirtle and Dr. Tanya Golash-Boza outline their own approaches to time management and include samples of their semester plans.[6] I'd also recommend checking out both scholars' blogs (TheSociologyPhDandMe and Get a Life, PhD) for advice about navigating grad school and academia more generally.

The semester plan and weekly calendar approach to time management can work well if you're juggling multiple projects and professional commitments simultaneously, and if you often struggle to find enough time to get everything done. If the demands on your time are a little more straightforward, you might choose a simpler approach to time management. You might, for example, try out various checklist apps, such as Todoist or Trello, both of which allow you to sort tasks into projects, set deadlines, and keep track of what you've done. You might also look into the Pomodoro method, which is a strategy for breaking up large stretches of work time into smaller chunks with breaks in between.[7]

The Pomodoro method can be especially helpful if you have a big task that will take many hours to get done (e.g., grading a hundred student essays, studying for comprehensive exams, or writing your dissertation). With comprehensive exams, for example, you might have a long list of things to read and a whole summer to read them, and you might find it hard to stay focused and motivated to keep reading and taking notes. With the Pomodoro method, the idea is that you set a timer for a set amount of time (usually twenty-five minutes), keep working until the timer goes off, take a short break (usually five minutes) to reward yourself for the work you've done, and then set the timer again.

Ultimately, there are many strategies that academics use to track their progress and stay on track with work. You can try out those different approaches and see what works best for you and for the demands of your program. On his blog, Dr. Raul Pacheco-Vega has reviews of many time management and work tracking books and techniques.[8] Pacheco-Vega also offers his own suggestions for managing time and tasks in academia, especially those related to reading and writing about research.[9]

Whatever method you choose, I think the key is to see that big goals can be achieved through a series of short-term, small-scale efforts. Grad school, like an academic career, is full of big, amorphous, long-term goals (e.g., pass your comprehensive exams, finish your dissertation, get your degree). It's easy to treat those goals like single tasks. And it's easy to feel like you haven't accomplished anything until you finish one. But it doesn't have to be that way. You can achieve the big goals step by step. And you can celebrate along the way.

Master's Project

Time management skills are particularly important when you get to non-coursework parts of your program. In some programs, for example, you'll have to complete a master's project. That project is usually larger in scale and scope than what you would produce for a single class. And so if you don't have experience carrying out a large, independent project (like an undergraduate thesis), the master's project can seem like a daunting task. What the master's project entails—and whether you have to complete one at all—will depend on your field and your program. In the laboratory sciences, the social sciences, and the humanities, completing a master's project typically involves writing a paper based on research you carry out either independently or as part of a research team. In other fields, and especially in the arts, a master's project might take the form of a performance, an art piece, or a portfolio of materials that document your work. Most terminal master's programs require a master's project as the capstone for the degree. Some doctoral programs also require a master's project, while others waive the master's project requirement and give master's degrees effectively as "consolation prizes" to students who are unable to complete their doctoral degrees.

Completing a master's project, if you have to do one, is a chance to get experience designing and carrying out the kinds of research projects or creative activities expected for scholars in your field. In some fields you'll be responsible for the whole project, from start to finish—everything from designing the study to collecting and analyzing the data to writing the final report. In other fields you might be expected to work with your advisor or with other grad students to complete the project, but you'll probably be the one primarily responsible for overseeing the work and writing up the results.

It's easy to think of completing the master's project as just a box to check. But, if you're interested in pursuing a doctoral degree or a career in research, then completing your master's project can have other benefits as well. For example, your master's project might end up being the first paper you submit to present at a conference (more on this in chapter 9). Or it might be the first paper you submit for peer review in an academic journal (more on this in chapter 8).

Of course, you might never get to present or publish your master's project. I got scooped with mine—someone else published a similar analysis of the same dataset not long after I finished writing. By that point, I was in the process of starting my doctoral dissertation research, so I ended up abandoning my master's paper without ever publishing the results.

In the end, though, writing my master's paper and having a chance to get feedback from my advisors was still a useful experience. I learned that a literature review shouldn't be forty pages long. I learned how to tell a story with data (and that I enjoy telling qualitative stories more than quantitative ones). I learned how to frame that story in a way that highlights its contribution to the field. I had a chance to develop strong relationships with my advisors and grow my skills with a high level of hands-on support.

Exams

Like master's projects, exams in grad school also require a substantial amount of independent effort and serious time management skills. As we talked about in chapter 3, comprehensive exams, or qualifying exams, or oral exams—whatever your program calls them—generally involve putting together a list of readings from a particular subfield of your discipline, doing all those readings, getting a series of questions from your exam committee, and then spending two hours (if it's an oral exam) or seventy-two hours or maybe six months answering those questions. And in some departments (like where I completed my PhD), you'll have to go through the process more than once.

That whole exercise might seem pointless and painful. But there is a point to comprehensive exams, even if it's not always well articulated. First, comprehensive exams are intended to help you become an expert in a particular subfield. That usually means ensuring that you:

- Can explain the central theories and concepts used in your subfield (and how those theories and concepts have evolved over time)

- Can adjudicate key debates in the subfield (and situate your own work within them)
- Are familiar with the data and methods used by scholars in your subfield (and can use those data/methods in your own work)
- Recognize the standards of evidence in your subfield (i.e., what counts as evidence and how much is necessary to support an argument)

Second, and related, comprehensive exams are intended to help you act as an expert in your subfield. Now, you might be wondering—how is being an expert different from acting as an expert? Being an expert means knowing all the stuff an expert knows. Acting as an expert means being ready to share that knowledge or put that knowledge into practice, sometimes on a moment's notice. It might seem preposterous that anyone would ask you to give a lecture on a moment's notice, but, as we'll talk about in chapter 9, that can happen when you're doing media interviews about research. And it can happen when you're teaching as well.

To give you an example—in March 2019, news broke about a college admissions scandal involving celebrity parents who lied and cheated and paid bribes to get their kids into top colleges.[10] Some of my research is on privileged parents and the lengths they're willing to go to give their kids an unfair advantage in school.[11] Given that work, I started getting calls from reporters. One call—from NPR's *Marketplace Morning Report*—I got while walking with my toddler to pick up my older kid from preschool. I ended up doing the interview with my toddler in my lap from the preschool's office phone (the producers wanted me to use a landline for a better connection).[12] I didn't know the questions in advance, I had only about fifteen minutes to prepare, and I spent most of that time finding things that would keep my toddler quietly occupied during the interview. The interview went fine (well enough to lead to a few other interviews). But it went fine, in part, because I've learned how to think and write and speak under pressure.

All this is to say—while timed writing exams and oral exams can feel like a lot of pressure, it's the kind of pressure that you're almost certainly going to encounter in the future, whether you pursue a career in academia or a nonacademic career. Going through that process, then, can you help you figure out how you handle high-pressure situations and identify the resources and support you'll need to manage that kind of stress.

Along those lines, it's important to approach comprehensive exams not (just) as a chore but as an opportunity. It's a chance to spend months reading and thinking and learning—a chance you might not have again in your career. So, use that time to hone your reading skills—to learn, as we talked about in chapter 4, how to read strategically and how to systematically document what you've read. Use it as a chance to hone your rhetorical skills—to practice using evidence to make an argument. Use it as a chance to develop good work habits—like breaking down large, amorphous projects (like studying for comprehensive exams) into concrete tasks and structuring your own unstructured time.

Dissertation

Structuring your unstructured time is critical when you get to the dissertation stage. That's because completing a doctoral dissertation is a lot like using a butter knife to carve a ten-foot-tall boulder into a two-inch-tall statue. It's a huge amount of work. And it'll be a lot less painful if you work on it bit by bit over time.

Compared to a master's project, a doctoral dissertation generally requires at least three times as much work. Usually more. What that project looks like, however, and what steps you have to complete it will depend on your program and your discipline. To get a sense of what a typical dissertation looks like in your field and your program, I'd recommend taking a look at examples of previous students' work. As we talked about in chapter 3, you can get copies of previous students' dissertations by going to your university's library or by looking them up with ProQuest online.

Developing Your Project

Depending on your discipline, your dissertation might be based on a project you do independently, or it might stem from work you do on a project your advisor designed. That first, independent research model is more common in the social sciences, arts, and humanities. Under that model, you'll be the one fully responsible for designing a project, gathering (or at least getting access to) the data, analyzing the data, and writing up the results. The second model is more common in the lab sciences. Under that model, you won't be the one who initially designed the project, but you'll probably be responsible for carrying out some key part of that project, and you'll be the one responsible for writing about what you find.

Format-wise, dissertations also vary across departments and disciplines. In many fields, and especially in the social sciences and humanities, there's a good chance it'll look like a book—with an introduction, three or four substantive chapters, and a conclusion, all supporting one argument about a single topic. In some social science and lab science fields, it's becoming more common for students to write dissertations that look like a collection of (closely or sometimes loosely related) article-length manuscripts. Meanwhile, in more applied and creative fields, your dissertation might even take the form of a performance or a portfolio of work.

Different disciplines also have different norms around when students start their dissertation research. In lab science fields, you might start working on the project that will become your dissertation as soon as you start in your program. In the social sciences, arts, and humanities, you'll probably have to wait until you finish your coursework, and you'll probably have to write a proposal and get it approved before you're allowed to start doing your dissertation research.

The format of a dissertation proposal varies across different disciplines and degrees. In most cases, though, you'll be expected to:

- Identify a puzzle or problem that remains unsolved in the existing research (and use evidence from existing research to explain why that puzzle or problem is important to solve)
- Outline the steps you will take to solve that puzzle or problem (and use the existing research to explain your methodological choices)
- Describe the possible solutions to that puzzle or problem (and use the existing research and/or evidence from your preliminary research to explain those solutions)
- Provide a timeline for the completion of the work

Getting Feedback

Once you write your proposal, you'll probably need to have that proposal approved by your dissertation committee. That committee includes your dissertation advisor (or "chair") and usually at least two other faculty members (see chapter 2 for advice on choosing a committee). The committee will then approve (or not approve) your proposal as part of a proposal "defense." The point of that defense is to make sure you're ready to begin work on your dissertation project. Your committee wants to see that you have a well-formulated research question. That your hypotheses are well grounded in the literature. That you have the tools and knowledge you need to carry out your research and interpret what you find.

Before that defense, you'll probably meet with your advisor to review drafts of your proposal. Then when your advisor says you're ready, you'll send the draft proposal to the rest of your committee.

And you'll set a date to meet (in person or sometimes by teleconference) for the proposal defense. At the proposal defense, you'll probably be asked to provide a brief (ten to fifteen minutes) overview of your project. Your committee members will also ask you questions about your research and expect you to respond. At some point during the process, you'll probably also be asked to leave the room so your committee can discuss what they've read and heard. Then, when they're done discussing (which might take twenty or thirty minutes or more) they'll invite you back into the room. Finally, at the end of the defense, the committee will tell you whether or not you've "passed" your proposal defense and if there's anything you have to do next.

Now, if you've been having regular conversations with your committee, and if they've been giving you constructive feedback along the way, then your proposal defense will probably go smoothly. But even if you don't "pass" your proposal defense that first time, it isn't time to fret. It doesn't mean you're out of the program. Or that your dissertation is a failure from the start. Instead, it typically means that your committee wants to see certain changes to your proposal and that they will reconsider the proposal once those changes are made. In that case, you'll revise the proposal and get feedback from your advisor to make sure you're on track. Then you'll send the revised proposal to the rest of the committee. At that point, you might be required to have another proposal defense meeting. But, at least in my experience, that's rare. Instead, your committee members will likely review the updated proposal and then either request additional changes (without a formal meeting to discuss them) or decide that you have "passed."

Once your committee decides that you have "passed" your proposal defense, and once you've obtained other necessary approvals (e.g., from the IRB or IACUC), it's time to dig into your dissertation research. This could mean collecting and analyzing your own data—from archives, lab experiments, surveys, observations, clinical trials, and so forth. Or it could mean analyzing data that someone else has already collected. That process could take a few months. Or a few years.

As you're working on your dissertation, it's important to stay in regular contact with your dissertation committee and especially with your primary advisor. If you're working in a lab setting on the project of one of your professors, they might schedule regular meetings for progress checks. But if that's not how things work in your lab, or if you're working on an independent dissertation project, don't wait for your advisor to schedule meetings with you. Your professors are probably managing multiple students, multiple projects, multiple classes, and multiple service commitments, and you're much more likely to get the support you need if you're proactive about checking in and asking for help. I'd suggest checking in with your primary advisor at least once a month and with the rest of your committee at least once a semester. Those check-ins will be particularly useful for you and your committee if you give them updates on your progress. That could look something like this:

Dear Professor [LAST NAME],

I hope all is well. I wanted to write to check in about the progress I'm making on my dissertation. Just as a reminder, my dissertation project uses [DATA/METHODS] to examine [RESEARCH QUESTION]. Over the past [MONTH/ SEMESTER], I have:

- [LIST THINGS YOU HAVE DONE—E.G., CON-DUCTED A SERIES OF EXPERIMENTS, SPENT THIRTY HOURS OBSERVING AT YOUR FIELD SITE, INTERVIEWED FIVE PEOPLE, RUN A SET OF RE-GRESSION MODELS, APPLIED FOR A FELLOWSHIP, PRESENTED AT A CONFERENCE, WRITTEN A DRAFT OF A CHAPTER]

Based on the work I have completed so far, the primary conclusion of my dissertation will likely be [BRIEFLY STATE

CENTRAL ARGUMENT/CONCLUSION].[13] That conclusion is based on preliminary evidence showing that:

- [LIST THE PRELIMINARY FINDINGS AND BRIEFLY EXPLAIN HOW THEY SUPPORT YOUR CONCLUSION]

Between this [MONTH/SEMESTER] and next [MONTH/SEMESTER], I plan to:

- [LIST YOUR NEXT STEPS—E.G., CONDUCT ANOTHER EXPERIMENT, SPEND THIRTY HOURS OBSERVING AT YOUR FIELD SITE, INTERVIEW FIVE MORE PEOPLE, RUN A SET OF REGRESSION MODELS, APPLY FOR A FELLOWSHIP, PRESENT AT A CONFERENCE, WRITE A DRAFT OF A CHAPTER]

Would it be possible to schedule a meeting to talk about the progress I've made so far and about my plan for next steps? I am generally available [TIMES/DAYS]. That said, I understand that you are busy. Thus, if you are unable to meet, I would be grateful for any feedback you can provide by email, instead.

Thank you for your support with this project!

Best,

[YOUR NAME]

As the message above implies, there might be someone on your committee who never has time to meet in person. Maybe they're on sabbatical or traveling for research or dealing with a health problem or family situation that limits their ability to be on campus. As long as you're getting regular feedback from them by email or by phone, a lack of in-person meetings probably won't hurt your progress. That said, if you don't feel like you're getting the support you need, then you might consider looking for an alternate committee member or an alternate advisor. If you find yourself in that boat, I'd recommend going back and checking out the advice in chapter 2 on how to change things up and reach out to other professors who can better support your needs.

Writing Up the Results

As you continue working on your dissertation and getting feedback from your committee, you'll eventually reach a point where you're ready to transition from the data collection and analysis stage of the project to the stage where you start writing about what you found. That process, however, doesn't have a clear start date. Instead, when you start writing will depend on the progress you've made and the standards for research in your field.

In some disciplines and departments, you won't be expected or even allowed to write anything until the data analysis is completed; in others, you might be expected to start writing while you're still collecting and analyzing data. In that case, and if you've been meeting regularly with your advisor and discussing your progress on the project, they might tell you you're ready to write. More often, though, you'll have to figure that out on your own. A good signal to look for is that you've identified at least one key claim you can make with your data. That claim can form the basis of your first dissertation chapter or article, and you can start writing that piece (and possibly submit it for publication—more on this in chapter 8) while you continue gathering and analyzing the rest of your data.

Regardless of which approach is more common in your field, it's important to know that it can take as much time to write the dissertation as it takes to conduct the research. And sometimes more. Or even a lot more.

Of course, plenty of authors have already offered great advice about writing a dissertation: Joan Bolker's *Writing Your Dissertation in Fifteen Minutes a Day*, Scott Rank's *How to Finish Your Dissertation in Six Months, Even if You Don't Know What to Write*, and Paul J. Silvia's *How to Write a Lot: A Practical Guide to Productive Academic Writing*.[14] These books are especially helpful if you're struggling to stay on top of all the work and give structure to your unstructured time. Each offers a slightly different approach to research and writing and can help you figure out what strategies work best for you.

Now, these books about dissertations are designed to help you stay on track with your writing, but they don't offer as much advice about what to write or how to write it. That's because what a dissertation looks like varies so much across different departments and disciplines. Along those lines, I'll outline below some key questions you should be able to answer before you start writing. Of course, I don't expect you to answer these questions on your own. Instead, you can ask your advisor or your program's graduate chair/director or other grad students who are further along in the writing process. While asking these questions can feel intimidating, knowing the answers is critical if you want your committee to approve your dissertation and give you your degree.

- What do dissertations typically look like in my discipline/department?
  - What kinds of questions do they answer?
  - What kinds of data/methods/analysis do they use?
  - What kinds of conclusions/arguments do they make?
  - How are they structured?
- What approvals will I need to begin conducting my dissertation research?
  - Do I need IRB or IACUC (or other regulatory board) approval?
  - Do I need to write a formal proposal?
  - Do I need to complete a proposal defense?
  - What will I need to prepare for and do during the proposal defense?
  - Should I include evidence from my preliminary research (i.e., pilot data) in my proposal?
  - When should I begin conducting research?
- How should I write about what I find in my research?
  - What format should the final doctoral dissertation take?

- When should I begin writing?
- What should I write first?
- When and how often should I send drafts to my committee for review?
- Should those be full drafts or just drafts of key sections, instead?
- What is the process for completing my doctoral dissertation?
  - When should I send the final draft to my committee?
  - When should I schedule my dissertation defense?
  - What will I need to prepare for and do during the dissertation defense?
  - What happens if my committee does not approve my dissertation?

Now, when it comes to actually working on your dissertation, you might hear the advice to "write every day." That's not a bad strategy. But it requires that you always have something to write about. And depending on the type of research you do and where you are in the research process, writing—at least writing drafts of your dissertation or other manuscripts—might not always be the best use of your time. Instead, there might be days when you're gathering data. Or running regression models. Or conducting lab experiments. On those days, and as we'll talk more about in chapter 7, the "writing" you'll do is a different kind of writing: it's about documenting what you're doing and what you're finding as you go.

When you do get to the draft-writing stage, you might also hear the advice to track your word count—the number of words you write each day. That's also not a bad strategy, but I'd argue that it privileges any writing over good writing (we'll talk more about what I mean by "good" writing in chapter 7). It also discounts the importance of good editing in making your writing effective and easy to read. Thus, rather than focus on how many words I write in a day, I tend to focus on finishing specific writing tasks. That could mean writing an outline of the findings section of a paper.

Or writing a draft of the introduction. Or editing and cutting five hundred words from chapter 3. That way, and as we'll talk more about in chapter 7, you can feel like you're accomplishing something with your writing, even if you end up with a negative word count for the day.

Knowing When You're Done

As you move toward the completion of your project, you'll want to schedule meetings with your committee to talk about when you'll be ready to defend your dissertation and get your degree. If the whole committee can find a time to meet together, that can make sure everyone is on the same page. But scheduling is always complicated, so one-on-one meetings can work too.

During those meetings, it's important to be up front with your committee about your goals and deadlines. Let's say you want to go on the job market this upcoming year because your partner is also finishing their dissertation, and you both want to try to get academic jobs at the same research-focused school. If that's your goal, it's important to be blunt, to have a conversation that goes something like: "My goal is to go on the job market this year, and I'm hoping for an R1 job. Do you think that's feasible based on the progress I've made?" Hopefully, your committee will say "Yes, that sounds do-able." That said, it's also possible your committee will say "You need more time." Maybe you haven't gathered enough data to answer your question. Maybe you haven't published enough to have a decent shot at the kind of job you want. Maybe you're a very slow writer and your advisor is worried you won't be able to finish your dissertation in time. In that case, either you'll have to rethink your goals or your timeline or you'll have to convince your advisor and the rest of your committee that you can get it done.

When your advisor does decide you're ready, then it's time to schedule your dissertation defense. Typically, you'll want to schedule it at least three months in advance. You'll need to find a time when your whole committee can be in the same room (physically or virtually), and with academics that's no easy task. Scheduling far in advance also gives your committee time to read your dissertation and prepare comments and questions before your defense. In general, you'll want to give your committee members about a month to read your finished dissertation. Your advisor will also want to see earlier drafts of your dissertation, and some of your committee members might want to be more involved in that draft development process.

Format-wise, dissertation defenses are generally very similar to proposal defenses. This time around, though, the goal is to get your committee to approve your completed doctoral dissertation. And once they do sign off (whether at the defense meeting or, in some cases, after you complete some required revisions), and once you fill out a whole bunch of university paperwork, you'll have officially completed your degree!

Teaching

We've talked about time management skills in the context of coursework and research and writing, but those same skills are important for teaching too. Not all grad programs require students to serve as teaching assistants or instructors of record. That said, teaching experience, and especially designing and teaching your own classes, can be helpful if you're interested in an academic career. We'll talk a bit here about what you might be expected to do in terms of teaching, and then we'll talk more in-depth about being an effective teacher and how to balance effective teaching with all your other research and service and personal commitments in chapter 12.

Teaching Assistantships

In many graduate programs, and especially doctoral programs, you'll be expected to do work as a teaching assistant in exchange for support in getting your degree. Some programs use the term "teaching assistant" to refer to students who do any teaching-related tasks for a professor. Other programs distinguish "graders" or "readers" or "proctors" from "teaching assistants," with "teaching assistants" referring to grad students who lead their own lab or discussion section for students.

Along those lines, there are lots of different things you might be asked to do as a TA. You might just be asked to help with grading. Or you might be asked to do a whole range of things—developing the syllabus, preparing lecture materials, leading labs or discussion sections, handling communications with students, managing the course website, and maybe even teaching the class. When I was in grad school, the professor I was TAing for got sick, and for a few weeks that semester the other TA and I were responsible for preparing and giving twice-a-week lectures, on top of our other tasks (leading two weekly discussion sections of about thirty students each, answering student emails and holding office hours, and doing all the grading for the students in our sections).

Many programs have limits on the number of hours grad students are allowed to work as teaching assistants.[15] At Indiana University, where I work, for example, graduate teaching assistants are expected to work up to twenty hours a week. That might be twenty hours a week for one course. Or it might be ten hours a week each for two different courses.

Now, working twenty hours a week as a TA can feel like a lot to manage on top of your own coursework and projects, but if you're hoping for an academic career, then having a high level of teaching responsibility can be good preparation for the kind of work you'll do later on. In some cases, though, and as we talked about in chapter 2, the demands placed on teaching assistants reach the level of exploitation.[16] If you think you might be doing an inappropriate amount (or type) of work, it's okay to ask for help. Ask other grad students what they're expected to do. Or talk to your graduate program director. Or the department chair. Or, if you're lucky enough to have a graduate student union at your university, your union representative. Unions are designed to protect students from exploitation, so your representative will probably have a strong sense of what's appropriate for grad student work and can also offer advice on next steps.

Teaching Your Own Classes

Depending on your program, you might have the opportunity (or even be required) to serve as an "instructor of record." This means developing and teaching your own classes, with responsibility for selecting readings, developing the syllabus, designing lecture slides, writing lecture notes, leading class discussions and activities, writing assessments, and evaluating students' progress in the course.[17]

Teaching your own courses has a lot of benefits. If you're thinking of pursuing a job as a professor, and especially if you're interested in working at a small liberal arts college, a community college, or a regional campus of a state school, having taught courses as an instructor of record can be a great (or even necessary) addition to your CV. Teaching is also one of the best ways to hone your communication skills and deepen your knowledge of the discipline. And teaching can also be a way to earn a little (and often very little) money on the side.[18]

That said, teaching your own classes during grad school also has some drawbacks. It can take a significant amount of time and thought and energy to find or develop the materials for your own class. That's why, as a professor, I give my teaching assistants full permission to use, in their own classes, all the materials I've developed for mine. That includes syllabi, slides, notes, assignments, and exams. Having examples to use or model from can make that prep work substantially easier, particularly if you're also taking classes and doing research at the same time. If the professor you TA for doesn't offer to share their materials, it's okay to ask. And if they say no, or if that's not the course you plan to teach, it's okay to ask someone else (or look online for ideas). Most disciplines have teaching-related journals and websites and sometimes Facebook groups where scholars share teaching resources and ideas.

Even if you do find a wealth of materials to use, don't be surprised if teaching (at least initially) takes over a good chunk of your life. Doing readings, prepping notes and slides, grading assignments, emailing and meeting with students—it can all take a huge amount of time and energy, especially if you've never done it before.

Each time you teach a class, the prep work involved will probably get a little easier. That's especially true if you're careful to keep good records of what you do in class. As we'll talk about in chapter 12, I highly recommend digitizing all your teaching materials. Everything from lecture notes to comments on student work.[19] Even if you hand-write those materials initially, take a picture. Label it clearly. And store it in a file. That way, you have documentation of what worked (and what didn't). That way you can repeat it (or revise it) the next time around. And that way you'll have lots of great examples of your teaching-related materials to include with applications for teaching awards and academic jobs.

Research Assistantships

Serving as a teaching assistant isn't the only way you might work with professors in grad school. Rather, in some programs you might have the opportunity (or be required) to serve as a research assistant as well. However, and as we talked about in chapter 3, what it means to be a research assistant can vary substantially across disciplines and programs and also depending on the specific professor for whom you work. That includes variations in whether or how you'll be paid, how many hours you'll be expected to work, whether or not you'll receive authorship credit for your work, and what type of work you'll be expected to do.

In some cases, your research assistantship might be your primary source of financial support in grad school (i.e., it pays for your tuition and your stipend, if you receive one). That model is particularly common in lab science fields where doctoral students are admitted to work with a particular advisor. It can also happen in other fields if your advisor gets a grant that covers research assistants (more on this in the next chapter). Under that model, you probably won't be expected to do other work like serving as a teaching assistant or teaching your own classes, and there might even be restrictions that prevent you from taking on extra work (like paid hourly work for another professor). You'll probably also be expected to work a fairly large number of hours each week (possibly twenty hours or more) on your advisor's research projects. In most lab science fields, if you work full-time as a research assistant, you can generally assume that your advisor will make you a coauthor on papers they publish that include some of your work. In other fields, though, authorship credit won't be guaranteed and will have to be negotiated with your advisor. If you're not sure where you stand, it's okay to ask. You might, for example, say something like: "Given my work on this project so far, I was wondering if you would consider allowing me to be a coauthor on a paper." You won't necessarily get a yes in response, but it will at least give you the opportunity to have a conversation about what level of involvement in research is expected for authorship credit in your field, clarify expectations, and avoid hurt feelings in the end.

In other cases, you might have the opportunity to do hourly work as a research assistant for your advisor or for another professor. Under this model, any money you earn will be paid hourly on top of what you get for your stipend (if you get a stipend). And your work as a research assistant will be on top of other work (e.g., as a teaching assistant or an instructor of record) that you're expected to do. There will probably also be limits on the number of hours you're allowed to work, with fewer restrictions during the summer months. These types of research assistantships can be a great way to make some extra money if you're short on funds, but it's important to avoid working so many hours you don't have time to work on building your own career. Under an hourly work research assistant model, you also shouldn't assume that you'll get authorship credit for the work you do on faculty projects, though you can certainly ask your advisor about that possibility, using language similar to what was suggested above.

In still other cases, a professor might ask you to work with them on a project without offering any sort of payment (stipend or hourly) in return. Now, you might be wondering—why would I ever agree to work for free? And you're right to be wary of these types of offers. In general, though, what you get out of this type of research assistantship is hands-on research training and, potentially, authorship credit as well. This model is particularly common in programs where faculty have limited research budgets (or no research budget at all) and in disciplines where papers typically have one or two or maybe three authors at most. If you're considering one of these opportunities, be sure to have a conversation, up front, about authorship credit and take time to consider whether the papers you publish with your professor will be worth the time you spend. As we'll talk about in chapter 11, hiring committees typically want to see that you have a clear research agenda and a clear identity as a scholar, and working on unrelated side projects can sometimes hurt that case rather than help.

Now, in terms of finding research assistantships in grad school, it's important to know that those opportunities aren't always officially advertised. Instead, they're typically shared by word of mouth. A professor who is looking for a research assistant might reach out to a student they know from class, or a student who has stopped by during office hours to express interest in their work. This isn't exactly a fair way of doing things,[20] but it means that if you're interested in research assistantships, you'll want to look for ways of increasing your chances of getting picked. If there's a faculty member you're interested in working with, make sure you know what they're working on, first. Read a few of the faculty member's more recent papers. Check out their website to find out about their current projects or ask other grad students who've worked with them. Also, take a class with that faculty member if you can. That class will give you a sense of whether the faculty member's current interests (and mentoring style) are a good fit for your needs. And it will signal to the faculty member that you're serious about working with them. Once you have a chance to get to know the faculty member you want to work with, make an appointment to chat with them or stop by during office hours. Then, when you get to the meeting, ask questions: Can you tell me more about your current project on X? What are you finding so far? Are you looking for any grad students to help with the project? The professor might not have space on their team right then, but they'll probably keep you in mind for future projects and remember your enthusiasm for their work.

In terms of the type of work you'll be doing as a research assistant, there are too many possibilities to fully explain. You might be compiling references and writing annotated bibliographies about topics related to the professor's research. You might be using statistical software to analyze survey data. You might be conducting in-depth interviews with research participants or conducting ethnographic observations in the field. You might be transcribing or coding interviews. Or you might be organizing files, cleaning lab equipment, or going out to get coffee for the research group. When you're signing up to work with a faculty member, ask up front (and ideally put in writing) what types of tasks you'll be expected to do and how many hours a week you'll generally be expected to spend and what you'll get in exchange.

Along those lines, and as we talked about with teaching assistant positions, it's also important to know that faculty sometimes exploit grad student labor. You might be asked to do inappropriate amounts or types of work. You might face emotional exploitation, with faculty members subjecting you to harsh verbal reprimands or manipulating you into working more for the possibility of rewards that never seem to materialize. Unfortunately, and as we talked about in chapter 2, the power dynamics of grad school (where grad students' careers often depend on their advisors' support) can make it difficult for students who are being mistreated to push back against the mistreatment they face. If you find yourself in an exploitative or harmful situation, and if you feel comfortable speaking up, certainly do so, and chapter 2 has some suggestions on where to turn. If you don't feel comfortable speaking up, though, please know that you don't deserve to exploited or harmed. And as suggested in chapter 2, please consider looking for other people and organizations who can help you persist through those challenges and get the support you need.

* * *

The path to a graduate degree is like an obstacle course, and the various program components and requirements are like the walls you'll have to climb and the mud pits you'll have to slog through along the way. If you don't know which obstacles come next, it can feel like you're running in the dark. And that darkness can slow you down—by making each step more tentative and making each obstacle feel scarier than it might actually be.

My hope is that this chapter will be your headlamp to light the way. That it'll help you stay on course and feel more confident as you navigate the obstacles you face in getting your degree.

Staying on course and making timely progress with the various program requirements will also give you more time to focus on doing your own research. That's where we'll turn in our next chapter, talking about how to do good research and how to find the money you'll need to support your research and support yourself while you're doing it.

Chapter 6
DOING RESEARCH AND FINDING FUNDING

1

 Matt Linick @mlinic1 · Jul 22, 2018

I had no idea how to use statistical program/software. So I 1) did a multivariate regression for my capstone project by hand using just a TI-85 and lots of sleepless nights, and 2) spent months copying and pasting data to change my dataset from wide to long for my dissertation.

Whether you're getting a master's in education or a doctoral degree in physics, there's a good chance you'll have to do some form of research as part of your degree. Maybe you're interested in examining human cells under a microscope. Or examining what Black feminist writers can tell us about how oppression contributes to inequalities in health. Maybe you want to work out complex math equations. Or talk to educators to understand how they implement a new math curriculum in school.

Even if you know what research looks like in your field, and even if you have a sense of the kind of research you might want to do, that doesn't mean you know how to do that kind of research or how to do it well. Like education scholar Dr. Matt Linick, author of the tweet included above, you might've taken a course on statistics. You might know what a regression coefficient is. And you might even know how to calculate one. But that doesn't mean you know how to get that regression coefficient the "right" way or the "easy" way (i.e., using statistical software programs like Stata or using various coding shortcuts in R). And if you don't know the "right" way or the "easy" way to do research, there's a good chance it'll take you a lot more time and energy and headache to get to the same result.

In this chapter, we'll talk about learning the tricks of the trade. And we'll talk about finding resources that can help you do your research and learn to do it well.

Learning the Tricks

Most disciplines and departments have formal courses on research methods. But those courses won't necessarily teach you everything you need to know about how to do research or how to do it well. You might learn how to run an ordinary least squares regression in Stata and how to interpret the results, but not what to do if you get a certain error message. Or you might learn how to design an in-depth interview guide and how to code the transcript for themes, but not what to do if your interview respondent keeps going off on tangents or if they're reluctant to say anything at all.

Those gaps in the formal curriculum of research methods are, in some ways, understandable, because your professors have only so much time. A single semester is almost never going to be enough time to learn all the ins and outs of a particular research method. Even with hands-on training in the lab or in the field, you'll never be able to work through every possible scenario of things that could go wrong. Instead, your professors will probably focus on painting the broad strokes—teaching you the overall philosophy of a given research method, teaching a few critical skills, and maybe walking you through how they've handled key problems they've encountered in their work. When you get to the field or the lab, however, you might encounter other problems you weren't explicitly taught how to solve.

Those gaps in the formal curriculum of research methods are where imposter syndrome seeps in. They can make you feel like "maybe I'm not cut out for this," even when the reality is that you've just reached the limits of your formal training. In those moments, it's important not to blame yourself for what you don't know. And it's okay to ask for help.

Let's say, for example, that you're working on a draft of your master's project. A professor on your master's committee tells you to add an interaction to your regression analysis. You have no idea what that means, let alone how to do it, or how to interpret the results once you do. You could check out a bunch of library books (or Reddit threads) on regression analyses and spend a month trying to figure it out yourself. And you might eventually figure it out. But you might not have a month to spare. Or you might still find yourself confused at the end. And that's why it's also okay to admit what you don't know and ask others for help.

Now, admitting you don't know something can be difficult, and asking for help might make you feel nervous. You might worry that your professors or your fellow grad students will judge you for not knowing something you're supposed to know. Or you might worry that you're burdening your professor with requests. But as we talked about in chapter 2, academia works (or at least should work) on a pay-it-forward model. Your professor has gotten plenty of help and support in their own career. And that means they should be willing to help you (or at least point you to someone who can help) as well.

The key is to frame your request in a way that is both honest about what you don't know and respectful of the time and effort it might take your professor to help you figure it out. For example, you might say: "You mentioned that you want me to add an interaction to my regression. But I'm not sure what that means, and I don't think we learned that in stats class. Would you be able to show me? Or maybe point me to some resources I can use to figure it out?" And, ideally, your professor will explain what an interaction is, how to add one (or more) to your regression models, and how to interpret the results. Or, at the very least, they'll direct you to another professor, or staff member, or advanced grad student who might be able to help.

But of course, it might feel too risky to ask. Especially if the professor in question has a reputation for being gruff or dismissive of grad student requests. Or, even if you do ask, and even if the professor does try to help, you might still walk away feeling confused.

If that happens, don't blame yourself. Instead, use it as an opportunity to build the team of mentors we talked about in chapter 2. Schedule a meeting with the professor who taught you research methods. Or find the research support offices on campus (a lot of universities have a dedicated team of people who consult with researchers about statistical questions, and grad students are welcome to use their services). Or talk to other, more advanced grad students who are doing similar types of work. You can even turn to Twitter. I know plenty of senior scholars who use social media as a platform to ask for advice about doing good research. Best practices in research methods are always changing (that's sort of the point of research), and it's important to stay on top of what works.

Doing the Work

Understanding research methods—and learning the more taken-for-granted tricks of the trade—is critical for doing research that is efficient, effective, and ethically sound. Efficiency and effectiveness are key if you don't want to spend ten years in grad school and if you want to make sure you can get a job when you're done. And ethics are important because, as scholars, we have a responsibility to conduct our research carefully, report our findings accurately, and avoid doing harm.

Outside of good methods training, there are also a few other things to keep in mind if you want to make your approach to research as efficient, effective, and ethically responsible as possible. That includes quality over quantity, showing your work, and knowing when you're done.

Quality over Quantity

In academia, it's easy to feel like you're being judged by the length of your CV. And if you're feeling that way, you're probably not wrong. A recent report found that publishing expectations for job candidates and tenure candidates in sociology have nearly doubled in recent decades.[2] In 1991 the average new hire (at the assistant professor level) had 2.5 peer-reviewed articles; by 2017 that number had risen to 4.8.

That focus on number of publications is, at least in part, a function of increasing competition for academic jobs.[3] As we talked about in the introduction, limited budgets have forced many colleges and universities to keep hiring costs low. That means limiting the number of new hires (especially tenure-track hires) and relying on large classes and adjunct instructors instead. As we'll talk about in chapter 11, those hiring limits increase the competition for academic jobs, and that competition increases the pressure on job candidates to try to stand out from the crowd.

The problem with that kind of competition, however, is that there's danger in playing the game. If academics keep racing to see who can churn out the most publications, we hurt ourselves, our students, and our colleagues.

There's already a strong culture of overwork in academia.[4] And that overwork can take a serious toll on your mental and physical health. In recent years, the culture of overwork in academia has been linked to mental and physical health problems among graduate students and faculty. That includes the suicide deaths of Malcolm Anderson, Will Moore, and Kelly Catlin as well as the death of adjunct professor Thea Hunter, who suffered from a number of physical health problems and struggled to get regular medical care because of a lack of health insurance and limited funds.[5]

The race to churn out as many high-profile publications as possible also undermines the whole purpose of good, scholarly work. Pressure to publish, for example, has contributed to the crisis of replicability and reproducibility in academic science.[6] Findings from numerous well-known experimental studies have failed to replicate, meaning that researchers following the data collection and analysis procedures outlined in previous research did not find similar results.[7] Scholars have also identified problems with reproducibility, wherein following the same procedures to analyze the same data fails to generate the same results.[8] Publication pressures encourage the kind of shoddy science that can limit reproducibility and replicability. Publication pressures also incentivize other forms of scholarly malpractice, including p-hacking (mining data for significant results), HARKing (hypothesizing after results are known), and even fabricating results.[9]

I can't tell you to ignore the pressure to publish—that would be unrealistic and irresponsible. What I can say, though, is that you should resist the pressure to publish so much research so quickly that you can't do good work. So don't focus on the number of publications on your CV. Focus on doing the best work you can. And when you do get to a position where you're evaluating others—for jobs, for tenure, for awards—use that same quality-over-quantity standard as well.

Showing Your Work

So, how do you do good work? The specifics vary across disciplines, but generally good work is rigorous and important to the field.

Rigor: Rigorous research is thoughtfully designed, ethically and carefully conducted, and effectively explained. The goals and the methods of the project are closely aligned. The research has been preapproved by all relevant agencies, and the personnel are well trained. The procedures have been dutifully documented, followed with precision, and fully explained. The citations are complete and accurate and reflect a thorough understanding of the field. The evidence is presented logically and supports clearly articulated conclusions. The writing is engaging and easy to follow.

Importance: Important research, meanwhile, contributes something useful to the field. In a lot of cases, that means finding something that's never been found before. Or pushing the field to think about something in a new way. That said, we should be cautious about equating innovation with importance. Privileging novelty discourages replication,[10] and replication (like publication of null findings) is critical for verifying and clarifying and explaining existing claims.[11]

Now, how do you show others your work is good? Of course, other people will make judgments about the quality of your work based on the status of the journal or press that publishes it (more on this in chapter 8). But there are also other, less status-driven ways of signaling that your work is rigorous and important, regardless of where it's been published or whether it's been published at all.

When it comes to showing rigor, good documentation is key. Preregistration is one form of documentation that's becoming increasingly common, especially with experimental research. That process involves saying, in advance, and through online public forms, what you're going to do and what you think you're going to find.[12] Of course, preregistration isn't always possible or practical, especially if you're more interested in generating hypotheses than testing them in an experimental way. In those cases, it's especially important to include other forms of research-related documentation instead. If you're doing ethnographic observations, for example, keep track of when you visit your field site and how long you spend there. Or if you're coding survey data, be sure to include notes in your coding files that explain the choices you make along the way (how you defined variables, how you dealt with missing data, which weights you used, etc.). That kind of documentation will allow you to write about your research methods in a more specific way. And that specificity will help your reader to trust the veracity of your claims and potentially replicate your research in other settings or with other data.

Showing importance happens mainly in the final writing process. We'll talk more about writing in our next chapter. For now, though, the key is to make your contribution explicit. When you're writing about your research, you should clearly answer the question "Why does this matter?" Maybe your research has implications for theory—challenging standard assumptions in your field, extending existing ideas to understudied cases, or developing new concepts. Maybe your research has more concrete implications as well—informing policy development or highlighting the effectiveness of particular practices in the field.

Knowing When You're Done

Once you learn how to do good research, and once you master the tricks of the trade, the process of gathering and analyzing data can start to feel familiar, even safe and comforting. If you're doing ethnographic research, for example, you might find yourself writing piles and piles of field notes or transcribing interview after interview. Or if you're doing quantitative or experimental research, you might find yourself tempted to try just one more variation on your models. All that work is research, and it does matter, but it's not enough on its own. And all that extra work can ultimately turn into a distraction from the larger goal. Thus, if you want to graduate, you'll eventually have to stop gathering and analyzing data and start writing about those data instead.

That's why it's important to know when enough is enough. And that's why it's important to start your project with a good research design. Because a well-designed project makes it clear when enough is enough. You'll have a sense up front of what questions you're trying to answer. And once you have the data necessary to answer those questions (and rule out alternative answers), you're done. Time to move on to writing—and chapter 7.

On the flip side, you might also be tempted to rush through the research to get to the writing stage. Maybe you want to graduate as quickly as possible because you need a job with a better income than your grad school stipend or because your kids or your partner are waiting on you to know where they'll be moving when you finish your degree. Maybe your research is contingent on funding and you can't extend the grant completion deadline or you've spent every dollar you've got.

That pressure to finish and finish fast can feel daunting, but it doesn't mean you have to cut corners with your research. You can still do quality research on a limited budget or with limited time— you just have to design your research around those constraints. If you know you need to finish fast, avoid planning a project (like an experimental study testing the effects of an elementary-school-based intervention on students' likelihood of going to college later on) that will take years to show any results. Or if you know your budget is limited, keep the research simple (adding an international comparison case might not be your best bet) or look for data you can access and analyze at little or no cost.

Of course there are trade-offs to scaling back your research. You might have a lower chance of publishing your work in a "top" journal. Or a lower chance of getting a "top" job. That's the reality of academia. But as we'll talk about in chapter 11, competing for those top slots might not be what you want. And that's okay—there are plenty of other journals and plenty of other jobs. Or, even if you do want one of those top slots, choosing trade-offs doesn't make you a failure. And it doesn't seal your fate. If you're pursuing a career in academia, you can always save what you couldn't do or didn't finish as fodder for future research. And there's nothing to stop you from using that future research to try to publish in a top journal or transition to a top job.

Whether you want to finish your research quickly or you have the luxury of taking your time, money will almost always make that process easier. And so in the next section we'll talk about how to apply for funding and what to do if you can't get the funding you want or need.

Finding Funding

In some fields it's possible to do research on a shoestring budget or no budget at all. I did my whole dissertation—more than three years of work, resulting in a book and a handful of other published articles—on about two thousand dollars in grant funding. I used that money to pay teachers and parents and students for participating in interviews and to get help transcribing some of my interviews.[13]

That said, and even if it's possible to do research with little or no funding, there's often a trade-off with effort and time. With more funding, for example, I would've been able to conduct more interviews and pay for more help in transcribing them. That would've meant more data and more time to analyze them. It would've meant less sleep deprivation (in grad school, I rarely got more than five hours of sleep a night, and I was drinking two liters of Diet Mountain Dew a day—not something I recommend). And it might've meant a shorter time between when I finished my dissertation research and when I finally published my first book.

Essentially, funding from grants and fellowships can help make your research as efficient and effective as possible. But especially in an era of tight university budgets and public skepticism toward science, there isn't enough funding to go around.[14] That scarcity generates both stiff competition and serious inequalities between scholars with funding and scholars without.[15]

Knowing Your Options

If you want to be able to compete for funding, the first step is to know what money is available and what stipulations come with those funds. Broadly speaking, there are a few types of funding and a few key terms to know.

Internal versus External Funding: One key distinction in research funding has to do with where the money comes from.

Some research funding is "internal" in that it comes directly from your university. There might be fellowships to allow you to spend a semester working on your research without having to fulfill other obligations like serving as a teaching or research assistant. Your department might also have money for travel funds or to pay for access to a dataset you need. Other research funding is "external" in that it comes from outside your university. Those external funding sources can be government agencies like the Department of Defense, the National Science Foundation, or the National Institutes of Health. They can be foundations like the Ford Foundation, the Spencer Foundation, or the William T. Grant Foundation. They can be professional organizations, like the American Political Science Association or the National Society of Black Engineers. Or they can even be for-profit companies, like technology or drug manufacturers.

Now, money is money, but when it comes to grant funding, the source of that money determines how easily you can spend it and what you can use it to buy. Internal funding, for example, usually has fewer application requirements, a faster turnaround time from application to award, and sometimes less competition, which means there's a higher chance that you'll get the award. Compared to external funding, though, the amount of money you can get from internal funding is generally much lower. External funding is also considered more prestigious and ultimately more valuable. That's because, unlike internal funding, external funding adds to or offsets university budgets instead of depleting those budgets. If you get an external fellowship, for example, your program and your university will no longer have to pay the cost of your graduate training. Or if your advisor gets a grant that includes money for training graduate students, the university also gets to keep a percentage of that money to help cover its own administrative costs.[16]

Because of those benefits, universities often expect faculty to pursue external funding for their research. That's especially true in lab science fields, where the costs of doing research (building a lab, buying all the necessary equipment and supplies, hiring teams of students, etc.) are often substantially higher than in other fields. Even outside the lab sciences, faculty are often expected to cover a portion of their own salaries—plus all the funding for their research and their graduate students—with external grants. Thus, if you're interested in a career in academia, and especially if you're getting a doctoral degree in a lab science field, it can be helpful to build up your experience applying for (and being rejected for— more on this in chapter 8) external grants.

Fellowships: Another key funding distinction is between fellowships and grants. Fellowships are programs with money attached. These programs are typically run by a foundation or a government office or sometimes a university or a corporation. The big fellowships are often prestigious and interdisciplinary, and they typically accept a cohort of "fellows" each year, with a standard application format, a standard deadline, and a standard amount of money for each fellow. In order to apply, you'll typically have to write a proposal outlining a research project you plan to complete during your fellowship year(s). Those applications then go through a process of review. We'll talk more about the peer-review process when we talk about academic publishing in chapter 8, but the peer-review process for fellowships (and for grants, which we'll talk about in the next section) is very similar. Other scholars in your field (often those who are former recipients of the fellowship) are asked to read your application, offer feedback, and ultimately make a recommendation about whether you should receive the award.

If you're selected for a fellowship, you'll get financial support (a stipend for living expenses and/or money for research), and you might also get mentoring or logistical support through the program. That support, though, does usually come with strings attached. During your fellowship period, you might have to attend annual or semiannual meetings where you present findings from your research and also network with other fellows, past fellows, and other program faculty and staff. If you get a fellowship, you'll probably also get regular requests from the funding agency to provide updates on your career and the progress you've made in your research. And you might also be asked to serve as a reviewer for future applications or to help organize annual meetings or workshops for future fellows. Responding to those requests is important. It takes time, but it's your chance to "pay it forward" and support the next generation of grad students in pursuing their degrees.

Essentially, while a fellowship might provide funding for only a year or two or three, your relationship with your funder can last much longer. And if your research is successful, it can give the funder a reason to trust you and invest more in you when you apply for additional funding with future projects after you get your degree.

Grants: Like fellowships, grants provide funding to support your research. They're typically funded by foundations, government agencies, universities, and corporations. There's also a standardized application process, and your application will generally be evaluated both by program staff and through a process of peer review.

Unlike fellowships, though, grants don't typically have a whole networking and mentoring program attached. Instead, grants usually provide just financial support for a particular project or initiative. How those grants work, though, and to whom they are awarded vary a lot across different types of awards. Understanding those variations is important because they affect your role in applying for and managing the grant funding and also determine what you can do with the money you get.

As a grad student, for example, your research might be fully funded through grants your advisor applied for and received. That's particularly common in the case of training grants. Training grants are awarded to faculty members or academic departments, and they provide financial support for the training of students, postdocs, and other research staff, usually as part of a specific, faculty-led project. Being funded through a training grant is helpful in that it can mean you won't have to apply for funding for your grad school research—your tuition costs and research costs and even your stipend might be covered through the grant.

In other cases, you might get a more limited amount of funding through your professors' grants. As we talked about with research assistantships in chapter 5, your advisor or other faculty members in your department might have received a grant to provide support for their own research projects. Those grants, in turn, might not include enough funding to cover your graduate tuition or stipend, but they might include money your professor can use to pay you on a semester or hourly basis for work on a specific project, or they might include money your professor can use to pay for you to travel with them to a conference and present your research.

In still other cases, you might want or need to apply for grant funds to cover your own research costs. Most large grants are available only to faculty or postdoctoral researchers. That said, there are many smaller grants (ranging from a few hundred dollars to tens of thousands of dollars) for which grad students can apply. As we'll discuss in the next section, these grants can be used to cover a wide array of research-related expenses, including equipment costs, costs associated with gathering and analyzing data, travel expenses for research and conferences, publication costs, and more.

That said, grants typically come with more rules than fellowships, and those rules dictate how you (or your advisor) can use the money you receive. Let's say, for example, that you start working on a project, and you realize that you need to go in a different direction or collect different data than what you originally planned. If you have a fellowship, that's usually okay—you don't typically have to get approval for a change of direction in your research. The fellowship is more of an investment in you than an investment in a specific research project. If you have a grant, on the other hand, you'll have to fill out lots of paperwork explaining how and why your plan changed and how exactly your budget will deviate from what you originally proposed.

All that paperwork can be a headache, but there are other perks to grants as well. For example, and unlike fellowships, the amount of grant money you can apply for isn't fixed in advance. Instead, you can tailor your application and your budget (within an upper bound) to the research you want to do. Furthermore, while getting one fellowship usually means you can't get another at the same time, you can often apply for and receive multiple grants to support one project and expand or extend it over time.

Finding Funding Sources

In addition to knowing the key terms, it's also important to know where to look for funding in your field. Early in your grad career, and especially if you're in a doctoral program and interested in an academic career, schedule a meeting with your advisor to talk about future funding plans. During that meeting, you might map out how you'll fund your graduate training and what funding you'll need beyond your graduate years. That might include postdoctoral fellowships, early career grants, and, maybe, big awards that you'll use to support your own grad students someday.

Before you do that, though, it's important to do your homework. Spend some time familiarizing yourself with the types of fellowships and grants you might apply for at various career stages and the different funding agencies you might turn to for support.

As you make that list, track everything in a spreadsheet. You can create separate tabs for funding at each career stage (predoctoral, postdoctoral, early career, midcareer, etc.). Within each tab, you can include key details like the name of the grant or fellowship, the name of the funding agency, any eligibility requirements, the maximum amount of the award, the application requirements and deadlines, names of other scholars who have applied for or received the award, and links to more information online.

In terms of gathering that information, there are a few key resources I'd recommend consulting.

Other People's CVs: A quick first stop for funding information is your advisor's CV. There will almost certainly be information on there about the various types of funding they've applied for and received throughout their career. The dates listed with those awards will also give you a sense of when they applied for what. You can also check out the CVs of other faculty, postdocs, and advanced grad students in your department and in similar departments at other schools. Make a list of all the grants, fellowships, awards, and funding agencies you see listed on those CVs.

Online Grant Databases: For a more systematic search, check out online funding databases. Pivot, for example, allows you to create a profile and find information about funding available to scholars at all career levels in your field. It also connects you to other researchers in academia, government, and industry who might be interested in collaborating on research. Most universities have subscriptions to Pivot, so you should be able to create a free account by heading to your university's library web page and searching for Pivot in their online resources.[17] UCLA's GRAPES database, meanwhile, is useful if you're looking for direct funding for your graduate training and research. It includes an incredibly comprehensive list of grants and fellowships for grad students and postdoctoral researchers across a wide range of disciplines.[18]

Other online databases provide information about projects that have already received awards. You can view successful proposals and also find out more information about your advisors' funded projects. Some of these resources include the NSF Award Search and the NIH Project Reporter.[19]

Program Officers: Once you have a list of potential funding sources, it can be helpful to contact those sponsors to get a sense of whether they might be interested in funding your project and if they have any recommendations about how to frame your application to increase its chances of success. Most grant and fellowship program websites list contact information for their program officers, and most program officers are happy to talk (albeit briefly) with potential applicants. That said, it's helpful to go into those conversations with both a clear sense of the project for which you're seeking funding and a clear set of questions you want to ask before you apply. You'll want to be able to describe your project and its aims in two to three sentences or less. And you'll want to state your questions clearly and succinctly.

If you're looking for advice on what to say in those conversations, or if you're not sure how to reach out, check out the guidelines from the National Institutes of Health.[20] They offer information about which questions should not be directed to program officers (e.g., budgeting questions should be directed to your university's grant specialists instead), how to avoid particularly busy times (e.g., in the final weeks before applications are due), and how to get the information you need as quickly as possible (e.g., by referencing the grant number or fellowship name in emails or when leaving a voicemail, and by indicating if your request needs an urgent reply).

University and Department Resources: Online databases and program officers are great for learning about external funding, but maybe you're not quite ready to apply for a big, external award. Maybe you're just looking for money to cover conference travel. Or maybe you're interested in a one semester fellowship that will give you some time to finish your dissertation research. In that case, internal grants or fellowships might be all you need. And if that's the case, then you'll probably want to start your search closer to home. If your department is doing its part to uncover the hidden curriculum, there might be a list of internal grants and fellowships right on your department website. If you can't find it there, then check out the university's office of research administration, which will probably have information about both internal and external funding for which you can apply. If you want more detailed information or want help figuring out what types of funding you qualify for, you can also schedule a meeting with the faculty or staff member in charge of your graduate program. Bring along a list of internal grants and fellowships you've seen online or on other students' CVs and then ask for their advice about when and how to apply.

Professional Organizations: Another good resource for information about funding is your discipline's professional organization. As we talked about in chapter 2, most fields have a national professional organization (or multiple) and sometimes regional organizations. Those organizations, in addition to hosting academic conferences and publishing academic journals, typically collect and share information about funding opportunities through their newsletters and websites. If you're not sure which professional organizations to look for (or join), check out the CVs of professors in your department. Once you join the organization, you'll usually start receiving email newsletters (sometimes far too many newsletters) with information about funding opportunities, job opportunities, and more. In some cases, these professional organizations will also offer their own funding for grad students and other scholars. They might offer small grants to cover the cost of travel to a conference. Or they might offer a cash award for the best grad student paper in a particular subfield. These small amounts of money might not seem like much, especially compared to big NIH or NSF grants. But when it comes to the costs of grad school, every little bit helps.

Choosing Costs to Cover

The whole reason to apply for grants and fellowships is to get financial support for your training and your research. Along those lines, and when you're applying for funding, you'll probably have to outline how you plan to use the money you get. Fortunately, or unfortunately, there are usually plenty of costs to cover.

- Time-related costs:
  - Stipend/salary for yourself
    - Academic year stipend/salary
    - Summer stipend/salary
  - Depending on the project and funding source, stipend/salary for coauthors or mentors

- Training-related costs:
  - Registration fees for training workshops
  - Travel costs associated with attending training workshops
  - Travel costs associated with trips to meet with outside mentors
- Research-related costs:
  - Equipment and software
  - Data-related costs (e.g., data access fees, participant incentives for research)
  - Research support (e.g., research assistants, transcription services, consultant fees)
  - Travel to field sites and/or to meet with external collaborators
  - Conference registration fees and travel expenses
- Publication-related costs
  - Professional editing/indexing
  - Manuscript submission fees
  - Publication/page fees

Getting Organized

Once you identify some possible funding sources and figure out what you'll need the money for, it's time to start putting together your application. Every funding agency has its own application with its own set of esoteric expectations. And every funding agency gets far more applications than it can ever afford to fund. That said, there are some things you can do to give yourself a better shot at getting money for your research.

First, get organized. Make a spreadsheet with all the grants and fellowships you plan to apply for and the key details for each one:[21]

- Grant or fellowship name
- Submission deadlines
- Budget constraints
- Eligibility criteria[22]

- Application components
  - Abstract
  - Proposal (short and/or long version)
  - CV/bio
  - Writing samples
  - Recommendation letters
  - Institutional approvals
  - Other statements and supporting materials
- Key words[23]
- Links to more information online

Having all these details in one place can help you compare and prioritize different sources of funding. You can also use the spreadsheet to track your completion of various application requirements and to help you avoid missing any important deadlines.

As you gather these data, create a set of digital folders where you store all the materials for each application. That includes materials provided by the funder, such as budget worksheets and proposal templates. It also includes materials you create for the application, such as your completed budget, your proposal, your CV, and your writing samples. Even if you use the same CV or writing sample for multiple funding applications, it helps to have copies of all the relevant documents stored together. That way, when it's time to upload everything, all the necessary files are in the same folder, and you don't have to spend two hours hunting them down before you click "submit."

Writing Funding Proposals

When you sit down to write your funding proposal, don't try to reinvent the wheel. Instead, look for examples of proposals that have been funded (and successful) in the past. As noted above, many funding agencies have searchable databases with links to their funded proposals. If the funder you're thinking of applying to doesn't do that, check its website for a list of people who've been funded in the past. Identify those whose research most closely aligns with your own, reach out to one or more of them (or ask an advisor to introduce you), and ask if they would be willing to share their proposal. It doesn't have to be a lengthy email—just a few sentences explaining who you are, what you're trying to do with your research, why you're applying for this funding, and why you think their proposal will be a good model for yours. If there are faculty members or other grad students in your department who have applied for similar funding, you're welcome to ask them too.

Once you have a few successful proposals to work from, model yours after them. That doesn't mean copying other people's proposals. It means mirroring the structure they use—what comes first and second and third. It also means adopting their style—what gets bolded or bulleted or put in footnotes. And it means following their logic—what types of evidence and arguments they use to make a case for their study.

Along those lines, the key to writing successful proposals is to build a strong case—for your study and for yourself as the PI. Why is your research question the right research question to be asking? Why are your hypotheses the right hypotheses to choose? Why are your methods and your data the right ones for answering the questions or testing the hypotheses you proposed? Why are you the right person to do this research? And why are you so sure that you're going to be successful in carrying it out? Your proposal should answer all those questions. And it should use data to support those answers. That support could include evidence from other people's research and, if you have it, preliminary evidence from your own research. That evidence could also include key details about your background and training that make you a good fit for the project. You want the selection committee to read your proposal and be confident that your research is going to be successful and important. And you want them to have that confidence even if you don't quite have it yet yourself.

When you're crafting funding proposals, it's also important to know—and to write for—your audience. The funding agency and its staff will have the final say in determining which proposals are funded. What that means, in turn, is that you want to make sure your goals align with theirs. And you want to make sure you echo those goals in your proposal. Let's say, for example, that you're applying for support from an organization whose primary mission is to end world hunger. If your proposal doesn't discuss how your project will move us closer to the goal of ending world hunger, and especially if it doesn't have the word "hunger" in it somewhere, there's a good chance it won't end up being one of the ones the organization chooses to fund.

At the same time, the funding agency isn't the only audience for your proposal. Rather, and as we talked about briefly when we defined grants and fellowships above, many funding proposals are vetted, in part, through a process of peer review. We'll talk about the peer-review process in more detail when we talk about publishing in chapter 8. The key thing to know here, though, is that you can't assume every reviewer will do or even be familiar with the kind of work you do. In fact, there might not be anyone on the review panel who is an expert in your particular subfield. Thus, in crafting your funding proposals, you should write for an audience of scholars who have general expertise in your field. That means avoiding acronyms and jargon, explaining key concepts, and defining key terms. You'll also want to explain why the findings from your project will be relevant not only to other researchers in your subfield but also to other scholars in your discipline and potentially to the public as a whole.

For more detailed advice about writing effective funding proposals, I'd recommend checking out:

- The University of Wisconsin's Writing Center website, which outlines the various parts of a grant proposal and offers tips for what to include and how to frame those various components. The website also has links to sample proposals, including one for the National Science Foundation Graduate Research Fellowship.[24]

- The National Institutes of Health seminars on grant writing, which demystify the whole grant application and grants management process.[25] Depending on your location, you might try to attend one of these workshops or keep an eye out for other similar workshops and webinars at your university or at other nearby schools.
- One of the many books about grant writing. Some are step-by-step guides to writing for a particular funding agency like the National Institutes of Health or the National Science Foundation.[26] Others include more general advice about writing effective grant proposals.[27]

Feedback on Funding Proposals

Getting feedback on your funding proposals—before you submit them—can substantially increase your chances of success. You can ask your advisor to read your proposal (just be sure to give them plenty of time before the deadline). You can also ask other grad students to read it. You can even ask your mom or your grandad or your friends from home. Ask them to tell you what makes sense and what doesn't. Ask them for suggestions on how to make your proposal as clear and strong as possible. Ask them to let you know if you're overselling your study or selling yourself short. You don't have to take every suggestion they offer, but you should take their feedback seriously, just as we talked about in chapter 2.

Getting feedback on your proposals can help you make sure the writing is as accessible and engaging as possible. That's important because, as we talked about a minute ago, the scholars reviewing your proposal probably won't (all) be experts on the thing you're planning to study. And they might only give your proposal a one-minute skim (at least to start). So you want to make sure you're making a clear case for your project and for the significance of what you might find.

Asking other grad students in your department for feedback on your proposals might seem strange or problematic. Grants and fellowship programs are usually competitive, and those other grad students might be applying for the same funds as you. Yet by reviewing each other's proposals, you'll probably both increase your chances of success. That way you can also focus on seeing each other as colleagues rather than competitors. As we talked about in chapter 2, that kind of collaborative environment tends to be much healthier for everyone involved.

Dotting i's and Crossing t's

In some cases, and before you finally click "submit," your funding application will need to be approved by officials at your university. You might need a letter of support from the dean. Or you might need to have the Office of Research Administration sign off that it has approved your budget and will help administer the funds. In some cases, and to get all these approvals, you'll need to submit a separate internal application for support from the university, and those applications are usually due months before the final application deadline. That internal application model is particularly common in the case of "limited submission" grants and fellowships, where only one person from a given university or division of a university is allowed to apply each year. In that case, university officials will review the internal applications and decide which proposal they will nominate for the external competition. Whether you're applying for one of those limited submission grants or not, it's important to make sure you leave enough time for approvals, that is, by having the full application and budget ready at least a month before the final deadline.

Finally, once you've got your proposal written and edited and edited again, and once you've got your budget outlined (and approved, if necessary, by the relevant university offices), it's time to dot your i's and cross your t's. Essentially, you want to check and double-check that you have filled out all the relevant forms, obtained all the necessary approvals and recommendations, and followed all the rules around font sizes and word counts and citation styles. The last thing you want, after all the prep work you've done, is to have your proposal rejected on a technicality. And on that front, a little diligence can go a long way.

* * *

Even if you follow all the steps suggested above, and even if you read half a dozen books on grant writing, there's a good chance your first grant or fellowship proposal won't be selected for funding. And there's a good chance your fifteenth proposal won't be selected either. As a grad student and a faculty member, I've gotten rejected plenty of times. I even finalized one funding proposal in the hospital after my second baby was born—he was two weeks early, and the university approvals finally came through the day he was born. I didn't get the funding in the end. And I'm not alone. Scholars with thousands or even millions of dollars in grant funding have all been rejected, probably dozens of times.

We'll talk more about dealing with rejection in chapter 8 and chapter 11. First, though, let's talk about how to write about the research you do. And we'll talk about how to navigate the world of journals and presses to publish the research you write.

Chapter 7

WRITING ABOUT YOUR RESEARCH

1

 Sarah Hegge @SarahLClothes · Jul 22, 2018

I had no idea what a lit review was when I started too! I felt like everyone in my classes already knew so I was too embarrassed to ask. It wasn't until later that I realized many of my classmates had been just as clueless 😄

As we talked about in chapter 5, getting a graduate degree almost always means doing some sort of research. But just doing the research won't be enough to get your degree. Rather, you'll also have to write about what you find. And you'll have to persuade your readers (or at least your dissertation committee) that what you found is both true and important.

In this chapter, we'll talk about writing about research—what academic writing looks like, what distinguishes good academic writing from bad academic writing, and what goals good academic writing should try to achieve.

Writing about Research
Academic Writing

If you remember back to your high school English classes, you might have learned that there are four primary types of writing—descriptive, narrative, expository, and persuasive. Let's talk briefly about each of these and where academic writing fits in the mix.

Descriptive writing can be fiction or nonfiction, and the goal is generally to paint a picture with words. Effective descriptive writing includes just enough detail and imagery that the reader can fully imagine what the author is describing without losing sight of the thing being described. Academic writing sometimes incorporates elements of descriptive writing. With qualitative research, for example, the author might include a descriptive paragraph that gives the reader a sense of the site where the research took place. However, academic writing is rarely purely descriptive in form.

Narrative writing can also be fiction or nonfiction, and the goal is to tell a story. That involves helping the reader experience some sequence of events from beginning to end. And, at least if it's good writing, it also involves entertaining the reader along the way. That entertainment, in turn, generally involves invoking some emotion in the reader—whether surprise, sadness, anger, elation, or fear. Academic writing sometimes incorporates elements of narrative writing. Structure-wise, for example, academic writing generally follows a story arc—it walks the reader through the story of the research from beginning (the research question and justification) to middle (the data collection and analysis) to end (the results and conclusions). Unlike with purely narrative writing, however, academic writing tends to be less concerned with entertaining the reader than with informing the reader.[2] And in that sense, academic writing is closer to expository writing.

Expository writing is generally nonfiction, and the point is to teach the reader something new. Good expository writing gives the reader the information they need to understand some fact or follow some procedure for themselves. Academic writing, in turn, might seem like a clear case of expository writing. And in some senses, that's true. Academic writing should help the reader understand something new about the world—something the authors have revealed with their research. Unlike more purely expository writing, however, academic writing also has to convince the reader that what the authors find is true. In that sense, academic writing also incorporates elements of persuasive writing.

Persuasive writing, in turn, is generally nonfiction and aimed at convincing the reader to believe the author's claims. That kind of persuasion requires a logical structure rather than a purely chronological one. As a result, good persuasive writing has a clear central argument, provides evidence that logically supports that argument, and presents that evidence in a systematic way. Consistent with that model of persuasive writing, the goal of academic writing is generally to persuade readers that what the authors found in their research is both important and true. That said, academic writing is also different from other forms of persuasive writing in that the evidence has to come from research—time spent systematically gathering and analyzing data—rather than just from the author's beliefs.

Ultimately, then, while academic writing can incorporate lots of different types of writing, it tends to be more instrumental (expository and persuasive) than sentimental (descriptive and narrative) in the end.

Avoiding the Trap of Bad Writing

Because of its instrumentality, it's easy to assume that the quality of academic writing doesn't matter. And judging by some of the research that gets published in academic journals, that would be a fair assumption to make. If you spend a little time reading in your discipline (or any academic discipline), you'll probably find plenty of bad writing. You might find books or articles with research questions and central arguments buried deep in the middle of page-long paragraphs. You might find paragraphs without topic sentences or transitions to guide the reader through. You might find dense, convoluted sentences with far more words and clauses than they need. You might find big words, buzz words, and quotations used only for effect.

Now I should make it clear here that when I talk about good writing and bad writing, I'm not talking about grammar. Sure, there are times when it's useful to use an Oxford comma (i.e., to distinguish whether you'll need two books or more if you're giving a copy of this book your colleagues, Aaliyah and Amy). In general, though, official grammar rules are arbitrary, especially in a language as convoluted as English. And there are plenty of great writers who play fast and loose with those rules.[3] Those official rules, in turn, also reflect the most privileged dialect of English—the one associated with highly educated white people.[4] As a result, strict enforcement of grammar rules has the effect of dismissing the contributions of students and scholars from systematically marginalized groups.[5]

Ultimately, then, when I'm talking about good academic writing, I'm talking about writing that makes a compelling argument, supports that argument with sufficient evidence, and presents both the argument and the evidence with clarity, brevity, accuracy, and consistency.

By that definition, it's certainly possible to publish bad writing, but you shouldn't set your own bar that low. As we talked about in chapter 4, bad writing fuels imposter syndrome by putting too big a burden on the reader. It makes readers, and especially student readers, feel like they're just not smart enough to get it, when really the writer just didn't work hard enough to make it clear. Arguably, bad writing also undermines public faith in academia because it makes it harder to disseminate the findings from research and increases the chances that a journalist or a policymaker or some person on Twitter will misreport what the research actually found.

Now, you might not think of yourself as a great writer or even as a writer at all. But the nice thing about academic writing—or at least academic article writing—is that there are clear formulas to follow. Creativity matters when you're coming up with your research projects. It matters a lot less when you're writing up the results, especially in article form. That means you don't have to wait for inspiration. You can rely on tried-and-true formulas to help you get started and push through writer's block.

Let's talk through some of those formulas and how to achieve good writing when you're writing about your work. Because article writing is shorter, more formulaic, and more similar across disciplines than academic book writing, it's easier to talk about in a book like this. So that's what we'll focus on here. That said, I'll also talk a bit about writing academic books and book chapters and other types of academic or academic-adjacent writing.

Finding and Writing Your Argument

First, good writing makes a compelling argument, and it supports that argument with sufficient evidence.

An argument is essentially an abstraction—it's a generalization you make based on your findings, which are in turn a generalization about the patterns you find in your data. To see what I mean, imagine a triangle. At the base of the triangle, there's your data—all the responses on a survey, or all the text you analyzed, or all the results of the tests you ran in the lab. Halfway up the triangle, there are your results—the patterns or relationships you find in your data. At the top of the triangle, there's your argument—what the patterns in your data tell us about how the world works or ought to work.

In some of my ethnographic research, for example, my data included field notes describing situations where elementary school students were struggling with some problem and then deciding whether or not to ask the teacher for help.[6] My results, meanwhile, were the patterns I found in those data. I found, for example, that students from middle- and upper-middle-class white families asked for more help and did so more proactively and persistently than did students from working-class families (e.g., by calling out rather than raising their hands, by continuing to pester the teachers until they got the help they wanted). I also found that while teachers could have denied those requests, they tended to grant them instead. In granting those requests, teachers also ended up rewarding the privileged students who asked, allowing those students to get their work done more quickly, more correctly, and with fewer problems. Finally, my argument was the generalization

I could make based on those findings. Specifically, I argued that because teachers were responsive to privileged students' requests, privileged students were able to use help seeking to maintain their unfair advantage in school.

Getting to the results of a research project is usually the (relatively) easy part. It's also the part of the process that you'll typically learn in your research methods classes. Maybe you'll be using regression models to identify patterns in quantitative or experimental data. Or maybe you'll be using qualitative coding strategies to identify patterns in interview transcripts or archival materials.

Getting to the argument is harder. The process of finding that argument will also depend on what type of research you do and what type of contribution you want to make to your field. Arguments, for example, are often easier to identify in deductive than in inductive research.[7]

Deductive research includes most laboratory science, experimental research, and quantitative, survey-based research. With deductive research, you start with a hypothesis. Then you test that hypothesis with your research. If your research supports your hypothesis, then your hypothesis becomes your argument. If your research doesn't support your hypothesis, then your argument becomes "not hypothesis" instead. To make this a little more concrete, let's say your hypothesis is that requiring weekly meetings between grad students and their advisors will reduce students' time-to-degree. You could run an experiment randomly assigning some grad students to the treatment condition (required weekly check-in meetings) and some grad students to the control condition (weekly check-in meetings not required). If students who got the required weekly check-in meetings have a significantly shorter time-to-degree, then your argument would be: *Requiring grad students to complete weekly check-in meetings with their advisors significantly reduces students' time-to-degree.* If, instead, students who got the required weekly check-in meetings don't have a significantly shorter time-to-degree, then your argument will instead be:

Requiring grad students to complete weekly check-in meetings with their advisors does not significantly reduce students' time-to-degree.

Now, you might be thinking—one of those arguments is a lot more interesting than the other. The first argument has clear implications for research, policy, and practice. It would suggest that students who take longer to finish might not be getting frequent enough support from their advisors. It would also suggest that faculty advisors should be meeting weekly with their grad student advisees and that grad programs should require those meetings, at least if they care about time-to-degree. Meanwhile, the second argument doesn't offer any strong implications, aside from suggesting that required weekly advisor meetings aren't enough, on their own, to reduce time-to-degree. That's why it's often difficult to publish "null" findings—the conclusions don't seem as powerful or as interesting.[8] And yet if you don't publish (or at least try to report) your null findings, then someone else might end up wasting time and resources doing the same experiment you did, only to get the same null result. Ultimately, then, it's important to publish (or at least try to report) null findings, even if they're not what you expected or hoped to find.

Inductive research doesn't typically have those kinds of publication bias problems, but it has its own challenges. Inductive research includes work using ethnography, interviews, archival research, textual analysis, and other forms of qualitative research as well as some forms of descriptive quantitative research. With inductive research, you start with a question rather than a hypothesis. Then you identify forms of data that you think will allow you to answer that question. Then you gather those data and analyze them to identify patterns. Then you develop an argument about the significance of those patterns. That last step is rarely easy. It sometimes takes five or six or fifteen tries to get it right.

How you get to your argument will also depend on whether you're trying to make a descriptive contribution to the literature or a more theoretical one. Descriptive research makes an argument about how things are, usually within the context of a specific case or population. You might describe the characteristics of some subject, substance, situation, or social group, or the relationships between different subjects, substances, situations, and social groups. In some fields, purely descriptive research is more common. In other fields, however, descriptive research won't be enough—at least if you want to get your argument published. In those fields, you'll be expected to make a more theoretical contribution instead. Theoretical research goes a step further in making an argument about why things are the way they are or why it matters that things are how they are, often by suggesting that the findings speak to something larger than the case or population studied in the research. Going that route, you'll not only describe some set of characteristics or relationships but also explain those characteristics and relationships or maybe reveal their consequences. As a result, the arguments in descriptive research focus on telling the reader how the world is, while the arguments in theoretical research focus on telling the reader either why the world is the way it is or why it matters that the world is the way it is. While descriptive arguments are usually deeply grounded in the data, theoretical arguments typically involve some degree of speculation. That speculation process, in turn, introduces a level of uncertainty that can make theoretical arguments harder to identify and harder to make.

Ultimately, and regardless of how you get to your argument, you'll want to make sure you have one. Because if there's only one thing your reader takes away from your writing, it should be your argument. And the reader's understanding of that argument should be the same as yours.

To achieve that goal, you'll want to state your argument with clarity, brevity, accuracy, and consistency. Clarity means putting your argument front and center, not buried in the middle of a paragraph. Brevity means keeping your argument short enough that it's easy to follow. Accuracy means making sure your argument is closely aligned with the patterns you find in your data. And consistency means repeating your argument systematically throughout the piece you're writing. Let's talk next about achieving clarity, brevity, accuracy, and consistency in your argument and in your writing as a whole.

Conveying Your Ideas with Clarity

When you're writing about academic research, you're usually trying to make a complex argument about complex ideas. And you might be tempted to make the complexity of the writing match the complexity of the argument and the ideas. But if you go that route, there's a good chance you'll just end up obscuring your ideas— making them harder for your reader to follow and more likely to be misunderstood.

The more complex your ideas, the more important it is to convey them clearly. Clear writing is easy to follow. It defines jargon terms and uses them consistently and sparingly. It conveys ideas in simple, straightforward sentences. It has a logical organization that guides the reader through the argument step by step.

Clear writing, in my view, also plays its cards face-up. Rather than wait to reveal your big conclusion, I'd recommend stating what you find up front. That means writing abstracts and introductions that overview the project as a whole (we'll talk about this more in the next section). It also means starting each paragraph with a topic sentence that tells your reader what to expect in the sentences that follow.

Conveying Your Ideas with Brevity

A lot of academics (myself included) have a tendency to overwrite— using fifteen words when five will do, and using big words when small ones work just as well. That kind of overwriting is problematic for two reasons. First, it runs the risk of confusing the reader, especially if the extra stuff makes the writing less clear. Second, overwriting makes it hard to stay within word limits and still include all necessary ideas. Most journals have strict limits on the number of words per article. And most presses have limits on the number of words they'll publish per book.

Given the problems with overwriting, brevity is an important (and undervalued) skill for academic writers. But it's not something you have to achieve with your first draft. If you need to overwrite to let the words flow, go ahead. Just don't get too attached to those extra words. Because, as we'll talk about later in this chapter, ruthless self-editing is key for ensuring that your writing is brief and clear.

When you're writing for brevity, though, it is still okay to include some repetition of ideas. As I'll discuss in the sample article outline below, you'll want to repeat your central argument multiple times in a given paper—in the abstract, in the introduction, in the results/analysis, and again in the discussion/conclusion. Repeating your central argument and repeating key details about your research and your findings ensure that your reader will get the gist of what you did and what you found, even if they read only part of what you write.

Conveying Your Ideas with Accuracy and Consistency

As a researcher, you can't bring your readers into the lab with you or out into the field. Instead, you have to explain what you did and persuade your readers to trust what you find. What that means, in turn, is that you have to write about your research as accurately and as consistently as possible.

To achieve that kind of accuracy and consistency, the first step is to be precise about what you did in your research. As we talked about in chapter 6, most disciplines view reproducibility and replicability as critical components of rigorous research.[9] If you want your research to be reproducible and replicable, then your methods section should read like a recipe for your work. It can be a fairly advanced recipe—written for an expert in your field. But it should be detailed enough for that expert to understand what you did, re-create what you did, and get the same results. Your methods recipe should also include some context, using prior research to justify the methodological decisions you made (e.g., why you used one statistical technique rather than another, or why you selected a particular case to study, or how you defined and measured the variables you use).

Second, be precise about what you found. Your descriptions of your results should be technically accurate and easy for your reader to understand. In statistical research, for example, odds ratios are notoriously difficult to interpret,[10] so you'll want to be cautious about how you describe those results, or possibly choose an alternative way of presenting your data. That might mean reporting average marginal effects instead of odds ratios, or presenting your findings in a figure as well as in the text.

Technically accurate doesn't just mean statistically accurate. It also means accurate in the sense of accurately capturing the phenomenon you're describing as it exists in the real world. To give you an example of what I mean, let's consider the case of medical research. Let's say, for example, that you have a dataset with a thousand hospital patients and data on their background characteristics and whether they experienced a hospital acquired infection (and probably some other variables, too, though those aren't relevant for this example). Now, let's say that you find in your regression model that women are significantly more likely than men to experience hospital acquired infections or that Black patients are significantly more likely than white patients to get those infections. There's a tendency in quantitative research to describe those patterns as "the effect of gender" or "the effect of race" on patient outcomes. But that's not accurate, for two reasons. First, it's not accurate because nonexperimental data can't definitively determine causality. They can only say that two variables are correlated. Second, it's not accurate because that's not how gender and race work in our society. Gender and race can't directly cause outcomes like experiencing a hospital acquired infection. Instead, those differences in infection rates are likely the consequence of systemic racism and sexism in society, which might impact patients' experiences in hospitals or the treatment they receive from hospital personnel. Writing with accuracy means acknowledging those more complex realities or at least avoiding language implying that women patients or Black patients are somehow to blame for their higher rates of infection.

Third, be consistent in describing what you found. Your argument should be logically consistent with the evidence you present, and your argument should be the same at the beginning of your paper or chapter or book as it is at the end. As you work on a given piece of writing, and especially a longer piece like a book, you will almost certainly find a clearer or briefer or more accurate way to state your argument. If so, go back and edit all other mentions of your argument to make sure they match at the end.

That's a good segue for talking about the importance of feedback and editing when you're writing about research.

Getting and Giving Feedback on Academic Writing

Like with grant proposals, feedback can substantially improve your academic writing. Getting that feedback from your advisor, from other professors, or even from other grad students can help you avoid leaving out relevant citations, identify parts of your argument that aren't clear, figure out where you need to add more data, or help you explain more persuasively the importance of what you found. You might feel some anxiety about letting other people read your work. But it's actually helpful to get feedback earlier in the writing process rather than try to produce a full perfect draft on your own. There's no such thing as a perfect draft, so getting feedback earlier in the process will help you avoid wasting time producing a full draft that you'll have to completely overhaul in the end.

If you have the time, an even better strategy is to get feedback at multiple stages of the writing process. That includes when you're developing the idea for the paper, when you're writing the outline of the paper, when you have a full first draft, when you're almost ready to submit the manuscript for publication, and when you've revised the manuscript in response to feedback from peer review. At each of those stages, it can be helpful to ask a trusted mentor, friend, or colleague to read the paper (or talk with you about the ideas) and offer their advice about what works and what could be improved. That doesn't mean, though, that you should ask the same person for advice at every stage. Different people have different strengths as readers, editors, and reviewers. Your advisor, for example, might be especially helpful at the idea generation stage but might never have the time to provide the kind of careful, line-by-line edits you need right before you submit for peer review. Meanwhile, you might find another faculty member who's great at helping you work out the logic and the framing of a paper at the outline stage. Your grad school classmates, in turn, might offer useful feedback at the first draft stage. And maybe your mom is the kind of stickler for spelling and grammar who can help you catch all the typos before you submit for review. Regardless of who fills what role, it can be helpful to have a team of people (like the broader team we talked about in chapter 2) who can help you with your writing, even before you submit a paper for review.

Along those lines, I highly recommend forming writing groups with other grad students. You might meet once a month (or more often if you have the time) and rotate who brings a piece of writing to share. Writing groups are a great way to practice getting and giving feedback. Your professors might even build that kind of informal peer review into your courses or into department workshops.

We'll talk more about how to give feedback in chapter 8. For now, though, it's important to note that when you're giving feedback to your peers, you should aim to build the paper up rather than tearing it down. That doesn't mean you should give only positive feedback. Pointing out the problems with a paper is part of giving good feedback. But it's not enough on its own. Rather, to give good feedback, you also have to explain why those problems are problems and offer suggestions for how to fix them. That's the model I try to follow whenever I'm giving feedback, whether it's to one of my students or one of my colleagues or as part of an anonymous peer review.

For some high-stakes publications (like a manuscript you're submitting to a top journal or a book you're publishing with an academic press), it might also make sense to get help from a professional editor. These editors can help you polish up your grammar, tighten up wordy prose, and generally make your writing as clear and effective as possible. Professional editing can be costly, but it can be especially helpful if you're writing in a language other than your first language, and you might be able to use grant funding to cover the costs.

Editing for Clarity, Brevity, Accuracy, and Consistency

Now, it's easy to look at a piece of published writing and assume that those words just tumbled perfectly out of the author's head. But I'd be willing to bet that most pieces of published writing have been through dozens of major and minor revisions before they make it to print. With the first article I ever published, for example, I rewrote most of the paper five times before I even submitted it for peer review. Then I rewrote big chunks of it another five times in response to peer reviews. And I probably made hundreds of small wording changes within each of those drafts along the way.

All that revision might sound daunting, but hopefully it's reassuring as well. It means that even people who think of themselves as pretty good writers struggle to write with clarity, brevity, accuracy, and consistency when they're writing their first (or even their tenth) draft. And it means that all that feedback we talked about in the last section will help you make your paper better in the end.

Ultimately, then, if you want your writing to be clear, brief, accurate, and consistent, you can't get too attached to any particular thing you write. There's a good chance you'll end up having to cut or change those words along the way. That said, there are ways to make the red ink feel a little less scary.

First, save *all* the drafts. These days, with unlimited cloud storage and easily searchable digital drives, there's no limit to the number of drafts you can save. Thus, every time I make a big change to a paper (e.g., reworking the wording or the framing of the argument, changing which examples I include), I save it as a new draft. That way, if I ever decide to revert back to something I wrote before, it's easy to search back through the previous drafts and find the wording or the examples I need. I also prefer to save the drafts with the date I start them (e.g., Calarco_Title_Year.Month.Day) rather than with the draft number (e.g., Calarco_Title_Draft#). I find that makes it easier to keep track of which draft is the most recent one. It also makes me feel less bad about being on draft 22.

Second, if I'm making a big revision, like changing the logical structure of the argument, or reworking the justification in the front end, I start over with a blank file. I write a new outline for the sections I'm trying to change. Then I copy in the parts of the old draft that still work. That way I'm not trying to tinker with sentences or paragraphs or whole sections that don't work. And I'm not wading through a sea of tracked changes to see what progress I've made.

Regardless of what approach you take to editing, it's critical to not treat the need for edits as evidence that you've failed. I've never written anything "perfect" the first time (and nothing I've ever published is "perfect," either). So now, after years of practice, I don't expect to write perfect first drafts or even halfway decent ones. I start by getting ideas on paper, and I trust that I'll get to revise them later on.

Revision makes writing better, but it's important not to get so caught up in the quest for perfection that you're never ready to click "submit." When I finish an early draft, I edit it to make my writing as clear and brief and accurate and consistent as possible. Then I get feedback from my colleagues and friends. Then I revise again. But I also keep in mind that, no matter what I write, especially with the first draft of a paper I submit, the editors and the reviewers are never going to say "This is great. Publish as is." For me, at least, knowing that I'll almost certainly have to revise again later makes it easier to not get too caught up in perfecting what I write. That's important, because in order to publish anything, you first have to let it go.

Writing with Coauthors

So far we've talked about writing and editing as a solo process, but that's not always the case. In some disciplines, manuscripts rarely have more than one author. In other disciplines, manuscripts almost always have more than one author, and the average number of authors might be closer to five or six rather than one or two.

Multiauthored writing comes with a lot of benefits. By working with a team, you have built-in outlets for feedback on your research and writing. By working with coauthors, you might be able to produce a larger volume of research at a faster pace than you could on your own because you can divide up the work and complete multiple projects simultaneously. In theory, at least, coauthoring is also a way to get credit for more papers, though the amount of credit you get will probably depend on whether you're first author, last author, or somewhere in between.[11]

Of course, multiauthored writing can also come with drawbacks. You'll have to negotiate author order, and those negotiations might not feel fair. Your advisor, for example, might ultimately claim the most prestigious authorship position, even if you and the other team members are doing all the work. Working with coauthors also means you'll have to work, at least in part, around other people's schedules. For example, if you really need to get a particular article published before you go on the job market, but the rest of your team are moving too slowly with their parts of the work, you might not make it in time.

Academic Articles: Models and Templates

Ultimately, and whether you're writing solo or with a group, it's important to have a sense of what a published manuscript in your field is supposed to look like and how to write one yourself. That said, and as we've talked about in previous sections, having read dozens or even hundreds of other people's manuscripts doesn't guarantee that you'll know where to start in writing your own.

If you struggle with knowing how to start getting words on paper or how to organize a solid draft, you're definitely not alone. Plenty of grad students struggle with writing. Plenty of professors do too. Not because they don't have good ideas but because they don't know where to start, or what to include, or how to organize their ideas in a logical way.

Finding Good Models in Your Field

What to include and how to organize the manuscript are field-specific decisions. Some fields, for example, lean toward longer journal articles that ground new research in an extensive discussion of existing research and theory (the "justification" or "literature review" section). In other fields, journal articles take the form of brief reports highlighting key findings from new research, with footnotes and supplementary materials providing more detailed and technical information. And in still other fields, scholars rarely write journal articles and focus on writing book manuscripts instead.

Ultimately, you'll want to familiarize yourself with the kind of academic writing that's most common in your field. You'll also want to carefully review the author guidelines listed by the journals where you might want to publish.[12] And you'll want to find articles published in those journals to use as templates for your own writing.

Beyond using published research as a model, I'd also recommend checking out the following sources for more information about academic writing in various fields:

- For lab science fields, check out the SciDevNet blog post "How Do I Write a Scientific Paper?" which outlines the key sections of a scientific journal article and explains what to include.[13]
- For advice on writing journal articles in economics and other fields that rely heavily on complex quantitative analyses, try the post linked in the endnotes from the Pomona College Writing Center as well as Deirdre McCloskey's *Economical Writing* and Robert Neugeboren's *The Student's Guide to Writing Economics*.[14]
- For advice on writing journal articles in history and other fields where books are often the primary outlet for academic scholarship, the Royal Historical Society has useful insights to share.[15]
- For general advice on writing articles for academic journals, check out with the *Guardian* piece linked in the endnotes, as well as books on academic writing by Paul J. Silvia and Wendy Laura Belcher.[16]

An Outline for (Social Science) Writing

When I'm writing my own academic articles and book manuscripts, I always start with an outline. I like outlines because they turn writing from an art into a science—from something amorphous and inspiration driven to something concrete and logical, something with clear formulas to follow in getting to the end result.

Over time, and building on writing advice I got from my own advisors, I put together the outline below. It's the outline I use in my own writing. It's also the outline I give my grad students for writing about their work. I initially developed this outline for writing about sociological research involving ethnographic fieldwork. That said, I would argue that the outline is readily adaptable for qualitative and quantitative research in the social sciences, and potentially in other fields.

When I'm writing, I typically start by outlining the analysis/results section. I work out, roughly, what I can argue with my data. Then I backtrack from there to outline the contribution I can make to the field. I get those two outlines "right" (or at least logically organized and consistent) before I write any full sentences or paragraphs. Then I write the introduction, which, for me, serves as a roadmap for the rest of the paper. Then I write the full analysis/results section, revise the overall outline based on any changes that happen in that process, and then write the background/justification section. Data/methods sections I find to be fairly easy to write (you're mostly describing what you did). So I save them for a day when my energy is low and I'm not feeling particularly excited to write. As I'll explain below, discussion/conclusion sections are my least favorite parts of a paper to write, so I save those for almost last. I also wait to write them until I have the rest of the paper well organized and well edited. Then, the actual last thing I do, at least before editing and word-cutting the whole paper, is write the abstract. It's the shortest part of the paper. But I want to make sure it is consistent with the rest of the paper and provides a clear overview of the paper as a whole. I find that it's difficult to achieve that kind of consistent, clear overview if I try to write the abstract first.

Regardless of which sections you write first, it's important to have a good understanding of the different parts of an academic paper and how they fit together to form a logical whole. Along those lines, here's a discussion of those different sections and a set of suggested outlines for what they might include.

Abstract: The point of the abstract is to provide a very brief overview of the paper. Different journals have different standards, but abstracts typically can't be longer than 150 or 200 words. Those word limits might make abstracts feel easy—"it's just 150 words." But those limits are also tricky because abstracts have to convey a lot of information in a very short form. With the abstract, you want to give your reader a basic sense of what you're doing, what you find, and why it's important. You want to leave the reader interested in reading more, but you also want them to understand and trust what you find, even if the abstract is all they read.

Along those lines, and when I'm writing abstracts, I typically follow this six-sentence formula that outlines the rest of the paper:

- Sentence 1: What we know
- Sentence 2: What we don't know
- Sentence 3: How you answer that question
- Sentence 4: What you found
- Sentence 5: What you conclude from those findings
- Sentence 6: Why those conclusions are important

Introduction: The introduction is where you start building a case for your study. You want to persuade the reader that you've identified an important gap in our knowledge of how the world works. That you've designed a study to fill that gap. That what you find has implications for research or policy or practice.

There are a few different ways to structure an introduction. In some fields, and especially in fields where articles are shorter and less theoretical, the introduction is where you put any necessary background information (e.g., definitions of key terms, references to relevant literature). In other fields, and especially for journals where editors expect a separate justification or background section, the introduction usually points to key ideas that you'll unpack later in the piece. With that model, there are two types of introductions—those that give away the punchline and those that don't. Under the give-away-the-punchline model, the introduction operates as an extended abstract—a lightly contextualized overview of the paper as a whole. You can include just enough information to give your reader a basic sense of what you're doing, what you find, and why it's important. Under the save-the-punchline-for-the-end model, on the other hand, the introduction just previews the front end of the paper—the justification/background section, the key questions or hypotheses, and the methods—without giving away what you find.

Personally, I prefer the give-away-the-punchline model, and that's the introduction model I outline below. Presumably the reader has already read the abstract, which includes the key findings and conclusions. That means there's no real reason to "hide" the findings until the end. I also think repetition is helpful in academic writing. If your reader has a clear sense of what you found going in, they'll know what to look for as they read further, and they'll be more likely to understand and believe your conclusions at the end. That said, some disciplines and some journals have strong don't-give-away-the-punchline norms. So familiarize yourself with your discipline's standards before deciding which way to go.

When I'm writing a give-away-the-punchline-style introduction, I typically follow a three-paragraph model. The first paragraph uses existing research (with a few key citations) to identify a gap in the literature (previewing the background/justification section). The second paragraph explains how the study fills that gap (previewing the methods and results/analysis sections). The third paragraph articulates why that solution is important (previewing the discussion and conclusion).

> Paragraph 1: Describe the gap in the literature you will address with your data.
> - What do we know? (*Prior research tells us that . . .*)
> - What do we not know? (*And yet, we do not know . . .*)
> - What do we suspect? (*Given prior research, however, there is reason to suspect that . . .*)
>
> Paragraph 2: Identify your research question and explain how you answer it.

- What question will you answer/hypothesis will you test? (*This study examines that possibility. Specifically, I ask . . .*)
- What data will you use to answer this question? (*To answer that question, I draw on data from . . .*)
- What do you find? (*In analyzing those data, I find . . .*)

Paragraph 3: Explain the importance of your findings.

- What is your central argument (i.e., the answer to your research question)? (*Given these findings, I argue that . . .*)
- How does this argument broaden, clarify, or challenge existing knowledge? (*These findings are important in that they . . .*)
- What implications do your findings have for research/ policy/practice? (*With respect to research/policy/practice, these findings suggest that . . .*)

Justification/Background: What this section looks like, and whether you need one at all, depends on the conventions in your field. In many disciplines, and especially in the lab sciences, all discussion of prior research goes in the introduction, and that justification is kept brief, with just a few highly relevant (and often very recent) references to prior research. In other disciplines, and especially in some social science and humanities fields, the justification or background section is longer and more concerned with tracing the theoretical origins of the study at hand.

Those extended justification and background sections are sometimes called the "literature review," but I don't like that term. The point of that section—whatever you call it—is not actually to review all the literature on the topic at hand. Instead, the point is to use the existing literature to make a case for why we need your study. And that's why I call it a "justification" section instead.

When you're writing that justification section, there are a few different approaches you can take to writing about prior research. As we talked about in chapter 4, that includes the author-first model and the idea-first model. Under an author-first model, you're essentially describing each study and highlighting its contribution to the literature. For example, you might say, "Johnson (2017) finds that spheres are round." Under an idea-first model, you're instead synthesizing the findings from various studies to support a larger contention. For example, you might say, "Some research shows that spheres are round (Johnson 2017; Gutierrez 2014)." Or even just "Spheres are round (Johnson 2017; Gutierrez 2014)." Each of these models has a purpose and a place in a justification section, but the first, in my view, is far overused.

The author-first model is great for highlighting specific examples that illustrate a point you're trying to make. But, if that's the only way you know how to write about research, it'll take you fifty pages and ten thousand words to get to your point. And with most journal word limits, that won't leave any space for your work.

The idea-first model lets you synthesize the existing research. You identify a common theme in the literature, then weave together various themes to build an argument for what we know, what we don't, and what we might find if we try. Ultimately, it's okay to weave in a few author-first references to illustrate key examples or define key terms. But I'd recommend using that model sparingly and keeping the focus on your research.

To keep the focus on your research, I'd also recommend keeping your justification section as short as possible while still following the conventions of your field. Even in fields where longer and more theoretical justification sections are common, for example, those sections should almost never be more than a thousand words, and ideally a lot less. Short or long, the justification section should also have a logical structure that makes it easy for the reader to follow the logic you're using to justify your study.

The specific components and ordering of that logic will depend on the type of contribution you're trying to make. Maybe you're trying to assess two competing explanations for some phenomenon. Maybe you're trying to determine whether a finding from one context holds in another. Maybe you're trying to provide a baseline description of some previously understudied case. Or maybe you're trying to offer a new explanation for something that has previously been found.

Once you figure out what type of contribution you're trying to make, I'd recommend starting broad, with key theories and concepts. Then narrow your focus, talking about how previous research has applied those theories to the problem or case you're studying. Next, identify a question that previous research hasn't fully or definitively answered about that problem or case. And finally, use the existing literature to suggest why it's important to answer that question and what we might find if we try. In my research (most of which is published in fields where it's standard to have a separate and often highly theoretical background or justification section) that typically looks something like this:

Section 1: Theoretical Context
- Identify the subfield(s), concepts, and terms most relevant to your research. (*The concept of X is central to research on Y...*)[17]
- Briefly explain/define those concepts/terms. (*Scholars who study Y have defined X as...*)
- Briefly note how those concepts/terms are relevant to your problem or case. (*These concepts are particularly relevant in the case of Z, because research shows that...*)

Section 2: What We Know and What We Don't
- Describe what Subfield A tells us about your problem or case. (*In the case of Z, research in Subfield A tells us that...*)
- Describe what Subfield A doesn't tell us about your problem or case. (*Less clear from Subfield A is how... [SOMETHING WE DON'T KNOW ABOUT Z].*)
- Repeat for Subfield B/etc.

Section 3: Your Question/Hypotheses
- State your research question. (*In light of these lingering questions, this study will examine...*)
- Identify and justify your hypotheses. (*While previous research has not answered this question specifically, it suggests that we might find...*)
- Explain why those findings would be important. (*If this is the case, it would mean that...*)

Data and Methods: As we talked about briefly above, a good methods section reads like a recipe for your work. It offers the reader enough detail that they could, at least in theory, reproduce your study or replicate it in another setting. Depending on your discipline, you might also include or link to supplemental materials, like the data you used or the code you used to analyze the data.

A good methods section, though, isn't just a list of the steps. Instead, a good methods section also justifies the decisions you made in carrying out your research. For example, if you're working with survey or administrative data, you'll probably have some missing data. Respondents don't always answer every question on a survey. And if they skipped answering one of the questions you're using to create the variables you're using in your analysis, then you'll have to decide whether to drop those respondents with missing data from your analysis or use another statistical technique (like multiple imputation) to approximate the missing responses, instead. If you're not sure which approach is the "right" approach, or if you're not sure how to justify the decisions you made, reach out to the methods person in the team of mentors we discussed in chapter 2. They should be able to help you make those decisions and ultimately help you make the case for what you've done.

Getting some help with your methods section is important because different disciplines, journals, and methods have different standards for how much detail and justification you should include. Beyond just asking your methods person, you can also look for examples of similar methods, published in the journals or by the presses where you want to publish, and then follow the standards and structures they use. When I teach qualitative methods courses, for example, I give my grad students a writing outline for their methods sections that looks like this:

Part 1: The Case
- Identify the specific case or problem you're studying. (*To answer my research question/test my hypotheses, I focus on the case of . . .*)

- Use existing research to justify your case selection. *(This is a useful case for answering that question/testing those hypotheses because...)*

Part 2: Data Collection/Selection

- Identify the types of data you're using.
- Explain how you chose and (if applicable) collected those data.
- Describe your data and your data collection strategies.
- Use existing research to justify your decisions.
- Note: If your paper is drawing on data from part of a larger study, only discuss the data relevant to the argument in this paper.

Part 3: Data Analysis

- Explain how you chose to analyze your data.
- Describe your data analysis strategies.
- Use existing research to justify your decisions.

Part 4: Limitations and Justifications

- Identify any limitations with the data or the study design. *(These data do have limitations, including...)*
- Explain the consequences of these limitations. *(Because of these limitations, this study is unable to...)*
- Use existing research to explain why these data are particularly useful for studying your problem or case. *(Despite their limitations, these data are still particularly useful for studying the case of Z, because...)*

Analysis/Results: This section is called different things in different fields. It might be the "analysis" section or the "results" section or even the "findings." Whatever it's called, and if you think of your manuscript as a work of art, this part is the picture inside the frame. It's where you present the findings from your research—sometimes with tables and figures or key examples and excerpts from your work. Ideally, this section is also where you use those findings to build a logical case for the conclusions you draw in your work.

The content and organization of that logic will depend on the specific type of argument you're trying to make. Maybe your argument is about how a particular drug impacts the function of the human heart. Or about how a new policy will improve heart health. Or about how writers use the metaphor of "heart." If your research project produced more data than can reasonably be included in one manuscript, having a clear argument can help you determine what belongs in this manuscript and what you can save for the next one. Regardless of how much data you have, having a clear argument, and knowing what that argument is, can also help you see how to present your findings in a way that logically supports your conclusions.

Of course, that doesn't mean you should ignore data that don't support your conclusions. Ignoring those data would constitute blatant scholarly misconduct. It would also contribute to the growing crisis of replicability and reproducibility in many scholarly fields.[18] As a scholar, you have a responsibility to carry out your research as rigorously as possible, to document that process as faithfully as possible, and to present the results as accurately as possible, even, and especially, if your results don't support your hypothesis. Ignoring or misrepresenting your results would be a disservice to science and to anyone who reads your research.

In my own writing, the analysis/results section typically starts with a one-paragraph overview of the findings. I start with a topic sentence that states the central argument. Then I identify two or three key patterns in the data that support that central argument. Following that overview paragraph, I then divide the analysis/results section into subsections, one for each key pattern in the data. Then I add a subsection at the end of the analysis/results section that discusses any caveats to or complexities in the larger patterns and explains what I conclude despite those caveats and complexities.

In my analysis/results section, each subsection describing a key pattern in the data typically looks something like this:

- Paragraph 1: Describe a key finding/pattern in your data and note (briefly) how it supports your argument.
- Paragraph 2: Identify one aspect of that finding/pattern.
  - State that aspect of the finding/pattern in your topic sentence.
  - In the remainder of the paragraph, explain how you identified that aspect of the pattern in your data (i.e., by running a regression model or interviewing a specific group of people).
  - Discuss evidence from your data that illustrates that aspect of the larger pattern (regression coefficients, key quotes, figure descriptions, etc.).
  - Explain how that evidence illustrates the relevant aspect of the larger pattern.
- Paragraphs 3–4: Repeat the above steps for one or two more aspects of the pattern.

In my analysis/results section, the subsection discussing caveats to the larger patterns typically looks like this:
- Paragraphs 1–2: Outliers
  - Start with a topic sentence that summarizes the types of outliers (i.e., unexpected/inconsistent evidence) you identified in your analysis.
  - Briefly describe one or two key examples of those outliers.
  - To the best of your ability, and drawing on previous research, explain what you think produced those outliers and explain why you believe your argument is valid despite those outliers.
- Paragraphs 3–4: Alternative Explanations/Conclusions
  - Start with a topic sentence that summarizes other possible explanations for your findings or other conclusions that could be drawn from your work.
  - Explain why you think your explanation/conclusion is a better fit than the alternatives, describing what you would

expect to see in your data if the alternative explanations/ conclusions were correct and referencing key examples from your data that support your conclusions better than they support the alternatives.

Discussion/Conclusion: At this point, you've made your argument and supported it with evidence. Now, in the discussion and conclusion sections, you have to tell your reader why your argument is important and what we ought to do because of it. In some disciplines, these discussion and conclusion sections are short and focused on the practical implications of your work. In other disciplines, these sections are long and speak beyond the data at hand to larger theoretical, methodological, or policy-related implications.

Personally, I find the discussion and conclusion sections of an article to be the hardest parts to write (followed by the justification/ background section). I think it's because these sections are the most speculative and the most loosely connected to the data at hand. In these sections you might speculate about how your findings fit into the larger body of research, what explains your findings (particularly if they are different from what previous research has shown), and what implications those findings have for research, policy, and practice.

If all that speculation leaves you feeling unmoored, a good outline can be your anchor. Before you can write that outline, though, you'll have to determine whether you'll need a combined discussion/conclusion section or two separate sections for discussion and conclusions. The conventions vary by discipline and even across different journals, so check out a few recent publications to see which model is more common in your field.

If you need separate discussion and conclusion sections, then the discussion will focus on summarizing, contextualizing, and explaining your findings, while the conclusion will speak to the implications of your findings. Discussion sections typically start with a brief summary of what you're trying to do with your research, what you find, and what you conclude. Next, discussion sections contextualize those findings and conclusions. That means comparing your findings to the findings from previous research and using prior research to speculate about what's causing the patterns you find. It also means acknowledging the limitations of your research and explaining why we should trust your conclusions despite those limitations.[19] Conclusion sections, meanwhile, take one step further away from the data. They explain how your findings clarify our understanding of some phenomenon or offer a new solution to some problem in your field.

When I'm writing discussion and conclusion sections, I typically follow an outline that looks like this:

- Paragraph 1: Overview
  - Remind readers of the question you are trying to answer or the contribution you're trying to make with your work. (*Building on research showing that . . . my goal in this article is to . . .*)
  - Remind the readers what data you're using and what patterns you find. (*Drawing on data from . . . I find that . . .*)
  - State your main conclusion. (*Given those findings, I argue that . . .*)
- Paragraphs 2–3: Contextualization
  - Start with a topic sentence that notes how your findings are consistent or inconsistent with some aspect of prior research. (*These findings are consistent/inconsistent with prior research on . . .*)
  - State what prior research in this area has found.
  - Explain how your findings are consistent/inconsistent with those prior findings.
  - Speculate (using research, if possible) about why your findings are consistent/inconsistent with prior research.
  - Briefly discuss why these consistencies/inconsistencies are important.

- Repeat as needed for one or two other major points of consistency/inconsistency with prior research.
- Paragraph 4: Explanation/Interpretation
  - Start with a topic sentence that offers a brief explanation for your findings. (*While it is beyond the scope of this study to explain why . . . there is reason to suspect that those patterns reflect . . .*)
  - Use prior research to support your tentative explanation for/interpretation of your findings. (*As previous research has shown . . .*)
- Paragraph 5: Alternative Explanations/Interpretations
  - Start with a topic sentence that acknowledges alternative explanations. (*Of course, there are other possible explanations for/interpretations of these findings, including . . .*)
  - Briefly note why some people might believe those alternative explanations/interpretations. (*Those explanations/interpretations are consistent with prior research showing that . . .*)
  - Explain why you think your explanation/interpretation is more fitting in this case. (*As this study has shown, however, . . . Thus, it seems more likely that . . .*)
- Paragraph 6: Limitations.
  - Start with a topic sentence that acknowledges the limitations of your study. (*Like all research, this study is limited in some ways.*)
  - Identify those limitations.
  - Explain why the reader should trust your conclusions despite those limitations. (*While it would have been ideal to . . . these data still allow me to . . .*)
  - Note how future research should try to avoid these limitations. (*In order to avoid similar limitations, future studies should . . .*)
- Paragraphs 7–9: Implications

- Start with a topic sentence that identifies one key implication of your study for research, policy, or practice. (*Despite its limitations, this study still has important implications for future research/policy/practice, including...*)
- Briefly restate key findings that support this implication. (*As previously discussed, this study shows that...*)
- Briefly explain what other researchers/policymakers/practitioners can learn from your findings and how they can use these insights in their own work. (*These findings suggest that...*)
- Repeat as needed for one or two other major implications.
- Paragraph 10: Conclusion
  - Start with a topic sentence that restates your central argument. (*As this study has shown...*)
  - Summarize your contribution to the literature. (*Given those arguments, I conclude that...*)

Bibliography/References: In theory, your bibliography is just the list of sources you reference in your work. In practice, there's more to it than that. Info gluts plus tight word limits mean that you'll never be able to cite everything.[20] So you'll have to make choices about who to cite. Let's talk through a few reasons why those choices are important.

Your bibliography shows who you're in conversation with. Within every field and subfield there are clusters of scholars working on similar topics. Within those clusters, there are often debates about the right methods to use or the right theories to invoke or the right kinds of conclusions to draw from evidence. Your bibliography shows how you position your research within those debates. And when it comes time for peer review, the editor is probably going to pick someone on your side of the debate and someone on the other side too.[21]

Your bibliography also shows whether you've done your homework. Readers, reviewers, and editors want to see that you've read the foundational work on your topic. That you understand the debates and concepts relevant to your research. And that you're up to date on the latest research on those topics. The authors of those latest and greatest pieces, in turn, are likely to be tapped as potential reviewers, especially if they've published in the same outlet where you're submitting your work. If you want to avoid the rage of the uncited reviewer, you'll want to double and triple check that you haven't missed any relevant research.

Your bibliography also reveals your blind spots. As we talked about in chapter 4, the formal curriculum in most disciplines privileges "foundational" work and especially the work of white men. That makes it easy to miss relevant new research and relevant research by scholars from systematically marginalized groups.[22]

Thus, when reviewing your bibliography, I suggest checking to make sure that you've cited:

- Relevant "foundational" works (i.e., the things everyone cites when they do research on your topic/problem)
- Discussions of relevant debates (e.g., annual review articles or edited volumes that speak to debates around your topic/problem)
- Very similar research (i.e., research that is very similar to yours in terms of its research questions, hypotheses, findings, methods, or conclusions, even if published in a lower status journal or a journal in a different field or subfield)
- Relevant recent research (i.e., research on related questions about your topic/problem from the last five to ten years, with a focus on research by scholars from marginalized groups, research published in the journal where you are hoping to publish, and research published in other high-visibility journals in your field)[23]
- Your own previously published work on the topic[24]

Footnotes/Endnotes: Footnotes (or endnotes) might seem like an afterthought, but they actually serve a very strategic purpose. They allow you to maintain the logical structure and flow of the main text while adding links to additional information, clarification, or justification for readers who want to know more. When defining a key term, for example, you might add a footnote explaining that other scholars have defined that term in different ways and justifying why you chose the definition you did. Or when describing a pattern you found in your data, you might add a footnote explaining how that pattern is similar to patterns found in other research. Footnotes usually contain interesting and helpful information, but they shouldn't contain any information that is necessary for the logic of your argument as a whole. That information belongs in the main text.

Along those lines, I recommend using the "distraction test" to determine whether a piece of information belongs in a footnote or in the main text. If a sentence distracts from the point of the paragraph, try moving it to a footnote. If the paragraph still makes sense without that sentence, you can leave it as a footnote or, if you're running up against tight word counts and need to cut words, let that be the first thing to go.

Appendices and Supplemental Materials: With some manuscripts, you'll want to give your readers access to more information than you can actually include in a published article or even published book format. You might, for example, write a methodological appendix that outlines your research procedures in a higher level of technical detail than can fit within journal or book word limits.[25] Or you might have appendices with supplemental analyses you ran to check the robustness of your conclusions. Or you might even want to give your readers a link to a website where you've posted your whole dataset and/or the statistical code you used to analyze it.

* * *

My hope is that this chapter will give you a sense of where to start when you're writing about your research. Whether you're using my outlines as a jumping-off point or turning to some of the other books and blog posts I've recommended, I hope it'll help you move past the moments of imposter syndrome and writer's block and start getting words on the page. I also hope this chapter and its resources will help you feel more confident asking for feedback on your writing and give you the tools to incorporate that feedback effectively into your work.

Of course, once you're done with all that writing and editing, I also hope you won't let what you've written just sit in a (literal or figurative) drawer. Instead, I hope you'll look for ways to publish the work you've written and share it with the world. That's where we'll turn in our next chapter, talking about the peer-review and publishing process and about how to find the right outlet for your work.

Chapter 8

PUBLISHING AND PROMOTING YOUR WORK

Wendy M. Christensen Ö ▤ ▬ ⊕ 🏛 ⚖ @wendyphd · Jul 22, 2018

Replying to @JessicaCalarco

Thanks for this! When I started grad school I — this is hard to confess — didn't really know what "peer review" meant. I thought it was a paper reviewed by other grad students. I was too embarrassed to ask so I had to covertly figure it out.

The whole point of writing about your research is to share what you find. Technically, one way to do that is to just write up your results and self-publish them or post them in an online repository for unpublished work.[2] If you want a job, though, and especially if you want an academic job, you'll probably have to go through the peer-reviewed, academic publishing process instead.

In this chapter, we'll talk about how to navigate that publishing process. We'll talk about the decisions you'll have to make, about the trade-offs involved in those decisions, about how to move forward after rejection, and about what to do when you finally publish your research. We'll also talk about reaching beyond a scholarly audience and writing for students, for practitioners and policymakers, and even for journalists and for the regular people who read books, newspapers, or online magazines.

What and Where to Submit

If you're looking to publish your research, some potential outlets for that work are considered more "reputable" or more "legitimate" than others. In most disciplines, there's a strong preference for "academic" outlets. In terms of journals, that means journals run by leading scholarly organizations (e.g., the *Journal of the American Medical Association*) and journals run by scholars affiliated with particular (usually high-status) universities (e.g., the *Harvard Education Review*). In terms of books, that means university presses (e.g., Princeton University Press), presses run by nonprofit foundations (e.g., Russell Sage), and, in some cases, for-profit publishers that are closely affiliated with academic research (e.g., Sage).

Those outlets are seen as more "legitimate," at least in part, because they publish peer-reviewed research. The peer-review process, which we'll talk about in detail, is supposed to prevent the publication of faulty or biased research. Of course, peer review doesn't always achieve that goal, and we could debate whether peer-reviewed research published in academic outlets is always higher quality than other forms of published or unpublished research. But, ultimately, what matters for you and your career is how those different forms of research are viewed and treated by hiring committees, tenure and promotion committees, grant funders, and other gatekeepers in academia.

Along those lines, the next few sections of the chapter will help you understand the various options for publishing academic research and the trade-offs those options entail. Those options include:

- Journal articles, with variations in terms of:
  - Peer-reviewed vs. pay-for-play
  - Gated vs. open-access
  - Field and subfield

- Status
- Timeliness and feedback
- Books, including those published by:
  - University and foundation presses (e.g., Harvard University Press, Russell Sage)
  - Textbook publishers and other academic-adjacent presses (e.g., Sage, Norton)
  - Trade presses (e.g., Knopf, Random House)
- Chapters in edited volumes, with similar considerations about different presses
- Policy reports
- Media articles (including blog posts, magazine/newspaper articles, op-eds, etc.)

Those different formats and outlets have different benefits and different drawbacks. There are trade-offs related to the depth and detail of the argument you can make. Trade-offs related to the amount of control you'll have over what gets published. Trade-offs related to status and fit. Trade-offs related to timeliness and quality of feedback. Trade-offs in terms of supporting the publishing industry versus public access to research. Ultimately, how you weigh those trade-offs should be a function of your goals.

Along those lines, let's talk through a few key decisions you might have to make and what to consider in the process.

Articles versus Books versus Book Chapters

The most obvious distinction between article publishing and book publishing is length. Academic articles are typically much, much shorter than books. The specific length varies considerably by discipline, but published articles are rarely more than thirteen thousand words and in some fields are typically less than five thousand. Academic books, on the other hand, typically include at least three substantive chapters, an introduction, a conclusion, and various appendices, and they usually have at least fifty thousand and sometimes more than a hundred thousand words.

Length is important because it determines the complexity of the argument you'll be able to make with a given piece of writing and also the amount of evidence you can include to support that argument. Whether you're writing an article or a book, you should still have one central argument. Given the length limits, however, academic articles have limited room for backstory, limited room for evidence, and limited room for unpacking the implications of that evidence. As a result, article arguments tend to be fairly straightforward, usually with only two or three key claims. Academic books, on the other hand, have more room for complexity. You can include more information about your case and your methods and your pathway into the research. You can also make more nuanced arguments, with a larger set of claims and more discussion of the evidence for and against those claims.

Because of the differences in length, articles typically take less time to write and publish. Counting from when I started writing, the quickest article I ever published went from first draft to in print in less than nine months. My first book took more than four years from the time I started writing to the time it came out in print. And that's not counting the time I spent writing the dissertation that later became that same book. Basically, even if you write a book-style dissertation, it can still take a year or five to rewrite your dissertation as a publishable book, and then another year or more before the book comes out in print. Because of the time involved, most fields encourage grad students to focus on writing articles rather than on writing books. And that's generally good advice, especially since materials published in article format can later be incorporated into a book (but not the other way around). That said, if a book is the best fit for your research, then you can try to get a book contract, even before you're finished writing or revising the book. Of course, there's no guarantee that a publisher will be willing to give you that contract, and, even if they do give you a contract up front, you might end up having to go through extra rounds of reviews.[3]

Article publishing is also a more standardized process than book publishing, which is another reason to focus on article writing with your early work. With article writing, you can submit an article to only one journal at a time. With books, it's normal (and sometimes encouraged) to submit a manuscript to multiple presses at the same time. With article publishing, and at least within a given journal, there's also a standard process and timeline. With book publishing, almost everything can be negotiated—the form and content of the book, the amount and type of writing you'll need to submit up front, the amount and type of feedback you'll get, and the number and type of revisions you'll ultimately have to complete.[4]

One limitation of article writing, however, is that you won't get quite as much control over what ends up in your published work. Because the process is highly standardized, and because there's so much competition for the limited space in (at least top-tier) academic journals, editors and reviewers have a great deal of control over what appears in print. Book publishers, meanwhile, generally give authors more leeway in responding to peer reviews.

Another limitation of article writing is that it's less lucrative than book writing, though maybe not by as much as you'd think. If you're publishing a journal article, you'll almost never get paid for the work you publish, and you might even have to pay page fees to have your article reviewed or published (if you're a grad student and the solo author on a paper, ask the editor to waive these fees). With book publishing, on the other hand, you can negotiate to receive a portion of the book's revenues in royalties. Especially if it's your first book, that percentage probably won't be higher than 10 percent, though you might be able to get a somewhat higher royalty percentage on certain book formats than others (e.g., digital vs. hardcover books). Ultimately, and regardless of the percentage, don't expect that you'll make a lot of money from publishing a book. Most academic books sell, at most, a few hundred copies (usually to libraries), and only a rare handful will sell enough copies to make an author rich. If you want to make money writing books, textbooks are a much better way to go, but only if your books end up being widely used, and only if you're willing to commit to writing regular updates to stay ahead of the used book market.[5]

We've focused so far on comparing academic articles to academic books, but those aren't the only outlets for academic research. Book chapters, for example, offer some of the flexibility of book writing while avoiding all the negotiations (the book editor will handle those) and keeping the turnaround fairly tight. Format-wise, book chapters are closer to articles, but the review and publishing process for book chapters is closer to that for academic books (or what are sometimes called "monographs"). Books with individually authored chapters are often called "edited volumes." The editors for those edited volumes are usually the scholars who had the original idea for the book. They handle soliciting and vetting submissions, and they negotiate a contract with a publisher. In some cases, the editors will put out a "call for submissions" that invites authors to submit abstracts or manuscripts for consideration as chapters in the book. In other cases, editors will invite submissions from authors they know are working on the topics they want to include in the book. If you're interested in publishing book chapters, it can be helpful to join professional organizations (and subsections of those professional organizations) and sign up to get email updates from those organizations, which will likely include notices about new calls for submissions in your area. It can also be helpful to use Twitter and other social media platforms to network with other scholars and share updates about your work. That way they'll be more likely to think of you when they're putting out invitations for manuscripts. Once the editors decide which chapters they want to include, the whole book will usually go through peer review. As you decide how to edit your chapter based on the reviewers' feedback, there will probably be some back and forth between you and the editors. But, eventually, once all the drafts are finalized, you (and all the other authors) will agree on final versions, and the book will go into production.

Publishing a book chapter in an edited volume can be a great way to contribute to a scholarly discussion on a topic you care about. Those edited volumes also tend to make great teaching tools because they give students a more in-depth look at a topic than they would get in a textbook without all the technical jargon and scholarly stodginess they might encounter in an academic journal article. That said, it's important to keep in mind that despite the peer-review process, and despite the work involved, book chapters are typically viewed (at least in most fields) as lower status publications than journal articles. And as we'll talk about in the next section, that difference in the status of your publications can matter in determining your status among your peers.

Status

Once you decide on a specific format for your research (articles vs. books vs. book chapters), the next thing you'll have to consider is where to submit. In most cases, and especially if you're interested in pursuing an academic job, you'll want to strive for the highest status outlet (either journal or press) you can get. That's because, as with so much of life in academia, status matters. A lot. Publishing an article in a top journal in your field can be your ticket to an R1 job—it was for me. I published the first article from my dissertation in the *American Sociological Review*, one of the top two journals in my field. And that article got me a lot of interest from potential employers, even in a tight job market year. Now, it's possible that I could have gotten my current job even if that article had appeared in a slightly lower ranked journal. But judging by the outcomes of other job candidates on the market that same year, there's a good chance I wouldn't have ended up at an R1 school, and there's a decent chance I wouldn't have gotten an academic job at all.

Of course, my intent here isn't to scare you away from publishing or make you worry about how the status of your publications might make or break your career. Instead, I'm trying to do for you what my advisors did for me—being realistic about how status matters and giving you some strategies to use when playing the status game.

So how do you figure out which outlet is the highest status outlet you can get? Every discipline has its own (sometimes tacit, sometimes more explicit) rankings of the "best" academic journals and the "best" presses for academic books. Those rankings are often closely linked to "impact factors," which indicate how often work published in a particular journal was cited in the past year.[6] You can find information about journal impact factors by going to Web of Science through your library web page and then using the Journal Citation Reports feature to search for specific journals or browse by category.[7]

In terms of journals, most fields have one or two or occasionally three top journals. Those journals are typically "general" journals that publish research from across the discipline and don't focus on a specific topic or method. Top journals also tend to publish research that makes a big (i.e., new, interesting, and important) contribution to the field. Below that, there's a tier of midrange journals. That list typically includes some general journals as well as top subfield journals that focus on a particular topic or method. Below that, there's a tier of lower range journals, which again includes a mix of general and subfield journals. And, finally, at the bottom, there are the pay-for-play journals, which we'll talk more about in a bit.

The status rankings around book publishing are similar, but they're usually more categorical than clearly ranked. There might be five or six top academic presses in your field, and they'll usually be affiliated with elite universities, but there won't always be a clear first or second rank. Below that there will usually be another, larger tier of middle-range academic and foundation-affiliated presses. Then a tier of lower status for-profit publishers, including those that specialize in textbooks and those that specialize in publishing research-based monographs for nonacademic audiences.

Those for-profit outlets generally have bigger budgets for marketing, which can mean bigger royalties, but they're typically seen as lower status by hiring and tenure committees, which can make them a risky bet for publishing, especially early in your career.

In most fields, publishing in a top journal or having a contract from a top academic press is treated as a big, important accomplishment. The status of those outlets is treated (rightly or wrongly) as a signal of the quality of your work. And it can significantly increase your chances of getting a tenure-track job at a research-focused university. In some departments, having an article in a top journal or a book published with a top press will also be an implicit or explicit requirement for promotion or tenure.

That doesn't mean, though, that articles published in non-top journals or books published in non-top presses are automatically less important or lower in quality than those published in top outlets. There are lots of factors that influence which research appears where. Many manuscripts also become clearer and harder hitting as they move through the review and revision process. Let's say, for example, that you initially submit your manuscript to a journal ranked number one in your field, and let's say it gets rejected there. At that point, you'll probably revise the manuscript based on feedback from the reviewers at the first-ranked journal. Then you'll probably resubmit to another journal, maybe this time one ranked fourth in your field. Maybe you're skipping second and third because they have notoriously long wait times, and you're trying to get this article published ASAP. At this point, and because of the revisions you made following your rejection at journal 1, you might get a fairly easy R&R that eventually becomes a really high-quality publication in journal 4. By that point the article you've written is going to be substantially better than the one you initially submitted to journal 1 and might even be more innovative or more important or better written than some of the research that does appear in journal 1.

Essentially, it's important to remember that the rankings of different journals and presses are what we like to call in sociology a "social construct."[8] Some journals and presses are high status because we view them as high status, and by viewing them as high status, we make them high status in their consequences.

Of course, recognizing rankings as a social construct doesn't make sociologists (or any other scholars) immune to status-based concerns. And that's why, when you're thinking about where to publish your research, status is something you'll have to consider.

Because of the rewards associated with publishing in top-tier outlets, those journals and presses receive an extremely large volume of submissions. Regardless of their status, though, most journals and presses publish only a small percentage of the manuscripts submitted to them each year.[9] Journals and academic presses keep those numbers low, in part, because of limits on their budgets and personnel.[10] However, those low numbers also allow journals to maintain their status—low acceptance rates make them more exclusive and thereby more elite.

Given the status hierarchies in academic publishing, a lot of authors (myself included) start by submitting their article manuscripts to the highest tier journal where they think they have a chance of getting a hit. And that's arguably a rational strategy, though it does come with trade-offs. Because of the high volume of submissions, the review process at top journals sometimes takes longer than at lower tier journals—in some cases even six months or more. Meanwhile, you can't submit the article manuscript elsewhere while you wait because most disciplines and most journals have strict one-submission-at-a-time rules. Which means that if your manuscript is ultimately rejected by a top journal, you'll have to start the submission process all over again. And if you're running up against a deadline (like going on the job market or going up for tenure), you might not have that kind of time to wait.

Now, if you're running up against one of those big deadlines, you might feel like "I just need to publish this manuscript now!" In those moments, it's especially important to be wary of "predatory" journals where scholars can pay to have their research published, often without peer review and with few or no questions asked.[11] Those pay-for-play journals are increasingly popping up to take advantage of the publish-or-perish pressures of academic work. And yet, while paying to add a line to your CV might feel worth it, hiring committees and tenure committees and grant and award committees generally know (or can easily find out) which journals operate as pay-for-play, and they might ultimately ignore those publications on your CV or, worse, judge you for trying to skirt the rules of the academic publishing game.

Gated versus Open-Access: The terms might seem similar, but it's important to distinguish pay-for-play journals from open-access journals. While pay-for-play journals make it easy for authors to publish, open-access journals make it easy for readers to access that published work. In that sense, open-access journals are different both from pay-for-play journals and from traditional academic journals, where access to research is gated.

If research is gated, it can be accessed (legally) only by those who pay a fee. If, for example, a journalist or a member of the public goes to a gated journal website and tries to read an article, they'll get a prompt saying they need to pay for access to that article (usually ten, twenty, or thirty dollars each). Scholars and students, meanwhile, typically have free access to gated research through their university libraries. As we talked about in chapter 4, though, that access isn't actually free. Universities pay hundreds of thousands of dollars annually to the companies (like Sage, Wiley, and Elsevier) that publish academic journals, in exchange for access to articles those companies publish.

Now, if you think those arrangements sound like a huge rip-off and an affront to the scholars who produce all those journal articles (and who never see a dime), I'm right there with you. And so are the scholars, policymakers, and university officials behind the open-access movement.[12] The open-access movement in publishing is designed to remove cost barriers and make research more accessible to the public and to non-university-affiliated students, teachers, researchers, journalists, policymakers, and practitioners who can use research in their work.

Unfortunately, though, there are costs associated with publishing research, and, at least in these early stages, the open-access movement shifts those costs away from readers (and universities) to the scholars who publish research. That includes costs associated with paying editors and deputy editors for the time they spend managing the journal. It also includes the costs associated with maintaining journal websites and having articles copyedited and formatted so they'll look "legitimate" when they're published online.

Those publishing-related costs, however, aren't exclusive to open-access journals. Many gated journals have submission fees, which you pay when you submit the manuscript for review rather than when it's accepted for publication. Some gated journals, especially in the lab sciences, also have publication charges or page fees, which you'll pay when your article is accepted. The amount of money you'll have to pay varies across different journals and different fields, but it's the kind of thing you (or your advisor) can use grant funding to pay for. If you don't have access to grant funding, and if, as a grad student, you're the first author or the only author of the piece, you might be eligible to have your fees waived. If the journal website doesn't specify that option, you can reach out to the editorial team to ask. You can just drop them a brief email, explaining that you are considering submitting a manuscript, that you are a grad student, that you don't have access to grant funding, and that you're asking if they would be willing to waive the fees. Ultimately, they might say no. But the answer is always no if you don't ask.

Beyond the cost factor, the decision between gated and open-access journals will probably depend on your career stage and on how open-access journals are viewed in your field. In some disciplines, the open-access movement is fairly new. As a result, those open-access journals might not have the same status as other, more established (and gated) journals in your field. Of course, and given the benefits of open-access publishing for consumers of academic research, my hope is that the status of open-access journals will increase over time. In the interim, though, and if you're a grad student in a field where open-access journals are not yet seen as comparable to the gated journals in the field, and especially if you're interested in pursuing a career in academia, it can be somewhat riskier to go the open-access route.

Academic versus Nonacademic

Another consideration in the publishing process is whether you want to go the academic or nonacademic route. So far, we've mostly talked about academic publishing—peer-reviewed articles and books published by scholarly organizations, university presses, and other university-adjacent outlets. That said, there are also other, nonacademic outlets for scholarly research. That includes trade books, policy briefs, research reports, magazine articles, blog posts, and newspaper op-eds.

The process of publishing nonacademic articles is, arguably, even more hidden than the academic one. For example, while the anonymity of the peer-review process is intended to avoid privileging well-known and well-connected scholars, your chances of publishing in nonacademic outlets often depend heavily on who you are and who you know. The first major nonacademic article I wrote, for example, was for the *Atlantic*. The magazine was launching a new "family" section, and the editor had reached out to my former advisor, Dr. Annette Lareau, a very well-known sociologist who studies inequalities in family life. The editor asked Annette to recommend scholars who might be interested in writing about their research for the magazine, and she passed along my name. Even then, though, the process wasn't automatic. It took a few months and a whole bunch of "pitches" for me to find a topic the editor liked enough to publish. And that piece, despite being less than a thousand words, ultimately went through five or six rounds of edits (with lots of tracked changes from the editor) before it made it to print.

Writing nonacademic articles also doesn't guarantee a big payday. For the article I published in the *Atlantic*, for example, I think I was paid $250. Not bad for a few days of writing and editing. But given how long it took to find a topic the editor actually wanted to publish, I wouldn't want to make freelancing my full-time gig. Trade books, meanwhile, typically sell more copies than academic books. But even then, the market for research-based books is much smaller than the market for narrative nonfiction (e.g., biographies), and only a handful of research-based books ever really make it big.

All this is to say that writing nonacademic articles isn't an easy or particularly lucrative alternative to the academic route. Furthermore, and compared to academic publishing, the nonacademic publishing market is even more concerned with hitting the right balance of novelty, palatability, and profitability. And that can be a tricky balance to strike, especially if you weren't taught to write that way.

That said, if you're interested in writing articles for nonacademic audiences, there are ways to build the connections and learn the skills that you'll need. As we'll talk more about at the end of the chapter, groups like the Scholars Strategy Network work to connect researchers with journalists, policymakers, and practitioners who might be interested in their work. Meanwhile, groups like the OpEd Project train researchers on how to translate their research into the kind of narrative format that works best for engaging nonacademic audiences in short form articles and reports.[13]

It's important to keep in mind that writing for academic and nonacademic outlets doesn't have to be either/or. As we'll talk more about at the end of this chapter, there are lots of ways to connect with wider audiences after you publish your research. Of course, that means you'll have to publish your research first. And that's where we'll turn next.

Publishing Academic Articles

Hopefully, at this point you have an idea of where you want to submit your manuscript and what kind of manuscript you want to submit. The next step is to navigate the submission process and, if you're going the academic route, get your paper peer reviewed. In the interest of clarity and brevity, I'll focus this section on the submission and peer-review process for academic articles. Then I'll talk a bit about the process for books and nonacademic articles (e.g., magazine articles, op-eds, blog posts, policy reports) as well.

Submission

Almost all journal submissions are now handled through online portals. That means that once you decide where you want to submit, your first stop should be the website for that journal.

In addition to the online submission system, the journal's website will probably have a set of guidelines for authors. That includes guidelines regarding what sections your manuscript can and cannot include (e.g., abstract, introduction, bibliography, footnotes/ endnotes). It also includes guidelines around formatting and length (e.g., word limits, font sizes, line spacing, headers, reference style).

Journal guidelines also typically include instructions for "blinding" your manuscript. Blinding means removing the authors' names from the manuscript and also removing any references in the text that would make it clear who the authors are. For example, the article you're submitting might build on findings from research you've previously published. In that case, you can directly blind the reference (e.g., "Building on my previous research (BLINDED), I find that . . .") or you can write about the research as if someone else published instead (e.g., "Building on previous research (Author, Date), I find that . . ."). You might also need to use the BLINDED option in your methods section if you're writing about how your study uses data from a larger project from which you have previously published research.

The point of blinding your self-citations is to maintain anonymity during peer review. The idea, at least, is that the reviewers won't know who the author is and thereby will be less likely to make decisions based on that author's status or connections in the field. In practice, though, that kind of anonymity is getting harder to maintain, especially with online CVs and with the push to post working papers in searchable repositories online. Thus, while it's important to follow journal guidelines around blinding, it's also important to keep in mind that if the reviewers are dogged enough, they'll probably be able to figure out who you are.

When it comes to enforcing submission guidelines, some journals are stricter than others. I've even had editors send a manuscript back to me and tell me they wouldn't consider it unless I cut it down to be even shorter than the official word limit posted online. Thus, it's generally good practice to read the guidelines carefully and make sure your manuscript is properly edited and formatted before you click "submit."

It's also important to make sure you include all the components necessary for review. Typically that includes the blinded manuscript, a separate title page with your name and contact information and information about who funded your research, a cover letter (more on this in a minute), and any supplementary files like tables or figures or appendices.

In an age of online submissions, cover letters can feel somewhat superfluous. But they can still be useful, and they don't have to be long. I typically treat the cover letter as an opportunity to help guide the editors in choosing potential reviewers. I rarely suggest reviewers by name (though some authors do), and I typically don't request that editors avoid specific reviewers (though some authors do that too). Ultimately, there's no guarantee that editors will grant your requests, and they might even do the opposite of what you suggest, especially if they think you're trying to bias the reviews. Instead, I use the cover letter to provide a brief overview of the study (an abstract of the abstract, if you will) and to high-light (1) the subdisciplines and debates within those subdisciplines to which my research speaks and (2) the methods I use in my research. By telling the editor where my research fits, both substantively and methodologically, I can give them a sense of the kinds of scholars who would be suitable reviewers, even without naming specific names.

My cover letters typically look something like this:

Dear Professor(s) [EDITORS' LAST NAMES],

I am writing to submit my manuscript, [TITLE], for possible publication in [JOURNAL]. This article examines [BRIEF SUMMARY OF RESEARCH QUESTION/ HYPOTHESES]. Using [DATA/METHODS], I find that [1–2 SENTENCE SUMMARY OF FINDINGS]. These results speak to research on [RELEVANT SUBFIELD(S)], and they are important in showing that [1 SENTENCE DISCUSSION OF IMPLICATIONS].

I have uploaded the various components of my manuscript and paid the submission fee. [NOTE: IF YOU ARE GOING TO REQUEST A WAIVER OF THE SUBMISSION FEE, DO THIS IN A SEPARATE EMAIL TO THE EDITOR, BEFORE YOU CLICK "SUBMIT."] Please let me know if there is any additional information you need regarding this submission, and thank you in advance for your consideration.

Sincerely,

[YOUR NAME]

Peer Review: Process

After you click submit (and, depending on the journal, pay the submission fee), your manuscript will go to the journal editor (or a deputy editor), who will do an initial "desk read" of the manuscript. At that point, the editors will decide whether to "desk reject" your manuscript or send it out for peer review. Desk rejections can feel painful, but they ultimately save everyone a lot of time. For the editors, desk rejections mean they don't have to spend the time (or the favor capital) getting reviewers for your manuscript. And for you, desk rejections mean that you're not waiting around for two months or six months or more for what would likely be the same result anyway.

We'll talk more about rejection in a minute; for now, let's talk about what happens if your manuscript does get selected for peer review. Editors rely on peer reviewers because they can't be an expert on every topic or type of research. Thus, when editors send a manuscript to potential reviewers, they typically ask the reviewers to assess the rigor of the research (editors don't want to publish research that's faulty or biased), the importance of the findings and their relevance to potential readers (editors want to publish research that will be widely read and cited), and the quality of the writing.

The peer-review process is either single or double blind. If it's single blind, the reviewers know who you are as the author, but you won't know their names. If it's double blind, the reviewers won't know who you are (unless they do some Googling, which is arguably unethical but hard to police), and you won't know who they are either (unless they intentionally or inadvertently out themselves).

Regardless of whether the process is single or double blind, editors try to find reviewers who are experts on the topic at hand. Ultimately, though, the reviewers you get might not be your first choice or your editor's first choice either. That's because reviewing is typically unpaid, unrecognized labor (though organizations like Publons are trying to change the unrecognized part).[14] As a result, there's limited incentive for scholars to say yes when asked to review, which can make it difficult for editors to find the right reviewers for your manuscript. Those challenges in finding good-fit reviewers are compounded by the fact that some subfields have only a small number of scholars working on a given problem or with a given method, which increases the chances for a conflict of interest.

In general, editors will avoid selecting peer reviewers who have a potential conflict of interest. What counts as a conflict of interest can vary across fields and across journals. In general, though, someone with a close connection to you (e.g., your advisor, your student, your department colleague, or someone you've ever co-authored with) probably won't be asked to review your work. In some cases, though, the editor might not be aware of potential conflicts of interest (e.g., a new coauthor with whom you haven't yet published, or a scholar who has been as an informal mentor for your work). And if that's the case, and they get invited to review anyway, it's up to them to acknowledge the conflict of interest (and usually politely decline to review).

Another potential conflict of interest comes from the review process itself. Let's say, for example, that you submitted your manuscript to Journal A and it got rejected after going through peer review. Then, you submit that same manuscript to Journal B, and it goes under peer review again. The editors from Journal B won't know which scholars were asked to review the manuscript at Journal A, and they might invite some of those same scholars to review your manuscript again. If that happens, then those scholars have to decide what to do. In general, there are no formal rules that prevent a scholar from reviewing the same manuscript for two different journals—it's not a technical conflict of interest in the same way that it would be a conflict of interest for your advisor or your colleague to review your work. That said, I do think it's important for a potential reviewer to be open with the editor of Journal B about the fact that they've reviewed a previous version of your manuscript. That way the editor can decide whether they want to include that scholar's review. In my experience as a reviewer, and possibly because it's so hard to find scholars willing to review, editors generally opt to include reviewers who've previously reviewed that same manuscript, rather than saying "thanks but no thanks" instead.

Because of that possibility, it's important to know that your manuscript might get the same reviewers at Journal B that it got at Journal A. That's why, as we'll talk more about in a minute, I'd argue that you should almost always make some revisions to a rejected manuscript before submitting it elsewhere. If your Journal A reviewers weren't happy with your manuscript when you sent it to Journal A, and those same Journal A reviewers get asked to review your unchanged manuscript again at Journal B, they're probably going to be even less happy the second time around, since you essentially wasted their time.

Eventually, the editor will find a set of scholars (usually three, but sometimes two or four) who agree to review your manuscript. Those scholars will get a copy of your blinded manuscript, and they'll be asked to read it and make a recommendation to the editor about whether the research should be published. In addition to that recommendation, the reviewers might be asked to answer questions about the manuscript (e.g., rating the soundness of its methods or the significance of its contribution to the field). Reviewer forms also have space for confidential feedback to the editor and for feedback that both you and the editor will get to see.

Peer Review: Outcomes

Once all the reviewers submit their reviews (sometimes after repeated reminders from the editor), the editor will make a decision about your manuscript.

The most likely outcome, by far, is rejection. This isn't to say that your research isn't good or important. It just means that, statistically speaking, most journals reject the vast majority of the manuscripts they receive. The journal *Nature*, for example, ultimately publishes less than 8 percent of the manuscripts it receives for consideration.[15] If your paper gets rejected, that means it won't be published in the journal that rejected it, but you're free to take the feedback from the reviews, revise the manuscript (or not), and then submit it elsewhere.

At the editorial decision stage, another possible (though far less likely) outcome is that the editor will invite you to "revise and resubmit" your manuscript. This is the R&R we talked about in chapter 3. If you accept the editor's invitation, then you'll have to revise the manuscript and resubmit it, at which point the editor will send the manuscript back out for another round of reviews. In general, journal editors will try to send the revised manuscript back to the same reviewers who reviewed your manuscript the first time. If those reviewers aren't available, then the editor will probably add some new reviewers. Those new reviewers will get to see the original reviews, the revised manuscript, and any "response to reviews" you include to explain the changes you made. Once those reviewers review the revised manuscript, the editor will consider their feedback and make another decision about whether to move forward with your manuscript or reject it.

A third possible outcome is that the editor will "conditionally accept" your manuscript. In most fields, it is extremely rare for a manuscript to be conditionally accepted on initial submission. If you're resubmitting an R&R, however, your chances of getting conditionally accepted might jump as high as 50 percent. Either way, a decision to conditionally accept your manuscript means that you'll still have to revise the manuscript, but only the editor will review the changes—the manuscript won't be sent out for another round of reviews.

The fourth possible outcome is that the editor will accept your manuscript as is. This outcome is almost unheard of as a decision for initial submissions, and it's not even all that common as a decision on R&Rs. Instead, most final acceptance decisions come after the manuscript is conditionally accepted, revised, and resubmitted for the editors to review.

If and when you get to the final acceptance stage, however, there's still more work to be done. At that point, the manuscript still has to go to the journal's copyeditor to be edited and formatted for publication. You'll have a chance to review and approve all those changes—and it's important to check the manuscript carefully at that stage. It's your last chance to make any necessary edits before the manuscript comes out in print.

Peer Reviews: Interpreting Reviewer Feedback

If the decision on your manuscript is anything other than "accept as is," then you'll probably have to spend some time (or a lot of time) revising your manuscript based on the feedback you get in the reviews. Typically, those reviews will be included in the email you get informing you of the editor's decision about your manuscript. You (generally) won't be able to see the names of the reviewers, but you will be able to see what they wrote about your manuscript.

It's important to know that the form and content of reviews can vary widely. That's, in part, because journals don't always provide reviewers with a template for writing reviews, and, even if one journal in your field does provide that kind of reviewer template, it's probably different from the template for every other journal in your field. With one manuscript I submitted recently, I got an R&R that came with one paragraph-long review, one four-paragraph review, and one four-page review. Some reviewers go through the manuscript in order and offer comments on each section (introduction, justification, methods, analysis, discussion). Other reviewers start by pointing out the major issues and then provide a list of minor issues as well. Some reviewers might focus on the theoretical contribution you're making with your research. Others might focus on the methods or the fit between the data and the argument or even whether you've caught all the typos before submitting your manuscript for review.

Reviews also vary in their tone and in their helpfulness. A lot of reviews are tough but fair—they point out (often bluntly) important flaws in the research or the writing, but they recognize those flaws as fixable, not fatal. Some reviews will even give you helpful suggestions for fixing the flaws. Other reviews are tough and mean—they dismiss your research as fatally flawed and sometimes even resort to name-calling to get their point across. Those reviews also tend to focus on pointing out the problems with your research rather than offering suggestions for how to fix them. Still other reviews are positive and supportive—they're usually fairly short (without much to critique there's not much to say), and the problems they identify (if any) are usually fairly small things, like references that should be added to the literature review or some typos that should be fixed in the text. These reviews don't do much to help you push the paper forward, but they are reassuring to receive, especially if the other reviews are tough or mean.

Now, what you do with those review comments depends on what kind of decision you've gotten on the manuscript. So, let's turn there, next.

Revise and Resubmit

Let's say you've opened your inbox and you see an email from the editor. And maybe it starts off all fine ("Thank you for submitting your manuscript . . ."), but then it takes a turn ("We are unable to publish the manuscript in its current form . . ."). Your heart sinks. But (hopefully) you keep reading. The next part might be a little confusing (". . . but we invite you to revise and resubmit your manuscript for further consideration"). Revise and resubmit notifications are notoriously tricky like that. And I wish that editors would just put the decision in big bold letters at the top of the email: **PLEASE REVISE AND RESUBMIT**. That would clear up a whole lot of confusion.

So if you've gotten an invitation to "revise and resubmit," what does that mean? First and foremost, that means your paper hasn't been rejected. At least, not yet. So congratulations! That said, there's still work, and probably a considerable amount of work, to be done. First, you'll need to read the editor's comments and the comments from the anonymous reviewers. Second, you'll need to decide whether to accept the invitation to revise and resubmit and let the editor know your decision. Third, you'll need to make a plan for how you're going to revise the manuscript. Fourth, you'll actually have to make those revisions. And fifth, you'll have to write a response memo that explains how your revisions address (or why they do not address) the reviewers' suggestions and concerns. Let's walk through each of these steps in turn.

First, reading the reviews. It's okay to jump in right away when you get that decision email. But it's also okay to give it a day or two or wait for a time when you're mentally ready to read some tough critiques of your work. Personally, if I get an R&R, I like to start with a quick skim of the editor's and reviewers' comments. I use that quick skim to decide whether the R&R is doable and then I let the editor know my decision (usually within two or three days).

Second, and along those lines, most editors will assume that if they give you an R&R, you're going to revise and resubmit the manuscript. That said, it's polite (and helpful) to respond to the decision email to let the editor (or at least the deputy editor or editorial assistant who handles email) know whether you're planning to revise and resubmit your manuscript and, if so, when you'll plan to return it to them. The only time I would suggest not accepting the invitation for an R&R is if one or more of the reviewers asks for something you simply can't give (e.g., adding more data that you don't have). Even in that case, though, an R&R is still usually salvageable—it might just mean reframing your research question or your argument so that the missing piece is no longer necessary. Your message back to the editor doesn't have to be long or detailed. Unless the editor gives you a specific turnaround time for the revisions (this is more common with "conditional accepts" than R&Rs), you technically have as much time as you need to write the revised manuscript. But it's good practice not to wait too long. I like to give myself two to three months, depending on what other commitments I have on my plate. That gives me time to think about the reviews, revise the manuscript, get feedback on the revised manuscript from colleagues, make some additional revisions, and then put together the response memo. But I've heard of some people who wait a year or more to resubmit an R&R. And I've heard of others who try to turn them around in a few weeks or less. So talk to your advisor or to other grad students to find out what timeframe is common in your field. Once you figure out a good timeline, here's a sample email you can use to let the editor know:

Dear Professor(s) [EDITORS' LAST NAMES],

Thank you for taking the time to review my manuscript, [TITLE]. I am grateful for the opportunity to revise and resubmit my manuscript for further consideration. I will plan to return the manuscript to you by [DATE]. However, if I encounter problems that will delay the resubmission, I will be sure to let you know.

Thank you for your consideration and your support of this project.

Sincerely,

[YOUR NAME]

After you send a note to the editor, the next step is to make a plan for revising the manuscript. Especially if it's your first time revising a manuscript, I'd recommend asking a friend or colleague or advisor for help. Someone else will be able to read the reviews with a more dispassionate eye and help you distinguish the harsh reviews from the ones that are tough but fair.

Once you have a sense of the reviews as a whole, the next step is to go through them point by point and develop a plan for revisions. My own strategy involves identifying, first, the common themes in the reviews and, second, the points of disagreement between the reviewers. To do that, I'll typically create a spreadsheet in Excel. Within the spreadsheet, I'll have a column where I copy and paste each comment from the reviewers, broken down by point. In some cases, if the reviewer comments are lengthy, or if they include multiple points in a single sentence, I'll paraphrase, rather than doing a direct copy/paste. Next to that, I'll also have a column indicating which reviewer made the comment. Because reviewer comments are sometimes harsh or hard to parse (e.g., including multiple critiques in one sentence), I'll add a column briefly summarizing each point made by the reviewers. That way I can put the reviewers' critiques or suggestions in my own words and (mostly) ignore the specific details of what they said. Next to that, I'll include a column identifying where in the manuscript the comment applies (framing, introduction, methods, writing, implications, etc.).

After I fill in that first set of columns, I sort the various rows by manuscript section. That way I can easily compare, for example, whether Reviewer 1 and Reviewer 2 had similar suggestions about the framing of the paper or whether their suggestions diverge. Once I identify those points of agreement or disagreement between the reviewers, I add a column outlining how I'm going to address the comments made by the reviewers or, if I'm not going to address them, how I'm going to explain that choice in the response to reviews. As I'm going through and making all those revisions, I then add a final column noting where in the manuscript the relevant changes appear. Table 8.1 shows a very short version of what that looks like in practice.

Now, when you're going through the reviews and making a plan for revisions, you might find places where the reviewers disagree about whether something is a problem or what to do about it. In those cases the editor will sometimes give you guidance on which reviewer's advice to follow. More often, though, that decision is up to you. You can try emailing the editor to ask for guidance, but there's no guarantee you'll get a response (or at least a timely one), and there's a good chance they'll say it's your call. In that case, you'll probably want to think strategically about which decision will best improve the manuscript and which will best increase your chances for getting the manuscript accepted in the end. In the sample review chart in table 8.1, for example, you can see that Reviewer 3 suggested adding a bunch of literature to the justification

TABLE 8.1. Sample Review and Revisions Spreadsheet

Reviewer	Comment	Section	Summary	Plan	Revision
Editor	As Reviewers 1 and 2 both point out, you need to frame your argument to make a larger, more significant contribution to the literature	Framing	Reframe the manuscript to make a bigger contribution to the literature	Following R2's suggestion, reframe the manuscript to show how these data challenge existing assumptions about . . . Revise the introduction, justification, analysis, and discussion, and abstract to incorporate this new framing.	The editor and reviewers asked me to reframe the manuscript to better illuminate the significance of its contribution to the literature. Following R2's suggestion, the revised introduction explains how this manuscript adds to the existing literature by challenging assumptions about . . . I have also revised the justification section, the analysis, and the discussion to further explain this contribution to the literature.
R1	What's the "so what" here? Why does it matter that . . . ?	Framing	Contribution isn't clear		
R2	The article would benefit from a broader framing that more clearly identifies the contribution to the literature. I would suggest focusing on how your data challenge existing assumptions about the importance of . . .	Framing	Reframe the manuscript to make a bigger contribution to the literature		

(continued)

R1	The author should have discussed the literature on . . . including . . . [long list of references].	Justification	Need to include literature on . . .	Given the reframing of the manuscript and its contribution, the suggested literature is no longer relevant.	While I appreciate R1's suggestions for incorporating additional literature on . . . the revisions to the framing of the manuscript make those existing studies irrelevant to the larger point of the manuscript. Thus, I have opted not to include them here.
R3	The example on p. 14 is really hard to follow and it's not clear how it supports the larger point the author is trying to make.	Evidence	Clarify examples and better explain how they support the argument.	Choose an alternate example that is easier to follow and more clearly highlights the key point of the paragraph on p. 14. Edit the language around that example to ensure that it clearly explains how the evidence supports the larger point.	In light of R3's questions about the example on p. 14, I have revised the analysis to include a shorter example that is easier to follow. I have also edited the text around that example to more clearly explain how it supports the larger point in that paragraph and in that section of the analysis.

section. That literature, though, doesn't fit the revised framing suggested by Reviewer 2. The editor and Reviewers 1 and 2 all called for a revised framing that would better highlight the manuscript's contribution to the literature. Thus, it's possible to justify not following Reviewer 3's literature suggestion because it becomes moot after following the suggestions from Reviewers 1 and 2. However, when you resubmit your manuscript, the editors will usually send it back to all the same reviewers who read your manuscript initially. And if Reviewer 3 agrees to review the revised manuscript, they might be frustrated to see that you didn't include their suggested references (especially if they are the author they want you to cite). If that's the case, however, then hopefully your clear justification for your decision not to include those references will lead the editor to discount Reviewer 3's potential anger and agree with your approach.

Once you have a plan in place for how to revise the manuscript, the next task is to actually make those revisions. If the revisions are major, and as I mentioned in chapter 7, I prefer to start over with a blank document rather than use track changes. The kind of reframing I talk about in the sample review chart above would definitely count as that kind of major revision. Any changes to the actual analysis or to the evidence you include would also count as a major revision. In those cases, I find it's easier to start with a new outline that clearly articulates the revised framing or the revised argument than try to fix whole sections or paragraphs that no longer work. Then I go back to the old draft, copy any sections or paragraphs or sentences that do still work, and paste them into the new draft. After tackling the major revisions, I then go through and fix any lingering smaller issues that were identified in the reviews. Some of those issues (e.g., typos, confusing examples, missing citations) end up getting fixed or becoming moot as I work through the major revisions. Others I just fix at the end. And I keep track of all those changes in the spreadsheet along the way.

Now, as you're reading the reviews and revising your manuscript, you might find you have lots of things to add—more references, more discussion of the literature, more evidence, more discussion of the implications. The problem with all those additions is that they'll probably leave you hundreds or even thousands of words over the word limit.

So how do you cut a manuscript down to size? I've found in my own editing that I can cut a manuscript 10 to 15 percent just by wordsmithing—going through sentence by sentence and finding shorter ways to say what I've said. If I need to cut more than that, then whole sentences, paragraphs, or sections will have to go. In that case, I start by cutting anything that feels redundant. Next, I use my argument as a guide, and I cut anything that isn't totally necessary to support, explain, or contextualize my central claim. If you have grant funding or just extra cash on hand, you can also hire a professional editor to make cuts for you. It'll probably make the paper better, but it'll probably cost a thousand dollars or more.

Once you finish all the edits and cuts, the last step in the revision process is to write a response memo that explains and justifies the changes you made (or didn't make) in your revised manuscript. The point of the memo is to persuade the editor and the reviewers that you've heard their concerns, addressed their concerns, and revised the paper to be ready for publication. Along those lines, it's important to know that your memo will be seen not only by the editor but also by the reviewers who get your manuscript for the second round of reviews. The editor will usually try to get the same reviewers for the second round. But if those reviewers aren't all available, then you'll get at least one new reviewer. That possibility of new and old reviewers has important implications for how you write your response memo. First, and because the original reviewers will see your memo, you want to write it in a way that shows gratitude and respect for reviewers' time and suggestions, even if you disagree with what they conclude. Second, and because you might get some new reviewers, you have to explain and justify your revisions in a way that will make sense to someone who didn't read (and probably won't see) the original manuscript.

So what should a response memo look like? Some authors go through each review in order, briefly describe each point the reviewer made, and then explain how and why they addressed (or didn't address) that point in the revised manuscript. That approach is very clear and thorough. But it can end up producing a memo that's as long as the manuscript itself. Or longer.

What I'd suggest, then, is a memo that focuses on what you did. That means breaking the memo down into three sections: major revisions, minor revisions, and additional points from the reviews. Within those sections, you can use your review spreadsheet to help you figure out what to write. In the first section, you can describe each major revision you made and then justify what you did based on the suggestions you got from the editor and/or the reviewers (e.g., "Based on recommendations from Reviewers 1 and 2, I have reframed the manuscript to focus on how . . ."). In the second section, summarize the minor revisions you made (bullet points are fine), and briefly explain how those revisions address concerns or suggestions raised in the reviews (e.g., "I have fixed all of the typographical and grammatical errors noted by Reviewer 3"). In the third section, you can talk about any reviewer suggestions that you opted not to include in the revised manuscript. The key here is to be respectful of the reviewer's expertise while also providing clear justification for your decision not to incorporate their suggestions. Here are a few examples of what that might look like:

- While I appreciate Reviewer 3's recommendation to include more literature on . . . , those studies are not relevant to the revised framing recommended by Reviewers 1 and 2. Thus, I opt not to include the literature on . . . because it would ultimately distract from the primary point of the revised manuscript.
- Reviewer 2 asked that I identify the mechanisms that produce the findings in my research. Unfortunately, the available data do not allow me to explicitly identify or test

potential mechanisms. That said, I do now include a paragraph in the discussion section using previous research to speculate about the mechanisms that might produce these findings. Those mechanisms include . . .

Ideally, you want the editor and the reviewers to read the memo first, and you want them to get from that memo the sense that you have fully understood, appreciated, and addressed all their previous concerns. If the editor and the reviewers like what you write in the memo, they'll be more inclined to read your manuscript through a positive lens. And they'll be less inclined to go in looking for more problems, instead.

Now, once you finish your memo, but before you resubmit everything online, take the time to check what you wrote. It's an easy way to avoid upsetting a fastidious reviewer who will see typos and grammatical errors as evidence that you're not serious about your research. (Side Note: Please don't be that reviewer.) I find that reading the manuscript and the memo aloud makes it easier to catch any small errors (especially the ones that spell check tends to miss). Reading it aloud also forces you to go slowly enough that you'll notice any sentences that aren't clearly phrased, any points that could use further justification, or any things you already said.

After you finalize your manuscript and resubmit everything through the online portal, the editor will read your memo and your updated manuscript and send it back out for another round of reviews. Then, after those reviews are complete, you'll get another decision from the editor. At that point, the possibilities are basically the same as the first time around. You could get a rejection, which is frustrating given the time you spent on the revisions, but which, statistically speaking, isn't all that unlikely. You could also get another invitation to revise and resubmit (what is often called a second or possibly third R&R). That outcome isn't as frustrating as an outright rejection, but it means that the future of the paper is still very much uncertain and that you'll have to go through the revision and resubmission and peer-review process all over again. The other possibility, and what you're really hoping for when you resubmit an R&R, is that the editor will either "conditionally accept" your manuscript for publication or, even better, accept it as is.

(Conditionally) Accepted

If your manuscript is "conditionally accepted," there's still a possibility that the paper could end up getting rejected, though that possibility becomes much smaller at this stage. A conditional acceptance also means there's still more work to do, though the amount of work is likely to be smaller than with a full R&R. You'll have to revise the paper again and write another memo explaining how you used the suggestions in the second round of reviews. This time, though, and unlike with an R&R, the memo and the revised manuscript won't go out for another round of peer review. Instead, the editor will read your memo and your revised manuscript and decide, without input from outside reviewers, whether to accept or reject the paper.

The process of revising a conditionally accepted manuscript is very similar to the process for an R&R. I'd recommend going through all those same steps that I outlined above. This time, though, you want to frame your "this paper should be published" argument squarely at the editor, and not just at whatever reviewer seemed hardest to convince. That means paying particularly close attention to any suggestions the editor makes in their decision letter. And it means you don't have to worry about detailing in the memo how you fixed every grammatical error caught by Reviewer 3.

Receiving a conditional acceptance on your manuscript isn't a guarantee that it'll eventually be accepted for publication. But at that point, it's a pretty good bet. And when you do get that final "accepted for publication" notification, it's definitely time to celebrate. Take a day off. Go out for a nice dinner. Have a party with some friends. Just make sure that when the copyeditor sends you the edited version of your manuscript, you check it (carefully—this is your last chance to make changes) and get it back in on time.

Dealing with Rejection

Big wins—like getting a paper accepted for publication—feel really good. But big wins are few and far between in academia. Rejection, unfortunately, is the far more frequent outcome. And that's true whether we're talking about manuscript submissions or grant proposals or job applications (more on this in chapter 11) or anything else in between.

Personally, I don't keep track of how many times I've been rejected, but it's probably well over a hundred if we're counting applications for grad school, jobs, fellowships, and awards as well as manuscript and grant proposal submissions. I've had papers rejected from three different journals before they found a home. I've had other rejected papers that I ended up just abandoning (or, at least, putting on the far-far-back burner) because I had new papers and projects that were less frustrating to work on.

And I'm certainly not alone. Every professor I know has been rejected dozens or even hundreds of times. Certainly there's a learning curve with academic work—the more things you submit, the better you get at getting things to stick. But even senior, well-known scholars get rejected. And some of them are even willing to admit on Twitter how much that rejection hurts.

All this is to say that rejection is normal, and it's normal to hate rejection too. It's also okay to spend the first few days post-rejection grumbling about the unfairness of the whole system and sniping about all those fussy comments from Reviewer 2. But be careful about airing those gripes on social media—you don't want Reviewer 2 writing angry subtweets about you. And be careful not to let the wallowing prevent you from moving forward with your work.

Of course, for some students, and even for senior scholars, the normal rejections of academia can trigger more serious episodes of depression or anxiety. So if you find yourself struggling to move forward or worrying endlessly about the consequences a given rejection might have for your career, please take the time to get help. Most universities have on-campus counseling centers, and some even offer a (usually limited) number of free visits per semester. In some cases, though, and because of high demand, you might have to wait a few weeks or even a month or more to schedule an on-campus appointment. If you can't wait that long, and you're in the United States, call the National Alliance on Mental Illness (NAMI) HelpLine (1-800-950-6264), email them at info@nami.org, or text NAMI to 741741. They can offer support and connect you to other resources, support groups, and mental health providers.[16] If you can't bring yourself to make that call, ask a friend to call for you. And please, if at any point you find yourself contemplating suicide, call the National Suicide Prevention Lifeline (1-800-273-8255) or contact the Crisis Text Line by texting HOME to 741741.[17]

Moving Forward after Rejection

Now, even if you are ready to move forward after your manuscript gets rejected, it's not always easy to know where to start or what to do next. Some scholars will just take the exact same paper, no revisions, and send it out to a different journal for review. And that strategy can work, especially if you originally sent the paper to a generalist journal and the primary feedback is that "this belongs in a topic-specific, subfield journal, instead." But as we talked about when we talked about peer review, that strategy is also risky, because you might get one or more of the same reviewers the second time around.

Given those risks, my recommendation is to use the reviews you got with your rejection and make a good-faith effort to revise the manuscript before sending it somewhere else. You don't have to make every change the reviewers recommend. And you don't have to write a response memo detailing all the revisions. You just want to make sure that if Reviewer 2 gets your paper a second time, they'll appreciate the progress you've made.

As you're revising your manuscript post-rejection, it's also important to strategize about where to send it next. If you initially sent the paper to a top-tier generalist journal and the feedback you got was that the contribution wasn't "broad" enough or "important" enough for a general audience, then you might consider sending to a more specialized subfield journal or a lower tier generalist journal as your next option. If your paper is already framed for a specialized subfield journal, then your next step post-rejection might be to go down a tier in terms of journal status, while sticking with the same subfield. Or if the revisions push you in a new direction, theory-wise or topic-wise, then you might consider switching to a different subfield journal.

Revising the paper and submitting elsewhere is usually the most sensible option for moving forward after a manuscript rejection. In some very rare cases, though, you might consider appealing the editor's decision. Maybe a reviewer fundamentally misunderstood your argument or your evidence. Or maybe a reviewer made an incorrect assumption about the existing literature or about the best methods for analyzing the kind of data you use. In those cases, you might consider writing an appeal to the editor. In that appeal, you should explain the reviewer's misunderstanding with evidence from the paper and from the review. You should also ask (very politely) if the editor will give you the opportunity to revise the manuscript to clarify the point that was misunderstood and then send it back out (either to the original reviewer or to new reviewers) for another round of reviews. Of course, even if the reviewer was wrong, the editor doesn't have to grant your appeal. They don't even have to consider your appeal. And they might have had other grounds for rejecting your paper that had nothing to do with the reviewer's misunderstanding. Appealing also runs the risk of angering the editor, which could hurt you if you want to submit other papers to that same journal in the future. Given those risks, I'd generally recommend against appealing editorial decisions. That said, part of uncovering the hidden curriculum is talking about those things that some scholars do to give themselves an extra advantage in their careers. Appealing editorial decisions is definitely one of those things.

In sum, rejection isn't easy, and it often feels unjustified. But there are plenty of journals out there. So even if it takes three tries, or maybe even ten, you can probably find your paper (or at least some version of your paper) a good home. Even if the revision process is painful, the paper will probably be better in the end.

Academic and Nonacademic Book Publishing

So far, we've talked mostly about the publishing process as it applies to academic journals. The process for getting a book published is similar in some ways and very different in others. And it also differs depending on whether you're trying to publish your book with an academic press or with a trade press. As I mentioned briefly above, trade press books have the potential to make more money, but hiring and tenure committees tend to see academic press books as higher status, so they can help you more in your career. Because of that, we'll focus here on the academic publishing process, with a bit about trade press books at the end.

Choosing a Press

Unlike academic journals, academic presses don't typically have a standard submission website where you upload your manuscript, fill out some forms, and then click "submit for review." Instead, submitting a book manuscript (or book proposal) to an academic press tends to be a much more informal process. In most cases, you'll end up emailing your manuscript or proposal to the editor who handles books in your field. That said, it isn't good practice to just email your proposal or your manuscript to that editor out of the blue. The whole process tends to go much more smoothly if you build a relationship with the editor first.

Along those lines, the first step in the book publishing process is to identify three to five academic presses that seem like they might be a good fit for your work. Then reach out to the editor at each of those presses who handles books in your field. You can reach out directly by sending the editor an email that briefly explains who you are (one or two sentences), briefly describes the book project you're envisioning (two to three sentences), and asks if they might be available to talk by phone or meet at an upcoming academic conference. An even better option, however, is to ask an advisor or other senior faculty member to send an email introducing you to editors they worked with on their own books. Then you can take the conversation from there and arrange a time to meet or talk with the editor about your work.

Now, you might feel reluctant to have those conversations until you have a full book manuscript or at least a full proposal ready for review. But waiting isn't always the best approach. Instead, it can be helpful to talk with editors while you're still at the book development stage. That way you can get a sense of the kind of feedback and support they'll give you during the writing and revision process. And especially if this is your first attempt at book writing, you can also use that early feedback from potential editors to help you when you're writing the proposal and the book.

Based on those initial conversations, the editor you talk with might invite you to submit either a book proposal or a full book manuscript for review. At that point, you might be tempted to say yes right away, especially if you're feeling pressured to get the book done and in print. That said, I'd encourage you not to rush. Unlike with academic article publishing, where you can submit your manuscript to only one journal at a time, with academic book publishing, you can be having conversations about your book with multiple presses, and you can even have your proposal or your manuscript under review with multiple presses at the same time.

Ultimately, if you decide to pursue multiple presses simultaneously, and if multiple presses are interested in offering you contracts, you might be able to use that interest to negotiate for (at least slightly) better terms (we'll talk more about those negotiations in a bit). That said, pursuing multiple presses simultaneously also means that you'll have to reject one or more presses that show interest in your work. And if you reject a press once, there's a good chance that editor won't be interested in working with you on future projects—editors hate rejection as much as authors do. Thus, it can be helpful to limit the number of presses where you submit your work for review.

Getting a contract with a trade press is an even more opaque process, given that most scholars don't have connections in that field. You could technically send an email to a trade editor, asking to schedule a meeting, but you probably won't hear back. That's because most trade editors deal exclusively through literary agents rather than working directly with authors. Getting an agent, in turn, isn't something an average scholar can just do. Instead, agents typically reach out to scholars they think might be interested in publishing trade books, usually after seeing those scholars quoted in major news outlets or interviewed on television. So if you're interested in writing a trade book, start by giving your research a more public face. More on that in a bit.

Writing a Proposal

Once you've talked with potential editors and narrowed down your list of presses, you'll want to put together a proposal to submit for review. Most presses will ask that you write a proposal even if you already have a full manuscript drafted. That's because the point of a book proposal isn't just to provide an outline of the book but to persuade the editor (and usually a larger committee of editors and higher-ups at the press) that your book would make an important contribution to their list.

So what are editors looking for in making that decision? First, they're looking for fit. Most presses are divided by field. That means there will probably be different editors and editorial teams for political science, history, and physics books, along with editors and editorial teams for an array of other fields. Within each of those fields, the editor might publish a wide range of books, or they might focus on books in a particular subfield (e.g., political theory) or using a particular method (e.g., comparative historical research). If your book doesn't fit within the press's area of focus, there's a good chance you won't get picked. That said, if your book is too similar to another book the press has published, especially in the past five years, there's a good chance you won't get picked in that case either.

Second, editors are also looking for books that are likely to make a significant contribution to the field. If your book goes on to win scholarly awards, if it ends up with hundreds or thousands of citations, or if it generates considerable media attention, that reflects well on the press that published your book, and it reflects well on your editor too. Of course, the editor won't know up front if your book will be a hit. But the editor will have a deep knowledge of your field, deep enough to have a sense of how other scholars will perceive and engage with your work.

Third, editors are looking for books that have a sizeable (or at least not tiny) audience. If your book will really matter to only the half dozen other scholars who study exactly the same thing you do, then it might not be worth it for the press to invest time and money in supporting your work. While academic presses are generally run as nonprofits, they have to be careful not to expend more resources than they take in on a given book. If your book sells only a handful of copies, the press might not recoup the costs of publishing your work (including publishing and printing costs as well as money for the editorial team's time). Thus, editors tend to look for books that, at the very least, speak to a whole subfield of scholars. And they're often especially excited about books that speak to a wider range of readers, including undergraduate students, scholars outside your subfield or your discipline, as well as practitioners and policymakers whose work relates to what you do.

Those audience-related considerations are especially important if you're considering publishing with a trade press. Trade presses make their money (or don't) based on the sales of individual books. That means that they're looking at your book primarily for its profit potential. In order to make a profit, your book has to have a clear (and sizeable) audience, and it has to fill a gap in the market that no other book has filled (or at least filled as well).

Given those various considerations, your goal in writing a book proposal should be to persuade the editor that your book is a clear fit for their list (without duplicating a book they've already published), will make a significant contribution to the field, and will have a sizeable (or at least not tiny) audience. In general, a book proposal will include the following sections:

- Significance: A brief overview of your book's contribution to the literature, with information about your central research question, the data you'll use to answer that question, and the central argument you'll make based on what you found
- Chapter Overview: Short summaries of what you'll include in each chapter, focusing on how each chapter contributes to the larger argument
- Audience: A discussion of who you see as the primary reader for the book, along with an explanation of how the book might be useful for other audiences (e.g., particular graduate or undergraduate courses)
- Comps: Short summaries of four to six comparable books (i.e., books about a related topic or making a related argument or drawing on a similar method/approach), with a discussion of how your book is both similar to and different from those comps
- Author Bio: A brief explanation of why you're the right person to write this book, focusing on your experience and training but also incorporating other relevant personal information
- Visibility: A discussion of your public visibility as a scholar (e.g., social media presence, media interviews, writing for

popular media, work with community organizations), with a focus on how you will leverage your existing engagements to support the marketing of the book
- Timeline to Completion: If you don't yet have a complete draft of the manuscript, you'll need to include a timeline explaining how long it will take you to finish writing and have a full manuscript ready for review

Getting a Contract

Once you've written your proposal and at least one or two sample chapters, and once you've narrowed down a list of presses, you might be ready to start looking for a book contract. A book contract is a legal agreement between you and the press that formalizes your commitment to publishing the book with that press and only that press and the press's commitment to publishing your book.

If you're going the academic publishing route, and especially if this is your first book, then you probably won't get a contract until after you go through peer review. That peer-review process is similar to the one we talked about with academic articles. The proposal and sample chapters (or, if you have it, the full manuscript) get sent out to a set of either single- or double-blind reviewers who read everything and offer their feedback. The editor or editors (if the book is under review at multiple presses simultaneously) will then use those reviews to decide whether to offer you a book contract. Once you sign a contract with one academic press, you should inform any other editors you've been in discussion with about the book. In very rare cases, something might go wrong in your relationship with your contracted editor or with your contracted press (e.g., a disagreement about how to handle suggestions from a particular reviewer, or an extreme delay in the publishing process), and you might need to look for another press. So it's important to stay on good terms with as many editors as you can.

If you're going the trade press route, then you'll need a literary agent to help you secure a contract, though you probably won't have to go through peer review. Instead, your agent will work with you to develop and revise your proposal and your sample chapters. Then when your agent thinks the book is ready, they'll contact trade presses that might be interested in your work and arrange an auction. Your sample materials will be sent to interested presses, and they'll read the materials and decide whether to make an offer on your book. If you get multiple offers, then your agent will help you decide which contract to sign or possibly work to negotiate better offers from one or more of those presses.

Now, having a contract is a legally binding commitment between you and the press, but it doesn't mean the press will automatically publish whatever you write. Before the book goes to publication, you'll almost certainly be expected to make edits. Those edits, in turn, will be based on feedback from your editor and, if you're submitting to an academic press, from peer reviews. Furthermore, if you got an academic book contract based on peer reviews of just your proposal and a few sample chapters, your editor might also decide to send the whole manuscript back out for peer review once you've completed it. And at that point you'll probably be expected to make more changes as well.

Even when your editor decides that your manuscript is "final," there will still be a bunch of cleanup work to do. You'll have to carefully review the copyedits (this is your last chance to catch and fix any errors in the book). You'll have to create an index of all the key topics you discuss in the book (or pay the press or an outside company to prepare the index for you). You'll also have to write marketing materials (e.g., chapter summaries and back-cover blurbs).

The book publishing process is complicated enough to fill a whole book. Because of that, and if you're contemplating going that route, I'd recommend checking out William Germano's *Getting It Published* and *From Dissertation to Book*.[18]

After You Publish Your Research

Once your research is accepted for publication, what do you do next? One option, of course, is just to move on with your next project. That's what plenty of scholars do. But, ultimately, what good is research if it just sits, unread, in a journal or on a dusty, dark library shelf?

Another option, then, is to try to engage your audience more directly. In most fields, there's a huge amount of new research being published every year, and it's hard for scholars and students and journalists to stay updated on all that new work. Meanwhile, academic journals and academic presses rarely have the budget for big marketing campaigns. That means it's up to you as the author to help your audience—or multiple audiences—find your work.

That kind of attention seeking can feel really weird and awkward, especially if you struggle with impostor syndrome. But remember why you did your research in the first place. Most likely, you think it's important. You think it has the potential to inform the work other people do or the decisions other people make. So, don't be ashamed of putting yourself out there. You know your work and its importance better than anyone, and, with a little effort, you can be a powerful advocate for your own work.

Connecting with Your Audience(s)

If you want to do the work of getting your work out there, the first thing you'll have to ask yourself is: whom do I want to reach? The most obvious audience for scholarly research is other scholars, and especially those in your same field and subfield. But that's not the only potential audience for your work. You might also be interested in connecting with policymakers who make decisions related to the topics you research. Or you might be interested in connecting with practitioners whose day-to-day work might be impacted by what you've found. Or you might be interested in connecting with journalists who are interested in writing about your research or, potentially, in connecting directly with public audiences by writing your own reports of what you found.

Once you figure out whom you want to reach with your work, the next questions you'll have to ask yourself are: How do I reach those audiences? And what do I want them to know? Here are a few options you might consider:

The Direct-Mail Approach: Some audiences can be reached directly. If you just published a new article or book manuscript, for example, you can email or mail a copy to key people you want to read your research.[19] That could be other scholars in your subfield who might ultimately cite your work and use it to inform their own. It could also be journalists who might write a piece about (or including mention of) your work. You can write a simple note to go along with the piece you send, briefly summarizing your work and explaining why you thought the recipient might be interested in reading it:

Dear [NAME],

I am writing to send you a copy of my new article/book, [TITLE], which was recently published in/by [JOURNAL/ PRESS]. To briefly summarize, my work shows [1-2 SENTENCE SUMMARY, HIGHLIGHTING THE FINDING OR ARGUMENT MOST RELEVANT TO THE RECIPIENT].

I thought you might be interested in receiving a copy because of your work on [RELEVANT TOPIC THEY HAVE DISCUSSED IN THEIR WRITING OR RESEARCH].

If you have questions about the article/book, or if you want to chat more, please let me know—I would be happy to do so. I can be reached at [YOUR CONTACT INFO].

Thank you for your time and for your great work on [RELEVANT TOPIC].

Best,

[YOUR NAME]

Now, if you send someone a copy of your new publication, there's a chance they'll read it and cite it and write about it in their own work. That chance will be much higher, though, if you take the time to build a relationship with potential readers first. That brings us to our second audience outreach approach.

The Relationship-Building Approach: If you want to increase the chances that journalists or other scholars will read and engage with your work, it can help to build a relationship with those potential readers. And it can help to start that relationship-building process long before you've even published any research.

As we talked about in chapter 2, professional organizations and academic conferences offer opportunities to connect with other scholars in your field. Presenting at those conferences is a great way to get the word out about your work, but that's not all you should do while you're there. Talk to the other presenters in your conference session and attend other related conference sessions. The scholars in those sessions are doing work similar to yours, and they're the ones who will probably be most interested in your work. Then once you establish a connection, stay in touch. Reach out after the conference to say how much you enjoyed chatting, and ask the other scholars to send you a copy of the research they presented. They might ask you for a copy of your paper as well. Then, once your paper is published, follow up to send them a copy of the final manuscript or report. You can just write a quick email with the PDF attached, saying, "I just wanted to let you know that the research I presented at [CONFERENCE] is now published in [JOURNAL]. Thanks again for chatting with me and for your feedback on the early draft of the work."

Beyond conferences and networking, joining professional organizations can also give you other opportunities to build relationships and get the word out about your work. Many professional organizations have periodic newsletters that feature recently published research, and you can submit your publications for inclusion in those updates. Your professional organization might also maintain a list of experts who are willing to answer questions from journalists about specific topics in your field, and signing up to be part of that database can help you connect with journalists who might later be interested in doing a story on your work.

Social media can also help you build relationships with other scholars, with journalists, and even with policymakers and practitioners whose work relates to yours. That said, there are more and less effective ways to use social media to engage your audience. So many scholars join Twitter when they have a new article or book coming out. They follow a few well-known academics and journalists, post a bunch of stuff about their new work, and wait for all the "likes." Those posts might get some traction, especially if they get retweeted or shared by people with more followers. But, that's not really how social media works. Twitter and Facebook and Instagram—they're all social *networks*. The point is to build a network of connections to other people and then sustain those networks with regular communication. And communication isn't just one-way. So if you think you might want to use Twitter (or another social media platform) to promote your own research, join now. Follow other scholars. Follow journalists who cover beats related to your work. Follow policymakers and practitioners and organizations that are interested in those topics. And don't just lurk in the background. Find conversations where you can contribute (ideally without being mean). Find and promote other people's work. Retweet and comment on the research they share, and share links to the articles you're reading, including ones from the popular press. That'll help you build connections to journalists, and those journalists might then start reaching out to you for background on stories relevant to your areas of interest, even if you don't have new research to share. With those relationships in place, you'll be in a much better position, network-wise, when it comes time to share your new research. By that point, the people in your network will be more inclined to follow the links you post and return the favors you've done for them by sharing your work with their followers.

Most of the strategies we've talked about so far start long before you've published your work. But there are also things you can do to promote your work during the publication process. Your university's public relations department, for example, can be a particularly helpful resource in spreading the word. I'd recommend emailing the PR team when your book or article is accepted for publication or even at the conditionally accepted stage. Depending on how busy the department is, there might be someone who will either put together or help you put together and send out a press release about your work. There might also be PR team members who can do media training and help you prep for interviews with journalists. Universities look good when their students and faculty members get research published, and so they have an interest (within budgetary constraints) to help spread the word.

The Public Writing Approach: Now, you might want to do more with your research than just get other scholars to read it and maybe write about it in their own work. Rather, you might want to use your research to try to influence policy or practice or public knowledge around a particular topic.

One way to achieve that goal is to look for opportunities to write for public audiences. Newspaper op-eds, for example, offer a platform for scholars who can connect their research to issues of broad public interest. If you're interested in going that route, see if your university is hosting an OpEd Project workshop or consider attending one of its public workshops, which cost a few hundred dollars and are hosted monthly in major cities around the United States.[20] Paying to learn to write an op-ed might seem silly, especially since you won't get paid anything for actually publishing one. But depending on your goals, those workshops can substantially increase your chances of getting an op-ed published and also leave you better trained for other forms of public writing.

Just drafting an op-ed, though, and even drafting one with the help of the OpEd Project, doesn't guarantee that your op-ed (or any other popular media pitch) will ever make it to print. Editors, especially for major news outlets, receive far more op-ed and free-lance writing submissions than they ever have room to publish. That means they can be very selective about what they publish, and they tend to print what's most relevant to current events. So if you're interested in doing any public writing, keep an eye on the news and have a back-pocket version of an article or op-ed that you can update to align with the story of the day.

Speaking to the story of the day might feel like a crass way of making your research matter. But writing for public audiences can also be a way of establishing yourself as a recognized expert in your field. Along those lines, and if you do have opportunities to share your research publicly, you should be ready for potential follow-up interviews with other media outlets that want your take. When I wrote my first piece for the *Atlantic*, for example, that led to a flurry of invitations for interviews with other news outlets.[21] In some cases, doing those interviews meant being ready on just a few hours' notice. Journalists work on tight timelines, and they'll move on if you don't respond.

The Getting-Involved Approach: Another option for making a more direct impact with your work is to get involved with people and organizations whose day-to-day work relates to the work you do. Let's say, for example, that you do research on solar technologies. One get-involved option would be to volunteer with local organizations that support low-income families in obtaining and installing their own solar panels.[22] Another get-involved option would be to testify at local, state, or federal government hearings about the importance of investing in solar technologies and making those technologies available to lower-income families.

Being publicly recognized as an expert can help pave the way for that kind of involvement. My public writing, for example, has led to invitations to speak at conferences for teachers and social service providers. Members of my local school board also reached out after hearing me on the local public radio station talking about my research, which led to a series of meetings about ways to reduce inequalities in the local public schools.

That said, even if you haven't done any public writing or built up a social media presence, there are ways to build connections related to your work. First, you can volunteer with local organizations. At my university, for example, faculty and students from across various lab science and social science disciplines plan and run an annual Science Fest for local youth.[23] Those scientists also coordinate with the local public schools to provide hands-on science lessons in the classroom (my kindergartner just brought home a bird's nest she made as part of an IU Biology lesson on animal habitats).

You can also partner with local organizations when doing your work. In education, for example, it's becoming increasingly common for scholars to form research-practice partnerships with local school districts, like the Houston Education Research Consortium, which is currently led by sociologist Dr. Ruth López Turley.[24] Similar partnerships are also emerging in the policing and criminal justice fields. In his work as the executive director of the Lab for Applied Social Science Research at the University of Maryland, for example, sociologist Dr. Rashawn Ray works closely with the Prince George's County Police Department to design and carry out effective implicit bias trainings and then study the impact those programs have on police and their interactions with Black communities.[25]

If you're not sure where to start in building those connections, I highly recommend joining the Scholars Strategy Network, a nonprofit organization that connects scholars with journalists, practitioners, and policymakers at the local, state, and national levels.[26] Those connections might lead to conversations with lawmakers or with the staffers who write and implement public policy. You might even be invited to offer testimony at legislative hearings. In the wake of the current climate crisis, for example, university experts, including Dr. Justin Farrell and Dr. Naomi Oreskes, spoke about how "dark money" (i.e., anonymous donations to front groups and trade associations) is being used to fund "climate obstruction" and how government oversight is necessary to prevent such interference.[27] A number of PhD scholars, including Dr. Tressie McMillan Cottom, also testified at a recent U.S. Senate committee hearing, where they urged lawmakers to protect students and taxpayers by restricting federal funding to for-profit colleges.[28]

The Risks of Going Public

If you decide you want to write for public audiences or do interviews with major news outlets or work closely with practitioners and policymakers, it's important to know that public engagement can also come with risks. That's because the more publicly engaged you are as a scholar, the more visible your work and your ideas will be. If, in turn, your work is at all political or controversial, then writing or posting or speaking publicly can elicit a negative response. Even if your work isn't especially controversial, writing or tweeting or speaking publicly means that other people might misinterpret your message or jump to criticize you, even for minor missteps.

That's certainly been my experience. When I wrote about free-range parenting for the *Atlantic*, for example, I got vicious emails questioning my own fitness for parenthood. Similarly, when I wrote about research questioning the conclusions of the classic "Marshmallow Test" of delayed gratification, I got emails and social media messages insisting that my conclusions were wrong. Posting regularly on Twitter and keeping my account public rather than private also open the door for all sorts of haters and trolls, who've criticized me for everything from the policies I advocate for based on my research to the kind of food I feed my kids.

Unfortunately, I'm not alone in that experience of public criticism. For some scholars, public pushback even escalates to violent threats. In a recent Twitter thread, for example, a number of high-profile scholars, many of them women of color, talked about receiving death threats and other violent emails, letters, social media messages, and phone calls. Those scholars also shared strategies they've used in dealing with those threats and, in some cases, talked about the support they have or haven't gotten from their universities in managing the threats they face.

If you receive violent or threatening messages, it can be tempting to just delete them, but I strongly urge you to report them to your university and to the police and other authorities (like the FBI). Depending on how the threats are sent, there might not be anything legal authorities can do to identify the sender. But it's important to have a record of all threats in case any escalate into further action. Your university, in turn, should take threats seriously. If they don't offer, you can ask your department chair, your university security office, or even your university's technology office to take steps to protect you, such as not posting your office number, your office hours, or your class times and locations on public-facing websites. Certainly, my hope is that you'll never receive these kinds of threats, but it's important to understand that going public comes with risks.

In some cases, those risks can also include risks to your career.[29] Universities generally appreciate public attention to the work their scholars are doing, but they don't love bad press, and they don't love scholars whose public writings or engagements might bring scrutiny on the university. That kind of scrutiny, in turn, could influence your chances of getting tenure, getting promoted, or getting considered for prestigious opportunities in your field.

Given the potential risks, you might decide that the best option for you is to avoid writing for public audiences or doing media interviews or sharing your views online. I can certainly understand that choice. At the same time, I'd urge you to consider why some scholars—and especially those from systematically marginalized groups—choose to remain publicly engaged, despite the risks. Along those lines, see a recent blog post from sociologist Dr. Victor Ray.[30] As Ray explains, he shares his views publicly, even as a pre-tenure Black scholar, because he thinks academics "have a responsibility to help translate their ideas to the public" and because he sees his work "as part of a long tradition of black activist scholarship that was never fooled by the idea that intellectual, practical and political work should be kept separate." Ray notes that by writing publicly, and also by editing *Inside Higher Ed*'s *Conditionally Accepted* blog, he can give voice to the experiences of scholars of color in the academy and also support the efforts of students and scholars pushing for change. If you decide to follow Ray's lead, also check out another of his blog posts, linked in the endnotes, which has great tips on how to write for public audiences and what you can get from doing so.[31]

* * *

Ultimately, and despite the risks involved, public scholarship can have tremendous benefits for society and potentially for your own career. If you decide to go that route, you'll want to be ready to talk about your research—or anything related to your research—at a moment's notice. And that's where we'll turn in chapter 9. We'll talk about how to present your research and talk about it with confidence, even when you're not feeling so confident yourself.

Chapter 9

TALKING ABOUT YOUR RESEARCH

 Erynn Masi de Casanova @Prof_Casanova · Jul 22, 2018

Was invited or volunteered to present in a working group first year of PhD, having only done 15-min conference presentation before. I read aloud 50 pages of my MA thesis before someone gently stopped me so we could have time for discussion.

"Tell us about your research!"

I remember the first email I got as a grad student telling me my paper was accepted for a conference presentation. My initial reaction was elation: "They care what I'm doing!" But as impostor syndrome crept in, that initial elation gave way to: "What should I say? How should I say it? Am I going to make a fool of myself?"

As sociologist Dr. Erynn Masi de Casanova's tweet makes clear, the answers to those first two questions will depend on where you're asked to talk about your work, and the answer to that third question is less likely to be yes if you go in well prepared.

Unfortunately, that kind of preparation isn't always part of the formal curriculum in grad school. So in this chapter we'll talk about different venues where you might present your research. We'll discuss how a good talk looks different in different venues (and different disciplines). And we'll consider some universal best practices for making talks effective and engaging. Finally, I'll share advice about preparing for what can seem like the scariest part of an academic talk—the Q&A.

Where to Talk about Your Work

As a grad student, there are a bunch of different venues where you might be asked to talk about your work:

- *In-class presentations*
- *Department workshops*
- *Academic conferences*, including small regional conferences and huge national or international conferences as well as different conference session types:
  - *Keynote sessions*, where you're the only person invited to speak formally and at length about your work in front of an audience
  - *Paper sessions*, where you're part of a panel of scholars each formally but briefly presenting research (usually on related topics) to an audience
  - *Poster sessions*, where you and dozens of other scholars share posters presenting your research and then stand with those posters during designated times while audience members walk through, look at the posters, and ask questions about the research
  - *Roundtables sessions*, where you meet informally with a group of scholars and sometimes a few audience members, often at a literal roundtable, and each talk briefly about your research (usually on related topics)
- *Job talks*
- *Guest lectures*
- *Interviews* on the radio or on TV

The basic presentation format varies across these different venues. And it varies in three dimensions: *structure, time,* and *props.*

Structure

Many academic talks operate, essentially, as monologues—you'll have a set amount of time to just talk to the audience about your research. This is the basic format for most in-class presentations, workshops, paper sessions, roundtables, job talks, and guest lectures. In some disciplines (looking at you, economists), you should be prepared for audience members to interrupt your talk with all kinds of questions and comments—you might not even get a chance to finish the talk. In other disciplines, you'll probably get the full time to speak, and audience members will hold their questions and comments (except maybe brief clarifying questions) for the end.

Some academic talks operate, instead, as dialogues—as a conversation about your research. Rather than just talking for five or twenty-five or forty-five minutes and then answering questions at the end, you'll be going back and forth with your audience or with a moderator. They'll ask you a question. You'll tell them a bit about your work. They'll ask you another question. And so on. This is the standard format for poster sessions. That dialogue format is also more common in more public-facing discussions of research, like if you get invited to do an interview about your work on the radio or on TV.

Time

Sometimes when you're asked to talk about your research, you won't get much time at all. Less than ten minutes. Or maybe even less than five. That includes some in-class presentations and most radio and television interviews, which might only be three or five minutes long. Poster presentations also tend to work this way. While the poster session might technically last for an hour or more, you'll rarely talk to any one audience member for more than a few minutes. And you might end up just standing around for long stretches in between.

Some academic talks fall in the midrange with respect to time, usually ten to twenty minutes. That includes most paper and roundtable sessions at conferences. It may also include department workshops if they have multiple presenters on one day. If you're invited to present at one of these types of events, a good way to estimate the time you'll have is to first figure out how long the session/workshop is supposed to last. It'll probably be in the program, and it'll probably be sixty to ninety minutes total. Then add up the various parts of the session. That includes all the talks, plus the discussant (if there is one—more on that later), plus the Q&A. Then divide the total time by that number, and you'll get a top-end estimate of the amount of time you'll have. For example, if your paper is accepted for a seventy-five-minute conference session and there are four papers and a discussant on the program, the presenters and the discussant will probably each have ten to twelve minutes to speak, and there will be ten to twelve minutes for Q&A at the end. Of course, if you want to double-check how much time you'll have, it's always okay to ask the person who organized the event. You can just send a short email that looks something like this:

Dear Professor [LAST NAME],

Thank you for inviting me to present my paper, [PAPER TITLE], at [EVENT NAME] on [DATE]. Could you please tell me how much time I will have for my presentation? I want to make sure that I include the right amount of content in my talk.

Thank you in advance for your clarification!

Best wishes,

[YOUR NAME]

The last category of talks is long form. These usually last around forty-five minutes, with time for questions at the end. It's the standard job-talk format, but it usually applies to guest lectures and to some conference talks (e.g., keynote addresses) as well. Like I mentioned above, and depending on the discipline, you might get that full time to talk and then answer questions at the end. Or you might be interrupted repeatedly with questions and comments. Going to talks in your department should give you a sense of the norms in your discipline, but if you're presenting outside your department and you want to double-check on the length or the format of the talk, it's always okay to ask.

A quick note on time: Formal presentations, and especially conference presentations with multiple presenters, will sometimes have a timekeeper. They'll give you a warning when you have five minutes or two minutes or zero minutes remaining. Whether there's a timekeeper or not, I highly recommend keeping your own eye on the clock. And please don't ignore the timekeeper's warnings. It's disrespectful to the other presenters and to the audience to use up more than your allotted time.

Props

With some types of talks, you're expected or even required to use props. That includes poster presentations. The poster is right there in the name, and you're definitely expected to have one, or at least have something that looks like a poster. More on that later. In most fields, it's also normal for presenters to use visual aids during paper sessions, job talks, and guest lectures. Most presenters use Power-Point, but there are other options, including Prezi, Tableau, and even basic PDFs.

With other types of talks, props are optional or excluded altogether. With roundtable sessions, for example, conferences don't typically provide projectors or screens. So PowerPoint, Prezi, and Tableau are all out. As an alternative, some presenters bring handouts with key tables and figures (ten to fifteen copies is usually more than enough). Other presenters opt not to use any visual aids and just talk.

A quick note on props: Computers, projectors, cables, and screens are a huge expense for conference organizers, so many conferences opt not to provide them. Thus, if you're presenting at a conference, bring your laptop and any cables you'll need to connect to a projector (especially if you use a Mac). You might not need to use your own laptop or cables, but it's better to have them than to end up without the tools you need. I'd also recommend bringing your presentation on a thumb drive or saving it on a cloud drive for backup.

Giving Good Talks

Whatever you're talking about, and wherever you present it, there are some basic tips and tricks you can follow for giving an effective academic talk. That includes putting in the prep work to ensure that what you say is clear and well organized, that your props are accessible and effective, and that you'll be able to present in an engaging way.

Planning Good Talks

For monologue-style talks, I strongly recommend planning and practicing (and maybe even writing) the talk in advance. When your time is limited, it helps to know how much time to spend on each section and what to say when. Table 9.1 presents a few guidelines for how much time to spend on the various sections of your talk.

No matter the length, the focus should be on your research— not what previous research has found. Save the bulk of your time to talk about your study, your results, and your conclusions. People aren't coming to hear about what's been done before. They're coming to hear what's new. And if your talk is at eight o'clock in the morning, they might not come at all. I've been there. At one of my first conference presentations, an early-morning session, there were only three people in the audience. I've heard stories from other academics about sessions where the various presenters just presented to each other, with no audience at all. If this happens to you, you might feel as though the conference was a waste of time and money, but ultimately presenting is still good experience and good practice for the future, even if only a few people heard what you said.

TABLE 9.1. Minute-by-Minute Breakdown of Academic Talks

Talk Section	Conference Talk (10–15 minutes)	Job Talk (45 minutes)
	Talk Type	
Introduction/acknowledgments	0.5 minutes	1 minute
Background/justification	1–2 minutes	5 minutes
Research goals/questions	1 minute	2 minutes
Study design/data/methods	2 minutes	5 minutes
Overview	1 minute	3 minutes
Findings/results	4–7 minutes	20 minutes
Discussion/implications	1 minute	5 minutes
Thanks	0.5 minutes	1 minute

Most academics don't script their talks in advance, the way a politician with a speech writer might do. That said, they do typically plan in advance (or sometimes on the plane on the way to the conference—an approach I strongly discourage) what they're going to say. Along those lines, let's think about what to include in each section of the talk.

Thanks: When you're planning your talk, leave time to give thanks. At the beginning, introduce yourself and your project (if there's no one introducing you). Then add a few acknowledgments—thank any agencies that gave you funding, any coauthors who aren't presenting with you, any organizations that supported your work, and so on. Then take a few seconds to thank the session organizer (the person who organized the talk), the presider (the person who introduced you and/or the person who is keeping time), the discussant (the person who will be giving comments about the presented papers), and the audience for sharing their time with you.

Background: Don't just summarize the literature—make a case for your study. What's the gap or puzzle or problem in the literature you're going to address? Why is that an important puzzle or problem to solve? (Note: Aim higher than "because no one has looked at this before.") In a longer talk, you might also get into what research says about possible answers to your research questions or what your hypothesis is and why you think it's the right one.

Methods: Don't just describe what you did—make a case for your study design. How are you going to test your hypothesis or answer your research question? Why is your case/sample/dataset the right one for your research question? Why is your method the right method for analyzing the data you have?

Results: When it comes to results, I recommend a "sandwich" approach that starts and ends with the key point you want to make (the bread) and puts the evidence (the fillings) in between. That approach looks like this:

- State your point.
- Describe the pattern or analysis in the data that supports your point.
- Introduce an illustrative quote/excerpt/table/figure (and if you're using qualitative data, don't be afraid to act it out—if the person you're quoting or describing is frustrated, put some frustration in your voice too).
- Explain how the quote/excerpt/table/figure illustrates your point.

Repeat that sandwich process as many times as needed to present all the key points you need to make your argument. Or at least all those you have time to include.

Discussion: End your talk by answering the "so what" question. What should we take away from these findings? How do they build on/challenge/contribute to existing research? What implications do they have for policy/practice? What are the next steps?

Thanks Again: Close your talk by thanking the audience for listening. Saying thanks, especially if you have a "thank-you" slide with your contact info, also signals you're done. That signal can be helpful to avoid the awkward moment where the audience hears you stop talking but isn't sure if you're finished talking and thus doesn't know whether to clap. If you say thanks and no one claps, though, don't stress. It doesn't mean your presentation was a flop. Some disciplines don't have a strong clap-after-each-presentation norm, and academics are notoriously awkward about that kind of social stuff.

Giving Good Talks

Now let's think for a minute about actually giving the talk, or saying it aloud. It's easy to watch a TED Talk or a seasoned professor and think "Wow. They're just so knowledgeable. I could never talk that clearly or comfortably or authoritatively about anything." But remember—clarity and comfort and authority don't (or at least usually don't) come naturally. Most scholars achieve that level of ease with public speaking only after years of experience, and they often spend weeks or months planning and practicing for high-profile talks.

Along those lines, I'd recommend checking out Three Minute Thesis.[2] It's a competition that started at the University of Queensland and now has more than six hundred participating universities across more than sixty-five countries. Participants in the competition present their doctoral thesis in a three-minute, publicly recorded talk. Winning the competition is a big deal, but just participating is a great opportunity to practice distilling your ideas, engaging an audience, and talking confidently about your research.

Of course, even if Three Minute Thesis isn't quite your speed, there are still things you can do to hone your speaking skills and get ready to give your talks. Here are a few key things I'd recommend:

Preparation: Planning your talk, and maybe even writing it out, can help you craft the kind of compelling story that will keep your listeners engaged. As good journalism shows us, a well-structured story can keep the reader or the listener engaged, no matter what the story is about. Along those lines, there are a few structures that work particularly well for academic talks:

- The Uncertain Explanation: Start by introducing some phenomenon that previous research hasn't fully explained, then lay out how you explain that phenomenon with your research.
- The Uncertain Outcome: Start by introducing some phenomenon where the consequences have been unclear, then explain how you reveal those consequences with your research.
- The Evocative Example: Start with an evocative example from your research or from the real world, then explain how that example illustrates the larger patterns you find in your research.

If you pick a structure and plan your talk in advance, it'll help you avoid rambling or freezing up. Planning ahead means you'll go into the talk knowing what you need to say, knowing how each thing you say leads into what you'll say next, and knowing you won't run too long or too short.

So what does good planning look like? At the very least, it means working out the clearest and most compelling way to tell the story of your research and then jotting a few notes about what to say in each part of your talk. Figuring that out usually involves an iterative process where you draft the talk, practice it, and then revise. (We'll talk more about practice in a minute.)

If you're worried about fitting a lot of material into a short amount of time, or avoiding awkward transitions between ideas, you might also consider scripting your talk. If you go that route, follow these guidelines:

- Write your talk like you'd say it (use short, declarative sentences).
- Aim for a hundred words per minute (any more than that and you'll have to talk as fast as I do).

- Print it out in fourteen-point font or bigger (any smaller and you'll struggle to keep track of where you are when you're giving the talk).
- Practice it aloud (and edit, edit, edit until it feels comfortable to say).
- Keep practicing until you're confident (but bring your script, just in case).
- Try to stay eyes-up as much as possible (and don't forget to breathe).

Now, you might worry that a scripted or well-prepped talk will end up feeling stiff or hollow—less than genuine. In reality, though, it's easier to speak from the heart if your heart isn't racing with anxiety. At a recent academic conference, for example, I was asked to speak on a panel offering tips to grad students attending the conference for the first time. The organizer told me and the other panelists not to worry about prepping anything in advance. And, normally, I would've ignored that advice and prepped something anyway. But I knew I was going to be late to the panel (I had an overlapping meeting), and I had other talks to prep, so I decided I'd talk "off the cuff," instead. And I did talk. But I have no idea if what I said was useful because I felt like I was just repeating myself and rambling and rattling off a bunch of clichés. You've probably seen a talk like that, and you probably forgot that talk ten minutes later (unless it was *really* bad). That's because the point of the talk probably got lost somewhere in all the rambling. Or because the point wasn't there at all.

And of course, a scripted talk can come across feeling stiff and hollow. But that's much less likely to happen if you write it like you'd say it. And if you practice enough.

Practice: With practice, even a fully scripted talk can look and feel like it's "off the cuff." That's, in part, because practicing your talk can help you get the script just right. When you say your talk aloud, and especially when you practice your talk for an audience, you (and your audience) can hear what works and what doesn't.

You can hear if you repeat things. You can hear if something is confusing or if the logic doesn't flow. If you take time to practice, you can go back and edit those less-than-great parts to make them smoother for the next time around.

As you practice, try out different ways to organize your ideas and transition smoothly between them. Then script the one that works best. As you practice, listen for the tricky concepts and terms that trip you up. Then work out how best to explain those concepts or use different terms instead.

All that practice will help you feel more comfortable. At that point, you've already said it a dozen times (or at least four or five). You'll look like you're speaking off-the-cuff, which some people perceive (rightly or wrongly) as a sign that you really know your stuff. And you'll be confident in what you want to say, even if you're not totally confident yet in saying it.

Enthusiasm: Good storytellers keep their audience engaged. That engagement comes, in part, from the structure of the story, but it also comes from the storyteller's own enthusiasm for the topic. When you're animated about your research, your audience will get excited too, and they'll be more likely to remember what you say. Focusing on your excitement for the project will also help you keep your voice loud and clear, which is especially important if you can't rely on a microphone and have to do your best to project. Of course you might not always feel that kind of excitement, especially if your stomach is tied in knots. In that case it's okay to fake a little excitement for effect. When I'm in that boat, and I need a little extra enthusiasm boost, I like to imagine that I'm reading a story to a class of preschoolers. They're the kind of audience for whom a little extra excitement goes a very long way.

A Note on Nerves

I teach a 250-student Introduction to Sociology class twice a week. That means I'm used to speaking in front of big crowds. I actually like the "theater" part of my job, but I still get nervous, especially before big talks. When I get nervous, I start talking faster and faster and sometimes find myself talking so fast I can't catch my breath.

If that happens to you—it's okay to take a (short) break. Take a sip of water. Glance through your notes (or pretend to). Ask the audience to look at something on your slides. It might feel like an eternity in your head, but the audience won't mind the break. If anything, they'll be more engaged when you start speaking again.

Also, look for the "nodder." Usually, there's someone in the audience who (like me) is a habitual nodder. When you're feeling nervous, look to that person. Let their nods give you confidence you're on the right track. That you're making sense. That you're doing okay.

Audiences and Accessibility

When you're prepping or giving a talk, it's easy to focus on what will make you feel most comfortable. But you also need to think about presenting your information in an accessible way. The gold standard for accessibility is what's often called "universal design." Essentially, that means designing things (like talks, classrooms, or assignments) to be fully accessible to as many people as possible, ideally without the need for individualized accommodations.[3]

So how do you make your presentations as accessible as possible? Building on recommendations from the National Endowment for the Arts, I would suggest:

- Informing your audience of what will be expected of them during your presentation (e.g., Will there be a video? Will they have to answer questions or move around?)
- Presenting essential information in multiple ways (e.g., verbally and in written form)
- Making essential information as audible and legible as possible:

- Use a microphone if one is available (and encourage audience members to use a microphone when asking questions or making comments)
- Face your audience and stay eyes-up as much as possible
- Speak slowly and clearly
- Minimize background noise (e.g., keep doors closed during presentations)
- Turn on captions when presenting audio or video clips
- Adjust light settings to improve the visibility of presentation screens
- Avoid small font sizes and choose easy-to-read fonts (24-point is the minimum I'd recommend for slides, with 28 or 32 even better)
- Choose colors that highlight contrast and maximize accessibility for those with color blindness[4]
- Use images to illustrate key concepts and ideas
- Bring large-print copies of slides and handouts for anyone visually impaired
- Giving your audience time to process information:
  - Minimize the amount of information on each slide
  - Spend adequate time explaining each idea or slide
  - Pause before presenting new ideas or new slides

Now, accessibility is important for audiences, but it's important for you as the presenter too. If you're scheduled to give a talk or attend a talk, and you need accommodations (e.g., a wheelchair ramp, an interpreter, or a floor microphone), don't be afraid to ask. Some conference websites allow you to indicate your needs when you're registering to present or attend. Unfortunately, though, filling out those forms doesn't guarantee you'll get the accommodations you ask for. And those forms rarely exist for smaller-scale presentations like department workshops or job talks. In that case, reach out to the organizer, let them know about the accommodations you'll need, and ask for contact information for someone you can reach out to if the accommodations aren't available when you show up for your talk.

In my case, for example, I gave a few talks not long after I gave birth to my kids, and I needed space and time to pump breastmilk during my visit. I was pretty nervous about asking for those accommodations, and it didn't always work out perfectly. I ended up pumping in a few bathroom stalls, which is less than hygienic, and I ended up with a few embarrassing leaks and a few long, uncomfortable stretches because I didn't have time to pump. That said, most people I talked to tried their best to help.

Regardless of what type of accommodations you might need, there are ways to ask that can increase your chances of success. In general, you don't need to explain the whole backstory or give a lot of details. Just say what you need (e.g., "I'm currently breastfeeding, and I'll need a private place to use a breast pump for 30 minutes every 3–4 hours"). Then ask for help ("Would it be possible for [CONFERENCE/UNIVERSITY/ORGANIZA-TION] to provide those accommodations?"). And add a little gratitude in advance ("Thank you in advance for your help in looking into this").

Prepping Good Props

Visual aids aren't technically necessary for a good talk. That said, they can help guide the audience through your argument, and they can take the pressure off by giving the audience something to look at besides just your face. Props like posters, handouts, and slides can also make your presentations more accessible to your audience, and especially to audience members with disabilities— but only if they're done well. So let's talk about what good props look like in different forms.

Posters: The first time I presented at a poster session, I had no idea what the poster was supposed to look like. I didn't know what to include. Or how big it should be. So I looked up the conference information, and the only details I could find were the dimensions of the poster space—essentially, the easel I'd get to hang it on. And that easel was four feet by six feet. So that's what I went with. My poster was *huge*. It cost a fortune to print. And it got me some strange looks from other presenters. Because the background on my poster was bright green. Not white like theirs.

In hindsight, three feet by five feet or even smaller than that would have been fine. If you're short on cash, it's also okay to just print the various parts of your poster on sheets of regular paper and arrange them in a poster format.

As for what to include, posters should have the same basic elements as an academic talk—title, author, acknowledgments, background/justification, research goals/questions, study design/data/methods, overview, findings/results, discussion/implications. Keep the text as minimal as possible (bullet points and figures are great). And keep fonts legible—ideally twenty point or larger.

Along those lines, there's actually a movement in the science world to completely reimagine what counts as good poster design.[5] With this kind of poster, you'll want to state the main conclusion of your paper in a single sentence in big, bold print, on a brightly colored background. Paste in a QR code that links to your full paper online. And add a column on one side of the poster with more detailed information, printed in smaller text on a white background. I like this poster model because it's designed to draw in the audience and give them just enough information to spark a conversation about your ideas. I also like it because my original bright green background would fit right in.

Handouts: I find that handouts are most useful as supplements rather than full overviews. That means key tables. Or figures. Things that can't be condensed or simplified enough to fit (legibly) on a slide.

Slides: I love good slide design, and I think my slides are pretty decent (you can check out my website for a few examples), but they're nothing compared to the slides my spouse regularly makes for his job in university administration. He made one presentation, about cybersecurity, entirely of GIFs and memes. It was clear, engaging, and hilarious—even without hearing the talk. My slides will probably never be as innovative or as engaging as his. But I can try.

Along those lines, a few tips for designing effective, engaging slides:

- Give each slide a clear purpose.
- Summarize key points; don't write it all out.
- Only use 24-point font or larger for text.
- Shapes with text printed in them are more engaging than bullet points.
- Key phrases are more effective than long blocks of text.
- Figures are better than simple tables, which are better than detailed tables.
- Use images to illustrate key ideas.

Images add depth to a presentation, especially when coupled with minimalist text. Along those lines, a few tips on finding and selecting good images to use:

- Go with the highest resolution you can find (if it looks blurry in presentation mode on your computer, it'll be *really* blurry on the big screen).
- Find images labeled for reuse, or take your own (you can find free, unrestricted-use images at sites like unsplash, freeimages, pixabay, etc.).
- Mix up the layouts; try some full screen images with text shapes on top.

If it wasn't already obvious, I really enjoy giving talks. As someone who (very briefly) considered art school, I also love designing slides. And as a former drama geek, I love the performance-art aspect of presenting (and teaching). Despite all that, I still get butterflies, especially before the Q&A. And that's where we'll turn next.

Mastering the Q&A

With most academic talks, there will be time for questions at the end. Mastering the academic Q&A is definitely part of the hidden curriculum of grad school. I don't think I've ever seen a class that explicitly taught students how to answer questions about their work. Instead, it's the kind of thing you're expected to learn by doing or by watching speakers answer questions during their talks. (Of course, that's more difficult to do if your department doesn't regularly host speaking events.)

The challenge (and arguably the fun) of the Q&A section is that you don't know in advance what questions you'll be asked. That said, there are things you can do to be better prepared.

- Know Your Data Well: For qualitative data (e.g., interviews, ethnographic observations, document analysis), it's great to be able to offer examples (from memory) as answers to questions or to illustrate patterns you didn't have time to include in the talk. For quantitative data (surveys and experiments), it can help to know the basic results of supplemental and descriptive analyses you ran.
- Anticipate Potential Questions: Practice your talk with friends. Their questions will probably be similar to those you'll get from other people. Take notes and plan rough responses to those questions (and maybe even prep extra slides).
- Prompt Specific Questions: You don't have time to cover the whole paper or project in your talk. If you allude to parts of the analysis you're leaving out, you're more likely to get questions about those left-out parts. And you can easily prepare notes in advance.
- Always Be Ready for Questions about Mechanisms and Implications: There are a few types of questions that regularly come up during talks, and they usually have to do with mechanisms, implications, and alternative explanations.

What explains your findings? Is your explanation the right explanation? What about this other explanation? Why should we care about what you found? Prepping answers to those questions can make for a much smoother Q&A.

- Reflect on the Implications of Your Decisions: Be able to explain why you chose your case/data/methods. At the same time, be ready to explain (citing relevant research) how and why a different case/data/method might (or might not) lead to different results.
- Acknowledge the Limits of Your Data: It's okay to speculate a bit, especially about mechanisms and implications. But it's also okay to say "my data can't answer that question," especially if you can follow it up with "but other research would suggest X."
- Acknowledge the Limits of Your Knowledge: In general, when you get a question, it's better to say something (even if you're not quite answering the question that was asked) than to say nothing at all. Along those lines, if you get a question and you don't know the answer, you might answer a related question instead, saying something like, "I'm not sure about [THE THING YOU ASKED ABOUT], but I do know [RELATED PIECE OF INFORMATION]." If you think you know the answer, but you just need a moment to think, take a beat to write down the question that was asked (it's helpful to have a pen and paper ready). That will give you a bit of time to collect your thoughts and hopefully come up with the answer. If, at that point, you still don't know the answer, it's okay to say "That's a great question. I don't have the answer right now / I can't recall the specifics on that / I haven't run those models yet, but if you come chat with me after, I'd love to get your contact information so I can follow up once I have a chance to look into it."

Especially if it's your first time presenting, the Q&A might feel like an attack. It's important, though, not to get defensive. Instead, focus on using your responses to highlight your ability to think on the fly. That kind of on-the-fly thinking is a critical skill both in presenting research and, if you're aiming for an academic job, in teaching.

* * *

We'll talk more about teaching in chapter 12. Before that, though, let's talk a bit about the non-presenting side of academic conferences. Specifically, let's talk about how to navigate the financial, social, and logistical hurdles involved in attending big events.

Chapter 10

GOING TO CONFERENCES

—

 Roxy Brookshire @RoxyBrookshire · Jul 21, 2018

#hiddencurriculum both grad and some undergrad may have funding for you to go to conferences BUT they will reimburse you - so the assumption is you have a credit card. Also if you need care for a child/elder/disabled family member you will be on the hook for making that $$$.

As we talked about in chapter 2, academic conferences can be a great opportunity to present and get feedback on your research. They also give you a chance to build connections with other scholars and learn about new research in your field.

At the same time, and as sociology grad student Roxy Brookshire suggests, just getting to the conference can be a big hurdle for many students. Between airfare and a couple of days' hotel costs, attending an academic conference can easily costs hundreds or thousands of dollars, especially when those conferences are held in major cities where you'll pay seven dollars for a coffee and seventeen for a sandwich and a drink.

Because of those costs, and as we'll talk about in this chapter, it's important to be strategic in deciding when to start going to conferences, how often you'll go, which ones you'll attend, and how long you'll stay. We'll also talk in this chapter about the other tricky decisions you'll have to make when you're attending an academic conference. Decisions about what to do with your time when you're not presenting your research. Decisions about how to navigate all the awkward small talk you'll encounter while you're there.

Deciding When and Where and How Often to Go

As we'll talk more about in chapter 12, going to conferences is particularly important when you're looking for a job. In some disciplines, first-round interviews for academic and even some nonacademic jobs are held during professional conferences. Even in disciplines where the interview process is less centralized, informal meetings during conferences can give candidates a leg up over the other applicants in the pool.

So what if you're not on the job market just yet? When should you start going to conferences? Which ones should you choose? And how often should you go?

In terms of when to start going to conferences, my recommendation is to wait until you have to go or until someone else will pay your way. Conferences are expensive. You'll have to pay for transport to and from the conference and for someplace to stay while you're there. You'll also have to pay a registration fee to attend the conference, and you might have to pay an additional membership fee to join the organization hosting the conference. Altogether, those costs can easily add up to more than a thousand dollars per conference, especially if you have to fly to get there and if you're staying more than two nights. Your department, your university, or even the conference you're attending might have funds you can apply for to help you cover conference costs. But they rarely cover the full cost of attendance.

If those conference costs are too much to manage, it's okay to be strategic about when you go. You don't have to start going to conferences your first year of grad school, and you don't have to go every year. Yes, conferences are a great place to network and learn about new research and get feedback on your work. But there are other ways to do that. Even professors skip conferences if they have family obligations or if their teaching schedule conflicts with the conference or if they don't have research funds to cover the costs. And now, with the rise of conference Twitter hashtags and online livestreaming, you can often follow along with what's happening at conferences even if you're not there.

You can also be strategic about which conferences you attend. In addition to big national or international conferences, for example, many disciplines also have smaller regional or subfield conferences. They're typically held in smaller, less expensive cities. They're usually a short drive or train ride or bus ride away. And they're typically more casual and more friendly, with fewer attendees overall, fewer "big name" scholars, and bigger proportions of students and professors from regional campuses and community colleges. Because of those differences, I highly recommend trying out a regional conference as the first conference you submit to and attend. Getting a sense of how conferences work, in a relatively low-stakes environment, can help you feel more prepared for the big conferences you might go to later in your career.

When I was in grad school, my department didn't provide any standard travel funds for grad students, and my starting stipend was something around thirteen thousand dollars a year. Because of that, I waited until my fifth year of grad school to go to my first national sociology conference (the annual meeting of the American Sociological Association, or ASA). I went for only one night and stayed with another grad student at a very run-down, bug-infested motel about a mile from the conference. The conference was in Atlanta in August, and by the time I walked to the conference hotel for my roundtable session, I was a sweaty, disheveled mess. But I got through the presentation, and I got a pretty good sense of what not to do when I went back to that same conference on the job market the following year.

Along those lines, I would argue that universities, disciplines, departments, and individual faculty members should help students cover the costs of attending conferences, especially as they get to the dissertation stage. With that kind of help, you can stay at the conference hotel rather than having to schlep across the city at the beginning and end of each day. You can also stay long enough to appreciate the conference rather than just give your presentation and run.

Unfortunately, though, and because many state and federal governments have reduced their investment in research and higher education,[2] many universities, disciplines, departments, and faculty members don't have money for grad student travel. If you're in one of those departments, there's a good chance your professors are paying out of pocket to attend conferences and limiting the trips they take. And so if you can't find outside funding, and if the conference is one you really can't miss, you'll have to figure out how to manage those costs on your own.

Now, we've talked about how the costs of conferences might keep you from going. And we'll talk more about strategies for keeping costs low in a bit. First, though, let's consider why, despite the high costs of academic conferences, you might still want to attend.

Submitting to Conferences

One of the main reasons to go to conferences, at least early in your career, is to present and get feedback on your work. To do that, you first have to have a paper or, for some conferences, an extended abstract of a paper you want to present.

Different disciplines have different norms (and sometimes formal rules) about what stage of research you can present. In some disciplines, for example, conferences will accept only manuscripts that haven't yet been accepted for publication. The idea with that model is that conferences should be an opportunity to get feedback and improve your work. The problem with presenting unpublished work, though, is that you run the risk of getting "scooped." Essentially, unscrupulous scholars might hear you present and then use your ideas to conduct a similar analysis and submit their results for publication before you have a chance to do the same. The high premium on novelty in academic publishing means they might get all the credit, even if you had the idea first.

If you're worried about protecting yourself against the possibility of getting scooped, there are a few things you can do. First, and before presenting at conferences, you might register your research as a working paper or preprint. As we talked about in chapter 8, online repositories like NBER Working Papers or SocArXiv allow you to make your work public before it has been published and do so in a searchable and citeable way. Second, if your research involves the development of new procedures or technologies, you can also talk to your university's technology transfer office about the steps you can take to protect what you discover or invent in your work.

Regardless of whether you take those first two paths, I'd also recommend thinking strategically about when to submit and present your research. Most conferences, for example, require that you submit a paper or abstract well in advance of the actual conferences—sometimes three months or six months or even nine months ahead. If you're strategic about it, you can use that extended timeline to get your project published or close to published by the time you present. Along those lines, I'd recommend familiarizing yourself with the conference submission deadlines in your discipline and, to the extent possible, planning your projects around those deadlines. In general, that means submitting your paper to a journal either right before you submit it to the conference or not too long after.

Of course, submitting a paper to a conference isn't a guarantee you'll get accepted. That said, there are things you can do to increase your chances for getting on the program. As we talked about in chapter 9, most conferences will have paper sessions and roundtable sessions and possibly poster sessions as well. Paper sessions are the most prestigious, in part because they often represent the smallest number of slots on the program. As a result, those paper sessions (which involve standing up in front of an audience and giving a talk about your research) typically go to well-known scholars and to more junior scholars doing really timely, innovative, and well-developed research. If you're a grad student (especially early in grad school), or if your project is at a very early stage of development, you'll have a much better shot at getting your paper into a roundtable or poster session. Those sessions typically have more slots for presenters, and they're well suited for presentations of early-stage work. If you're submitting to a conference, and you really want to be able to present, make sure you indicate on your submission form that you're willing to present at a roundtable and/or poster session and not just at a formal paper session.

Affording to Go and Eat while You're There

If you get accepted for a conference, the next step is to figure out how you'll afford to go. Along those lines, there are a few potential funding sources:

- Your School/Program: Universities, schools within those universities, and departments or programs within those schools sometimes have travel awards for grad students. Ask your department administrator or graduate program director if there are any internal funds you can apply for to help you pay for travel. The maximum award might be only a few hundred dollars (if that), but it's still worth applying—every little bit helps.
- Your Conference/Professional Organization: Some professional organizations (and sections of those professional organizations) have grad student travel awards that can be used to help offset the cost of traveling to that organization's annual meeting. Check the website for the organization (and various sections of that organization) to look for information about travel awards. The applications

are typically fairly short—maybe just a copy of your CV, the title of the paper you'll be presenting, and a brief statement about why you deserve the award. Organizations typically receive a large volume of applications for these awards, and they typically grant them to students who are on the job market or finishing their dissertations. That means that if you don't get one, it's not a knock on you or your work, and you should definitely apply again in future years.

- Your Advisor/Coauthor: If the paper you'll be presenting is coauthored with your advisor or with another faculty member, ask them if they have funds to help cover the costs of your travel to the conference. It doesn't have to be a lot of money—even a hundred dollars can help.

If you're lucky enough to get help with travel costs, it's important to know that you probably won't get that money up front. Instead, you'll have to collect receipts for all your travel-related costs and then submit them for reimbursement after the conference. In the short term, that means you'll have to be able to pay, up front and out of pocket, for things like membership fees, conference registration fees, airfare, hotel rooms, and subway, bus, or taxi rides. And even after you submit your receipts, it could take a month or more after the conference for the check to come through. Depending on your finances, that might mean you have to spend a few months saving up before each conference or putting the expenses on a credit card you can afford to pay off when you get reimbursed down the road.

If you don't have help with travel costs, you might have to be even more careful about how you save and how you spend. Personally, I don't think it's worth going into debt to attend an academic conference. But there are trade-offs to not going, like missed social connections, missed opportunities to learn about new research, and the possibility of social judgment from your professors and your peers. Along those lines, and if you decide to go anyway, here are a few tips for making it work without breaking the bank:

- You Might Not Have to Stay for the Whole Conference: If you got a travel award or other travel funds to help with the costs of attending, you might be required to stay for the whole conference or at least stay for a set number of days. If you're funding your travel yourself, or if your travel award doesn't come with stipulations on how long you have to stay, you might consider cutting things short rather than staying the whole time. Hotel rooms are one of the biggest expenses for conferences, and each day you stay just adds more fees. If you know, well in advance, what day you'll be presenting, plan your travel around that day. You might stay one night before (especially if your presentation is in the morning) and potentially one night after (especially if your presentation is in the afternoon/evening). If the conference schedule isn't announced until a few weeks before, see if there are topic days you can use as a guide. In some disciplines, for example, each subfield gets a day of the conference, and most events and talks for that subfield are held on that day. So even if you don't know exactly when you'll be presenting, you'll know that it'll probably be sometime on that day.
- Double (or Triple or Quadruple) Up: Splitting a hotel room with other grad students can help cut down on costs. Unfortunately, if you're staying at the official conference hotel, there's a good chance you'll be charged extra if you want to share a room. In that case, it's worth looking into other housing options, instead. You can usually find an affordable Airbnb or hotel room in another part of town, and if you're staying in a city with good public transit, you'll be able to get to the conference and back quickly and easily for a couple of dollars each way.

- Take Public Transit: Trains, buses, and subways aren't just an option if you're staying at a hotel in another part of town. They can also save you a lot of money when you're traveling to and from the airport, or even when you're getting to the conference. I recently went to a conference in New York City. Rather than take a taxi from JFK to Midtown, I took the air train to the subway, which dropped me off just a block from my hotel. That trip cost me less than ten dollars. A taxi ride would've cost more than fifty dollars, and that's before the tip.
- Get Creative with Flight Options: If you live in a city with a major airline hub, you'll probably be able to get a decently priced flight, provided you're willing to book far enough in advance and fly at off-peak times. If you live in a non-hub city, like I do (the closest airport to Bloomington is Indianapolis, which doesn't have many direct flights to places other than Chicago), it can be harder to find cheap flights. If you're willing to drive a bit, though, you can sometimes find a much better deal. In my case, for example, I can usually save a lot of money by driving to Cincinnati or Chicago and flying from there instead.
- Avoid Overpriced Food: Conferences tend to be located in the most expensive parts of cities. That means if you're trying to grab a cup of coffee or a sandwich between sessions, you'll pay double what you'd pay just a few blocks away. One way to avoid breaking the bank on food and drinks is to bring basics from home. When I go to conferences, I always pack protein bars, trail mix, and a reusable water bottle. Then when I get to the conference, I find a grocery store and buy some yogurt and fresh fruit. It'll be more expensive than what I'd pay at home in Indiana (big-city prices and all), but still a lot cheaper than what I'd pay at the hotel or a nearby coffee shop. And probably healthier too. Then, in the evenings, I'll get some food at

the various conference receptions (there are plenty, and they're usually free) and, if I'm still hungry after, grab a snack from a food truck or convenience store on my way back to my room.

How to Spend Your Time

We talked in chapter 9 about how to present your research at conferences, but that covers only an hour or two of your time. Even if you go to the conference for just a day, you'll still have plenty of hours to fill. So what should you do with the rest of your time?

One option, and a good option, is to check out other research sessions. During a conference there are sessions—sometimes dozens of them all running concurrently—from early in the morning to late in the evening each day. Online programs make those sessions easily searchable. You can look for specific topics of interest or check out specific scholars' work. Going to sessions is a great way to learn about new research, new methods, and new teaching strategies in your field. Sessions are also a great place to network. After the session, you can go up and ask the presenters a question, or just say you liked their work. If that feels too scary, though, or if there's a long line, that's okay.

Sessions are a great place to network with other audience members as well. Those audience members, whether they're faculty members or grad students, are there for the same reason you are—because they're interested in the topic. So look left or right or behind you. Find someone else who's standing a little awkwardly, looking like they're not sure what to do next, and strike up a conversation with them. Ask what they thought about the session. Or just remark on what you liked and let the conversation go from there. You might end up finding a new friend or coauthor or mentor, but even if you don't, you'll have found a friendly face you can smile at the next time you pass in the hall. When you're spending days surrounded by thousands of people you don't know, those little moments of connection can make you feel a little more at home.

Another less formal option is to check out the conference book exhibit. At the book exhibit, presses, including academic presses and academic-adjacent trade presses, set up tables featuring new and best-selling books in their line. You're welcome to wander through and browse. If you find books you like, you'll be able to buy them at a steep discount off what you would pay in the bookstore or online. That's especially true on the last day of the book exhibit, when many presses slash prices to avoid having to schlep books back home. In addition to browsing for books, you can also use the book exhibit as a chance to make connections with potential editors, though you'll want to go at strategic times. Editors often spend most of the conference in meetings, but they'll typically be at their press booth during key events like book release parties or meet-the-author hours. Those events are a good time to stop by, as there might be free food, and you might have a chance to chat briefly with the press's editor or with authors who have published with that press. Then you can follow up with an email after the conference reintroducing yourself, thanking them for chatting with you, and asking if you can arrange a time to talk in more depth.

Yet another less formal option is to check out the more socially oriented conference events. Social events—including receptions, sponsored meals, and informal gatherings at the bar—are actually where much of the "business" of conferences happens, especially in terms of networking. Maybe you're the kind of person who really thrives in that kind of social scene, but if you're not, that's okay too. As someone who doesn't drink alcohol and prefers a good night's sleep to staying up late making small talk, I'm not a fan of the conference social stuff. At my first big national conference, I was supposed to meet one of my advisors at a reception for sociologists who study education. I'm also the kind of person who gets very stressed about being late, so I showed up ten minutes before the reception even started, and there was no one else there. I stood awkwardly in the corner for a while. Then another grad student showed up and awkwardly took a different corner. I was too shy to say anything, so we both just waited there silently until other people arrived. Even then, though, I didn't see anyone I knew, so I got a few veggie sticks and some crackers from the food tables, made a slow lap around the room (in case the advisor I was supposed to meet was somewhere in the crowd), and went back to my corner again. Finally, about twenty minutes into the event, my advisor arrived, and I rushed over to meet her, feeling incredibly relieved. She introduced me to a few other scholars she knew and then started chatting with a friend she hadn't seen in years. It seemed like it would be weird to keep hanging around, so I took that as my cue and called it a night.

Now, that story might make receptions seem incredibly awkward and uncomfortable. But they do get easier over time. Almost ten years after that first big conference, receptions are now the place where I go to catch up with old friends (though I still rarely stay out past ten). If I go to a reception for sociologists of education, I'll usually know or recognize at least a third of the people in the room—they're people I've been on panels with during conferences, people I've served on committees with, people I've chatted with on Twitter, and people whose papers I've read or reviewed. Having those connections makes it far easier to say hello.

Before you get to that stage, though, I'd recommend using the buddy system for social conference events. If you go with someone you know, you can give each other the confidence to approach other scholars and say hello. Or, at the very least, you'll have someone to talk to when you're standing awkwardly in the corner, and you'll have someone who can make sure you get back to your room safely at the end of the night.

Between presentation sessions, business meetings, and social gatherings, conference days can stretch from eight in the morning (or earlier) until well past midnight. That whole time you'll have to be "on," and you'll be surrounded by people you don't know—many of them senior scholars from elite universities. In that kind of environment with that kind of schedule, it's normal to feel exhausted and overwhelmed. If you're feeling that way, or if you're worried you might, don't be afraid to take breaks. Go for a walk or a run (my favorite thing to do when I'm traveling is find a new route to run). Get yourself an ice cream or a donut. Take a nap in your room. Find a quiet corner to rest and recharge (figuratively and literally—if you're looking for me at a conference, I'm usually sitting next to an outlet, recharging my laptop and phone). Schedule time with friends you trust and who'll make you feel whole again.

In terms of taking breaks, it's also important to block off time right before you present. You'll want at least twenty or thirty minutes to review your notes, gather your thoughts, and breathe. If that means skipping out halfway through another session, that's okay. Just sit in the back and leave as quietly as you can.

Notes on Networking

We've talked a bit about approaching other scholars and striking up conversations at conferences. That said, there are also other ways to connect that don't rely so heavily on serendipity.

One option is to reach out to other scholars and set up meetings in advance. Maybe there's a scholar whose work you really admire. Or another grad student you've met on Twitter. Or a professor you haven't seen since undergrad. Or a scholar in a department where you're thinking of applying for grad school or for a job. It's okay to reach out to those people before the meeting (even if you don't know them personally) and ask if they have time to meet. You might not get a message back, or they might say no, but I don't know any scholar who isn't flattered to be asked.

If your list includes more senior scholars, reach out about a month in advance of the conference. More than that, and there's a risk the meeting will never materialize. The other scholar probably doesn't know their conference schedule yet, so they might respond back saying "I'll check back in with you as we get closer to the conference." Then life gets busy and they forget. Less than a month out, and especially by the week of the conference, the other scholar's schedule will probably be full. So try to hit that sweet spot right around a month, and try to keep it brief. Also, be sure to let the other scholar know what you want to talk about. Maybe you're looking for advice about how to use a particular method or dataset, or how to frame your dissertation, or how to navigate the job market. Or maybe you just want to hear more about how they did their research. Essentially, you'll want the other person to know what they're getting into, and you'll want to have questions ready to avoid awkward silences when you meet. An email like this works well:

Dear Professor [LAST NAME],

I'm a big fan of your work on [TOPIC], and I would love to talk with you about [THE THING YOU WANT TO KNOW]. If you're planning to attend [CONFERENCE], do you have time in your schedule for a brief meeting? I am available [YOUR AVAILABILITY DURING THE CONFERENCE].

To tell you a little bit about myself, I'm a grad student at [UNIVERSITY] doing research on [YOUR RESEARCH TOPIC]. [IF APPLICABLE] I'll be presenting my paper, [TITLE], at [TIME] on [DATE]. If you have time in your schedule, I would be honored if you would consider attending.

Thank you in advance for your consideration!

Sincerely,

[YOUR NAME]

When you send an email like that, don't feel like you have to offer to buy the other person coffee or alcohol or a meal. Senior scholars know (or should know) that grad students are working on a limited budget. They don't (or shouldn't) expect you to treat them. Instead, the best way to show appreciation for their time is to thank them and to pay it forward in your own career.

Along those lines, some conferences have mentoring programs that pair grad students and other junior scholars with more senior scholars in the field. Keep an eye out for email notifications about those programs. You'll usually have to sign up a few months before the conference, but those events can be a great way to build a connection and get advice and information that go beyond what you can access in your own department. Those mentoring programs are also a great way to give back later—if you benefit from mentoring programs as a grad student, be sure to volunteer as a mentor when you're on the other side of the desk.

Now, the temptation with networking is to focus on networking up—making connections to more senior scholars in your field. That makes sense, on some level, because those senior scholars will probably be the ones making decisions about your career. That said, senior scholars aren't the only scholars you should know, and knowing them won't necessarily make conferences feel like "home." Instead, that feeling comes, primarily, through lateral connections—connections to other scholars at roughly the same career stage as you. It's easy to see those scholars as your competitors—for grants, publications, jobs, or awards. But seeing other scholars as competitors will probably just make you bitter and jealous and paranoid. If you go that route, you end up perpetuating both the hidden curriculum and the problematic cultures that created it. Instead, then, I would recommend seeing those other laterally positioned scholars as your support group. They're the people who understand best what challenges you're facing. They're the ones you can commiserate with and the ones you can work with to make academia—future academia—the kind of place you want it to be. So, if someone else wins the award or gets the job or gets that article published, cheer them on; don't tear them down or smear them behind their back. That way they'll be more likely to do the same for you.

What to Wear

One of the questions I often hear about conferences is "What should I wear?" Ultimately, the answer depends on your discipline and on where you are in your career. Academics in general aren't known for being especially stylish, but there are some disciplines where standard dress is more formal (i.e., business suits) and others that are *very* casual (i.e., T-shirts and jeans). Most professors don't have special outfits for conferences—they'll wear the same things to conferences that they wear to teach. So you can use their teaching outfits as a guide.

That said, there's also plenty of clothes-choice variation within every discipline. And you can use that variation to choose the version of "appropriate" that makes you feel most confident. If putting on a business suit makes you feel powerful and smart, go with that. If you don't wait until the last minute, you can usually find suits at a fairly affordable price. My spouse works in university administration, in an office where suits are the norm. He signs up for emails from places like Express and Banana Republic and J. Crew and then waits for the big sales (usually twice a year) to replace the ones that are worn. If a suit will make you feel awkward and uncomfortable, though, that's okay too. There are plenty of other options that work just as well. A well-fitting pair of dress pants or even dark jeans, a dress shirt or blouse, and a sweater or blazer is almost always fine.

Layering actually works well for academic conferences. It might be hot and humid outside, but the conference rooms are usually on the chilly side. The last thing you want when you're already feeling nervous is to be shivering cold.

While we're on the topic of comfort, let's talk shoes. Buying a stylish new pair for your first big conference is sure to end in blistered and bandaged feet. At the very least, take some time before the conference to break them in. Or, better yet, opt for a trusty old pair you know will be comfy. When you're hiking around the conference center or back and forth to different hotels, there's a good chance you'll be logging thousands of steps a day. You'll make it a whole lot farther and faster if you're not hobbling in pain.

The same thing goes for bags. Especially if you're not staying at the conference hotel, you might want a bag to carry around all the stuff you'll need throughout the day—presentation notes, laptop, charger, notebook, pens, business cards, tissues, bandages, stain wipes, water bottle, snacks, and so on. You can opt for a shoulder bag to carry all that, but if your bag is as full as mine, you'll probably end up with a sore, red shoulder by the end of the day. If a backpack will get the job done and be more comfortable, just go with that.

* * *

These tips on what to wear and what to bring will help you when you're heading to conferences, and they're similar to what you'll need for job interviews too. Along those lines, chapter 11 will turn to the topic of job hunting. We'll talk about how to identify the (academic or nonacademic) jobs you want and how to write your applications to show employers they want you too. We'll talk about formal and informal interviews, negotiating job offers, dealing with long waits, and staying calm along the way.

Chapter 11

NAVIGATING THE JOB MARKET

 W. Carson Byrd @Prof_WCByrd · Jul 25, 2018

I don't hide this reality [the fact that non-tenure-track positions now account for over 70% of all instructional staff appointments in American universities] from grad students, but talk to them. As @JessicaCalarco kicked off, the #HiddenCurriculum builds imposter syndrome and misinforms students about academia's labor market and alt-ac jobs, making it more difficult to be successful/ employed and understanding why.

As we talked about in chapter 1, grad school should be a means to a bigger end, not the end in itself. Unfortunately, though, going to grad school doesn't guarantee you'll get the job you want, at least not right away, and maybe not at all.

Employment prospects for students with graduate degrees just aren't as good as they once were.[2] In academia, for example, the percentage of tenure-track positions has decreased in recent years.[3] Instead, universities are hiring more "contingent" faculty, including those with non-tenure-track positions and those, like adjuncts, who are employed only part-time.[4] Even outside of academia, going to grad school doesn't guarantee you'll get a great job or even a job right away. Surveys of recent doctoral degree holders have found that more than a quarter of students don't have jobs lined up when they finish their degree.[5]

Now, those numbers might seem scary, but they don't mean you shouldn't go to grad school or that you should drop out before you're done. Workers with advanced degrees (e.g., master's degrees, professional degrees, and doctoral degrees), at least in the United States, still have higher median earnings and lower unemployment rates than do workers with just a bachelor's degree.[6] Essentially, going to grad school won't guarantee an immediate job offer, and it won't guarantee you'll get the exact job you want, but it can still be the right choice in many fields. That's especially true if you're realistic about your options and strategic in aligning your short-term and long-term goals.

In this chapter, we'll talk about the job options you'll have with your degrees. We'll talk about how to choose between those options and how to tailor your application materials for the different routes you might pursue. We'll talk about what to do if you get an interview and what to do if you don't. We'll talk about negotiating final job offers, dealing with waiting-game anxiety, and being flexible about where the future might go.

In those discussions, we'll go into more detail with academic job options than nonacademic ones. That's because the range of nonacademic jobs you can do with a graduate degree is so wide that it could fill a whole book. So I'll give some general advice here and suggest few additional resources you should check out as well. That includes Imagine PhD and myIDP, both of which are free online career exploration tools that can help you identify career options and plan your path post-degree. You might also check out Christopher Caterine's *Leaving Academia: A Practical Guide*, Susan Basalla and Maggie Debelius's *"So What Are You Going to Do with That?" Finding Careers outside Academia*, and Karen Kelsky's *The Professor Is In: The Essential Guide to Turning Your Ph.D. into a Job*.[7]

Academic Jobs

Doctoral degree programs are generally designed to prepare their graduates for careers in academia. While universities hire lots of employees with graduate degrees (lawyers, graphic designers, human resources managers, computer network engineers, etc.), we'll focus here on jobs involving teaching and/or research in a college or university setting. What those academic jobs entail—and how you go about getting one—depends on the institution you'll work for and the type of academic (e.g., professor, lecturer, researcher, postdoc) you'll be. Along those lines, we'll start by talking about different categories of academic jobs. Then we'll talk about the process of applying for those jobs and the things you should consider in deciding which job to take.

Institution Types

In the United States alone, there are thousands of colleges and universities, and each one has its own faculty culture. That said, schools can be divided into broad categories, and those categories roughly correspond to differences in faculty life. Those categories include major research universities, regional colleges and universities, liberal arts colleges, community colleges, and for-profit colleges. Let's break down each of those in turn:

Major Research Universities: These schools include a mix of elite private schools and large public schools (i.e., state "flagship" institutions). They typically have well-developed graduate and undergraduate programs, with students pursuing bachelor's degrees, master's degrees, other professional degrees, and doctoral degrees. Research expectations for tenure-track faculty are generally very high, and teaching loads tend to be somewhat lower than at other types of schools (with lots of variation based on titles, tracks, and departments).

Regional Colleges and Universities: These schools, which are generally public schools, include branch campuses of major state universities as well as smaller, local schools. These schools typically focus on undergraduate education, with most students pursuing bachelor's degrees, though they might have graduate programs as well. Research expectations for tenure-track faculty are typically lower than at major research universities, and teaching loads are higher.

Liberal Arts Colleges: These schools, which are typically private rather than public, focus on undergraduate education, with the vast majority of students pursuing bachelor's degrees. Research and teaching expectations for tenure-track faculty vary with the selectivity of the school. At the most selective liberal arts colleges, research and teaching expectations are similar to those for faculty at major research universities, though liberal arts college faculty typically focus on undergraduate rather than graduate teaching. Less selective liberal arts colleges have teaching and research expectations more similar to those for faculty at regional colleges and universities.

Community Colleges: These schools, which are typically publicly funded and operated, also focus on undergraduate education, but with most students pursuing associate's (two-year) degrees or completing other certificate programs. These nonselective schools offer low-cost education for local residents and typically enroll (almost) anyone who wants to attend. Expectations for faculty center almost exclusively on teaching, though some do engage in research, either in their discipline or in the science of teaching and learning.

For-Profit Colleges: These schools, which are private rather than public, and which include a mix of online and brick-and-mortar schools, offer a range of degree and certificate programs for students. Like community colleges, these schools are typically nonselective, but because of their high costs and deceptive marketing tactics, they've been widely criticized for exploiting the students (and especially the students from marginalized groups) they serve.[8] These schools typically hire and pay faculty on a per-course basis and generally don't provide faculty any support for conducting research.

Variations and Expectations

As the above descriptions suggest, different categories of colleges and universities vary in their research expectations, teaching expectations, and support for faculty research. Let's unpack why those variations are important.

Teaching Loads: Teaching loads are typically lower at higher status institutions than at lower status institutions. At the most prestigious research universities and selective liberal arts colleges (sometimes called SLACs), faculty have relatively low teaching loads, such as 2–2 or even 2–1. These numbers indicate the number courses you're expected to teach each year and how those courses are divided across semesters (i.e., 2–2 means teaching two courses each semester, for a total of four courses a year, while 2–1 means two courses one semester and one course in another, for a total of three courses a year).[9] If you work at a research-focused school and you have grant funding, you might also be able to "buy" yourself out of some of your teaching responsibilities and spend the extra time on research.[10]

At less-selective liberal arts colleges, less-prestigious research universities, and regional colleges and universities, faculty typically have higher teaching loads, such as 3–3 or 4–4. Faculty and instructors at community colleges and for-profit colleges, meanwhile, sometimes teach upward of six classes per semester, especially if they're being paid on a per-class basis (more on this in a minute).

Research Expectations: Higher teaching loads means less time for research—there are only so many hours in a day. Because of that, research expectations for faculty also vary across different types of schools. At the most prestigious research universities and selective liberal arts colleges, for example, you'll probably be expected to spend at least 40 percent of your time doing research, and you'll be evaluated for hiring, tenure, and promotion almost exclusively on that part of your work.

At less-prestigious research universities, regional colleges and universities, and less-selective liberal arts colleges, you might be expected to have some engagement in research, but the expectations for research productivity will be lower, and your teaching will probably count more toward hiring and tenure than it would at other schools. Meanwhile, at a community college or for-profit college, the research expectations are minimal, and your job will depend almost entirely on the courses you can teach.

Support for Research: Research and teaching expectations are also closely aligned with universities' financial support for faculty research. Major research universities, for example, often provide at least some support for research, including (initial) funding for research and research infrastructure (e.g., lab space), administrative support with grant writing and grant management, research libraries and computing infrastructure, and the opportunity to hire grad students and postdocs to serve as research assistants. These "start-up" funds and other forms of support are typically offered as a part of a recruitment package and are intended to jump-start research productivity.

That support, however, can come with strings attached. The more start-up funds you get, for example, the stronger the expectation to secure external grants. If you get an external grant, some of that money goes back to your university. Universities tack on an "indirect rate" to grant funding that works like a tax and is used to fund support and services related to faculty research. If you got start-up funds, they might have come, at least in part, from the indirect returns on someone else's grant.

If you end up at a major research university, you might also be expected to cover a substantial portion of your salary with grants. Academic positions are typically paid on a nine- or ten-month basis—any "summer salary" you get will have to come from grants. Meanwhile, with some research-only positions, you'll have to find grants to pay your whole salary. Being dependent on grant funding (or what's often called "soft money") can be stressful, as it forces you to be constantly applying for grants. As we talked about in chapter 6, those grants are extremely competitive, and the chances of success are often very low.

Meanwhile, at other colleges and universities where research expectations are lower, you probably won't face as much pressure to get grants. That said, you probably also won't get start-up funds, and the university will probably offer more limited support for research. That lack of support can make it difficult to do and publish research. At the same time, your salary will still probably be paid only over nine or ten months. And so if you can't make that money stretch over the full year, you might still find yourself applying for grants or taking on additional work (like teaching summer classes) to make ends meeting during summer months.

Variations across Titles and Tracks

As we've talked about so far, what it means to be a faculty member depends, in part, on where you teach (or don't teach). That said, there are also variations within institutions, based on your title and track. Broadly speaking, those variations break down into four categories: tenure-track faculty, full-time non-tenure-track research faculty, full-time non-tenure-track teaching faculty, and part-time faculty. Here's an overview of what those categories mean in terms of salary, job security, support, and responsibilities:

Tenure-Track Faculty: These faculty have already received or are eligible for tenure (for a discussion of what tenure means, see chapter 3). Some tenure-track faculty are hired exclusively to do research or engage in other "clinical" types of work. Others are expected to do a mix of teaching and research. Still others focus almost exclusively on teaching. Across those categories, though, tenure-track faculty are generally paid more and have more job security (especially post-tenure) than other, non-tenure-track faculty at the same school.

Full-Time Non-Tenure-Track Research Faculty: Such faculty are employees of the university, and they usually get employment benefits like health care, but they aren't eligible for tenure. Instead, they are typically hired to work on short-term contracts as part of grant-funded projects. These positions usually have decent salaries, but the salaries come from "soft money," which means the job isn't guaranteed long term. When the funding for your project runs out, you'll have to either apply for additional grant funding or find another job.

Full-Time Non-Tenure-Track Teaching Faculty: Like non-tenure-track research faculty, such faculty are employees of the university, and they usually get employment benefits like health care, but they aren't eligible for tenure. Instead, these faculty (often called lecturers) are hired on short-term contracts that commit them to teaching particular classes and that rarely provide support for research. Lecturer contracts are generally renewable—you might end up teaching at the same college or university for your whole career, but you might never get a promotion or a sizeable raise.

Visiting Assistant Professors: These non-tenure-track faculty members fall somewhere in between the research faculty and teaching faculty categories. They are typically hired to teach particular classes, but they might also receive some support for research. Unlike lecturer and researcher contracts, though, visiting assistant professor contracts are typically nonrenewable. Instead, you'll generally be expected to work at the university for one or two or three years and then find another job elsewhere.

Part-Time Faculty: These faculty (often called adjuncts) don't typically receive employment benefits from the colleges or universities where they work. Instead, part-time faculty are hired and paid on a per-course basis (often for only a few thousand dollars per course),[11] and they're not guaranteed employment from year to year or even semester to semester.[12] In order to make ends meet financially, you might end up teaching four or more classes a semester, spread across multiple colleges and universities, which will likely make it difficult to find time for research.

Now that you have a sense of the different types of academic jobs you might consider, let's look at the process of finding and applying for those jobs.

The Academic Job Market

As a grad student, I knew I wanted an academic job. I had done a few summer internships outside of academia (one in education policy research, one in market research). I liked the applied work I was doing in those jobs, but I missed having the freedom to pursue my own research interests, and I missed working with students. Essentially, I wanted the kind of perfect-balance-of-research-and-teaching professor job I had seen as an undergrad and that had inspired me to go to grad school in the first place.

That said, I also knew that my chances of getting that kind of job, at least statistically speaking, were slim. There were well over a hundred sociology and sociology-adjacent jobs posted the year I went on the market (I tracked them all in a spreadsheet). But only a portion of those were jobs for which I was a clear or even partial fit. That included "open" sociology jobs looking for the "best" candidate they could find, regardless of research focus or method. It also included jobs looking for the kind of sociology I do—someone focused on education or family or inequalities, or someone who specializes in qualitative methods. There were also some jobs in education schools and schools of social work that were open to sociologists doing the kind of work I do. Even for those clear fit jobs, though, I knew I would be only one of hundreds of qualified applicants.

Ultimately, and after considering location-related constraints (more on this later), I narrowed my list to about sixty jobs, plus a few postdoctoral fellowship positions. In the end, I got two phone interviews, three on-campus interviews, and two job offers.

Now, I was extremely lucky to get two job offers. I knew plenty of other grad students who didn't get any interviews at all. And yet my family couldn't understand why I would want to take a job so far from home. "There are plenty of colleges around here," they told me. "Why would you want to move so far away?"

Nearly ten years later, my family still doesn't really understand the academic job market. But it helped a little when I explained it with the analogy of someone training to be an elementary school art teacher. Some elementary schools can't afford to have a full-time art teacher, and those schools that can afford an art teacher usually only have one. Most teachers, in turn, have twenty-five- or thirty-year careers, which means that even an elementary school that can afford a full-time art teacher probably won't hire one very often. So if you're training to be an elementary school art teacher, it could take a while to find a job, especially if you want the kind of job you trained for. Having a degree from a more prestigious school might help, and being an especially good artist or an especially good teacher might help, but it's not a guarantee. And so if you want or need a job right away, you might end up having to move long distances, take a part-time job with limited salary/benefits (i.e., substitute teacher), or take a job in a different field.

Now, an analogy like this one can help you explain the basics of the academic job market to skeptical family members and friends. But there might still be some parts of the job market you don't understand yourself.

Career Trajectories and the Variable Value of Postdocs

If you're feeling a little confused, then the first thing to know is that academic hiring operates differently across disciplines and across different types of schools. Everything from what qualifications you need to be eligible for an academic job to what materials you'll need to submit with your applications and what the hiring process looks like—all of that can vary.

In the lab sciences, for example, it's rare for grad students to get an academic job immediately after finishing their degree. Instead, most finish a postdoc (or multiple) before they get their first academic job. Some research-based nonacademic jobs in the sciences are also more likely to hire postdocs than newly minted PhDs. Thus, if you're in a lab science field, and if you're interested in faculty (or nonacademic research) jobs, then a postdoc should probably be your first stop after you finish your graduate degree.

When you're considering various options for lab science postdocs, it's important to choose carefully. As in grad school, you'll probably be applying to work with a professor in their lab. Unlike in grad school, though, you'll probably be expected to develop your own project for your postdoctoral research. Thus, even more so than in grad school, the environment where you do your post-doc, and the kind of project you complete while you're there, should be clearly aligned with the kinds of research environments you want to work in and projects you hope to complete, long term, in your career. For example, if your long-term goal is to be a professor at a selective liberal arts college, it makes sense to develop a postdoctoral research project that can be accomplished with the resources (core facilities, laboratories, personnel, etc.) that are typically available at those institutions. When you're considering various postdoc options, you should talk candidly with your potential advisors about what elements of your postdoc research you'll be allowed to take with you to start your own lab. You should also revisit those conversations periodically as you continue toward the completion of your project and toward your first academic (or nonacademic) job.

In the social sciences, arts, and humanities, getting a postdoc can sometimes improve your chances on the job market, especially if you're interested in tenure-track jobs at major research universities. That said, postdocs aren't generally required for faculty jobs in social science, arts, and humanities fields. Instead, and unlike in the lab sciences, postdocs in these fields often operate as a backup option for students who are interested in tenure-track positions but whose CVs aren't quite full enough when they finish their degrees. In line with that backup-option status, postdocs in the social sciences and humanities typically provide only one or two years of funding, usually without an option to renew. What that means, in turn, is that you'll be applying for the postdoc in the fall of one year (usually while you're finishing your dissertation), moving to a new university that next summer, and then immediately going back on the job market again either that fall or the following.

With all those transitions, it can be hard to focus on using your postdoc to finish and submit the publications you need to build up your CV. That's especially true if your postdoc comes with teaching obligations, which will leave you with even less time for research. Thus, if you're a student in a non-lab-science field, I would recommend considering postdocs only if you are deeply committed to pursuing a tenure-track job at a major research university, and only if an extra year or two has a high chance of significantly increasing the number of published manuscripts (and especially highly placed manuscripts) on your CV. If you're considering that option, I'd strongly urge you to sit down with your advisor to talk about the kinds of jobs you want long term, how far along you are with various manuscripts, and how much you'll likely be able to get done with one or two extra years.

Getting the Inside Scoop

When you're ready to go on the academic job market—whether you're getting a postdoc first or not—it's important to have a sense of how things work in your field and what kinds of academic jobs you might want in the end.

Thankfully, some parts of the academic job market are relatively transparent. In most disciplines, for example, academic job postings (at least for more junior positions) are publicly posted and follow a standard timeline for applications, interviews, and hiring. If you join your discipline's professional organization, you can probably sign up to receive email notifications about open positions. In many fields, those notices start going out between July and October, with applications due, usually, between August and December. On-campus interviews typically happen between November and February, with job offers going out a few weeks after that, and with the whole negotiation process usually wrapped up by March or April. That said, the hiring timeline also varies across disciplines and across schools.

To help applicants make sense of those variations, some disciplines have online job market forums. These include official forums, usually sponsored by major professional organizations, where universities post information about their open jobs. These also include unofficial forums where (mostly) anonymous scholars share information (and sometimes speculate) about which positions are available, who is on the market (including grad students, postdocs, and professors looking to move), who is on the "short list" for various positions, who is getting interviewed, and who will get what job. Those unofficial forums might seem helpful, especially if you're desperate to know where you stand. But I'd recommend avoiding them if you can. The information on unofficial forums can be inadvertently or even deliberately wrong. Users hoping to increase their own chances of success sometimes post misinformation to lead their competition off track. Furthermore, and because of the competitiveness of the academic job market, those unofficial forums can sometimes turn into a cesspool of jealousy-induced and often deeply harmful posts about individual scholars or departments or about the job market as a whole. Thus, if you decide to use those online forums, enter knowing that the information you encounter might be biased in ways that are intended to hurt you or someone else.

Regardless of where you find information about academic positions in your discipline, it can be helpful to do some digging before you decide to apply. Look at official school and department and faculty websites. Follow scholars from those departments on Twitter and possibly reach out to grad students there for inside scoops. Ask your advisors for info they can get through their social networks, and ask if they can set up meetings for you to chat with scholars or grad students at those schools.

That kind of digging can help you decode what the job ads really mean. Some job ads, for example, are vague, even though what the department wants is actually very specific. The job listing might say that a department is looking for someone who specializes in "quantitative methods." Given that language, it's easy to assume that anyone who uses quantitative methods in their work would be qualified to apply. In reality, though, the department might actually be looking for someone who is recognized in the *development* of cutting-edge quantitative methods, but they're keeping the language vague just in case no one with those qualifications applies. Other job ads are specific when what they really want is actually vague. The job listing might state that the area of specialization is "Education, Religion, Race/Class/Gender." Now, the department might want someone who can teach classes in all those areas, or they might have a specific scholar in mind. Another possibility, though, is that the hiring committee couldn't agree on what type of scholar to hire, so the job ad includes all the various options they'd consider.

Doing a little background digging can also help you get a sense of the climate you'll encounter in a particular department or school. In this case, I mean not meteorological climates (though that might matter in your decision) but social and work climates. What's the balance of senior faculty to junior faculty, and are decisions made democratically or from the top down? Is there a lot of infighting between faculty, or do people mostly get along? What does the faculty look like in terms of its racial/ethnic and gender composition, and are faculty from marginalized groups as likely to get tenure as their more privileged peers? Does the university have family-friendly policies, and are faculty actually encouraged to use them? Can faculty afford to live near campus, or do most people commute from far away?

These are only a few of the questions you'll want to ask when you're considering different schools, but getting some information up front can help you narrow down the list before you even apply. That kind of information can also be particularly helpful for when your own decisions are limited in some way.

Choices and Limits

In any given year, there might be a hundred or more academic jobs to which you could reasonably apply. Maybe you're in a position where you can apply to all those jobs and take the highest status one you can get.[13] But maybe you're not. Maybe your partner is also on the academic job market, or maybe they have a job already and don't want to move. Maybe you have kids, or you're planning to have kids, and you want to live near your extended family. Or maybe your parents or your siblings need you nearby to help. Maybe you're already exhausted by the constant competition for grants and publications and you would prefer a more teaching-focused or lower-pressure program. Or maybe you want to avoid particular geographic locations or schools because of the social climate (or the meteorological climate) you might find there.

Essentially, there are good reasons why you might want to limit your job search, and it's okay to decide that way. Your job is only one part of your life, and you want to find a job (or at least set yourself up to get a long-term job) where you won't be miserable every day. The kind of job where you'll be able to achieve the balance between work and nonwork life that we'll talk more about in chapter 12.

That said, if you make your job decisions based on factors other than the status of the program, you might get funny looks (or even snide comments) from faculty members or other grad students in your department. That's because the status of your grad school or postdoc department is determined, in part, by how well it places its students. Essentially, to rise in the rankings or maintain its current ranking, your department needs as many students as possible to land in tenure-track jobs at major research universities. Because of those status concerns, your department might focus on preparing you for only those jobs. Faculty members or fellow grad students might even show disinterest (or even outright hostility) if you intimate that you're interested in nonacademic or teaching-focused jobs or jobs at lower status schools.

Given those risks, it might be tempting to imply to other people in your program that your options are open, even if they're not. And ultimately that may not be a bad strategy to take. At the same time, and if you think you're interested in nonacademic or nonelite jobs, you can also look for advisors and mentors who have experience preparing students for those other career tracks. Because, ideally, you want at least one or two people in your corner who won't shame or ignore you because of the kind of academic (or nonacademic) job you ultimately take. To find those supportive mentors, I'd recommend checking out faculty CVs. Many faculty members will list their current and former students on their CVs. Look for faculty members whose former students haven't all taken the fast track. Talk to those faculty about how they helped students prepare for different types of careers. And reach out to those former students. Get their take on how to navigate the formal systems of status-driven advising to get the support you really need.

Tailoring Your Materials

Whether you're primarily interested in research jobs or teaching jobs, support from faculty can help you get the experience you need for the job you want. Schools with a focus on teaching, for example, don't just want the runners-up—the research-focused applicants who didn't publish enough manuscripts or get enough grant money to be picked for a job at an elite research school. Those schools want applicants who care about teaching, who have experience teaching, and who have demonstrated themselves to be high-quality teachers and mentors. So if you're interested in teaching jobs, you want to make sure you have those qualifications, and you want to make sure your applications materials reflect your commitment to supporting the students they serve.

That said, and given the realities of the academic job market, you might want to apply for a wide range of jobs—some research-focused, some teaching-focused, and maybe even some nonacademic positions. In that case, you want to tailor your materials for each type of job. That tailoring process takes time—you might spend a full month or more prepping, revising, and adapting your job market materials. But it's worth the time to show potential employers that you're as interested in them as they should be in you.

Along those lines, I'd recommend asking around for examples of recent (and ideally successful) job applications in your field. You can ask the junior professors in your department. Or other students who graduated in the past few years. Those examples can give you a sense of your discipline's norms regarding how much to write and how detailed to be. They can also help you see how other scholars have tailored their materials for different types of jobs.

Cover Letter: Your cover letter is your sales pitch, and the product you're selling is you. So don't sell yourself short, and be sure that the product you're selling is the product your buyers need. That means tailoring your cover letter—and especially the first and last paragraphs—to show you're the right person for the job.

How do you make that case? By linking your experience and qualifications to key words from the job ad. And by using the evidence from your record to back up your claims. So, for example, if the job listing is for an expert in quantitative methods, describe yourself in those terms (provided that's true of course). You might say, "Given my contribution to the development of cutting-edge quantitative methods, and given the breadth of quantitative methods employed in my published research, I am keenly interested in and well qualified for the assistant professor position in your department."

Don't get too technical, at least in the first paragraph. You want that first paragraph to make sense to anyone who reads your cover letter, which might ultimately include faculty members, grad students (who, in some departments, serve on hiring committees), provosts, and deans. There's a good chance the administrators in that group won't be scholars in your field, and the faculty and grad students probably specialize in different subfields, which is why they're hiring someone like you. So keep the front end of your letter focused on why you're a good fit for the position, and then get into the rest of your record later on.

Now, it might feel uncomfortable to write about your own accomplishments, particularly in a sales-pitchy kind of way. If that's the case, pretend you're writing about someone else—someone you really admire. Then ask a close friend or fellow grad student to read your materials, help you cut any self-deprecation and strengthen your "this is why I'm a great fit" claims.

CV: Your cover letter might technically be the first file in your application, but there's a good chance that before even reading your cover letter, the hiring committee will flip to your CV. As we talked about in chapter 3, a CV is essentially an academic résumé. But rather than offer a one-page summary of your accomplishments and qualifications, it lists all the accolades you've gotten and all the research, teaching, and service you've done.

There are lots of ways to organize a CV, but you don't want to think too far outside the box. Instead, look for examples to follow (including the ones in Appendices A–C). Find the web pages of recently hired assistant professors and check out the format they use. In general, you'll want to include:

- Your academic appointments, if you've had any[14]
- Your degrees and expected degrees, the schools that granted those degrees, and when you got or will get them
- Your published, conditionally accepted, and forthcoming research (with separate sections for research that is and isn't peer reviewed)[15]
- Your in-progress research (including pieces that are currently under peer review and/or are developed enough that you would feel comfortable sharing them with the committee)
- Any grants or fellowships you've received
- Any patents you've filed
- Any awards or honors you've received
- Any guest lectures, presentations, or academic talks you've been invited to give[16]
- Any conference presentations you've given
- Any teaching experience you have
- Any students you've mentored
- Any service you've done for your department, your university, or your discipline (e.g., serving on committees, coordinating workshops, organizing conference events, reviewing manuscripts)

- Any professional organizations you belong to
- Any relevant work experience (e.g., as a research assistant to a faculty member, as an employee or intern at a research organization or in another related field)
- Any relevant community engagement (e.g., work with volunteer organizations, advocacy groups, practitioners, or policymakers as well as public writing)
- Any media coverage of your research

There's not a whole lot of job-specific tailoring you can do with your CV. But you can play around with the ordering to emphasize the parts of your CV that are most relevant to the position. And you can also (sparingly) use bolded or italicized text to highlight key words.

Research Statement: Your research statement gives context to your CV. Rather than just list all your publications and in-progress work, it summarizes your contributions to your discipline and makes the case that you're an emerging expert in a particular subfield. Of course, as a grad student or postdoc, you're probably not a nationally recognized expert—someone who gets quoted in the *New York Times* and asked to serve on all the panels and committees. But that's the kind of scholar that many universities (and especially major research universities) want because having scholars with that kind of visibility makes the university look good.

Along those lines, a good research statement makes the case that even if you're not yet a nationally recognized scholar, there's a chance you someday will be. To make that case, you want to show that you're able to secure funding for your research, publish your research in high-impact outlets, make important contributions to your field, and build on those contributions to identify new questions to answer in your research. At the very least, you want the reader to come away from your statement with the sense that you've been productive so far and that you'll continue to be productive in the future.

Because hiring committees might not read past the first paragraph, it's helpful to start with a one-paragraph overview of your research-based accomplishments and contributions to the field. You can start with something like: "As an emerging expert in the area of [RESEARCH], I have published in high-impact [FIELD] journals and also won an award from [ORGANIZATION] for my research." After that, it's helpful to point to the primary theme of your research and to explain (briefly) why that theme or phenomenon is important to understand.

Now, maybe you're struggling to find a single theme that captures all your research; it's okay to have wide-ranging research interests. That said, it's also important to show that you can make a clear contribution to one area of work. That kind of focus gives you a clear identity as a scholar, and it's perceived (rightly or wrongly) as a sign that you'll become the kind of well-known, highly respected expert that many universities want.

That said, there are ways to bring diverse interests under a larger umbrella. In my own job-market research statement, for example, I talked about how my research primarily uses qualitative methods to examine inequalities in education and family life. Within that larger framework, I then have multiple lines of research focusing on specific mechanisms that produce those inequalities (e.g., parent-child interactions, student-teacher interactions, and peer interactions).

Once you identify the broad theme of your research and the various lines of research that fit into that theme, you can then organize the rest of the research statement into subsections around those various lines of research. Within each subsection, identify the research questions you've answered and the questions you plan to answer with future work. Point to specific publications and in-progress projects that answer those questions. And explain the contributions those publications and projects have made or will make to the field.

In terms of tailoring, you can reorder the various sections of your research statement, starting with the lines of research most relevant to that particular job. Beyond that, you can also add key words from the job ad (where appropriate) to highlight the link between what you do and what they want. And you can point to specific attributes of the department or school that will allow you to be successful in your future research. For example, if the department has other scholars working in your subfield, you could mention those scholars by name and say that you're interested in collaborating with them on future projects. Or if the university has a research center that relates to your work, you could write about wanting to get involved with the center and connect with other scholars doing similar research. Ultimately, you want to show the hiring committee that you're as interested in them as they should be in you.

Teaching Statement: With your teaching statement, the goal is to show the hiring committee that you'll be an effective teacher and that you can teach the kinds of classes they need. Again, because hiring committees have to consider large numbers of applications, it helps to summarize the most relevant information in the first paragraph. That means pointing to the areas mentioned in the job ad and your qualifications for teaching graduate or undergraduate courses on those topics. From there, you'll also want to include a brief overview of your teaching philosophy, your teaching experience, any awards you've received for teaching, and any contributions you've made to the science of teaching and learning. Then, in the rest of the statement, unpack each of those points in turn.

In terms of your teaching philosophy, identify the core goal or ideal that motivates your teaching. Maybe your primary goal is to help students develop critical thinking skills. Or be better writers. Or take action to address the injustices in our world. Whatever your philosophy, provide clear evidence to back up your claims. Say how you've achieved that goal in your classes or, if you haven't taught your own classes, how you would plan to do so in the future. Point to specific activities or assignments you've used (or would use). Discuss what students learned (or could learn) from those efforts. Then tie it all back to your teaching philosophy at the end.

In terms of your approach to teaching, talk about how you engage (or will engage) your students. Given the benefits of active learning,[17] many universities and departments prefer to hire instructors who do more than just lecture in class. If you're not familiar with active learning pedagogy, or if you think you could use a primer, I'd recommend visiting your university's teaching center (or at least visiting its web page). Most teaching centers will have workshops you can take and possibly even certificate programs you can complete. If your university doesn't have a teaching center, or if you want to go beyond the programs offered there, I'd also recommend checking out a few books on teaching, including Barbi Honeycutt's *Flipping the College Classroom*, Norman Eng's *Teaching College*, and Ken Bain's *What the Best College Teachers Do*.[18]

In terms of your teaching experience, don't just list the courses you've taught (or assistant taught). Instead, use evidence from the courses you've taught (or helped teach) to make the case that you are (or will be) an effective teacher. Identify the learning objectives for each of your courses, and explain how you achieve those objectives in class. Do you lecture or engage students in small-group activities? Do your students take exams or write papers or complete final projects? Whatever approach you take, explain how that approach aligns with your goals for that specific course and with your teaching philosophy more generally.

In talking about your teaching experience, it's also helpful to point to the progress you've made. No one expects you to be an award-winning teacher the first time you teach a class. But they do want to see that you're able to handle challenges in the classroom (large class sizes, limited support, mandated textbooks, students with varied levels of preparation, etc.). And they want to see that you're learning from any mistakes you make.

Along those lines, let's talk a bit about teaching evaluations. We know from research that those evaluations are both biased against instructors from systematically marginalized groups and also not particularly effective for distinguishing between more competent and less competent teachers.[19] And yet hiring committees and deans will almost certainly look at your evaluations and use them to judge your teaching skills. If your evaluations aren't as great as they might be, use your teaching statement to contextualize and explain those results. Maybe you set high standards in your classes, and your students were frustrated that they couldn't get an easy A.[20] Or maybe you had to keep students engaged despite being required to use a textbook or teach in a space that students didn't like. The goal here isn't to be defensive about your evaluations. Instead, focus on providing context for those numbers and reframing them in terms of the work you've done and will continue to do in class.

Thankfully, teaching evaluations aren't the only evidence you can use to show whether you're an effective teacher. Teaching awards, teaching certificates, participation in teaching-related workshops, and contributions to the science of teaching and learning (i.e., publishing in a teaching journal or publishing teaching materials in online databases) are all good signals of your strengths as a teacher and your commitment to quality teaching in higher ed. So be sure to include those accomplishments in your teaching statement.

Teaching Portfolio: In addition to your teaching statement, most job postings will request that you submit a teaching portfolio. This is essentially a curated set of documents that provide evidence of the kind of teaching you've done and the kind of teacher you'll be. You can include syllabi you've developed. Assignments you've created. Lecture slides. In-class activities. Teaching-related publications. And copies of any emails or handwritten notes you've gotten from students thanking you for a good class. The goal here isn't to share all the teaching materials you've ever created but rather to offer evidence of the best work you can do.

Diversity Statement: Some job postings will also ask that you submit a diversity statement with your application. In a recent Twitter thread, computational ecologist Dr. Samniqueka Halsey offered a particularly helpful discussion of these sorts of statements.[21] Halsey explained that these statements are a place to explain "your values related to diversity," "your experiences working with diverse populations," and "your future plans related to inclusivity." Halsey also noted that the schools and departments requesting these types of diversity statements typically have a strong commitment to supporting students and scholars from systematically marginalized groups and that they're looking to hire new faculty members who will also support that commitment.

Along those lines, a good place to start in a diversity statement is by stating your own commitment to diversity, equity, and inclusion. If those words are all you have, though, there's a good chance you won't get the job. There will be plenty of other excellent scholars out there who not only care about diversity and equity and inclusion but also have actively demonstrated that commitment in their career. Essentially, and as with all other parts of your job application, evidence is key.

If you want to be able to show your commitment to diversity, equity, and inclusion, you have to do the work. In terms of research, choose projects that illuminate systems of oppression or have potential benefits for people from marginalized groups. Carry out those projects with a keen understanding of your own positionality (i.e., recognizing the power you have relative to that of the people you're studying).[22] Critically interrogate your own default assumptions about which types of data to gather, how to gather those data ethically, and how to report those data responsibly. Think beyond your own networks to identify potential collaborators (including faculty, grad students, and undergrad students) from systematically marginalized groups, encourage those collaborators to take a leadership role, and be sure to give them credit for that work. Also, when writing about your work, be sure to cite the work of other scholars from marginalized groups.

In terms of your teaching, support diversity, equity, and inclusion in your classroom and help your students understand why diversity, equity, and inclusion are important to achieve. Build your syllabi around the work of scholars from systematically marginalized groups. Emphasize that work when you're talking about research in class. Talk with your students about the hidden curriculum in college and how it unfairly privileges students and scholars from already privileged groups. Educate yourself about the resources available on campus and point your students to those resources—including resources for students struggling with food insecurity and housing insecurity, depression and anxiety, learning disabilities, personal and family emergencies, bias and discrimination, or sexual harassment and abuse. Serve as a resource for your students. Encourage them to visit you during office hours. Encourage them to share their questions, their ideas, and even their suggestions for improving the course. As a professor, I can learn as much (or more) from my students as they do from me, but that learning happens only if I put aside my own ego and make it clear to students that I am open to really hearing what they have to say.

In terms of your service, work to support people from marginalized groups on campus, in your community, and in society as a whole. Look for student groups and community organizations that are doing the kind of work you value. Volunteer your time and your expertise. In doing so, though, take time to really listen. Especially if you're a member of a more privileged group, don't assume you know what they need better than they do, and don't assume they'll automatically want your support.

If you do the work of diversity, equity, and inclusion, then writing your diversity statement should be fairly easy—just talk about what you've done and what impact you've had in the process.

That said, there are also some things to avoid in writing such statements. As political scientist Dr. Ian Hartshorn recently pointed out on Twitter,[23] scholars sometimes use diversity statements to talk about their "vicarious exposure to underrepresented minorities," saying things like "my best friend is [A PERSON OF COLOR]" or "my wife is [A PERSON OF COLOR]." While that kind of vicarious exposure might've shaped your views about people from marginalized groups, and while it might've increased your commitment to supporting diversity in higher education, it isn't evidence of that commitment in and of itself. Writing your statements that way amounts to "virtue signaling"—it suggests that you want to be seen as someone who wants to support diversity, equity, and inclusion without providing any evidence to back up that claim. Thus, and as sociologist Dr. Zawadi Rucks-Ahidiana went on to argue in that same Twitter thread,[24] if you are going to mention your interactions with people from marginalized groups, you should focus on "the students of color and colleagues of color you do research with. The students of color you've taught and mentored."

When you're writing a diversity statement, you also want to avoid language that might be perceived as out of date or out of touch. As Halsey explained on Twitter,[25] she and other scholars use the term "minoritized" rather than "minority" to refer to people from marginalized racial and ethnic groups "because we are not born to be discriminated against, it is something, done to us."[26] Similarly, and in a recent blog post, grad student Nadirah Foley discussed critiques of the phrase "women and people of color," which, because it conflates womanhood with white womanhood, "constitutes an act of erasure, or at least a lack of attention to the intersection of racial and gendered disenfranchisement that we [Black women] experience."[27] Of course, language is a fluid thing, and it's possible that the terms we're using now will be considered inappropriate ten or twenty or fifty years from now. But that doesn't mean you should just throw up your hands and use whatever words you choose. Instead, it's important to educate yourself (i.e., by reading the work of scholars from marginalized groups) and to make your language choices fully informed.

Statement of Faith: If you're applying for a job at a religiously affiliated school, you might also be asked to write a statement of faith. These schools typically have a religious mission and they want to know that you're, at the very least, aware of that mission and willing to support it in your work. What "supporting the mission" means, though, varies a lot from school to school. At some schools you might be expected to follow and promote a particular religious faith in your teaching, research, and even personal conduct. At other schools, the expectations might be looser, or they might be only minimally enforced.

Along those lines, it's important to know what the rules are and how they're enforced before you decide to apply. Read the school's mission statement carefully. Talk to your advisor and find out what they know. Also check out the CVs of the faculty at those schools and the lists of courses they teach. Try to get a sense of whether the kind of research and teaching you do (or want to do) would raise any red flags.

If, after getting more information, you still want to apply, then it's time to write your statement of faith. In most cases, it's okay to keep these statements brief. You don't need a lot of detail about how you'll "support the mission" in your work. Just write a brief statement explaining that you understand the university's values (echoing the university's language) and that you pledge to uphold those values as an employee.

In some cases, though, you might be asked to write a little more. Specifically, you might be asked to discuss your own relationship with religion and spirituality. If you're a member of the faith affiliated with the school, or if you're a member of a closely related faith, writing a statement like that might be fairly easy and comfortable. You can talk about your experiences as a member of that faith and how they inform your values or your work.

If you're not a member of that faith, you have some harder choices to make. One option is to openly state that you aren't a member. Another option is to be vague about your own religious affiliation (if you have one at all). Either way, you can still pledge to uphold the school's religious values. That decision, though, might ultimately be one that you don't morally feel you can make. And if that's the case, then you can certainly be honest about your misgivings about supporting the school's religious mission. That choice might ultimately hurt your chances of being hired, but you have to weigh that risk against the risk to your own integrity. And you might ultimately decide that if the school won't accept you for your moral commitments, it's not the kind of place you want to be.

After the Application

After all the time and effort you put into researching various positions and tailoring your application materials, it can feel like a relief to finally click "send." At that point, and at least for a short time, the whole hiring process is (mostly) out of your hands. That said, the time between when you send in your application and when you hear anything back can start to feel like an eternity. Especially since some hiring committees might never contact you at all.

The longer that wait drags on, the more you might find yourself spiraling into anxiety and self-doubt. And it's okay to feel nervous or frustrated, but it's also important to take care of yourself. Talk to the people in your life (as best you can) about why you're feeling worried or stressed. Ask them for patience and understanding and some extra TLC. Commiserate with other grad students on the job market, and commit to supporting and cheering each other on, no matter what the outcome might be. And especially if it gets to the point where your fears and frustrations prevent you from continuing on with your work, consider seeking professional counseling as well (see chapter 8 for whom to contact and how).

Getting help with those anxieties is important because you'll need to use the time while you're waiting to hear back about job applications to press forward with your work. You'll need to prep and practice your job talk so you'll be ready if you get an interview (more on this in the next section). You'll need to keep working on your dissertation. You'll need to work toward finishing more manuscripts to send out for review.

If all that research work turns into new R&Rs or new grant funding or a new award, you can email the hiring committees to let them know. Send your updated CV and a brief email explaining that you applied for the open position in their department and that you wanted to make sure they have the most up-to-date information possible when considering your application. That said, it's important to save the updates for major news—publications, grants, awards. If you send hiring committees an update every time you make a slight edit to your research statement, there's a good chance they'll get annoyed. It's also important to remember that there are people behind those processes. Those people aren't just human resources representatives. They're the faculty (and sometimes grad students) who will be your future colleagues, and they're probably going to use their interactions with you—including their digital interactions with you—to make a judgment about what kind of colleague you'll be.

Interviews

While you're waiting to hear back about your application, you'll probably want to start prepping a presentation about your research. Now it can feel strange to prep a job talk (or what's sometimes called a "chalk talk") before you get any invitations for interviews. But you'll want to leave plenty of time to write, revise, and practice what you'll say. And once you do get a call or an email asking you to visit for an interview, things move fast. You'll have only a week or sometimes only a few days before you'll have to get on a plane.

Job Talks and Chalk Talks

If you get an on-campus interview for a tenure-track academic job, you'll almost certainly have to give a talk about your research. In some disciplines, job talks focus on current research. You'll be expected to describe what you found in your dissertation or other recent research, and you'll be expected to talk briefly about how your future research will build on what you found. In other disciplines, chalk talks are the norm, and they focus on future research instead. You'll be expected to outline (literally by writing on the board) the specific aims of the grant proposals you're planning to submit and the research you're planning to do with those grants.

Regardless of which form these talks take in your discipline, the point is to show your potential future colleagues what kind of colleague you'll be. They'll be looking for evidence that your research (or your proposed future research) complements and extends research already being done in the department. They'll be looking for evidence that you can communicate clearly and be an effective teacher. And they'll be looking for evidence that you can think on your feet and respond to constructive criticism. Essentially, the faculty, staff, and students attending your talk are looking for evidence that you'll be a great researcher, teacher, and colleague.

We already talked a good bit about presenting your research in chapter 9, so I'll focus here on how to structure your job talk or chalk talk to highlight your strengths as a researcher, a teacher, and a colleague. I'd also recommend checking out the American Society for Cell Biology's blog post on designing and giving good chalk talks and "Tips for a Successful Job Talk" by education professor Dr. Stephen J. Aguilar in *Inside Higher Ed*.[28]

In terms of showcasing your skills as a researcher, your job or chalk talk should clearly highlight your contribution (or potential future contribution) to the field. Use what you know from existing research to point to an important and unanswered question in the literature. Use your expertise in research methods to explain why your approach is a good fit for the question at hand. Use your analytical skills to build an argument and present evidence that supports your claims. Show your research matters by talking about the implications for research, policy, and practice. Then situate the research you talk about in a larger research trajectory, explaining not only what you have done but also where you plan to go from here. That future-facing strategy gives your audience (and potential employer) a sense that you haven't run out of good ideas. That you're ready and motivated to continue with a long career of high-impact research.

Job talks and chalk talks focus on your skills as a researcher, but some schools will also want to get a sense of how you teach. During those interviews, you might be asked to give a separate guest lecture or teaching talk for students. In that case, the point is to show you can teach students about an important topic in your field and do it in an engaging way. If you've taught a class before, pick your best lesson and go with that, maybe with a few adjustments to better highlight how you can fill the department's teaching needs. If you haven't taught a class before, pick something close to home. Start from your own research and build out from there, using it to teach the class about an important topic or idea related to your work. Also, don't be afraid to get creative—small-group discussions, whole-class activities, and other innovative pedagogical strategies are all fair game, even if you're "teaching" a bunch of experts in your field. The key is to show that you can keep a group of students interested and engaged for an hour or more.

Even if you're not asked to teach an actual class, your job talk can still be a preview of what kind of teacher you'll be. Your talk, for example, should make it clear that you can present complex concepts in an engaging and easy-to-follow way. It might be tempting to go full expert—to name-drop every theorist and every jargon term you know. That might impress one or two people in the audience, but it runs the risk of alienating a whole lot more. Instead, then, define your terms and avoid jargon when you can. Plan your talk with a clear logical structure and walk your audience through your argument step by step. Make eye contact during your presentation and, to the best of your ability, call on people by name. That approach shows you're interested not only in doing the research but in communicating that research effectively.

Another place you'll showcase your teaching skills is in the Q&A. When you're teaching, you never know what questions your students are going to ask. You have to be ready for anything. And the Q&A works the same way. You might get hypothetical questions like "What would you have found if you studied Case B instead of Case A?" or "What would have happened if you used Method X instead of Method Y?" Or you might get questions that are framed more like comments and that never seem to come to a point. The key in those moments isn't to show you know the right answer but to show you can think on your feet. That you can identify the heart of what the person is actually asking or trying to say (e.g., "Do your findings generalize to other cases? Did you think carefully about your methodological choices? Do you know the relevant research on this topic? Did you consider other possible explanations for what you found?"). And that you can respond in a way that demonstrates your knowledge, your respect for your future colleagues, your willingness to engage in academic debate, and your confidence in your own expertise.

The more you practice your job talk and the better you know your data, the easier it will be to come up with effective responses to tough questions. If you get stuck, though, it's okay to admit what you don't know. In that case, you can say: "That's a great question. I don't have the data in front of me to answer right now, but I will certainly get back to you with an answer by email ASAP." Or: "That's a great suggestion. I hadn't considered that possibility, but I'd love to talk more about how to go about testing it with future work." Along those lines, be sure you have paper and pen handy during your job talk and jot yourself notes about the questions people ask. That way you can collect your thoughts a moment before answering and also follow up after with more information as well.

Ultimately, you want to use your job talk to show your potential future colleagues what a great colleague you'll be. Try not to get defensive if someone criticizes or questions your work. Try to show you appreciate constructive feedback and that you can be respectful and grateful for that feedback, even when you disagree. Try to show that you're open to the possibility of collaborating with colleagues and working with grad students, too.

The On-Campus Interview

Your job talk or chalk talk isn't the only thing people will use to get a sense of what kind of colleague or teacher or researcher you'll be. Instead, and if you get invited to give a job talk on campus, you'll probably have two or three days full of meetings with deans, faculty, staff, grad students, and sometimes undergraduate students. Everything you say in those meetings—and in the emails or phone calls leading up to and following those meetings—is on the record. That means that almost everything you say and do could matter for whether you'll get the job.

It's important to do your homework and go in well prepared. When I went on interviews, I made myself cheat sheets with pictures of every faculty member in the department and descriptions of their research, and I studied them on the plane. That way I would remember who I was talking to and have things I could ask them about if they ran out of questions for me. I also tailored my job talks to include key references to work by department faculty and recent department grads. I spent time researching the schools where I was interviewing and the communities around those schools. From the job candidates I'd seen in my own department, I knew that it could break a case if an applicant didn't have a good answer for "why do you want to work here?"

Being prepared for the on-campus interview also means being prepared for the long slog the whole visit entails. You might have a few slots of downtime during your visit, but you'll probably need to be "on" for hours at a time. So whenever anyone offers you a bathroom break, take it, even if you don't need to go. It'll give you a minute to clear your head. Also bring a bag or backpack with a few essentials—breath mints, bandages (you'll probably do a lot of walking around campus), notebook, pens, and maybe a protein bar in case there's a long stretch between meals or in case you're asked to talk through your meals and don't get a chance to eat.

There will probably be meals with department faculty and students. If you have allergies or other dietary needs, tell the staff person who helps you with the logistics for your interview. Especially if you're polite and grateful, that person will probably be happy to help to find restaurants that'll work for you. At dinner and maybe even at lunch, the faculty you're with might propose having some alcohol. It's okay to drink if others are drinking, but if you don't drink or don't want to drink, that's totally fine. If that's your choice, you don't have to explain—the faculty or students you're out to dinner with will probably just assume you want to be totally lucid during the interview.

During your on-campus meetings, and especially during informal meetings like meals, you might encounter inappropriate questions or comments about your life outside work. You might, for example, be asked about your family situation—such as whether you have a spouse, a partner, or kids, or whether you're planning to have kids in the future. In many places it's illegal for employers to ask prospective employees those questions. The idea is that keeping those details secret will prevent the hiring committee from making decisions about you based on factors other than your qualifications for the job.[29] Those laws, however, aren't enough to prevent faculty members or deans from asking inappropriate questions or making inappropriate comments (e.g., "I see you're wearing a wedding ring") during interviews. If you get those questions, you can choose not to answer, but seeming cagey could (unfortunately) hurt your chances of getting the job. Instead, then, you might think about how to answer those questions if you get them. And you might think about decisions you could make (like not wearing a wedding ring) to reduce the chance you'll get those questions at all.

At the same time, you might want to talk with potential employers about your family situation. You might want to know: "Is my partner eligible for a spousal hire? Is there affordable child care near campus? What are the university's policies regarding family leave?" As the job candidate, you're allowed to ask those questions, though I'd recommend waiting to ask them until after you get an offer because at that point, you're in a far better bargaining position than before you get the job.

While you might want to wait to ask some questions, there are plenty of others that you can and should ask during your job interviews. Questions to learn more about your potential colleagues. And questions to learn more about the school and the local community.

With deans and with faculty, you might ask about:

- How many courses you'll teach each semester
- How many new courses you'll be expected to prep before tenure
- What kind of teaching support you'll get (e.g., graduate or undergraduate teaching assistants)
- What the students are like
- What the department and university expect, research-wise, for tenure
- What support the department provides for research (e.g., start-up funds, research assistants)
- How often faculty get sabbaticals (if they get them at all)
- What types of departmental and university service are usually assigned to junior professors
- How decisions get made in the department
- What faculty meetings are usually like
- What the department's relationship with the administration is like
- What they like best about the department
- What they would change about the department if they could
- What types of mentoring support are available for new faculty
- Where most faculty live
- What the community around campus is like

With students, you might ask instead about:

- How the graduate program is structured (e.g., coursework, teaching, exams)
- What the undergraduate students are like
- What kind of support they get for their research
- What they're looking for in their professors and advisors
- What relationships among grad students and between grad students and faculty are like
- How faculty involve (or don't involve) students in their teaching and research
- What they like best about the department
- What they would change about the department if they could
- Where most grad students live
- What the community around campus is like

Once you finish your visit, it's good form to send brief "thank-you" emails to each person you met during your visit. The notes don't have to be long. Just two or three sentences is fine. But personalizing them a bit shows you're really interested in the position and the people you met. Something like: "Thanks for taking the time to meet with me during my visit. It was great chatting with you about . . ." or "I really appreciated your question about . . ." or "Thanks for the suggestion about . . ."

After the interview, you'll probably also have to deal with navigating reimbursement requests. Some departments will purchase your flight and your hotel for you and cover all your airport shuttle rides and meals. That makes it much easier, logistically, in that you don't have to pay anything (or at least not more than transport to and from your home airport) up front. Other departments, though, will ask that you pay those costs yourself and save the receipts for reimbursement at the end. If you don't have the money to cover it, or if you can't wait three months to be reimbursed, it's okay to tell the staff member or the faculty member coordinating your visit. They might be able to pull some strings to get it all worked out. That said, university rules around money tend to operate like steel traps, so there might not be anything they can do.

Off-Campus Interviews

Now, not all schools or departments have money for a full round of on-campus interviews. Those schools typically invite a handful of students to do phone interviews or videoconferencing interviews or in-person meetings at conferences. Then they use those interviews to either make a final decision or choose one candidate for an on-campus interview.

The prep work for off-campus interviews is less intense than for on-campus interviews, but you still want to be prepared. Do enough research to get a sense of the school, the department, the faculty, and the students. Then tailor your interview answers to match their needs. Departments with limited budgets, for example, are typically smaller than big-budget schools. That means higher teaching loads, more course preps, and more service as well as less time devoted to research. Thus, you'll want to show when you answer questions that you understand what those departments are looking for and that you're ready and willing to work within the constraints they face.

As with on-campus interviews, it's polite and respectful to send brief thank-you emails to the faculty you spoke with during your interview. Departments with small budgets don't want to feel like your second choice. And if they get the sense you're treating them as your backup option, they might treat you as their backup option too.

Negotiating Offers

Maybe all those interviews will turn into a job offer. Maybe even more than one. The first thing that usually happens in that process is that you'll get an informal offer, with some rough details about salary, teaching loads, and support for research and teaching. At that point, you'll have the opportunity to negotiate—to ask for changes to your contract. If you have only one job offer, it might feel risky to negotiate. You don't want the job offer to suddenly disappear. That said, negotiation is a normal part of the process, even if you have only one offer. And the dean or department chair will usually be willing to negotiate, at least a little, because they've invested time and resources in recruiting you and they don't want you to suddenly disappear either.

Ultimately, and regardless of how many offers you get, it's important to approach negotiations with respect for the people involved and with a clear understanding of each department's constraints. At public colleges and universities, for example, you'll typically have less room to negotiate salary than you would at a private school. Departments at public colleges and universities often face strict limits on their regular budgets. At those schools, salaries might also be publicly listed, which creates pressure to keep pay fairly consistent across faculty, particularly within the same rank. That said, departments at public colleges and universities may still have some room for negotiation, particularly around one-time expenses and other types of support.

Along those lines, things you might consider negotiating include:

- Salaries: It can feel awkward and uncomfortable to ask for a higher salary than what you're offered. But raises in academia, and especially at public colleges and universities, are few and far between. You might not have another opportunity to negotiate your salary until you get tenure or until you get a job offer from another school. Thus, it's important to ask for a base salary that will let you make ends meet and achieve the kind of financial security and stability that will help you be successful in your job.
- Start-Up Funds for Research: Some schools can provide start-up funds for research-related expenses (lab equipment,

research assistants, access to data or other materials, books, etc.). These funds vary widely across disciplines, and they tend to be *much* higher in the natural sciences than in the social sciences and humanities. Because these are one-time expenses, they are sometimes more negotiable than salary.

- Travel Funding for Conference Attendance: As we talked about in chapter 10, conferences are expensive. Thus, if your department expects you to attend academic conferences, you can ask for money (either in lump sum or each year) to help offset those costs.

- Moving Expenses: Taking an academic job usually means changing cities or, sometimes, moving halfway across the world. Given the expense involved, it's appropriate to ask for help covering some or all of your moving costs.

- Office/Lab Equipment: Most schools will provide you with a basic setup—office space, computer, desk, and chair. If you want anything fancier, though, or if you need specific equipment for your work, you can negotiate for that up front as well.

- Course Releases: You might request a one- or two-course reduction in your teaching load during your first year. If you're able to get a reduction, I strongly recommend taking it during the second semester of your first year rather than during the first. It might feel overwhelming to teach your first semester, but with moving and getting set up at a new school, you're probably not going to get much research done that first semester anyway. And so if you want to use your course releases to focus on research, you'll be better off doing that once you're feeling settled in.

- Research and Teaching Assistants: Depending on the size of the department and the number of graduate students, you might be able to negotiate for help with your teaching and/or your research.

- Course Requests: Prepping new courses takes a huge amount of time and effort. Along those lines, you might ask

for limits on the number of new courses you'll be expected
to prep, especially in your first few years. You might also
request to teach specific classes that align well with your
research and teaching interests. And you might ask to teach
those classes at specific days and times.

- Spouse/Partner Accommodations: If you're being recruited
for a tenure-track faculty job, you can ask about the possibility of hiring of your spouse or partner as well. These
types of spousal hires are most commonly used for couples
where both partners are academics, but in some cases the
university might be able to help find jobs for nonacademic
partners who could work in staff or administrative roles
(e.g., lawyers, accountants, human resource officers,
marketing and design professionals, IT professionals).
Those spousal hire positions, though, are rarely guaranteed.
Instead, what you're negotiating for is the opportunity for
your spouse or partner to interview for a job in a department or school or administrative unit relevant to their
work. After your spouse or partner's interview, that department or school or administrative unit will decide (in
conjunction with the university administration) whether
your spouse or partner will be offered a job. If, in the end,
only one of you is offered a job, you'll have to decide
whether it's worth it.

There's no guarantee your negotiations will be successful. That
said, a few successful requests can go a long way toward making
life a little easier and making you more effective in your teaching
and research.

Dealing with Disappointment

Of course, there's a chance things won't work out as planned. You
might not get your dream job. You might not get a job at all. That
kind of rejection can feel like a devastating blow, but it doesn't

make you a failure, and it doesn't mean you should give up hope. Instead, it just means you'll need to be strategic about what you do next.

Let's start with the scenario where you don't get any academic job. One option is to delay getting your degree and go back on the job market again the next year. This can be a particularly attractive option if you have manuscripts in the pipeline that just haven't hit quite yet. Waiting an extra year can give you time to push more of those manuscripts toward publication—maybe turn an R&R into a conditional accept or a draft into an R&R. Waiting an extra year, though, can also come with real costs. Your department, for example, might not be willing or able to fund you for another year of research. That might mean taking out thousands of dollars in loans.

If you're in that situation, it might be worth looking into other short-term options instead. Postdocs, for example, can act as a bridge between your degree and your first academic job. The hiring process for postdocs varies across disciplines and departments. In some cases you might apply for a postdoc the way you'd apply for an academic job, with a very similar set of required materials and a similar process for on-campus interviews. In other cases postdocs are negotiated informally, through back-channel conversations between your grad school advisor and faculty at other schools.

As we talked about at the beginning of the chapter, postdocs are effectively required in many of the lab sciences, and they're becoming increasingly common in other fields. In those fields, postdocs can give you a year or two or three to work on building up your CV. That said, and as we also talked about in detail at the beginning of the chapter, it's important to be cautious about postdocs if they're not the norm in your field. Getting a postdoc, for example, almost always means relocating. If you have family obligations or location restrictions, that might not be an option for you. In some fields, postdocs are also so short (one or two years) that it's hard to get much done. By the time you move to a new city, get settled, and get started with your research, you have to immediately go back on the job market again.

Given those limitations, and if a postdoc won't substantially increase your chances of getting an academic job, you might also consider looking for nonacademic jobs instead. We'll talk more about the nonacademic job market in the next section.

In the meanwhile, let's consider another short-term option for moving forward if you didn't get your academic dream job. In that situation, you might take an academic job that isn't the one you want long term. Maybe that's a tenure-track job at a school in a place you don't love—maybe because your partner or your extended family lives in a different city or because the community in that place isn't friendly toward people like you. Or maybe you have a visiting assistant professor position where you'll have to move in a year or two, even if you want to stay. Or maybe you like where you live but you're working as an adjunct teaching multiple classes and still struggling to make ends meet.

If you want to move, and especially if you want to move to a higher status school, you'll have a steep road ahead. You'll have to do more research, publish more research, and publish more high-visibility research than your colleagues have to do. Essentially, you'll have to show, with your research productivity, that you're a good fit for a higher status position than the one you already have. And you'll probably have to do it without the support of your colleagues, because there's a good chance they won't be thrilled to help you prove you deserve something better than them. Meanwhile, you'll also have to keep going back on the job market. Maybe not in the first year. But probably by the third year and possibly again and again every year after that.

That's a hard battle to keep fighting. And, eventually, if you're stuck and you're really not happy where you are, you might find yourself looking for nonacademic options instead.

Nonacademic Options

Thankfully, having a master's or doctoral degree opens the door to all kinds of careers—careers in research, business, nonprofits, government, policy, education, and health care, to name just a few. Which careers specifically though will depend in large part on your discipline and your degree.

Unfortunately, your advisors might not be much help when it comes to navigating the nonacademic job market or helping you find a nonacademic job. On the nonacademic job market, your networks often determine which jobs you know about and which jobs you can get.[30] Many professors, in turn, aren't well connected to experts outside of academia. They might have a few friends from grad school who went the nonacademic route. Or they might have contacts from their preacademic careers or nonacademic consulting. But, ultimately, the bulk of the searching will probably be up to you.

That said, there are resources to help you identify and map out paths into various nonacademic careers. That includes online career development tools you can use to explore career options and create a plan for pursuing those jobs post-degree:

- **Imagine PhD** is a free online career planning tool that'll help you identify careers related to your discipline, make and follow a professional development plan to get on the right track for those careers, and ultimately find jobs that are a good match for your interests, training, and skills. Imagine PhD is geared toward doctoral students (or graduates of doctoral programs) in the humanities and social sciences.[31]
- **myIDP** is another free online career planning tool that'll help you identify your career-relevant skills, interests, and values, then map them onto particular careers. It'll also help you plan and carry out the steps to take in pursuing the kind of career you want, and it'll help you identify open

jobs in those fields. This resource is geared toward doctoral students (or graduates of doctoral programs) in the lab sciences, engineering, and mathematics.[32]

These online resources are especially useful for big-picture career planning. They'll help you identify which skills and credentials you'll need for particular jobs. They'll help you put together a timeline for acquiring those skills and credentials. They'll point you to resources you can use along the way.

Along those lines, you might find that if you want a particular job post-degree, you'll need some training or experience that isn't offered as a standard part of your graduate or postdoctoral program. Maybe you'll need an internship in government or industry or in the nonprofit or arts sector. Maybe you'll need additional training on cutting-edge research methods that your professors don't yet know. If you find yourself in that position, then the summers during grad school can be good opportunity to get the extra experience or training you need. In terms of finding those opportunities, you can ask your advisor for recommendations, and you can also check out some of the resources below.

Depending on your field, you might be able to find relevant internships or summer work opportunities through online lists and search tools, including:

- USA Jobs,[33] an online search tool for finding jobs and internships with the federal government, including through:
  - The Pathways Programs for current college and graduate students and those who recently completed their degrees[34]
  - The Presidential Management Fellows Program for students pursuing advanced degrees[35]
  - Washington Headquarters Services, which places current students and recent graduates in administrative and operational support jobs[36]

- New York Foundation for the Arts, which maintains an updated list of open jobs and internships in the arts[37]
- On Think Tank's list of policy "think tanks," with links to information about internships and careers[38]
- Bridgespan's Nonprofit Job Board, which has current listings for jobs and internships at nonprofits and NGOs (nongovernmental organizations) in the United States and abroad[39]

You might also check out a few specific organizations that regularly hire grad students and postdocs:

- The National Institute of Standards and Technology (NIST)
  - NIST Professional Research Experience Program (PREP)[40]
  - NIST NRC Postdoctoral Research Associateships Program[41]
- National Endowment for the Humanities Internship Program[42]
- Smithsonian Office of Fellowships & Internships[43]
- Pew Research Center, an organization that conducts public opinion polls and demographic and data-driven social science research[44]
- Gallup, a research and polling organization[45]

If you need additional training beyond what you can get as part of your graduate program, you might also look into nondegree workshops and training programs, including:

- The ICPSR Summer Program in Quantitative Methods of Social Research[46]
- Duke University's Machine Learning Summer School[47]
- The University of Michigan School of Public Health Big Data Summer Institute[48]
- The University of Chicago Summer Institute in Social Research Methods[49]
- Emory University School of Public Health Summer Qualitative Research Workshops[50]

- European Consortium for Political Research Summer School in Methods and Techniques[51]
- Research Talk's Qualitative Research Summer Intensive at the University of North Carolina[52]
- Syracuse University's Institute for Qualitative and Multi-Method Research[53]

These are only a few among many options you might consider for outside experience and training during grad school. For more discipline-specific opportunities, I'd recommend heading to your professional organization's website, which is likely to have information about internships and training programs specific to your field.

Your professional organization and your university career office can also point you to specific nonacademic job postings. The University of Michigan's Career Center, for example, has a great list of resources on its website, including tools for identifying which types of jobs best match your skills, links for accessing job postings across various fields, and blog posts about navigating the whole nonacademic job search process.[54] Columbia University's Career Center, in turn, has links to career-related resources broken down by field, including higher education administration, government, nonprofits, publishing, consulting, marketing, and more.[55] Whether you turn to your career center, your professional organization, or websites like CareerBuilder, ZipRecruiter, or LinkedIn, you'll want to visit frequently and keep an eye on the new online listings because the available offerings can change week to week and even day to day.

Prioritizing Options

While the academic job market has some options in terms of location, status, and work-role expectations, the nonacademic job market is far more varied. Thus, as you're considering your various career options, it's important to think strategically about what matters most to you in your career. You might be particularly interested in having a job with flexible hours or one that doesn't come home with you at night. You might be interested in a job that allows you to continue doing research without academia's pressure to publish. Or you might be interested in having a job with a more direct impact on the world, maybe in policy development or administration or nonprofit work. Identifying your priorities can help you narrow down your options and start prepping early for the kind of career you want.

* * *

Whatever job you take, the transition from grad school to work will probably be a little bumpy. New colleagues. New routines. Maybe a new home and a new city (or even a new country). All that change can be overwhelming, even if you end up with the job of your dreams.

Managing all those changes will be easier if you already have good strategies in place for juggling the different parts of your job and for balancing work and life outside of work. To develop those strategies, you'll want to start early, while you're still in grad school. That's where we'll turn in our final chapter. We'll talk about how to be an effective teacher and colleague while still finding time for research. And we'll talk about getting all that work done while still making time for yourself.

Chapter 12

BALANCING TEACHING, RESEARCH, SERVICE, AND LIFE

Devon R. Gross @DevonRGross · Jul 22, 2018

Replying to @JessicaCalarco

On my visit to my grad school program, I let myself be convinced that the program requirements to teach a 2/2 every semester (!) after your MA were an "advantage because all the teaching experience you'll have will help you get a job."

One of the things I love most about having a career in academia is that I get to wear a lot of hats. Not literal hats, of course, but hats in the sense of different roles. I get to read and spend time dreaming up new research ideas. I get to design those projects and do the work of gathering and analyzing data. I get to write about research for academic and nonacademic audiences. I get to design and teach classes and mentor students. I get to review manuscripts and give other scholars feedback on their work. I get to serve on committees with thoughtful colleagues, and I get to give back to my department and my university and my discipline while also pushing those organizations to be the kinds of organizations I want them to be.

With all those different hats to wear, my job is never boring. But wearing all those hats can also be challenging—for professors and for grad students and for postdocs. It's hard to keep track of all those hats and remember to wear the right one at the right time. The more hats I acquire (especially with parenthood and post-tenure service expectations), the more I become the kind of absent-minded academic I swore I'd never be. Having to wear all those different hats also means that there's always more work to be done than time to do it. To get the edits for this book done on time, and amid other writing deadlines, teaching assignments, service commitments, and personal stuff, I spent four months getting up at four or five o'clock so I could work for an extra hour or two before my kids got up for the day.

Given the challenges of wearing all those hats, you might find yourself tempted to do nothing but work, or you might find yourself too tired and overwhelmed to do any work at all. That's where we turn in this final chapter. We'll talk about how to keep track of the hats you'll wear in grad school and in the rest of your career. We'll also talk about why it's hard to balance research and teaching and service and how to be more efficient and effective with all three. Finally, we'll talk about the pressures of academia—the pressure to be the best, to love your work, and to work all the time. We'll talk about how those pressures can make it hard to justify making time for yourself, your family, your friends, and your community.[2]

Of course, which hats you wear and when will depend on your discipline, your department, what kind of degree you're getting, and what kind of career trajectory you're planning post-degree. In terms of teaching, for example, you might teach your first class in grad school or when you get your first faculty job, or you might never teach at all. In terms of administrative responsibilities, you might be leading a research team as a grad student or as a postdoc, or you might do solo work your entire career. In terms of service, you might be asked as a grad student to serve on committees for your department, your university, or your professional organization, or you might be able to skirt those obligations until you get your degree. These variations are important to consider when you're choosing a program up front and also when you're considering different career options down the road. My hope is that this chapter will help you understand why those variations matter and what it takes to be good (or good enough) at all the parts of your job.

Managing Your Wardrobe

When you have closet full of hats—student hats, research hats, teacher hats, service hats, and personal ones—it's important to plan which one you'll wear when. If you don't take time to plan, you might end up just wearing your favorite hat all the time or the one that's hardest to take off.

So how do you plan your wardrobe? Here, it helps to imagine that we're planning our wardrobe for a trip. The first step is to choose a destination—decide where you want to go in each hat. The second step is to figure out how you're going to get there, including the stops you have to make along the way. The third step is to figure out when you'll take each leg of your journey. And the fourth step depends on how much time, if any, you'll have left over when you finished the journey you've planned. If the route you've planned will take more time than you have, then the fourth step is to figure out how to cut back—either on the number of stops on your route or on the amount of time you spend at each stop. If, instead, you have more time than you need to make all the stops you've planned, then the fourth step is to decide which hat you want to wear a little longer and how to find more stops you can make in that hat. Let's talk through each of those steps in turn.

Choosing Your Destination

To figure out which hat to wear and when, you first have to know where you're going. For that, you have to think about your longer term goals. The National Center for Faculty Development and Diversity recommends starting with a five-year plan that lays out your key personal and professional goals. Applying that approach to our hats and trips metaphor, you'll want to think about all the destinations you want to get to and which hat you'll be wearing when you're there. That might look something like this:

- Student/Academic Hat: Finish your coursework; finish your qualifying exams.
- Teacher Hat: Teach your first course.
- Researcher Hat: Finish your dissertation; get an academic job.
- Personal Hat: Run your first marathon.

Mapping Your Route

Once you know where you want to get to in each hat you wear, you can start mapping the routes you'll need to take to get there. The goals above, for example, including finishing your dissertation, starting to teach your own classes, getting an academic job, and running your first marathon along the way. Each of those big goals involves dozens of smaller steps. And certainly you don't have to break down each of those tasks into what you'll do day by day, at least not at this stage. But it can be helpful, for each of your big goals, to map out roughly what you'll do and when.

Let's say, for example, that one of your goals for the next year is to pass your qualifying exams. You might break down that goal into concrete steps as follows:

- Develop reading list.
- Read everything and take notes.
- Take practice exam.
- Take final exam.

Now, that's a good place to start, but it's not enough to really get you to the level of knowing what you have to do each month or each week or each day. So I'd suggest breaking it down further. That more detailed list of concrete steps might look something like this:

- Develop reading list.
  - Find sample lists (e.g., from friends).
  - Review sample lists.

- Develop list outline (organized by thematic section).
- Add relevant items from sample lists.
- Add relevant items already read.
- Add relevant items not on sample lists.
- Meet with advisor to discuss list.
- Revise based on advisor's feedback.
- Send final list to advisor for approval.
- Read everything and take notes.
  - Find sample note outline.
  - Revise sample note outline as needed.
  - Read items in Area A.
  - Enter Item 1 into citation software.
  - Read Item 1 strategically.
  - Complete note outline for Item 1.
  - Repeat for Items 2–N.
  - Write memos for Area A.
    - Key concepts
    - Key theories
    - Key debates
    - Key methods
  - Repeat for items in Areas B–N.
- Take practice exam.
  - Find sample questions.
  - Revise sample questions as needed.
  - Send sample questions to advisor.
  - Ask advisor to conduct practice exam.
  - Write practice exam.
  - Meet with advisor to discuss practice exam.
- Take final exam.
  - Meet with advisor to schedule exam date.
  - Confirm exam date with committee.
  - Send reminders to committee.
  - Complete assigned exam.
  - Meet with advisor/committee to review completed exam.

If you plan your routes with this level of detail, you'll have a much better sense of how to get where you want to go. If you're not sure how to get to that level of detail, though, it's okay to ask for help. In chapter 2, we talked about finding an advice person who understands the ins and outs of academia and who can help you strategize about which steps to take in achieving your goals. If you're stuck at the not-so-detailed planning stage, bring your rough draft plan to your advice person and ask them for help in filling out the rest. You can also ask them for advice about how much time to plan for each step you'll have to take along the way.

Adding Necessary Pit Stops

Now, you can build a whole route around getting to your big goal destinations. But if you focus just on getting to the destination, you might miss some necessary stops you have to make along the way.

In each of the hats you wear, there will probably be some tasks you have to do, even if they don't build quite as directly into your larger goals. In your student hat, for example, you might have to attend class meetings, read for class each week, write weekly memos or do weekly problem sets, and finish a bunch of course papers by the end of the semester. Meanwhile, in your research hat, you might have a must-do list of tasks for the professor you work for along with your own set of must-do tasks like getting IRB approval or filing the paperwork for your grant renewal. If you have a teaching hat, you'll have must-do tasks for that role too. If you're a teaching assistant, for example, you might have to attend class meetings, do the readings, prep discussion questions, meet with students, grade papers and exams, and do whatever other teaching-related tasks your professor assigns to you. Meanwhile, if you're teaching your own classes, you might have to design the syllabus, write your teaching notes, prep slides and in-class activities, write the exams and other assignments, and do all the other things you'd have to do as a teaching assistant too. In terms of your service hat, you might have to go to committee meetings or help plan department events. And finally, in your nonacademic hats, you'll have plenty of must-do tasks too. That includes regular tasks like laundry, dishes, and grocery shopping, taking care of your family, your pets, your houseplants, and of course yourself.

When you're planning the routes you're going to take to get to your bigger goals, it's important to include these necessary pit stops you have to make along the way. These must-do tasks might not build directly (or at least feel like they're building directly) toward your larger goals. But not doing them can sometimes run you off track and keep you from getting where you want to go.

That's why it's especially important to schedule the pit stops you need for taking care of yourself and other key people in your life. Maybe your personal pit stops involve taking a walk or going for a run or doing yoga every day. Maybe you need to have dinner with a friend once a week. Or schedule regular appointments with a therapist. Or attend religious services. Or just zone out for an hour in front of the TV each night before bed. Maybe you need to spend the weekends with your kids. Or take your grandma to her doctor's appointments each week. Or eat breakfast with your partner each day.

Schedule your necessary pit stops before trying to figure out the rest of your trips. Otherwise, it's easy to let work fill up your time and leave no time left for yourself.

Scheduling Your Trips

Once you've mapped out your route and all the stops you need to make along the way, you can move on to the second step in managing your wardrobe of hats. That second step involves scheduling when you'll wear each hat and what you'll do while you're wearing it.

First, make sure you have all your time-specific commitments on your calendar for the week ahead. Maybe you have classes on Tuesdays and Thursdays and Wednesday afternoons, and maybe you have a doctor's appointment on Wednesday morning and a department event on Friday. Block off all those times and set yourself reminders so you'll know where to be and when.

Second, schedule time for the tasks you have to accomplish that week. Maybe you have to read four articles for class, write a response memo, finish a problem set, and grade thirty papers. Plan when you'll do each of those tasks, and don't budget more time than you think you'll actually need. That way, and especially if those tasks aren't your favorite, you won't be tempted to scroll through social media or put away the dishes instead. Also, if you need extra motivation to get these must-do tasks done quickly, reward yourself for the work you do. When you finish each reading for class, take a quick five-minute walk. Or for each five papers you finish grading, treat yourself with a piece of chocolate or a five-minute Twitter break.

Third, look at your larger planning maps and choose which steps in your larger routes you'll try to finish this week. Start with the most important task and find a blank space on your calendar where that task will fit. If that task will take more than one slot to complete, try breaking it up into smaller tasks and slotting each of those into separate spaces. That way you have a clear sense of what to do and when. Then move on to the next most important task, and the next, and the next, slotting those into blank spaces on your calendar as well.

Of course, to know which tasks you can schedule and where on your schedule they'll fit, you have to know, at least roughly, how long it takes (or should take) to finish each task. Learning to estimate those times takes practice. It's totally normal if, the first few weeks you try this, you end up wildly under- or overestimating how much time each task will take. Maybe you'll leave yourself thirty minutes to write an abstract, but it ends up taking two hours. Over time you'll get better at aligning tasks with slots in your schedule. And you'll get faster with routine tasks too.

Along those lines, and especially if you're new to careful scheduling, allot yourself somewhat more time than you'll probably need for each task. That way you won't feel stressed about staying within the schedule, and that way you can celebrate if the tasks you plan take less time than you think you'll need.

Also, don't forget to build in breaks and transition times. If it'll take you fifteen minutes to walk across campus and get set up before class, put that on your schedule. If you have a two-hour block to read four articles for your qualifying exams, block off a five- or ten-minute break between each one.

Planning ahead like this makes it easier to avoid wasting time figuring out what you could be or should be doing. Maybe you have an hour between classes on Tuesdays. If you don't plan what you're going to do in that hour, it's easy to let it slip by—to spend it scrolling social media or catching up on the latest gossip in the grad student lounge. But if you need that time to get everything done, and if you plan ahead, you might use that hour to read two articles you have to read for class. Or you might use that hour to write a cover letter for a fellowship application.

Even small chunks of time become more valuable when you're planning ahead. If I know I have fifteen minutes between meetings, for example, that's when I plan to wear my email hat. Most days, I get more messages than I can manage. For me, that makes it tempting to just ignore them all. Especially since most of the emails I get require more than just a quick response. But if I plan ahead, I can use my small chunks of time to triage the email coming in—responding to messages that just need a quick reply and filing for later those that involve a more complex task.

Planning Tricks and Tools

When you sit down to do all your route mapping and pit-stop planning and calendar scheduling, there are lots of great tools you can use. If you prefer a tactile approach, you might opt for a paper notebook and a physical calendar or planner. Dr. Raul Pacheco-Vega has a terrific set of recommendations for starting and maintaining an "everything notebook" complete with file tabs and color-coded entries.[3] If, like me, you prefer digital options for staying organized, then you might try out tools like Trello for big-picture planning,[4] Todoist for checking off day-to-day tasks,[5] and Google calendar for managing your schedule. Whether you opt for paper or digital, I'd recommend color-coding your calendar to match each of your hats. Maybe you've got a green hat for teaching and mentoring, blue for research, purple for service, and yellow for your personal life. If you color-code, you can quickly glance at your calendar and get a sense of which hat you'll be wearing when.

Of course, things come up last minute. Sometimes you'll have to abandon or completely rework your scheduled plan for the day. For me, for example, a snow day at my kids' school or an urgent request from a student can leave me scrambling to change up what I planned. If that happens, it'll be okay. The better you get at scheduling your time, the better you'll get at rearranging things when you have a sudden change of plans.

At the same time, having a schedule can make it easier to resist the not-so-necessary distractions that threaten to pull you off course. If I have a specific hour blocked off for working on an R&R, for example, or if I have thirty minutes blocked off to prep for class, it's easier to say no if a student requests to meet with me during that time or if a colleague stops by to chat. That's also why I try to work from home two days a week. If I'm not in the office, I'm much less likely to encounter unexpected distractions on days when I need to get a lot done.

Now, route mapping and pit-stop planning and calendar scheduling are helpful, but it's important to remember that they're not ends in themselves. To keep all that planning from becoming a procrastination tool—a way to feel like you're working without actually getting work done—it's important to be strategic about how you plan. That means scheduling a specific time and a limited amount of time each week (ideally thirty to sixty minutes) when you're going to plan. Depending on my own schedule, I typically do my weekly planning either on Friday afternoon (while I still have a good sense of what I've accomplished for the week and what comes next) or on Monday morning (before I jump into new tasks for the week). The National Center for Faculty Development and Diversity recommends Sunday nights as a good time for planning. But for me, with two small kids at home and weekends full of birthday parties and soccer games and trying to get the little one to take a nap, Sunday night is peak exhaustion. So it works better for me if I use that time to rest instead.

Rethinking Your Wardrobe: Cutting Back

Your fourth step in managing your wardrobe of hats will depend on how things go with the third step. After filling up your calendar for the week, you might find you have tasks you need or want to accomplish that just don't seem to fit. In that case, you might be trying to wear some hats more than you reasonably have time for. And, in that case, you'll probably have to find ways to cut back. That might mean cutting back on the number of destinations you plan for each hat. Or it might mean cutting back on the amount of time you spend in each hat getting to where you want to go. Let's talk through each of these in turn.

One way to cut tasks is by stepping back from responsibilities that take up too much time. Maybe you've been serving on an events-planning committee for your department and you've been spending hours a week contacting potential presenters, coordinating rooms and scheduling, and handling all the day-of-event logistics. If those hours are cutting into the time you need for research and class prep and taking care of yourself, then it might be time to pass the torch to someone else (or multiple people). During grad school, I'd recommend not taking on more than one major service commitment at a time, and possibly avoiding any big service commitments at critical points in your program (e.g., when you're studying for qualifying exams or finishing your dissertation or teaching your first class). If you're not sure how to go about stepping back, check out the discussion of cutting ties in chapter 2.

Even if you can't cut back on any of your current responsibilities, you can cut back by saying no to new tasks coming in. Maybe a professor asks you if you're interested in doing some hourly work on one of their research projects. Sure, the extra money would be nice, and you might learn some things from working with the professor. But if you're already overloaded, then adding that extra task might not be worth it in the end. So how do you know which new tasks are worth it? Think about your bigger goals. If adding that new task won't help you move closer to achieving one of your bigger goals, and especially if it runs the risk of pushing you off course, then the easy response is "I have too much on my plate at the moment, but I really appreciate you thinking of me." If you're not sure if the new task will help you, and even if you think it might, don't say yes right away. Instead, reach out to your advice person from chapter 2. If you got the request in an email, just forward it along and ask: "What do you think I should do?" Having someone else give you the go-ahead can make it far easier to say no and can help you figure out when it makes sense to say yes. If you do say yes, however, then it's important to strategize about how you'll cut back in other ways.

If you've cut the tasks you can cut and you've still got more work than time, then the only remaining option is to cut back on the time you devote to each task. In that case, you might recalibrate your standards for work. Focus on doing work that's good enough, at least for some tasks, rather than doing the best you can do. If you're prepping a new class, for example, you don't have to spend days or weeks crafting the perfect syllabus from scratch. Ask a colleague you trust to share their materials and tweak what they've already done. If you ask graciously and respectfully, there's a good chance they'll be willing to share, especially if others shared materials with them. You might say something like: "I've heard from students/TAs who've worked with you that they really enjoyed your class on [TOPIC]. I'm prepping a new class on [TOPIC], and I was wondering if you might be willing to share a copy of your syllabus/assignments/lecture slides for me to use as an example to build on."

Now, there might be some stretches in grad school (and later in your career) when you just can't make enough time. That's especially true if you're juggling academic work with caregiving responsibilities or running a community organization or working another full-time job. During those stretches, it's especially important to rely on the support person we talked about in chapter 2. In those moments of time crunch, it can be helpful to talk to someone who just says "Being that busy really sucks" or "How can I help?" rather than shaming you for being busy or giving you advice on how to be less busy. In those moments of time crunch, it's also okay to just let some things go. I've had monthlong stretches when the laundry piled up taller than my kids. Eventually things ease up, and I dig myself out and get back on track.

Rethinking Your Wardrobe: Adding More Hats

We've talked so far about what to do if, at the end of your calendar scheduling step, you have more tasks than time. But it might not always be that way. Instead, there might be times in grad school when you have more time than tasks. That's especially likely if you're at a phase of your program when you have a long stretch of unstructured time to complete a big, amorphous goal. Maybe you have three months over the summer when you're supposed to be studying for your qualifying exams and not much else you have to do. Or maybe you have a yearlong fellowship and your only major goal for that year is to finish your dissertation research.

As we talked about in chapter 5, those long stretches of unstructured time can be hard to manage, especially if you're not scheduling your own time. The more unstructured time you have, the more tempting it can be to spend that time scrolling through Twitter or doing laundry or bingeing shows on Netflix.

In that case, it can be helpful to add more structure to your time. A good first step might be breaking down your big, amorphous tasks into even more discrete chunks than we talked about in the second step above. If you're studying for qualifying exams, for example, you might put each individual reading on your calendar and allot yourself just enough time to get each reading done. Or if you're working on writing your dissertation, you might start by outlining one chapter down to the paragraph level (the way we talked about in chapter 7), making each paragraph from that outline a task on your schedule, and completing those tasks before moving on to repeat the whole process for the next chapter and the next one and the next.

When you're dealing with long stretches of unstructured time and big, amorphous goals, it's also important to remember to schedule time for wearing your personal hats. When you have a big task on your plate (like studying for qualifying exams or finishing your dissertation), it's easy to feel pressure to work all the time. But if you don't explicitly make time for yourself, you'll probably be more tempted to fall into distraction. And those distraction tasks (like reformatting your CV or revising your teaching notes or reorganizing your closet) generally don't leave you feeling as though you've accomplished any personal goals.

Now, it's possible that even after you've structured your unstructured time and made time for your personal needs and goals you'll end up with more time than you need. In that case, and in the interest of staying motivated without feeling overtaxed, it can sometimes be helpful to add a few new tasks.

So how do you know which new tasks to add? To make that decision, think about which hat you want to wear more often and then add a new goal—a new destination—for that hat. Maybe your research hat is the one you like best. If that's the case, then you might consider adding a new project as a goal. You might even reach out to a professor or a grad school classmate and suggest a project to work on together as coauthors or plan a time to brainstorm ideas. Or maybe your teaching hat is the one you want to wear more often or more effectively. In that case, you might set a goal of prepping a new class or revising one that needs a good update with new assignments or new ideas. Or maybe you want to get more involved in service. For that, you might reach out to editors of academic journals you read and volunteer to serve as a reviewer. You might volunteer to help with committees in your department or your university or your discipline. Or you might get involved with local community organizations. Of course you might also be feeling burned out on research and teaching and service. In that case, you might opt to spend more time in one of your personal hats, picking a goal like learning to knit a sweater or writing a blog.

Whatever hat you decide to wear more of, just be thoughtful about how you add tasks. One at a time is better than many at once. And check in with yourself periodically to make sure that the tasks you've said yes to still meet your bigger goals.

Dealing with Distraction

Planning your wardrobe and making time for your personal hats can help you stay on track to achieving your goals. That said, and especially during those moments when you're not wearing your favorite hat, or when one hat takes you on a route you'd rather not have to travel, it's easy to get distracted or procrastinate on finishing must-do tasks. I'm certainly not immune to distraction and procrastination. If I have a writing project I'm stuck on, or a phone call I don't want to make, or an inbox overflowing with requests, it's easy to find myself scrolling Twitter, looking for a colleague to chat with, doing another load of laundry, or saying "I'll just finish this podcast, first." Now, occasional dips into distraction and procrastination are fine—your brain needs a break from time to time. But if you find that distraction and procrastination are keeping you from meeting your goals, then you might consider trying another approach.

One distraction management approach I really like is called "temptation bundling." This approach, tested by economist

Dr. Katherine Milkman and her colleagues Dr. Julia Minson and Dr. Kevin Volpp, involves "bundling" the things you have to do with things you really want to do and find yourself doing too much.[6] So, for example, if you hate going to the gym but you know you need to work out more, then you can save your favorite TV shows and say you're going to watch them only while you're on the treadmill or the elliptical machine. Or if you're weeks behind on laundry, then you can choose to listen to your favorite podcast only while you're working through that pile of clothes. I do this with Twitter too—I try to scroll only when I'm doing the cool-down walk after my run in the mornings, when I'm walking around campus, and when I'm walking to pick up my kids from school. Essentially, by putting limits on your procrastination-temptation activities, you can do those things you enjoy and complete the tasks you have to do as well.

That said, it's also important to know that struggling with procrastination isn't a sign that you're lazy or not cut out for academic work. Research shows that when we procrastinate, and especially if we persistently procrastinate on certain things, it's because of how we feel about those particular tasks. As psychologist Dr. Tim Pychyl explained in a recent interview with the New York Times, "Procrastination is an emotion regulation problem, not a time management problem."[7]

Say, for example, that you get an email from your advisor asking for a status update on your dissertation. If you're feeling insecure about the amount of work you've accomplished since your last check-in, then you might be tempted to just ignore the email because responding would mean acknowledging the limited progress you've made and confronting the negative emotions (e.g., insecurity, shame, and self-doubt) that go along with that limited progress. Three days later, if that email is still sitting in your inbox, then you're probably feeling not only insecure about the progress you've made but also embarrassed about not responding sooner and worried that your advisor will be angry at you. And in that case, you might opt to just keep ignoring the email—letting it get pushed down by the incoming messages until it disappears.

Of course, email isn't the only task that elicits negative emotions, and insecurity and shame aren't the only emotions that might push you to procrastinate on important tasks. You might be feeling frustrated with a paper you're writing, and that frustration might lead you to push off that project for another day. Or you might be feeling confused about an assignment you're supposed to do for class, so you avoid it rather than admitting your confusion to your professor and asking them for help.

Whatever the cause, though, it's important to recognize those cycles of procrastination when you're in them, and it's important to look for a way out. While procrastination might make you feel better in the short term, chronic procrastination can affect your well-being and even your physical health.[8]

So, how should you deal with chronic procrastination? In that recent *New York Times* article,[9] journalist Charlotte Lieberman offers advice based on evidence from procrastination research.[10] Specifically, Lieberman suggests practicing both self-compassion and self-forgiveness. That means recognizing that perfection isn't possible, being kind to yourself when you make a mistake, not dwelling on past regrets, and seeing your own past moments of procrastination as something you did, not someone you are. In terms of more concrete steps, Lieberman also suggests focusing on just the next step in some bigger task rather than on the process as a whole, and she suggests setting up obstacles that make it harder to procrastinate. That could mean using apps like Freedom that block your access to the internet for predetermined stretches of time. Or it could mean being strategic about where you work. If, for example, your go-to procrastination involves conversations with colleagues, then working from home might help you cut back. If instead your go-to procrastination involves doing laundry, then you might want to work from a coffee shop or the library rather than at home.

* * *

Now that we have a sense of how to manage your hat-filled wardrobe, let's talk about what wearing each hat entails. In grad school, the two hats you'll probably wear most often are your student hat and your researcher hat. Chapter 5 is all about wearing your student hat—staying on track in your program and getting your academic must-dos done. Chapters 6 through 10, in turn, cover the various tasks you'll do in your researcher hat—how to find funding, plan and carry out your research, and write, publish, and present what you've found. Rather than try to rehash all that here, I'll turn to the hats we've spent less time talking about. We'll cover wearing your teacher and mentor hats and wearing your service-related (or what we might call your "good citizen") hat.

Wearing Your Teacher and Mentor Hats

I could probably spend all my time thinking about teaching: developing new syllabi and creative, fun assignments, tinkering with my class notes, coming up with more effective discussion questions and more engaging slides. But just because I could spend all my time that way doesn't mean that I can or that I should. So, instead, I focus on being as effective a teacher as I can be while still getting the rest of my work done.

Being an effective teacher is important because, as a professor, the most direct impact I will probably ever have with my work is on the students I teach (and the students I mentor, but more on that in a minute). Thus, and despite the advice I got as a grad student, I spend far more time on teaching than the bare minimum would require. I spend time reading about what good pedagogy looks like in higher education and why that good pedagogy matters. I spend time developing and reworking my classes to make them effective and engaging for students. That time and effort matters to my students, and it's valuable for me too because there are few things more rewarding than seeing the look on my students' faces when they realize something (especially about themselves and their own lives) that they've never realized before.

At the same time, and when it comes to teaching, I know I have to be effective in an efficient way. That was especially true when I was a grad student and a pre-tenure professor—if I spent all my time on teaching, I wouldn't be able to do enough research to keep my teaching job. Even post-tenure, though, I know I have to be efficient if I want to be able to wear all my other hats. And so, even when I'm tempted to go down a daylong rabbit hole, searching for the perfect new activity for my class, or when I'm kicking myself for taking too long to respond to the dozens of student emails in my inbox, I try to settle for good enough instead.

So, what does it look like to teach effectively and efficiently? The answer to that question will depend on the number of courses you teach, the size of those courses, the level of those courses (i.e., whether they're introductory courses, advanced undergraduate courses, or grad courses), and the content of those courses. That said, there are some general strategies you can use, most of which I learned from years I spent as a researcher observing in elementary and middle schools.

Effective Course Design

Effective (and efficient) teaching starts long before you even set foot in the classroom. It starts with clear goal setting. Essentially, you want to have a clear goal for what students will take away from the course, from each class period, and from each activity you do in class. Those goals don't have to be lofty. The point of a given activity, for example, might be for students to deepen their understanding of a particular theory or concept.

Even if the goals are small, it's important for you as the instructor to know what they are and to communicate them to students. It's a lot like writing a research paper. As we talked about in chapter 7, knowing what argument you want to make can help you develop a clear, logical plan for conveying that argument. It can also help you more quickly and more easily identify the evidence you need to support your claims. Furthermore, by having a clear argument, by presenting that argument logically, and by supporting that argument with appropriate evidence, you're much more likely to convince your students to believe what you tell them and to keep them from getting lost along the way.

Students want to know why they're learning what they're learning. As the instructor, you can and should answer that question for them.

The first step in that process is to figure out what you want your students to learn. Those objectives might be knowledge or skill based. In my Introduction to Sociology class, for example, I want students to understand how their lives and others' lives are shaped by larger social forces. Meanwhile, in my ethnographic methods course, I want students to learn how to gather, analyze, and write with qualitative data. Whatever your objectives, state them clearly on your syllabus.[11] Then, organize the rest of the course—topics, assignments, activities, assessments, etc.—around those objectives and do so in a way that logically builds from one step to the next.

Of course, getting that logical structure "right" isn't easy, especially the first time you teach a course. There might be lessons that left students feeling confused, activities that just fell flat, or exam questions that were too vague or difficult to really gauge what students know. That's why it's important to keep a journal as you're teaching. Document what worked and what didn't. Or, better yet, take thirty minutes right after each lesson and rework things for the next time you teach that class. Find a reading that will work better than the one you assigned. Work out a better way to explain that tricky concept. Or rewrite that question that generated twenty "what does this mean?" queries during the exam.

In my own classes, I've found that I can save a huge amount of time by editing for next time while I'm still teaching the current semester's class. I do that by storing all the materials for my current class in one folder, dated for that semester. At the beginning of the semester, I make a copy of that folder and date it for the next semester I think I'll be teaching that same class. Then, as I go through the current semester's class, I start editing the materials in the folder for the future semester's class (syllabus, class notes, slides, exams, etc.). That way I have a copy of the materials I'm currently working from (to make sure I know what students were actually taught), but I can also edit those materials to make them more effective for future use while it's still fresh in my brain.

Inclusive Course Design

The most effective courses are also inclusive courses. That's because effective teaching is teaching that achieves its goal. So if your goal is to have students learn and develop new skills, then you have to create an environment where that kind of learning can happen. And that means making students—all students—feel welcomed and understood.

Essentially, what I'm recommending is that you build your courses on the principles of "inclusive" or "universal" design.[12] We talked about universal design and accessibility in terms of presenting research in chapter 9. In the realm of teaching and learning, inclusive/universal design is the idea that tools for learning and achievement should be equally accessible to all students, regardless of their backgrounds and regardless of the abilities they bring to the course.

Along those lines, let's think about a few places where you can apply those principles of inclusivity and universal design:

Course Syllabi: As we talked about in chapters 4 and 5, it's easy to design a course that relies exclusively on readings and other materials produced by white (and usually cis-gendered, heterosexual) men. If you go that route, though, you risk alienating a large portion of your students, making them feel like they don't belong in your class or in your discipline as a whole. Thus, when you're writing your syllabus and gathering materials to use and talk about in class, think outside the box. Be explicit about incorporating the work of scholars from systematically marginalized groups. Be intentional about how you engage their work and highlight their contributions to the field.

Course Policies: College students face all sorts of challenges—challenges that are often invisible to you as the instructor—that make it harder for them to succeed in class.[13] By making your course policies as inclusive as possible, you can help students manage those challenges and do so in a way that doesn't force them to tell you what they're going through or ask for special accommodations for the challenges they face. With attendance policies, for example, you might consider giving all students a set number of "free" absences that they can use for any reason—illness, family obligations, work conflicts, car trouble, and so on. Under that model, students don't need to submit any documentation when they're absent from class, and you don't have to be the arbiter of who "deserves" to be excused. Similarly, and with respect to policies around coursework, you might consider building in flexibility that students can access without having to ask. If you give students multiple exams, for example, you might automatically drop their lowest grade. Or you might offer extra assignments that students can complete to make up any they miss or on which they get particularly low grades. Those kinds of course policies might make things a little more complicated for you as an instructor (though learning management systems like Canvas make it fairly easy to do things like drop the lowest grade on a set of assignments or exams), but they can go a long way in giving your students the flexibility they need to succeed.

Course Materials: Another place where inclusivity and universal design matter is in the course materials you create. With respect to assignments and assessments, for example, students with attention-deficit/hyperactivity disorder and other learning disabilities sometimes find it very difficult to take timed, in-class exams.[14] It's difficult for those students to focus when they're sitting elbow to elbow with twenty or fifty or two hundred other students. They might also experience extreme anxiety related to the pressure of finishing an exam in a short amount of time. Disability-related accommodations like separate space or extra time are supposed to alleviate those pressures and give students with diagnosed learning disabilities a more equal chance to succeed. That said, not all students who need those accommodations have been tested for them before they get to college.[15] Thus, if you want your courses to be truly inclusive, you might consider designing assessments that avoid the need for accommodations. That could mean using projects or portfolios to assess students' knowledge rather than timed exams. Or it could mean designing exams that can be completed as take-home exams rather than while sitting in class.

You can also make your courses more inclusive by setting clear expectations up front. In my own classes, for example, I give students outlines to use when taking notes in class. The outlines correspond with the slides I present in class, and they include spaces for defining key terms, explaining key concepts and theories, and identifying relevant examples. My goal is to teach students to be more effective note takers by helping them synthesize and summarize what they learn (rather than just writing down everything I say). I also give my students detailed review guides for each exam. The review guides include key terms students should be able to define, key concepts and theories they should be able to explain with examples, and key skills they should be able to demonstrate. I then encourage students to work together to complete the review guide so they'll be well prepared for the exams. With projects and writing assignments, I also give my students detailed instructions and outlines to follow and rubrics that show how I'll grade what they submit. By making my expectations explicit up front, and by giving students models to follow, I can avoid giving a bad grade to a student who knows their stuff but doesn't have as much experience conveying it in college-standard ways.

Now, all these rubrics and note outlines and review guides might seem like a lot of hand holding for college students. But I'd argue that they're necessary for inclusive teaching. Students come to college with varying needs and abilities and varying levels of experience with college-type tasks.[16] Some of your students might have been doing library research, writing evidence-based papers, and using bibliographic citations since they were in fifth grade. Others might have made it all the way to college without ever writing a paper longer than a page. If your assignment says just "write a five-page paper about a topic related to the class and be sure to include a bibliography," students in that latter group might not know that you expect their five-page paper to make a clear argument, support that argument with evidence and quotations from research, and use in-text citations to reference the works they cite. If those students don't know what you actually expect, there's a good chance they'll do it "wrong." And you might end up grading them based on the privileges life has denied them rather than on what they've learned in your class.

Effective and Inclusive Instruction

Once you design an effective and inclusive course, you still have to teach that course in an effective and inclusive way. Hundreds of books and articles have been written about college pedagogy— everything from "flipped" classrooms to culturally responsive teaching to end-of-class debriefs.[17] There's too much to summarize here. Thus, I'll focus instead on outlining a set of strategies that I've found particularly effective for helping students value what we're learning and feel valued in class.

If you want your students to learn, and especially if you want your students to value learning, it's important to treat them with dignity and respect. Along those lines, and in addition to the kinds of inclusive course design strategies we talked about in the last section, there are also a few strategies you can use when you're interacting with students in class:

Learn Students' Names: Learning students' names is a small gesture that can make them feel seen and valued in class. In my biggest classes (about 250 students), I learn students' names, in part, through large-group discussions (more on this in a minute). When I call on students for answers, I ask their name and then repeat it back to them to make sure I've got it right. In my "smaller" undergraduate classes (about 80 students), I use that same discussion strategy, and I also take attendance every class period by calling names aloud. It takes about five minutes of each class period, but it's the fastest way for me to learn students' names. By the third week I can usually remember the names of about 60 percent of the students in my smaller classes and about 15 percent of the students in my bigger classes.

Be Mindful of How You Interact with Students: It's easy for teachers to focus their attention (and especially their positive attention) on students from privileged backgrounds. In my own research, for example, I've found that because of their comfort interacting with (and demanding things from) authority figures, privileged students are able to persuade their teachers to give them all kinds of unfair advantages in school—extra assistance and accommodations, more attention to their ideas, more leeway around rules, and more praise for their efforts.[18] Building on those findings, I'd recommend being mindful of how you interact with your students. Think about whom you call on in class. Think about which students you praise. Think about whom you say yes to when they ask you for an extension or ask you to bump up their grade.

Uncover the Hidden Curriculum: Respecting students means acknowledging the challenges they face. Some of those challenges, in turn, have to do with their own struggles to navigate the hidden curriculum of college. As a teacher and a mentor, you can help uncover that hidden curriculum and make it part of the formal curriculum. Take time in class to talk about the hidden curriculum and how it perpetuates inequalities in college, in grad school, and in society as a whole.[19] Tell them about things like office hours, about how to get involved in faculty research projects, and about where to find information about grad school, pipeline programs, scholarships, and careers in your field. Essentially, you want to try to "lift as you climb."[20]

These strategies can create a foundation of respect for students in your classes. That kind of respect, in turn, can also help students feel more comfortable participating in class. In my undergraduate classes, for example, I can tell that the semester is off to a good start when I can get students to voluntarily share personal stories aloud, even in a class of 250, when I have to cut off the discussion because too many students want to share and when students stay after class because they want to talk more.

That kind of discussion, though, doesn't just happen organically. Rather, there are things you can do as an instructor to encourage students to contribute and to feel comfortable and confident in class. Specifically, I'd suggest:

Set the Tone Early: Don't use the first day of class just to review the syllabus. Start with a mini lesson that gets students thinking and talking and sharing. Include small-group or partner discussions and a few questions that ask for more public responses.

Start with Low Stakes: Ask brainstorming questions that produce a list of responses and don't require knowledge of the assigned readings. On the first day of my Intro to Sociology class, I start with an activity designed to help students recognize how people's choices are often shaped by forces outside their control. I ask students to work in small groups and brainstorm a list of reasons why a student might not finish high school. Then we combine those lists as a class, and we easily end up with twenty or thirty reasons, everything from laziness and lack of motivation to bullying and homelessness and teen pregnancy. Helping to create that list makes students feel invested in the activity and in the discussion that follows, where we unpack which explanations for leaving high school are agency-based explanations (those that blame the student for leaving) and which are structurally based (those blaming forces outside the student's control).

Provide In-Class Discussion Materials: Blog posts and video clips and short podcasts are great. For students, those materials provide a concrete, easily accessible, culturally relevant jumping-off point for a discussion. On the first day of my Intro to Sociology class, for example, and after we generate that list of reasons why a student might not finish high school, I show a thirty-second stay-in-school ad about what happens to students if they drop out, featuring LeBron James. After the video, we talk about its message about why students drop out of high school (i.e., because they're lazy and don't care enough about school), and we compare that message to our class-generated list of other reasons why students might drop out. I then use that discussion as a springboard to talk about how sociologists try to look beyond agency-based explanations for social behavior and examine the larger structural forces that shape people's choices.

Share Your Experiences: Sharing relevant personal stories is a great way to show students how to engage with the material. And if they're funny or embarrassing stories, that's sometimes even better. Letting yourself be seen as human and fallible helps students feel comfortable coming to you for support. In my Sociology of Childhood class, for example, we read sociologist Dr. Allison Pugh's work on children's "economies of dignity" and the shame kids feel when they can't join the conversation with their peers. I tell students about how, in sixth grade, my language arts teacher asked for "brand names" for a mad-lib-style group writing assignment. The teacher went around the room, and my classmates suggested things like Gap and Reebok and Esprit (it was the nineties). When it got to me, I had no idea what to say, so I slipped off one of my shoes (which I had gotten at Payless) and read the label— Lower East Sides. That prompted peals of laughter and incredulous claims of "I've never heard of that!" from my peers. I was mortified, sinking red-faced into my chair. Sharing such a story illustrates the concepts at hand and also helps students feel more comfortable sharing their own stories (and thus making their own connections to the material).

Choose Your Questions Carefully: If you want to have a large-group discussion, open-ended questions work best. Essentially, if you ask a question with a single correct answer, you're putting students on the spot. Students who are worried about getting the answer wrong (even if they actually know it) won't raise their hand, and they'll end up feeling locked out of the discussion. Thus, if you want to ask a closed-ended question, try doing so privately instead of publicly. Online polling tools like Top Hat and Poll Anywhere are great for that. You can easily get a sense of whether students understand a concept without making them risk publicly getting it wrong.

Validate Students' Answers: During large-group discussions, it's important for you as the instructor to play the role of moderator. Depending on the class setup, for example, it might be hard for students at the back of the room to hear things said by students up front. Thus, after each student makes a comment, you can reiterate what they say for the class. That allows you to summarize and clarify long-winded answers. And it also allows you to redirect if the student's point was off topic, unclear, or problematic in some way. Moderating the discussion that way also allows you to connect a student's point to the larger discussion/topic before moving on to the next student. Like learning students' names, this approach helps students feel seen when they contribute—when you repeat and summarize what they say, you're essentially validating their contributions to the class. That approach is also beneficial for the students who are listening. It helps them see the connection between what their classmates share and what they're supposed to get out of the lesson. And it reassures the listeners that you as the instructor aren't going to let racist, sexist, or otherwise problematic responses go unaddressed.

Acknowledge Your Limits: It's important for students to know that, as instructors, we don't know everything, can't do everything, make mistakes, and don't always achieve what we set out to achieve. So talk about the times when things didn't work out the way you planned. Apologize if you make a mistake. And be honest about what you don't know. Essentially, model for your students that it's okay not to be perfect and that mistakes aren't the end of the world.

Avoid Putting Students on the Spot: Now, while it's important to help normalize the idea that it's okay to make mistakes, it's also important to avoid intentionally creating opportunities for students to fail. In class, for example, I never cold-call students—I don't want them to be afraid to come to class. If I ask a question and no one raises their hand, that's on me. It could mean they didn't do the reading, but, in my experience, it more often means that the question wasn't clear or that students are afraid of looking stupid if their answer is wrong. Not cold-calling also avoids asking students (intentionally or unintentionally) to speak for their entire group (race, ethnicity, gender, sexual orientation, disability status, etc.). Essentially, I find that in-class discussions are most useful and engaging when students have control over when and how they share.

I should add here, though, that I do expect my students to participate, and I do make participation part of my students' grades. That said, I also design my participation assignments to accommodate differences in students' preferred mode and timing of participation. In my smaller classes, for example, students can get participation points either by contributing to in-class discussions or by posting relevant comments and questions to an online class message board. Similarly, in my bigger classes, I use online tools to engage students throughout each class period with opinion polls, open-ended discussion questions, and comprehension checks. I've found that having the option of online participation works well to engage students who might never feel comfortable speaking in front of the group, no matter what I do in class.

Effective and Inclusive Mentoring

The work of teaching, or at least good teaching, goes well beyond what happens in the classroom. If your students trust you, they might turn to you for support and mentoring as well. In those moments, it's easy to question whether you're really up for the task.

You might find yourself thinking of your most trusted mentors and wondering if you could ever fill their shoes. Thankfully, though, good mentoring is something you can learn. Your university might even have workshops or classes you can take on how to be a better mentor for your students. I'd highly recommend taking those workshops if you can, but I'll also offer a few suggestions on how to be an effective mentor while maintaining the time you need for yourself and for your own career success.

Effective mentors provide regular, constructive feedback to their students. Take time to review your students' work—carefully and thoroughly—and show them how to improve. Don't just say "this is wrong" or "fix this." Don't just give them harsh feedback so they'll be ready for Reviewer 2. Instead, explain why the problems are problems, identify possible solutions, and explain why those solutions are better. As we talked about in chapter 2, mentors shouldn't contribute to the culture of cruelty in academia. You wouldn't want harsh or degrading mentoring from your advisors, and your students don't want that kind of mentoring from you.

Effective mentors are also fierce advocates for their students. Some of your students might be reluctant to advocate for themselves.[21] As a mentor, you can play that role for them. Nominate your students for awards. Encourage them to consider grad school (if it's appropriate). Encourage them to submit their manuscripts for publication and to apply for grants and awards. Use your networks to help introduce your students to scholars from other departments and other disciplines and get inside information about grad school, postdocs, and jobs. Write the kinds of recommendation letters you'd want to receive, and write those letters in ways that avoid perpetuating stereotypes and implicit biases about students from marginalized groups.[22]

Being an effective mentor can be incredibly rewarding, but it can also come with costs. That includes time, emotional, and career costs.[23] That's why if you want to be a good mentor, you have to ensure that you're getting your own needs met too. We'll talk more about how to achieve that kind of work-life balance in a minute. Before that, though, let's talk about one other part of your work life that you might have to balance with your teaching and your research.

Wearing Your Service Hat

As a grad student, and certainly if you go the academic route after getting your degree, your work will include not only teaching and research but also service. That service is a function of academia's model of faculty governance.[24] The point of faculty governance is to promote academic freedom—to prevent government officials or other nonacademics from telling professors what to research or what to teach. To achieve that kind of freedom, though, faculty have to be the ones making decisions. That means that, in addition to doing research and teaching, faculty (and in some cases post-docs, grad students, and undergrads) also have to do the work of running (or at least helping to run) a department, a university, and a discipline.

That work is what academics call "service." At the department level, you might be asked on serve on committees (e.g., hiring, undergraduate affairs, graduate recruitment, public relations, climate). You might also, especially post-tenure, be asked to serve in department leadership positions, such as director of graduate studies or department chair. At the university level, there's a similar set of service roles to fill, including committees, task forces, and leadership positions (like the dean and provost positions we talked about in chapter 3). Meanwhile, at the discipline level there's another set of service to be done. That includes service related to research—reviewing articles and grant proposals, serving on editorial boards, or even editing an academic journal. There's also service involved in running professional organizations—organizing conference sessions, planning special events, serving on awards or nominations committees, and doing other logistical and managerial tasks.

All that service is necessary to keep departments and universities and disciplines running—at least if academics want to maintain a level of control over how those departments and universities and disciplines are run. And yet there's very little incentive for individual scholars to do the service that needs to be done. It's a classic "public goods" problem—everyone benefits from the service that gets done, but there's no direct benefit to contributing, and there's very little cost to not doing your part.[25] As a result, the service work in academia tends to be very unequally distributed, with scholars from systematically marginalized groups doing a disproportionate share of the work.[26]

Given the inequalities in academic service, and the limited rewards for doing that work, you might have been told to "just say no." In reality, though, and especially if you're a member of a systematically marginalized group, saying no might not feel like an option. As sociologist Dr. Zawadi Rucks-Ahidiana has argued, "Being a faculty member of color comes with a responsibility to students"—a responsibility to create within universities, and especially predominantly white universities, "a safe and supportive space" for students of color.[27] You might feel that same sense of responsibility to contribute to the service of academia. By serving on hiring committees or on graduate admissions committees, or by agreeing to review journal manuscripts or grant proposals or awards nominations, you have the chance to help make academia a safer and more supportive space for other scholars, and especially for more junior scholars and scholars from groups long excluded from academia's ivory tower.

Of course, the service work in academia wouldn't be so unequally divided if scholars from more privileged groups stepped up to do the work of making academia a safe and supportive space. And so if you are a scholar with more privilege, I would urge you to think critically about the benefits you get from other people's service. I would urge you to give back at least as much as you get. And I would urge you to be mindful to avoid creating or perpetuating problems (like bias in teaching or mentoring or admissions or hiring or awards) that other people's service will have to solve. Instead, in your service roles, you can establish yourself as the kind of professor whom students and colleagues—and especially students and colleagues from marginalized groups— can trust. Not by proclaiming it from the rooftops, but by the more subtle choices you make.

At the same time, and given the toll that service work can take on you and your career, it's important to remember that you don't have to do everything or be everything to everyone. So how do you know *when* to say no? To answer that question, I'd urge you to consider the plan that Dr. Rucks-Ahidiana laid out for herself in her first year as new assistant professor.[28] As she explained,

> I will set boundaries that allow me to prioritize the demands of tenure without sacrificing work that gives me life. I will limit the requests on my time based on a certain number of people or certain amount of time per semester. I will meet with small groups of students when possible to respond to the demand for interaction while not overcommitting myself. I will explain how they can support my journey to tenure and what earning tenure means not just for me but also for students like them.
>
> I will be selective about when I say "Yes!" and "Not right now," so as to prioritize what I can do now versus what I would like to do but just can't at that moment. Finally, I will find ways to make sure my engagements are acknowledged in my tenure file by associating them with my service work as much as possible. But, no, I will not say no to paying forward what those three black professors gave me.

Essentially, be strategic with your yesses, but know that those yesses are necessary and that they can make a huge difference in the lives of your students and your colleagues and in shaping what academia will look like for generations of students and scholars to come.

Balancing Life and Work

Those strategic yesses can help you achieve at least some level of balance between all the various parts of your work (teaching, research, service, etc.). Even with those strategic yesses, though, you might still struggle to find enough time to wear all your work-related hats. If you're feeling that crunch, you might be tempted to steal some extra work-hat-wearing time from your nonwork life. Especially with the overwork culture of academia, that "I'll just work more hours" approach might feel like the only option you can take.

The problem, though, is that constant work can take a serious toll.[29] It can affect your health and your mental health. It can affect your friendships and your family and your relationships. Personally, I've dealt with all of those firsthand.

In grad school, for example, I was always working or commuting. I almost never went out or took breaks, and even when I spent time with my partner on the weekends, it was usually me on the couch doing work while he played video games or watched TV. There were a couple of times, driving between DC and Philly, when I could feel myself falling asleep at the wheel. There were also times when I got really sick. As I mentioned in chapter 5, there was a summer in grad school, right after I started the fieldwork for my dissertation, when I ended up hospitalized with a serious infection that left me feeling tired and sick for months. I can't say for certain that working so much made me more likely to get sick or made it harder to recover, but that's essentially what the research suggests.[30]

Even now, as a tenured professor, I find it hard not to work too much. During those weeks (or months) when I'm rushing toward deadlines, my family feels it too. I have pictures my kids have drawn of me working at my laptop. Sometimes they even make their own laptops out of paper and cardboard and stickers to "work" alongside me at my desk. My partner, whom I've been with since college, is understanding (though he's not an academic), but my work takes a toll on him (and us) too.

Given all that, maybe I'm not the best person to give advice about balancing work and life. But I'll tell you what I try to do. Mostly, it involves creating a solid routine. Work, for me, already involves plenty of thinking. The less I have to think about the other stuff, the less stressed I know I'll be. For me, that means doing the same things and following the same routine almost every day. I eat the same breakfast and lunch every day. I go for a run every day. If it's a teaching day, I wear one of the five or six "professional" outfits I keep on rotation (usually dresses so I don't have to bother with matching shirts and pants). For dinners, we shop and cook on Sundays, making a giant batch of something (from a spreadsheet of favorite recipes) with enough leftovers to last at least until Thursday, then do pizza or mac and cheese or occasionally go out to eat. I also build my own routine around a routine that works for my family. That means snuggling with my kids and reading books on the couch in the morning. It means walking my kids to school most mornings (if I don't have early meetings) and walking to pick them up and play at the park most afternoons (if I don't have to stay on campus late). It means having dinner together as a family every night and, usually, not doing any work between four and nine in the evening.

Working around that routine, I use the time I have left (which does include early mornings and evenings and during my kids' "quiet time" on the weekends) to get my work done. I'm lucky that being an academic gives me the flexibility to work that way. I don't have to be in the office from nine to five or eight to six on weekdays. I can take an afternoon off to go on a fieldtrip with my kids. Or get up early to do work before the kids wake up and then go for a run after the kids go to school. Very few jobs have that kind of flexibility. My partner's certainly doesn't, and that imbalance of flexibility comes with some trade-offs too. If the kids get sick, for example, and we can't find a sitter, I'm almost always the one who stays home with them or who takes them to class or to meetings with me. Balancing work and life with small kids is tricky,[31] but I also know that I'm far more privileged than most.

Along those lines, work-life balance is considerably easier to achieve if you have resources to support that balance.[32] Enough money for food and housing and transportation. A flexible schedule and supportive colleagues who don't judge when or how you work. Access to paid family leave, money for child care, or family willing to help nearby. Money for house cleaning services or grocery delivery or help with other household tasks. Being able to afford a gym membership or a treadmill in the basement or a house in a neighborhood where it's safe to exercise outside. Without those resources, work-life balance can be extremely difficult to achieve.

Even with those resources, you might face temporary or ongoing challenges that upset the balance between work and life. Maybe you or a friend or family member gets sick. Maybe your car breaks down or your basement floods or you're going through a divorce. In those moments, it's important not to judge yourself for what doesn't get done. And it's important to ask for help.

Now, I get that it can be scary to speak up in those moments of struggle. It's easy to worry that others will see you as a failure— that they'll judge you for not being able to do it all on your own. That's certainly a risk. But know that most departments have resources and flexibility—even if those resources and flexibility aren't openly advertised—to help students and faculty in need. And so in those moments when nonwork life is using up all your reserves, ask if there are ways to reduce the pressure on the work side instead. Maybe that's asking for an extension on a deadline. Or asking a coauthor or colleague to step up and do more of the work. Maybe it's scaling back the number of assignments you give your students (and that you'll ultimately have to grade). Or maybe it's not taking on new service commitments or new students or new course preps.

Ultimately, the goal with work-life balance shouldn't be to keep your work and life commitments perfectly level at all times. That's just not realistic, given how life and work actually happen. Instead, and in my view, the goal should be a flexible routine. The routine is for the easy days—the days when you can do what you need to feel fulfilled and still have enough time for work. The flexibility is for the harder days—the days when life or work demands more of your energy and when the other side has to give.

CONCLUSION

 p.s. kehal @prabhbob · Jul 22, 2018

Seeing the wide array of replies to this important thread really reveals how much academia is built on exclusion and continues to operate as such. I love & appreciate excavating the #hiddencurriculum but at what point do we move beyond illuminating to reconstituting?

Academia is full of inequalities—inequalities in who gets admitted and who gets pushed out, who gets funded and who has to scrape by, whose work gets published, cited, and awarded and whose goes unrecognized, who gets hired, tenured, and promoted and who ends up having to settle for a job that isn't the one they hoped to get with their degree.[2] When grad school's hidden curriculum stays hidden, those inequalities get amplified, and their source stays hidden too. Essentially, the hiddenness of the hidden curriculum makes it seem as though the people who win in grad school are just "better suited" to play the game.

My hope is that this book will challenge that view. That it will push departments and disciplines, administrators and faculty members to recognize that the students they see as the best and the brightest might've started with an ace up their sleeve, while the students they think "can't hack it" just need help learning the rules. The same help the supposedly best and brightest students probably got long before they got to grad school.

Along those lines, my hope is that this book will spark a bigger conversation about dismantling the hidden curriculum of grad school and making it part of the formal curriculum. I've done what I can here—uncovering as much of the hidden curriculum as possible given the variations across schools and disciplines, the limits on my own knowledge, and the number of words I'm allowed to include. But there will still be parts of the hidden curriculum left hidden when you get to the last page. Those school- and discipline-specific parts of the hidden curriculum are the parts you'll have to uncover for yourself. But my hope is that you won't have to do that uncovering alone.

Rather, and as we'll talk about in this conclusion, I want faculty in it with you. I want departments and universities and whole disciplines to commit to dismantling the hidden curriculum. To make explicit the knowledge and skills and strategies necessary for success in academia. To eliminate the incentives to hide all that knowledge from view.

Uncovering the Hidden Curriculum

Faculty can help uncover the hidden curriculum, in part, by including it in the formal curriculum. But what does that mean? What would that look like in practice?

The first step is for faculty to identify the hidden curriculum in their own disciplines and departments. Essentially, faculty should ask themselves: What types of informal knowledge, skills, and strategies do students need to know to be successful in our program and our discipline? Are we explicitly teaching those things to students? Or are we assuming that students already know those things or will learn them on their own?

The second step, then, is for faculty to incorporate the hidden curriculum into the formal curriculum. That might mean creating new courses or workshops for graduate students (and possibly for postdocs and junior faculty as well). It could also mean redesigning existing courses and workshops to cover the hidden curriculum as well as the more formal one. Essentially, faculty should ensure that all students can access the hidden curriculum, regardless of who they are, which courses they take, and whom they have as an advisor.

And yet even if the hidden curriculum is taught to all students in formal courses, demonstrating those skills and knowledge might still be harder for some students than for others. You might, for example, learn that you need to ask for help and be your own advocate in school. You might even learn what types of help and support are available and whom you need to ask to get that support. And yet if you don't trust the faculty in your department and your university and your discipline, there's a good chance you still won't ask.

A third step, then, is to ensure that all students have access to mentors they can trust. As you're probably well aware, just having an advisor isn't enough. Rather, you deserve effective, committed mentors—faculty who've been trained to meet regularly with students, discuss students' questions and concerns, and give clear, unambiguous feedback.[3] You also deserve mentors who won't stigmatize, stereotype, silence, exclude, abuse, or otherwise mistreat you.[4] And you deserve to know that your advisors won't stand silently by when other students or faculty engage in that kind of misconduct against you or against anyone else.

The problem, unfortunately, is that your university, your department, and your discipline might not have enough of those good mentors to go around. We know that scholars from systematically marginalized groups already do a disproportionate share of the mentoring in academia.[5] And yet even as the number of grad students from those groups has grown, faculty from systematically marginalized groups remain seriously underrepresented in many fields.[6] That disproportionality, in turn, creates an even bigger mentoring load for faculty who are already overburdened with requests for support, and that overload might make it hard for you to get the mentoring you need to succeed.

Given the huge imbalance of mentoring (and especially high-quality mentoring) in academia, faculty from more privileged groups need to step up. They need to be the kinds of teachers and mentors that students can really trust. In reality, though, faculty, and especially faculty from privileged groups, have rarely been prepared to teach and mentor students or to work with and support colleagues from backgrounds different from their own.[7] Given that lack of preparation, faculty from privileged groups run the risk of saying and doing things, even inadvertently, that contribute to academia's culture of cruelty and harm.

Because of that risk, the push for change can't just stay at the individual level. We need structural solutions too. Departments and universities should offer high-quality training programs and offer support to faculty who want to get better at providing support for their students. At Indiana University, for example, the Office of Diversity and Inclusion recently launched the iTEDs program, a teaching exchange where faculty members can observe highly effective instructors and learn how to approach teaching and mentoring in a more inclusive way.[8]

Training programs and teaching exchanges are a great way for faculty to improve their skills as teachers and mentors. And yet, given the demands on professors' time, and given the low value most schools place on good teaching and good mentoring, most faculty have little incentive to participate in those programs and lots of reasons to just keep doing what they've always done.

Dismantling the Hidden Curriculum

To fix that problem, we'll have to change the whole incentive structure of academia. We'll have to dismantle not only the hidden curriculum but also the structures of inequality that hid that curriculum in the first place and that work to keep it hidden from view.

For that to happen, universities will have to put their money where their mouth is when it comes to diversity, equity, and inclusion.[9] Universities, and especially the kinds of research universities that train grad students, need to dramatically increase the representation of faculty from marginalized groups. To do that, universities will have to specifically designate positions for diversity in hiring and back up those positions with ample resources and support.

Of course, those top-down efforts are critical, but they won't be enough on their own. Faculty from systematically marginalized groups won't want to take a job in a department or a university or a community where they feel unsafe or unwelcome or unvalued. And even if they do take a job in one of those places, they might not get the support they need to stay.

To fix those problems, we'll also need to change the culture of academia. That includes the value we assign to different kinds of academic work (i.e., research vs. teaching vs. service) and the expectations we have for how much work academics should do. Changing that culture won't be easy. That's because academia's culture of cruelty stems, at least in part, from academia's status as a racialized, gendered, and classed institution.[10] Those inequalities are reinforced by academia's emphasis on status, hierarchy, and competition. And that obsession with status, hierarchy, and competition reflects academia's structure of rewards.

Thus, if we want to dismantle the hidden curriculum of grad school, we have to eliminate the incentives that created the hidden curriculum and that work to keep it hidden from view.

One way to change those incentives is with a substantial government investment in higher education. Enough money for public colleges and universities to dramatically increase their number of tenure-track faculty and reduce their reliance on exorbitant tuitions, large class sizes, and underpaid lecturers and adjuncts. Increasing the number of tenure-track academic jobs will reduce competition for those jobs, thereby reducing the pressure on grad students and junior faculty to publish as much as possible. That reduced pressure to publish, in turn, will reduce the incentive to minimize the amount of time spent on teaching, mentoring, and service.

Even without a big public investment, universities, departments, and disciplines can take their own steps to change academia's incentive structure and reduce the pressure to publish. At least at this point faculty still have some control over decision making in universities, departments, and disciplines.[11] That means faculty still play a big role in setting the standards for hiring, tenure, promotion, grants, publications, and awards. Faculty should use that power to reward scholars who strive for a balance of teaching, research, and service and who emphasize quality over quantity in that work. That means rewarding scholars who do careful, thoughtful, and impactful work—in the classroom, in the lab, in the field, and in committee meetings—rather than work that just fills out their CV.[12]

Along those lines, and by reducing the pressure to publish, universities, departments, and disciplines can also work to increase the incentives for good teaching and good mentoring. Carrot-wise, those incentives could include reduced course loads for faculty who mentor large numbers of students. Or monetary rewards for faculty who are nominated by students and colleagues as particularly effective teachers and mentors. Stick-wise, those incentives could also include sanctions (like a tax on research funds) for faculty who don't do their fair share of teaching and mentoring work.

Ultimately, my hope is that academia will get to a place where teaching and mentoring and service work are valued as much as research. To get to that point, though, we have to proceed with care. We can't, for example, just ratchet up teaching and mentoring expectations without decreasing expectations for publishing and grant-getting. If we go that route, we'll just strengthen the dangerous culture of overwork that already exists in academia.[13] We also have to be careful about how we evaluate good teaching and good mentoring and decide who deserves those rewards. Student evaluations, for example, might be an easy metric to use, but they're also highly inaccurate as a measure of teacher effectiveness and extremely biased against instructors from systematically marginalized groups.[14]

Conclusions

When I started grad school, I had only a vague sense of the hidden curriculum or that there was a hidden curriculum at all. And I certainly wasn't alone, though it felt like that at times. As you've seen in the tweets throughout this book, plenty of other grad students and former grad students have struggled with the hidden curriculum. Struggled with the gaffes and missteps and self-doubts that come from not knowing what you're "supposed" to know.

If this book helps you avoid even one of those gaffes or missteps or self-doubts, then I'd say the effort was worth it on my end. But of course one book—even a book as long as this one—can't tell you everything you need to know. There will be discipline- and department-specific parts of the hidden curriculum you'll have to uncover on your own. My hope is that this book will help you see those gaps in your knowledge and not blame yourself for not knowing what you were never taught. That it will help you build a team of trusted mentors and feel more confident asking for help.

At the same time, I don't think it's fair that you have to do all that work of uncovering the hidden curriculum for yourself. When your university and your department and your discipline rely on you to do that work, they're effectively ignoring the hiddenness of the hidden curriculum and the role that hiddenness plays in making academia such an unequal place.

My hope, then, is that this book will find its way into the hands of deans and department chairs, directors of graduate studies and other professors too. Not because those faculty members need a refresher on the hidden curriculum of grad school, but because they're the ones with the power to do something about it. They're the ones with the power to uncover the hidden curriculum for their students. The ones with the power to dismantle that hidden curriculum and make it part of the formal curriculum. And the ones with the power to change the structures and cultures and incentives that hid the hidden curriculum and keep it hidden from you.

APPENDIX A: SAMPLE CV—MASTER'S DEGREE

Jessica McCrory Calarco
University of Pennsylvania, Department of Sociology
3718 Locust Walk, Philadelphia, PA 19104-6299

August 2009

EDUCATION

University of Pennsylvania

    M.A., Sociology   2008

    Thesis: "Structured Opportunity: The Impact of School and Neighborhood Composition on College Attendance among Youth"

Brown University

    B.A., Sociology and Education Studies, *Magna Cum Laude, Honors*   2006

RESEARCH INTERESTS

Education, Children & Youth, Friendships, Social Class

AWARDS AND HONORS

Research Fellowship in Education and Adolescent Health, American Educational Research Association   2008

Institute for Education Sciences Pre-Doctoral Fellowship/Training Program   2007–2009

Samuel Lamport Prize for Outstanding Research in Sociology, Brown University   2006

IN-PROGRESS RESEARCH

The Rules: How Children Navigate and Negotiate Rules and Behavioral Expectations (Dissertation)

"Is It Always Better to Have Friends in High Places? Effects of Friends' Socioeconomic Status on Future College Attendance among Youth" (with Grace Kao)

CONFERENCE PRESENTATIONS

"Is It Always Better to Have Friends in High Places? Effects of Friends' Socioeconomic Status on Future College Attendance among Youth" (with Grace Kao), Population Association of America Annual Meeting   2009

"Structured Inequalities: The Effects of School and Neighborhood Status Composition on Adolescents' Subsequent Educational Attainment," American Educational Research Association Annual Meeting   2009

TEACHING EXPERIENCE

American Society, University of Pennsylvania (Teaching Assistant to Prof. Charles Bosk)   2009

    Responsible for leading two discussion sections of 25 students each

APPENDIX B: SAMPLE CV—JOB MARKET

Jessica McCrory Calarco
University of Pennsylvania, Department of Sociology
3718 Locust Walk, Philadelphia, PA 19104-6299

October 2011

EDUCATION

University of Pennsylvania

    Ph.D., Sociology (expected completion May 2012)

    Thesis: "Negotiating Opportunities: Social Class and Children's Help-Seeking in Elementary School"

    M.A., Sociology   2008

Brown University

    B.A., Sociology and Education Studies, *Magna Cum Laude, Honors*   2006

RESEARCH AND TEACHING INTERESTS

Education, Social Class & Stratification, Family, Health, Children & Youth, Friendships, Social Class, Ethnography, Research Methods, Social Networks, Social and Cultural Capital

PEER-REVIEWED ARTICLES AND BOOK CHAPTERS

Jessica McCrory Calarco. "'I Need Help!' Social Class and Children's Help-Seeking in Elementary School," *American Sociological Review.*   Forthcoming

    *2011 David Stevenson Award for Best Graduate Student Paper, Sociology of Education Section, American Sociological Association

    *2011 Candace Rogers Award for Best Graduate Student Paper, Eastern Sociological Society

Annette Lareau & Jessica McCrory Calarco. "Class, Cultural Capital, and Institutions: The Case of Families and Schools," Chapter 4 in Susan T. Fiske & Hazel Markus, eds., *Facing Social Class: Social Psychology of Social Class*, New York: Russell Sage.   Forthcoming

MANUSCRIPTS UNDER REVIEW

Jessica McCrory Calarco, Grace Kao, & Sebastian Cherng. "Along for the Ride: Best Friends' Resources and Adolescents' College Attendance," *American Educational Research Journal.* (Revise & Resubmit)

Jessica McCrory Calarco & Annette Lareau. "Where's My Cupcake? Class Cultures and Consumerism in Elementary Schools." (Under Review)

AWARDS AND HONORS

David L. Stevenson Award for Best Graduate Student Paper, Sociology of Education Section, American Sociological Association   2011

Candace Rogers Award for Best Graduate Student Paper, Eastern Sociological Society   2011

Dissertation Completion Fellowship, School of Arts & Sciences, University of Pennsylvania   2011–2012

Otto and Gertrude K. Pollak Summer Research Fellowship, University of Pennsylvania   2010

Research Fellowship in Education and Adolescent Health, American Educational Research   2008
    Association

Institute for Education Sciences Pre-Doctoral Fellowship/Training Program   2007–2009

Samuel Lamport Prize for Outstanding Research in Sociology, Brown University   2006

ARTICLES IN PREPARATION

Jessica McCrory Calarco. "Developing Dispositions: How Parents Teach Children to Negotiate with Institutional Authorities." (Working Paper)

Jessica McCrory Calarco. "Can I Do It My Way? Social Class Differences in Elementary Students' Efforts to Seek Customized Classroom Accommodations." (Working Paper)

Jessica McCrory Calarco. "Gender Replay: The Changing Role of Gender in Children's Peer Relations." (Working Paper)

BOOK MANUSCRIPTS IN PREPARATION

Jessica McCrory Calarco. *Negotiating Opportunities: Social Class and Children's Efforts to Shape Their School Experiences.* (Manuscript in Preparation)

SELECTED CONFERENCE PRESENTATIONS

"Developing Dispositions: Parents' Class-Based Socialization of Children's Classroom Help-   2011
    Seeking Behaviors," Eastern Sociological Society Annual Meeting

"Can You Help Me Get Ahead? Class Differences in Children's Requests for Assistance and   2010
    Accommodations from Teachers," American Sociological Association Annual Meeting

"Is It Always Better to Have Friends in High Places? Effects of Friends' Socioeconomic   2009
    Status on Future College Attendance among Youth" (with Grace Kao), Population
    Association of America Annual Meeting

"Structured Inequalities: The Effects of School and Neighborhood Status Composition on   2009
    Adolescents' Subsequent Educational Attainment," American Educational Research
    Association Annual Meeting

TEACHING EXPERIENCE (INSTRUCTOR)

Social Problems and Public Policy, University of Pennsylvania   2010

20-student introductory course using theories of social constructionism to examine how issues come to be seen and addressed as social problems

Teaching Evaluations:
3.92/4.00 (overall quality of instructor); 3.58/4.00 (overall quality of course)

TEACHING EXPERIENCE (GUEST LECTURER)

Introduction to Sociology, University of Pennsylvania   2011

American Society, University of Pennsylvania   2009

Sociology of Gender, University of Pennsylvania   2009

TEACHING EXPERIENCE (TEACHING ASSISTANT)

American Society, University of Pennsylvania (Teaching Assistant to Prof. Charles Bosk)   2009

Responsible for leading two discussion sections of 25 students each

Teaching Evaluations: 3.42/4.00 (overall quality of instructor)

PROFESSIONAL AND DEPARTMENTAL SERVICE

Graduate Student Editor, *Anthropology & Education Quarterly*	2008–2011
Graduate Student Representative, Department of Sociology, University of Pennsylvania	2006–2008
Workshop Participant and Presenter	2006–2011

Education & Inequality Workshop, University of Pennsylvania

Urban Ethnography Workshop, University of Pennsylvania

Family & Gender Workshop, University of Pennsylvania

Occasional Peer Reviewer:

Ethnography, American Educational Research Journal, Anthropology & Education Quarterly

PROFESSIONAL MEMBERSHIPS

American Sociological Association

Eastern Sociological Society

APPENDIX C: SAMPLE CV—PRE-TENURE

Jessica McCrory Calarco
Indiana University, Department of Sociology
1020 E. Kirkwood Ave, Bloomington, IN 47405-7103

January 2018

ACADEMIC APPOINTMENTS

Indiana University

    Assistant Professor of Sociology   2012–Present

EDUCATION

University of Pennsylvania

    Ph.D., Sociology   2012

    Thesis: "Negotiating Opportunities: Social Class and Children's Help-Seeking in Elementary School"

    M.A., Sociology   2008

Brown University

    B.A., Sociology and Education Studies, *Magna Cum Laude, Honors*   2006

RESEARCH AND TEACHING INTERESTS

Education, Family, Social Class & Stratification, Children & Youth, Culture & Social Interaction, Social Psychology, Ethnography, Research Methods, Social Networks

BOOKS

Jessica McCrory Calarco. *Negotiating Opportunities: How the Middle Class Secures Advantages in School.* New York: Oxford University Press.   2018

PEER-REVIEWED ARTICLES AND BOOK CHAPTERS

Jessica McCrory Calarco. "Social Class and Student-Teacher Interactions," Chapter 7 in Thurston Domina, Benjamin Gibbs, Lisa Nunn, and Andrew Penner, eds., *Education & Society.* University of California Press.   Forthcoming

Brea L. Perry & Jessica McCrory Calarco. "Let Them Eat Cake: Socioeconomic Status and Caregiver Indulgence of Children's Food and Drink Requests," in Sara Shostak, ed., *Food Systems and Health (Advances in Medical Sociology)*, Vol. 18, p. 121–146. Emerald Publishing.   2017

Jessica McCrory Calarco. "Coached for the Classroom: Parents' Cultural Transmission and Children's Reproduction of Inequalities," *American Sociological Review* 79, no. 5: 1015–1037.   2011

    *Reprinted in Jeanne Ballantine, Joan Spade, and Jenny Stuber. 2017. *Schools and Society: A Sociological Approach to Education*, 6th Edition. Sage.

    *Featured in 2013–2014 Indiana University Annual Report on Research.

Jessica McCrory Calarco. "The Inconsistent Curriculum: Cultural Tool-Kits and Student Interpretations of Ambiguous Expectations," *Social Psychology Quarterly* 76, no. 2: 186–209.   2014

Jessica McCrory Calarco. "Help Seekers and Silent Strugglers: Student Problem-Solving in Elementary Classrooms," *American Educator* 38, no. 1: 24–31.   2014

Sebastian Cherng, Jessica McCrory Calarco, & Grace Kao. "Along for the Ride: Best Friends' Resources and Adolescents' College Completion," *American Educational Research Journal* 50, no. 1: 76–106.   2013

Annette Lareau & Jessica McCrory Calarco. "Class, Cultural Capital, and Institutions: The Case of Families and Schools," Chapter 4 in Susan T. Fiske & Hazel Markus, eds., *Facing Social Class: Social Psychology of Social Class*, New York: Russell Sage.   2012

Jessica McCrory Calarco. "'I Need Help!' Social Class and Children's Help-Seeking in Elementary School," *American Sociological Review*.   2011

> ***2011 David Stevenson Award for Best Graduate Student Paper, Sociology of Education Section, American Sociological Association**
>
> ***2011 Candace Rogers Award for Best Graduate Student Paper, Eastern Sociological Society**

MANUSCRIPTS UNDER REVIEW AND IN PREPARATION

Amy L. Gonzales, Jessica McCrory Calarco, and Teresa Lynch. "Technology Problems and Student Achievement Gaps: A Validation and Extension of Technology Maintenance Theory," *Communication Research*. (Revise & Resubmit)

Jessica McCrory Calarco and Natasha Quadlin. "A Theory of (Socioeconomic) Relativity: The Role of Relative Advantage in Educational Attainment." (Working Paper)

Jessica McCrory Calarco. "Gender (Re)Play: Systems of Power and Children's Resistance to Cultural Norms and Stereotypes." (Working Paper)

Jessica McCrory Calarco, Weihua An, and William R. McConnell. "Save Me a Seat: Segregation in Elementary Students' Lunchroom Seating Networks Over Two Years." (Working Paper)

Jaclyn Tabor and Jessica McCrory Calarco. "The Novelty of the 'Child Free': Cartoon Depictions of the Desirability of Children and Parenthood from 1925–2006." (Working Paper)

OTHER PUBLICATIONS AND REPORTS

Jaclyn Tabor and Jessica McCrory Calarco. "To See Why Attitudes on Having Children Have Changed, Look at… *New Yorker* Cartoons?" *The Conversation*.   2015

Jessica McCrory Calarco. Review of *The Broken Compass: Parental Involvement with Children's Education*, by Keith Robinson and Angel Harris, *Social Forces*.   2014

Jessica McCrory Calarco. Review of *Schooling Girls, Queuing Women: Multiple Standpoints and Ongoing Inequalities*, by Helen A. Moore, *Contemporary Sociology*.   2014

Jessica McCrory Calarco. "Classroom Interactions: Teachers and Students," in James Ainsworth, ed., *Sociology of Education: An A-to-Z Guide*. Sage.   2013

Jessica McCrory Calarco. "Teacher Expectations," in James Ainsworth, ed., *Sociology of Education: An A-to-Z Guide*. Sage.   2013

Jessica McCrory Calarco. "Study: Middle-Class Students Are Better at Asking for Help," *The Learning Curve*. NBC News, *Education Nation*.   2011

GRANTS (SUBMITTED)

Spencer Foundation, Lyle Spencer Research Award, Co-PI (with Thurston Domina, Andrew Penner, and Emily Penner). "The Developmental Consequences of the National School Lunch Program." Requested Amount: $1,000,000. Status: Request for Full Proposal.

Indiana Clinical and Translational Sciences Institute, Networks, ComplexSystems and Health PDT.PI. "Parent Network Study." Requested Amount: $20,000. Status: Revise & Resubmit.

AWARDS AND HONORS

Doris Entwisle Early Career Award, Sociology of Education Section, ASA	2017
Trustees Teaching Award, Indiana University	2017
Finalist, Spencer Foundation Postdoctoral Fellowship	2016
Outstanding Junior Faculty Award, Indiana University	2015
Trustees Teaching Award, Indiana University	2014
Outstanding Reviewer Award, Sociology of Education Section, ASA	2013
Finalist, Robert Wood Johnson Foundation Scholars in Health Policy Program	2012
David L. Stevenson Award for Best Graduate Student Paper, Sociology of Education Section, American Sociological Association	2011
Candace Rogers Award for Best Graduate Student Paper, Eastern Sociological Society	2011
Dissertation Completion Fellowship, School of Arts & Sciences, University of Pennsylvania	2011–2012
Otto and Gertrude K. Pollak Summer Research Fellowship, University of Pennsylvania	2010
Research Fellowship in Education and Adolescent Health, American Educational Research Association	2008
Institute for Education Sciences Pre-Doctoral Fellowship/Training Program	2007–2009
Samuel Lamport Prize for Outstanding Research in Sociology, Brown University	2006

INVITED TALKS

Emory University	2018
Working Class Studies Association Conference	2017
University of North Carolina	2017
Brown University	2017
Indiana University, School of Informatics and Computing	2016
University of Pennsylvania	2016
Hamilton College	2013
University of Notre Dame	2012

SELECTED CONFERENCE PRESENTATIONS

"A Theory of (Socioeconomic) Relativity: The Role of Individual and Local Advantage in Educational Attainment," American Sociological Association Annual Meeting (with Natasha Quadlin)	2017

"Class Act: How Teachers Translate Students' Non-Cognitive Skills into Social Class Inequalities in School," American Sociological Association Annual Meeting	2016
"Can I Do It My Way? Social Class and Accommodation-Seeking in Elementary School," Midwest Sociology of Education Research Symposium	2015
"Save Me a Seat: Segregation in Elementary Students' Lunchroom Seating Networks Over Two Years," American Sociological Association Annual Meeting (with Weihua An and William R. McConnell)	2014
"The Inconsistent Curriculum: Situational Variability in Teachers' Expectations and Its Consequences for Educational Inequality," American Sociological Association Annual Meeting	2013
"Training Squeaky Wheels: Social Class and Parents' Development of Children's Self-Advocacy Skills," American Sociological Association Annual Meeting	2012
"Developing Dispositions: Parents' Class-Based Socialization of Children's Classroom Help-Seeking Behaviors," Eastern Sociological Society Annual Meeting	2011
"Can You Help Me Get Ahead? Class Differences in Children's Requests for Assistance and Accommodations from Teachers," American Sociological Association Annual Meeting	2010
"Is It Always Better to Have Friends in High Places? Effects of Friends' Socioeconomic Status on Future College Attendance among Youth" (with Grace Kao), Population Association of America Annual Meeting	2009
"Structured Inequalities: The Effects of School and Neighborhood Status Composition on Adolescents' Subsequent Educational Attainment," American Educational Research Association Annual Meeting	2009

TEACHING EXPERIENCE (INSTRUCTOR)

Course	Students	Level	Years
Introduction to Sociology, Indiana University	120–210	U	2016–2018
Qualitative Methods: Ethnography, Indiana University	11–15	G	2015–2017
Sociology of Childhood, Indiana University	65–85	U	2013–2018
Summer Ethnography Workshop, Indiana University	10	G	2013
Social Problems, Indiana University	50–65	U	2012–2014
Social Problems and Public Policy, University of Pennsylvania	15	U	2010

TEACHING EXPERIENCE (GUEST LECTURER)

Sociology of Culture, University of North Carolina (Graduate)	2017
Proseminar, Indiana University (Graduate)	2013–2017
Research Methods, University of Pennsylvania (Graduate)	2011
Introduction to Sociology, University of Pennsylvania	2011
American Society, University of Pennsylvania	2009
Sociology of Gender, University of Pennsylvania	2009

Teaching Experience (Teaching Assistant)

American Society, University of Pennsylvania (Teaching Assistant to Prof. Charles Bosk)	2009

Responsible for leading two discussion sections of 25 students each

Student Mentoring

Dissertation Committee Chair

Maritza Steele, Indiana University (co-chair)	2017–Present

Dissertation Committee Member

Kristin Kelley, Indiana University	2018–Present
Nik Summers, Indiana University	2017–Present
Emma Cohen, Indiana University	2017–Present
Peter Lista, Indiana University	2017–Present
Eric Sevell, Indiana University	2016–Present
Chris Turner, Indiana University	2016–Present
Mai Thai, Indiana University	2015–Present
Jason Blind, Indiana University	2013–Present
Alyssa Powers, Indiana University	2013–Present
Emily Wurgler, Indiana University	2013–2017
Mobile Qualitative Research Specialist, Over the Shoulder, Chicago, IL	
Kody Steffy, Indiana University	2014–2016
Assistant Professor, Center for Integrative Studies, Michigan State University	
Jane Van Heuvelen, Indiana University	2013–2016
Assistant Professor of Sociology, University of Illinois Urbana-Champaign	

Master's Thesis Committee Member

Callie Cleckner, Indiana University	2019
Colleen Johnston, Indiana University	2015
Felicia Helvey, Indiana University	2014

Qualifying Examination Committee Chair

Felicia Helvey, Indiana University	2016

Qualifying Examination Committee Member

Annie Russian, Indiana University	2018
Maritza Steele, Indiana University	2017
Eric Wright, Indiana University	2016
Mai Thai, Indiana University	2016
Colleen Johnston, Indiana University	2015

First-Year Faculty Mentor

Sam Regas, Indiana University	2016–2017
Muna Adem, Indiana University	2015–2016
Colleen Johnston, Indiana University	2013–2014
Felicia Helvey, Indiana University	2012–2013

Career Mentoring Program, Sociology of Education Section, ASA

Casey Stockstill, University of Wisconsin-Madison	2016
Jennifer Nelson, Emory University	2015
Kari Kozlowski, UNC-Chapel Hill	2013
Kia Sorensen, University of Wisconsin-Madison	2013

Career Mentoring Program, Sociology of Children and Youth Section, ASA

Yader Lanuza, University of California, Irvine	2016
Alex Manning, University of Minnesota	2015

PROFESSIONAL SERVICE

Council Member, Sociology of Education Section, ASA	2017–2019
Distinguished Book Award Committee, Race, Gender, and Class Section, ASA	2017–2018
Chair and Organizer, Regular Sessions on Sociology of Education, ASA	2017–2018
Social Media Committee, Inequality, Poverty, and Mobility Section, ASA	2017–2018
Nominations Committee, Sociology of Family Section, ASA	2017–2018
Editorial Board, *Social Psychology Quarterly*	2017–2019
Chair and Organizer, Roundtable Session, Sociology of Family Section, ASA	2016–2017
Nominations Committee, Children and Youth Section, ASA	2016–2017
Discussant, "Sociology of Education" Session, ASA Annual Meeting	2016
Chair, James Coleman Award Committee, Sociology of Education Section, ASA	2015–2016
Graduate Student Paper Award Committee, Children and Youth Section, ASA	2015–2016
Chair and Organizer, Roundtable Session, Children and Youth Section, ASA	2015–2016
Career Mentoring Program, Sociology of Children and Youth Section, ASA	2015–2018
Editorial Board, *Sociology of Education*	2014–2016
Editorial Board, *Research in the Sociology of Education*	2014–2016
Pierre Bourdieu Book Award Committee, Sociology of Education Section, ASA	2014
David Lee Stevenson Award Committee, Sociology of Education Section, ASA	2012
Graduate Student Editor, *Anthropology & Education Quarterly*	2008–2012

Occasional Peer Reviewer:

American Sociological Review; American Journal of Sociology; Sociology of Education; Social Psychology Quarterly; Ethnography, American Educational Research Journal, Anthropology of Education Quarterly; Sociological Methodology; Research in the Sociology of Education; Social Forces; Social Problems; Sociological Forum; National Science Foundation

DEPARTMENTAL AND UNIVERSITY SERVICE

Undergraduate Affairs Committee, Sociology Department, Indiana University	2017–2018
Peer Teaching Observer, Sociology Department, Indiana University	2017–2018
Outstanding Junior Faculty Award Selection Committee Member, Indiana University	2017
Public Affairs Committee, Sociology Department, Indiana University	2016–2017
Presenter and Participant, IU Faculty Colloquium on Student Success, Indiana University Office of the Vice President of Academic Affairs	2016–2017
Participant, Top Hat Pilot Program, Indiana University	2016–2017
Organizer, Symposium on Race and Education, Sociology Department, Indiana University	2016

Participant, Faculty Research Experience Mapping Focus Group, Indiana University Office of the Vice Provost for Research	2016
Graduate Recruitment and Evaluation Committee Member, Sociology Department, Indiana University	2015–2016
Organizer, Symposium on Race and Health, Sociology Department, Indiana University	2014
Graduate Affairs Committee Member, Sociology Department, Indiana University	2013–2015
Faculty Coordinator, Gender, Race & Class Workshop, Sociology Department, Indiana University	2013–2018
Presenter, New Faculty Orientation Panel on Professional Development and the Faculty Success Program, Indiana University	2013
Schuessler Award Selection Committee, Sociology Department, Indiana University	2012–2014
Sutherland Teaching Award Committee, Sociology Department, Indiana University	2012–2018
Library Coordinator, Sociology Department, Indiana University	2012–2013
Social Action Award Committee, Sociology Department, Indiana University	2012–2013
Graduate Student Representative, Sociology Department, University of Pennsylvania	2006–2008

PROFESSIONAL MEMBERSHIPS

American Sociological Association

American Educational Research Association

Midwest Sociology of Education Association

Eastern Sociological Society

Working Class Studies Association

MEDIA INTERVIEWS

CBC – Interview with Carol Off and Jeff Douglas (26 August 2015)	2015
BBC – Interview with Peter Allen (21 August 2012)	2012
CKNW – Interview with Michael Smyth for the *Simi Sara Show* (22 August 2012)	2012

MEDIA COVERAGE OF RESEARCH

Shaunacy Ferro. "Changing Parenting Attitudes, as Seen through New Yorker Cartoons," *Mental Floss* (3 September 2015).

Ben Richmond. "Researchers Studied New Yorker Cartoons to See What Rich People Think about Kids," *Motherboard News* (25 August 2015).

Erika Beras. "Poorer Kids May Be Too Respectful at School," *Scientific American* (3 December 2014).

Rebecca Klein. "Working-Class Kids Ask Fewer Questions in Class, And Here's Why," *Huffington Post* (10 September 2014).

Claire McInerny. "Difference Between Kids Who Ask for Help and Kids Who Don't: Money," *State Impact Indiana* (9 September 2014).

Sarah D. Sparks. "Want Students to Ask for Help? Talk to Parents," *EdWeek* (2 September 2014).

Barbara Harrington. "Social Class Impacts Children's Educational Outcomes," *WFIU* (1 September 2014).

Jesse Singal. "Why Working-Class Kids Don't Ask Enough Questions in School," *The Science of Us* NYMag.com (28 August 2014).

Annie Murphy Paul. "Why Parenting Is More Important than Schools," *Time* (24 October 2012).

Zosia Bielski. "Working Class Parents Coach Kids to Problem-Solve, Middle-Class Promote Asking for Help," *The Globe and Mail* (20 August 2012).

Graeme Paton. "Working-Class Pupils Lost Out Because They Are Too Polite," *The Telegraph* (20 August 2012).

"Middle Class Children: Squeaky Wheels in Training," *Science Daily* (19 August 2012).

Stephen Hurley. "How Do YOU Teach Self-Advocacy to Your Children, *Teaching Out Loud* (22 August 2012).

Tara Malone. "Asking for Help Isn't Easy for Some Students," *Chicago Tribune* (4 January 2012).

Brea Stover. "Children—Seen and Heard," *SAS Frontiers* (24 January 2012).

Rhonda Rosenberg. "Seeking Help Is Harder for Some Children," *United Federation of Teachers* (19 January 2012).

"Middle-Class Students Ask for More Help than Working-Class Peers, Create Own Advantages," *Huffington Post* (7 December 2011).

Jaclyn Zubryzcki. "Middle-Class Students Seek and Get More Help," *Education Week* (14 December 2011).

Sarah D. Sparks. "Middle-Class Students Are Better at Asking for Academic Help," *Inside School Research* Education Week Blog (7 December 2011).

"Middle-Class Students Ask for Help More than Working-Class Peers, Study Finds," *Science Daily* (7 December 2011).

Dan H. Friedman. "Middle-Class Students Seek Help," *Raising Arizona Kids* (7 December 2011).

Don McLenaghen. "Science Sunday #26," *Radio Freethinker* (11 December 2011).

NOTES

Introduction

1. Research on the hidden curriculum reveals how the structure and culture of schooling systematically advantage privileged students over their peers from systematically marginalized groups (Anyon 1980; Giroux and Penna 1979; Wren 1999). While the content of the hidden curriculum varies across different levels of schooling, scholars have found that some form of hidden curriculum exists from preschool (Martin 1998; Peach 1994) through college (Margolis 2002) and even into graduate school (Cribb and Bignold 1999).

2. Research shows that scholars marginalized by racism, sexism, and other forms of discrimination are often systematically excluded from "top" opportunities in academia (Clauset, Arbesman, and Larremore 2015; Kennelly, Misra, and Karides 1999; Lundine et al. 2018; Ozlem and DiAngelo 2017; Reskin 1993; Rivera 2017).

3. Research on first-generation college students reveals that they often feel torn between the kinds of skills and habits they are expected to demonstrate in college and those valued by their family and friends at home (Lee and Kramer 2013; Lehmann 2014).

4. Affluent, white parents teach their children that they deserve support and special accommodations—from teachers, from health care providers, and from society as a whole (Calarco 2014a, 2018; Lareau 2011). They coach their children to ask for and even demand support from institutional authorities, and they model that behavior for their children in their own interactions with teachers, doctors, and other professionals.

5. Experimental audit studies have found that professors (consciously or subconsciously) discriminate against students from systematically marginalized groups (Beattie, Cohen, and McGuire 2013; Eaton et al. 2020; Moss-Racusin et al. 2012).

6. Unlike their affluent, white peers, students from marginalized groups are often reluctant to speak up when they are confused or struggling (Calarco 2011; Jack 2016). That reluctance is justified because, unlike their affluent, white peers, students from marginalized groups have to worry about how they might be judged for needing help and how they might be punished for seeking it (Calarco 2014a, 2014b, 2018).

7. There's also the possibility that at least some privileged people intentionally kept (and still keep) the hidden curriculum hidden. That way they can ensure that only students who look like them (and act and talk and do research like them) have a chance to succeed in academia.

8. The rapid rise in graduate enrollment appears to have slowed since 2016. One report from the Council of Graduate Studies found that graduate enrollment increased by only 0.5 percent from Fall 2016 to Fall 2017 (Okahana and Zhou 2018).

9. According to the National Center for Education Statistics, the increase in graduate school enrollment between 2000 and 2016 was substantially higher among Black students (100 percent) and Hispanic students (134 percent) than among white students (7 percent) (NCES 2018).

10. Students from systematically marginalized groups have the most to gain from higher education (Brand and Xie 2010), and mentoring can help those students do better and go farther in school (Brown, Davis, and McClendon 1999; Davis 2007; Griffin et al. 2010). That mentoring is particularly effective when mentors have similar backgrounds to those of their students (Davis 2012; Mason 2009). As a result, academia often relies upon faculty of color, faculty from low-income families, faculty who were first-generation college students, and women faculty to mentor and support marginalized students (June 2015, 2018).

11. Students (and especially students from marginalized groups) rely heavily on faculty from marginalized groups as mentors. As a result, faculty from marginalized groups do an outsized share of the work of teaching and mentoring students. Because teaching and mentoring are often undervalued, particularly in institutions with graduate programs, that "invisible labor" can make it more difficult for faculty members from marginalized groups to get tenure by limiting their time for research (June 2015; Matthew 2016; Rockquemore 2016c).

12. https://twitter.com/bellhookedme/status/1021514148872507392.

13. I use the term "lab sciences" to refer to the physical sciences, natural sciences, and engineering.

14. https://twitter.com/JessicaCalarco/status/1020741749852000256.

15. Research on impostor syndrome reveals that many graduate students and faculty—and especially those from systematically marginalized groups—experience feelings of "intellectual phoniness" or concerns that others might perceive them as undeserving of their position (Dua 2007; Gardner and Holley 2011; Gibson-Beverly and Schwartz 2008). Those feelings of self-doubt are also linked to higher rates of depression and burnout in high-status fields (McGregor, Gee, and Posey 2008; Sonnak and Towell 2001; Villwock et al. 2016).

16. https://twitter.com/LCHSayer/status/1037017288313061376.

17. Scholars have argued that there is a "crisis of mental health" in graduate education, with students experiencing disproportionately high rates of depression, anxiety, and even suicidal thoughts (Evans et al. 2018; Garcia-Williams, Moffitt, and Kaslow 2014; Levecque et al. 2017).

Chapter 1

1. https://twitter.com/devon_cantwell/status/1071550405564399616.

2. In sociology we have this concept of "credentialism" (Collins 1979), the idea that as more people in society obtain a particular degree (like a bachelor's degree),

the market value of that degree goes down. As a result, employers start requiring (or at least hiring people with) more advanced degrees. And that puts pressure on students to stay in school longer to get those increasingly necessary credentials.

3. Corporations like Google, Facebook, Apple, and Comcast are increasingly hiring social scientists to help them analyze the almost terrifying amount of data they collect about their customers (Zhou 2014).

4. https://journalism.columbia.edu/cpc.

5. www.brown.edu/academics/public-health/ctr/certificate.

6. https://bootcamp.unc.edu/data.

7. One recent report, for example, found that there are stark differences between the students who pursue microcredentials and those who ultimately earn them (Burke 2019; Hollands and Kazi 2019). While nondegree programs often target students from systematically marginalized groups (Cottom 2018), those who ultimately earn microcredentials are primarily white and Asian men with high levels of education and income (Hollands and Kazi 2019). The same report also found that only a small minority of microcredential recipients reported positive career outcomes related to their microcredential.

8. At least some nondegree programs operate in a predatory manner, preying on the high aspirations of students from marginalized groups, promising them an easy and cost-effective path to career mobility and ultimately leaving them with substantial debt and no certificate or degree (Cottom 2018; Seamster and Charron-Chénier 2017).

9. Some programs that bridge the line between the "hard" sciences and the social sciences (e.g., Statistics) will offer both MS and MA degrees.

10. This pressure to achieve ever higher levels of education has increased as more and more students complete college degrees (Collins 1979).

11. If you're interested in applying for prestigious doctoral programs, and especially if your GRE scores or grades aren't as high as you might want them to be, or if you're switching fields from your bachelor's to your doctoral degree, getting a master's degree first can sometimes improve your chances of acceptance.

12. In some cases, colleges will hire instructors with only a master's degree. Such positions, however, often involve high teaching loads (e.g., five or six or seven courses per semester) with limited salary and benefits.

13. National Science Foundation 2018.

14. Flaherty 2019a.

15. Having student loan debt is now the norm among college graduates, and that debt is particularly consequential for students of color (especially Black students) and those from low-income families (Addo, Houle, and Simon 2016; Houle 2014).

16. For the 2019–2020 school year, the University of Chicago Bursar's Office lists tuition and fees for MA students in the social sciences at a rate of $20,100 per quarter for students taking three classes per quarter. https://bursar.uchicago.edu.

17. https://ssw.umich.edu/programs/msw/tuition/fall-2021#as-mm-resident.

18. In some countries, taxpayers fund higher education. For those students, getting a degree is essentially free (Teixeira 2016). In countries like the United States, and particularly since the 1990s, state and federal governments have shifted the cost of higher education from taxpayers to individual students and their families (Stivers and Berman 2016). That shifting of the cost burden significantly increased tuition and student loan debt. However, even with sky-high tuition rates, many colleges and universities still struggle to make ends meet financially.

19. Given high levels of economic inequality in society, and given persistent racial gaps in wealth (Dwyer 2018; Oliver and Shapiro 2006; Seamster and Charron-Chénier 2017), the costs associated with attending unfunded grad programs are likely to be challenging for many students.

20. If your employer is helping you pay for grad school, they'll typically expect you to continue working full-time. That means going to school part-time, which generally means a longer time-to-degree.

21. While a full professor at an elite, private, doctoral-degree-granting institution might make more than $200,000 annually, an assistant professor at a public university might make only $60,000 annually, and an adjunct professor might make just $3,000 for each course they teach (Flaherty 2019a).

22. Many colleges and universities struggle with tight budgets (Berman and Paradeise 2016). Faced with those budget constraints, colleges and universities often rely on graduate students for low-cost teaching and research labor. Given the work they do, however, some graduate students have formed unions (and even gone on strike) to push for fair working conditions and fair compensation for their labor (Duffy 2019).

23. At most universities, tuition and fees are substantially reduced once doctoral students complete their required coursework and are considered "ABD" (i.e., when they have completed everything except their dissertation). Thus, if you need an extra year to finish beyond what your program can fund, you might have to pay only one or two thousand dollars rather than tens of thousands.

24. Because of their endowments and the money they collect from undergraduate tuition, private universities generally have more money to spend on graduate training. In 2018, for example, Harvard University's endowment was $38.8 billion, Yale's was $29.4 billion, and Stanford's was $26.5 billion (Suneson 2019).

25. Grant funding in the sciences has had a tremendous influence on organizational decision making in higher education (Berman 2011).

26. Doctoral programs typically admit only a small number of students each year. Those small numbers lead to a high concern with yield—a measure of the percentage of admitted students who ultimately decide to attend. If most of the students admitted opt not to attend, the program won't be viable—there won't be enough students to fill classes or to serve as research and teaching assistants. Thus, programs

sometimes offer "recruitment bonuses" (in the form of higher stipends or summer salary) to woo students who have also been admitted to other programs and who might thereby need persuasion to attend.

27. The National Science Foundation Graduate Fellowship Program provides three years of support (including tuition, fees, and stipend) for students pursuing doctoral degrees in science (including social science, psychology, and STEM education and learning), technology, engineering, and mathematics. Students are typically eligible to apply for this program during the first and second years of their graduate training. www.nsf.gov/funding/pgm_summ.jsp?pims_id=6201&org=NSF.

28. NSF Dissertation Research Improvement Grants can be used to cover specific costs involved in carrying out dissertation research. These grants are discipline-specific and are generally available to students in disciplines where they are expected to conduct independent research rather than research as part of a grant-funded faculty project (e.g., political science, sociology, anthropology, linguistics). www.nsf.gov/funding/education.jsp?fund_type=2.

29. The National Science Foundation Faculty Early Career Development Program provides research support for early career faculty members as they carry out projects intended to establish themselves as experts in a given field. www.nsf.gov/funding/pgm_summ.jsp?pims_id=503214.

30. The National Institutes of Health (NIH) Training and Career Development Grants provide financial support for grad students and postdocs in the biomedical and health sciences. Some of these grants are awarded to faculty members who can then use them to support grad students or postdocs working in their labs. Other grants are awarded directly to individual grad students, postdocs, or early career scholars to support them in carrying out independent projects. More information can be found on the NIH website. For information about graduate training grants from the NIH, see https://researchtraining.nih.gov/career/graduate. For more information about postdoctoral funding from the NIH, see https://researchtraining.nih.gov/career/postdoctoral-residency.

31. The NIH Dissertation Award can be used to cover specific costs involved in carrying out dissertation research in the biomedical and health sciences. https://researchtraining.nih.gov/programs/other-training-related/R36.

32. The National Institutes of Health Career Development (K) Awards are intended to help early career researchers transition from a mentored research model (i.e., as a grad student or postdoc) to an independent research model (i.e., as a faculty member) and are open to advanced postdocs and early career faculty members doing health-related research. www.nichd.nih.gov/grants-contracts/training-careers/extramural/career.

33. The Fulbright Programs are international educational exchange programs that fund U.S. students and scholars to study, teach, or conduct research abroad. Related programs also fund non-U.S. students to study in the United States. The

Fulbright U.S. Student Program is open to students in a variety of disciplines, including visual and performing arts. The Fulbright-Hays Program, meanwhile, is funded through the U.S. Department of Education and supports U.S. grad students and postdocs in pursuing research or training opportunities related to foreign languages and area studies. https://eca.state.gov/fulbright.

34. The Marshall Scholarship is a program that funds U.S. students for either one or two years of graduate study in the United Kingdom. The program is open to students interested in pursuing graduate training in a variety of disciplines. Students can apply to attend any British university, though the program determines students' final placement. www.marshallscholarship.org.

35. The Rhodes Scholarship program funds students from the United States and other countries to attend graduate school at Oxford University in the United Kingdom. The program funds two years of graduate study in a variety of disciplines. www .rhodesscholar.org.

36. The NAEd/Spencer Dissertation Fellowship Program is funded by the National Academy of Education and the Spencer Foundation, and it provides a stipend for students conducting dissertation research on topics related to the improvement of education. The program is open to students from a wide range of academic disciplines and professional fields. https://naeducation.org/naedspencer-dissertation -fellowship-program.

37. The William T. Grant Scholars Program supports the career development of early-career researchers. The program provides five years of funding for the completion of a major research project that will significantly expand the researcher's methodological or substantive expertise. The program also pairs scholars with senior mentors who can support them in developing the expertise necessary to carry out the proposed project. http://wtgrantfoundation.org/grants/william-t-grant -scholars-program.

38. The Robert Wood Johnson Foundation's Health Policy Fellows Program provides one year of support and up to $104,000 for midcareer scholars doing research relevant to health policy in the United States. www.rwjf.org/en/library/funding -opportunities/2019/health-policy-fellows.html.

39. For additional links to funding programs, including those that provide targeted support for students from systematically marginalized groups, see this list from the McNair Scholars Program: https://mcnairscholars.com/funding.

40. The Ford Foundation Fellowship Programs aim to increase the diversity of college and university faculty in the United States and the number of professors who can and will use diversity as a resource for enriching the education of all students. To that end, the Ford Foundation, in conjunction with the National Academies of Sciences, Engineering, and Medicine, awards fellowships to support grad students and postdocs, covering tuition, fees, and stipends along with research-related expenses. Grad students can apply for predoctoral funding before entering a doctoral

program or during their initial years in the program. Grad students can also apply for Dissertation Fellowships, which support them while carrying out their dissertation research. https://sites.nationalacademies.org/pga/fordfellowships.

41. The Alfred P. Sloan Graduate Scholarship Programs are aimed at increasing the diversity of students in the STEM (science, technology, engineering, and mathematics) fields by supporting graduate students from systematically marginalized groups and preparing them for careers in academia. http://sloanphds.org/?pageid=30.

42. AAUW American Fellowships support women scholars at various stages of their careers. These fellowships provide money for dissertation completion, postdoctoral research, and short-term funding related to the publication of research. www.aauw.org/what-we-do/educational-funding-and-awards/american-fellowships.

43. AAUW Career Development Grants support women bachelor's degree holders (and especially women of color) in pursuing degrees and opportunities that will allow them to change or advance in their careers. www.aauw.org/what-we-do/educational-funding-and-awards/career-development-grants.

44. AAUW International Fellowships support students who are not U.S. citizens in pursuing graduate and postgraduate study in the United States. www.aauw.org/what-we-do/educational-funding-and-awards/international-fellowships.

45. AAUW Selected Professions Fellowships provide financial support for U.S. citizen women (and especially women of color) pursuing degrees at U.S. universities in architecture, computer science, engineering, mathematics/statistics, business administration, law, and medicine. www.aauw.org/what-we-do/educational-funding-and-awards/selected-professions-fellowships.

46. AAUW Publication Grants support women scholars in conducting research that will result in publications in engineering, medicine, and science. www.aauw.org/what-we-do/educational-funding-and-awards/research-publication-grant.

47. The Javits Fellowships provide support for students pursuing graduate training in the arts, humanities, and social sciences, with a focus on those with demonstrated financial need. www2.ed.gov/programs/jacobjavits/index.html.

48. Additional information about *U.S. News & World Report* rankings can be found on its website: www.usnews.com/best-graduate-schools.

49. Burris 2004; Caren 2013.

50. This does not mean, however, that you should always choose a higher-ranked over a lower-ranked program. As Fabio Rojas suggests in his book *Grad Skool Rulz*, the difference between a sixth-ranked program and a twelfth-ranked program is fairly arbitrary (Rojas 2011). That said, going to a program ranked in the top twenty in your field might give you an edge over students who attend lower-ranked programs (Burris 2004; Caren 2013).

51. Grad school can feel like a total institution—a setting, like a prison, military base, or boarding school, where inhabitants are largely isolated from the rest of

society and spend almost all their time with other inhabitants of the total institution (Goffman [1961] 2017).

52. Check Google Scholar to see if they've published anything in the past five years. Check the university's course listings to see which courses they've taught recently. And check that they're not currently working in a university administrative position (e.g., associate dean or vice provost) or listed as emeritus, which is the academic equivalent of retired.

53. Flaherty 2019b.

54. Small 2017.

55. As of December 2019, the *U.S. News & World Report* rankings of MPP programs in public policy analysis listed George Washington University (at number 10) as the only DC-based university in the top ten ranked programs (*U.S. News & World Report* 2019).

56. Harrington 2019.

57. Fischer 2017; Fountain 2017; Zhang 2019.

58. El Alam 2019; Sue and Spanierman 2020.

59. Caron 2018.

60. Anderson and Finch 2017; Balsam et al. 2011; Nadal et al. 2014; Smith, Hung, and Franklin 2011.

61. Flaherty 2019c.

62. With those supports in place, you'll be better able to persist in places that otherwise wouldn't meet your needs (Dyrbye et al. 2010; Small 2017; Wilks 2008).

63. Dancu et al. 2019.

64. Posselt 2016.

65. Posselt (2016) finds that the most important factors for graduate admissions are elite college attendance, GRE scores, and college grades. Graduate admissions committees perceive those measures as evidence of students' "merit," despite evidence that they are highly biased in favor of students from privileged groups.

66. Fedynich 2017; Ma et al. 2018; Moneta-Koehler et al. 2017.

67. Posselt 2016.

68. Jaschik 2018.

69. The Educational Testing Service administers the GRE and has useful resources for students on its website: www.ets.org/gre/revised_general/prepare.

70. Hall, O'Connell, and Cook 2017.

71. Research suggests that letters of recommendation and other forms of written evaluation often contain gendered (and other forms of biased) language (Biernat and Eidelman 2007; Isaac et al. 2011). Such biased language, in turn, confirms stereotypes and, in doing so, can hurt applicants' chances of being selected.

72. https://twitter.com/RoxieBrookshire/status/1020865730286415872.

73. Posselt 2016.

Chapter 2

1. https://twitter.com/JZPhilosophy/status/1022942339097133057.

2. Johnson and Huwe 2002; Lunsford 2014.

3. Lunsford et al. 2013.

4. June 2018; Matthew 2016; Rockquemore 2016c.

5. Lunsford et al. 2013.

6. Rockquemore 2016a, 2016b.

7. Small 2017, 8.

8. Research shows that peer mentoring programs are effective for reducing graduate student stress (Grant-Vallone and Ensher 2000).

9. Hyun et al. 2006; Oswalt and Riddock 2007.

10. The McNair Scholars Program is part of the Federal TRIO Programs and funded by the Council for Opportunity in Education. The program is named for Dr. Ronald E. McNair, an internationally renowned physicist who was invited to be part of NASA's *Challenger* mission and who was the second African American in space. Inspired by Dr. McNair's accomplishments, the program provides undergraduate scholarships for low-income students, first-generation college students, and students from marginalized racial and ethnic groups. The program's goal is to help those students pursue careers in academia. They do so not only by providing financial support but also through mentoring and professional development programs, assistance with grad school applications and admissions, and support in navigating the hidden curriculum of college, grad school, and academia as a whole.

11. The MMUF is funded by the Andrew W. Mellon Foundation and is named, in part, for Dr. Benjamin Elijah Mays, a former president of Morehouse College and a mentor to Dr. Martin Luther King Jr. The program's goal is to increase the number of undergraduate students from underrepresented minority groups who go on to pursue PhDs in the arts, sciences, social sciences, and humanities. It does so by providing scholarships and support programs for students during their undergraduate degrees.

12. The SSRC-Mellon Mays program is jointly run by the Social Science Research Council and the Andrew W. Mellon Foundation. The program builds on the MMUF Program to support MMUF fellows as they transition from undergrad to grad school and into their post-PhD careers. The program provides gap funding for the summer between college and grad school, funding for travel and research grants during grad school, and funding to complete dissertation projects. The program also hosts numerous workshops for graduate students, including seminars on proposal writing, dissertation development, dissertation writing, and transitions from undergrad to grad school to academic careers.

13. www.gc.cuny.edu/pipeline.

14. www.icpsr.umich.edu/icpsrweb/sumprog.

15. https://biosciences.stanford.edu/current-students/diversity/programs-for
-students/ssrp-amgen-scholars-program.

16. https://med.stanford.edu/coe/pre-med-students/summer-pre-med
-programs.html.

17. https://perryinitiative.org.

18. https://cleoinc.org/programs/plsi.

19. www.lsac.org/discover-law/diversity-law-school/prelaw-undergraduate
-scholars-plus-programs.

20. Calarco 2018; Jack 2019.

21. Brunsma, Embrick, and Shin 2017.

22. Harassment and discrimination can include "verbal and nonverbal behaviors
that convey hostility, objectification, exclusion, or second-class status" about members of a particular social group (women, racial minorities, LGBTQ people, etc.), as
well as "unwanted sexual attention" and "sexual coercion" (National Academies of
Sciences, Engineering, and Medicine 2018).

23. Fitzgerald, Swan, and Fischer 1995.

24. Most universities value academic freedom—the idea that professors should
be free to teach and do research with minimal outside interference. Because of those
values, however, universities are often reluctant to scrutinize what professors (and
especially tenured professors) do in the classroom or in their research. In that kind
of system, a formal report of misconduct is one of the only mechanisms for triggering
an investigation of problematic faculty conduct.

25. As we have seen in recent high-profile cases of sexual harassment in academia,
when there is one victim, there are often many (Anderson 2018). And when multiple
victims speak up, they often have a better chance of being heard.

26. You might also be worried about how the reporting process might reopen the
wounds of the trauma you've experienced and other past traumas as well.

27. Bergman et al. 2002.

28. Johnson and Huwe 2002; Lunsford et al. 2013.

29. Brunsma, Embrick, and Shin 2017; Lunsford 2014.

30. Flaherty 2019c.

31. Chamberlain and Hodson 2010.

32. That said, and like the hidden curriculum, that kind of informally shared
knowledge can also create problems (or allow problems to fester) when it isn't explicitly addressed. Other faculty and staff members, for example, might not be aware of
the problems that grad students assume "everyone" knows. Or even if some faculty
or staff members do know about those problems, they might feel less pressured to
address them if they assume that grad students are handling them informally on
their own.

Chapter 3

1. https://twitter.com/_jmnoonan/status/1021105871802249223.

2. Goffman 1956; Pugh 2011.

3. McGregor, Gee, and Posey 2008; Sonnak and Towell 2001; Villwock et al. 2016.

4. For more about the history of these laws and the university offices that oversee compliance with them, see Grady (2015) and Moon (2009).

5. https://grants.nih.gov/grants/forms/biosketch.htm.

6. https://research.med.psu.edu/research-support/concierge/biosketch-tips.

7. Grady 2015; Moon 2009.

8. In the name of "scientific" research, some scholars have caused considerable harm to the subjects of their work. Much of that harm, in turn, has been perpetrated against people from systematically marginalized groups. The Tuskegee experiments, for example, subjected Black men to syphilis and left them untreated in order to study the course of the disease (Green et al. 1997). Early gynecological research, meanwhile, involved surgeries conducted on enslaved women without anesthesia or consent (Owens 2017).

9. The Carnegie Classification of Institutions of Higher Education is now run by Indiana University's Center for Postsecondary Research. More information can be found here: http://carnegieclassifications.iu.edu.

10. McCormick and Zhao 2005.

11. At least in most cases. There are some postdoctoral fellowship programs for assistant professors. For example, the Spencer Foundation has a Postdoctoral Fellowship Program that provides funding for assistant professors doing research on education. The William T. Grant Foundation has similar programs as well. These are often referred to as "early career" programs.

12. AAUP 2017.

13. Basu 2012.

14. Associate professors without tenure do not have long-term job security and have to have their contracts periodically renewed, and they may have to find a job elsewhere if they are ultimately denied tenure.

15. Hall 2005.

16. Gerber 2014.

Chapter 4

1. https://twitter.com/JessicaCalarco/status/1035954741895938054.

2. These are sometimes called "qualifying" or "field" exams. Each discipline and department typically has its own set of rules and standards.

3. If your library doesn't have access to a particular book or article, you can also contact your librarian and ask for help in locating that particular resource through interlibrary loan.

4. Resnick 2019; Van Noorden 2013.

5. Chakravartty et al. 2018; Ginther et al. 2011; Grant and Ward 1991; Leahey 2007; Lincoln et al. 2012; Merritt 2000; Oliver 2019.

6. www.citeblackwomencollective.org.

7. Oliver 2019.

8. www.ssrn.com/index.cfm/en/rps/, www.nber.org/papers.html, and https://osf.io/preprints/socarxiv.

9. www.raulpacheco.org.

10. The University of Chicago Library has a handy reference for identifying which reference manager is right for you: http://guides.lib.uchicago.edu/c.php?g=297307&p=1984557.

11. www.raulpacheco.org/resources/literature-reviews.

Chapter 5

1. https://twitter.com/tamallery/status/1021010727052693507.

2. Gerber 2001, 2014.

3. Rivera 2011.

4. https://twitter.com/timhaneyphd/status/1021968589270786049.

5. Calarco 2018; Jack 2019.

6. Golash-Boza 2012a; Pirtle 2018.

7. Cirillo 2006.

8. www.raulpacheco.org/blog.

9. Pacheco-Vega 2019.

10. Calarco 2019; Medina, Benner, and Taylor 2019.

11. Calarco 2018.

12. In case you're curious, here's a link to the full interview on NPR's *Marketplace Morning Report*: www.marketplace.org/shows/marketplace-morning-report/03132019 -us-edition.

13. Depending on the structure of your dissertation, it might be easier and more useful to report separate conclusions/findings for each chapter or article rather than for the dissertation as a whole.

14. Bolker 1998; Rank 2015; Silvia 2019.

15. In many programs these limits are tied to FTEs, or "full-time equivalents." A graduate teaching assistant position might be considered 0.5 FTE (or the equivalent of a half-time position). Compensation would then be based on the number of hours expected for a half-time worker.

16. Those demands become especially exploitative when universities and departments don't have the money to pay teaching assistants adequately for the work they do. Protecting grad students from that kind of exploitation is one of the reasons why universities sometimes have graduate student unions.

17. That is, unless some of these elements (e.g., readings, exams) are dictated by the department or the school.

18. In a 2015 article in the *Chronicle of Higher Education,* one adjunct professor reported earning only three thousand dollars per class, without any health insurance, paid leave, or other benefits (Hall 2015). That's consistent with other research showing that the majority of adjunct faculty members in higher education are paid only a few thousand dollars per course, teach large numbers of courses, receive no employment benefits, and often have to teach at multiple colleges and universities in order to find enough courses to make ends meet (ASA Task Force on Contingent Faculty Employment 2019; Douglas-Gabriel 2019; House Committee on Education and the Workforce 2014).

19. Saving your comments on student work is helpful because your students might ask you for recommendation letters for jobs or grad school. That could happen a month after the class is over. But it could also happen a few years later. And having good documentation can help you write a better letter on their behalf.

20. Unfortunately, that kind of informal sharing of opportunities tends to perpetuate the inequalities in academia. Faculty from more privileged groups receive a disproportionate share of the grant funding for research (Ginther et al. 2011; Ginther, Kahn, and Schaffer 2016), and when they go to hire research assistants, they often choose students who look like them.

Chapter 6

1. https://twitter.com/mlinic1/status/1021089191793512448.

2. Warren 2019.

3. Ghaffarzadegan et al. 2015; Lederman 2016; Waaijer et al. 2018.

4. Flaherty 2014.

5. Flaherty 2017; Harris 2019; Krause 2018; Woo 2019.

6. National Academies of Sciences, Engineering, and Medicine 2019.

7. As a report from the National Academies of Sciences, Engineering, and Medicine explains, replication involves researchers following the data collection and analysis procedures outlined in previous research to determine whether new data produce similar results (National Academies of Sciences, Engineering, and Medicine 2019). If the findings from the replication are inconsistent with the original findings, the validity and reliability of the original study are in question. See also Resnick (2018) and Yong (2018).

8. In many cases reproducibility failures are caused by data and coding errors.

9. Konnikova 2015; Simmons, Nelson, and Simonsohn 2011.

10. National Academies of Sciences, Engineering, and Medicine 2019.

11. Gerber and Malhotra 2008; Hubbard and Armstrong 1997; Shrout and Rodgers 2018.

12. The Center for Open Science has an online platform for preregistering studies. https://cos.io/prereg. And there are other discipline-specific sites for preregistration as well.

13. I also spent at least a thousand dollars of my own money—on participant incentives, on books that I donated to the school libraries, and on equipment such as a voice recorder and qualitative data analysis software.

14. Berman 2011; Berman and Paradeise 2016; Gauchat 2012.

15. Waaijer et al. 2018.

16. The funds that universities siphon off from faculty grants are used to cover "indirect costs"—essentially the costs of providing the infrastructure and personnel needed to support research.

17. https://pivot.proquest.com/session/login.

18. https://grad.ucla.edu/funding/#.

19. www.nsf.gov/awardsearch/ and https://projectreporter.nih.gov/reporter.cfm.

20. National Institute of Allergy and Infectious Diseases 2018; www.niaid.nih.gov /grants-contracts/when-and-how-contact-program-officer.

21. Every grant and fellowship program has its own website, and most also require that applications be submitted through online forms.

22. Some grants and fellowships are open to only certain scholars. That might be grad students, pre-tenure faculty, or scholars from systematically marginalized groups. It's important to carefully check for and note any eligibility criteria.

23. Most grant and fellowship websites will have lengthy descriptions of the organization's overall mission and its goals with each funding program. As you read through these, you'll likely see key words and phrases repeated. You'll want to echo those key words and phrases in your application (where appropriate) to show how your research aligns with the funder's priorities.

24. University of Wisconsin 2019; https://writing.wisc.edu/handbook/assignments /grants-2.

25. https://grants.nih.gov/news/contact-in-person/seminars.htm.

26. Gerin, Kinkade, and Page 2017; Li and Marrongelle 2012.

27. Browning 2007; Karsh and Fox 2019; Schimel 2011.

Chapter 7

1. https://twitter.com/SarahLClothes/status/1021215031512494080.

2. That said, some academic writers do try to add an element of surprise to their writing by saving the "big reveal" (the results and conclusions) for the end.

3. Crystal 2015; Marsh 2013.

4. McWhorter 2017; Perry and Delpit 1998; Rickford and Rickford 2000.

5. Johnson and VanBrackle 2012.

6. Calarco 2011.

7. Arguments also tend to be easier to identify if your goal is to make a descriptive contribution to the literature rather than a theoretical one.

8. Ferguson and Brannick 2012; Franco, Malhotra, and Simonovits 2014.

9. National Academies of Sciences, Engineering, and Medicine 2019.

10. Davies, Crombie, and Tavakoli 1998.

11. Disciplines vary in how they view the status of different authorship positions, with some disciplines viewing the first author as getting the most "credit" for the work and other disciplines privileging the last author instead.

12. For example, the journal *Nature Physics* offers an "Elements of Style" guide for potential authors (*Nature Physics* 2007).

13. *SciDevNet* 2008.

14. McCloskey 1999; Neugeboren 2005; Pomona College 2019.

15. Royal Historical Society 2015.

16. Belcher 2019; Editors 2015; Silvia 2019.

17. Choose only those directly relevant to your argument—at most two or three subfields and two or three terms/concepts. More than that and you'll risk losing or confusing the reader.

18. National Academies of Sciences, Engineering, and Medicine 2019.

19. All research has limitations. Those limitations are not (necessarily) fatal flaws. Focus on explaining why your data are still useful despite these limitations.

20. Luker 2010.

21. This is my pet theory for why Reviewer 2 is always the snarky, angry reviewer. If Reviewer 1 is the first person the editor invites, then they're probably going to be the most obvious reviewer—the person you cite and agree with and whose work you build on with your own. But the editor doesn't want to pick just favorable reviewers. They also want someone who will scrutinize your work and find its flaws. So they invite Reviewer 2—the person whose work you criticize or who you could have cited but opted not to cite at all.

22. Even after controlling for where research is published (a rough measure of "quality"), articles by scholars from marginalized groups are cited less often than those written by scholars from more privileged groups (Chakravartty et al. 2018; Grant and Ward 1991; Merritt 2000), and those citation patterns have consequences for scholars' careers (Leahey 2007).

23. Editors often turn to authors who have recently published in their journal to serve as reviewers on similar topics.

24. Research shows that men are significantly more likely than women to cite their own published work (King et al. 2017), and those decisions contribute to larger patterns of citation-related inequality (Leahey 2007; Merritt 2000).

25. My first book contains a methodological appendix (Calarco 2018) that I wrote as a sort of insider's guide to ethnographic research. I'd also recommend checking out sociologist Dr. Annette Lareau's methodological appendices in her books as well (Lareau 2000, 2011).

Chapter 8

1. https://twitter.com/wendyphd/status/1021141549479071744.

2. In some fields scholars use online repositories to share "pre-prints"—drafts of manuscripts that have not yet been published and that, in most cases, have not yet undergone peer review. That includes the National Bureau of Economic Research's Working Paper repository (www.nber.org/papers.html) as well as SocArXiv (https://osf.io/preprints/socarxiv).

3. With my first book, *Negotiating Opportunities*, I got a book contract based on a book prospectus and two sample chapters. The editor sent my prospectus and sample chapters to a set of anonymous reviewers, who provided feedback. The reviews included a number of critical suggestions for improving both the sample chapters and the framing of the book as a whole, but they were generally favorable, so the publisher offered me a contract. I then revised the sample chapters, wrote the rest of the book, and sent it all back to the editor. The editor then sent the whole book out for another round of reviews. That second round of reviews included comments from some reviewers who had seen the original sample chapters as well as comments from new reviewers who had not seen the original chapters. Those new reviewers had a number of major suggestions for improving the manuscript, and the editor felt that it would be best to revise the manuscript again to address those concerns. So I did another round of revisions on the book and sent it back to the editor again. The editor then sent the revised manuscript back to the reviewers from the second round, who offered some additional suggestions for improvement. Based on those suggestions, I revised the manuscript again and then sent it back to the editor, at which point he finally approved it for publication. The whole process involved at least four rounds of revisions and took four years from when I wrote the prospectus and sample chapters to when the book finally came out in print. In hindsight, if I had written the whole manuscript first, it would have taken longer to get the initial book contract, but it probably would have significantly streamlined the revision process.

4. Sociologist Dr. Nicole Gonzalez Van Cleve has an excellent Twitter thread outlining various lessons she has learned in the book publishing process, with notes on what can and cannot be negotiated (Van Cleve 2019).

5. Mankiw 2019.

6. Garfield 2006.

7. You won't be able to access most features of Web of Science without a university account.

8. Berger and Luckmann 1967; Espeland and Sauder 2007.

9. The actual number of articles published annually varies across journals. Some journals are published quarterly and typically include about five articles per issue. Others are published weekly or monthly or annually.

10. Most academic journals have small budgets and are run by a small staff. They also rely heavily on volunteers, including faculty editors (who might receive a small amount of financial compensation for their role), editorial board members (who are typically unpaid), and reviewers (who are almost always unpaid). As we will talk about in a later section, academic journal and book publishing is also not particularly lucrative, which further limits the amount of work that can be published.

11. Cobey et al. 2018.

12. Some scholars, universities, professional organizations, and policymakers have begun negotiating with publishers or pushing for laws that will allow (or even require) scholars to make their research open-access, even when published in pay-walled journals (McKenzie 2019; Resnick 2019; Resnick and Belluz 2019).

13. For more advice on publishing op-eds, I'd recommend checking out a blog post from sociologist Dr. Tanya Golash-Boza, which has tons of helpful tips (Golash-Boza 2012b).

14. Publons is a free online service that tracks peer reviews. Some journals allow you to register your reviews with Publons as you complete them, but Publons also allows authors to submit their completed reviews for inclusion in their reviewer profiles. Publons does not publicly name the scholars who reviewed a given paper, but it does allow scholars to show publicly how many reviews they have completed and for which journals they have reviewed.

15. *Nature* 2020.

16. www.nami.org/find-support/nami-helpline.

17. https://suicidepreventionlifeline.org. If you are in Canada, text 686868. If you are in the United Kingdom, text 85258. For more information about the Crisis Text Line, see www.crisistextline.org.

18. Germano 2013, 2016.

19. Academic presses will sometimes distribute a small number of free books on your behalf. These free books can be sent to other scholars, to journalists who might be interested in writing about your research, or to members of selection committees for book awards. If you're writing a book manuscript, these are things you can ask for when you're negotiating your contract.

20. The OpEd Project trains scholars to write for public audiences and also con-nects them to a network of expert mentors. The organization hosts workshops in major cities around the United States and also at universities and other organizations that sign up to host. www.theopedproject.org.

21. www.theatlantic.com/family/archive/2018/04/free-range-parenting/557051.

22. In Bloomington, Indiana, where I live, Indiana Solar for All operates similarly to Habitat for Humanity, sponsoring local low-income families to obtain solar panels for their homes and linking those families with community volunteers who can help them install the panels. See https://insfa.org.

23. https://scienceoutreach.indiana.edu/news-events/science-fest/index.html.

24. https://kinder.rice.edu/houston-education-research-consortium.

25. https://socy.umd.edu/news/pgpd-discusses-collaboration-socy-kojo-nnamdi-show.

26. https://scholars.org.

27. Senate Democrats 2019.

28. www.help.senate.gov/hearings/reauthorizing-the-higher-education-act-strengthening-accountability-to-protect-students-and-taxpayers.

29. Sociologist Dr. Brooke Harrington, for example, was arrested by Danish authorities and charged with violating her work and residence permit (Harrington 2019). Why? Because she, as a noncitizen of Denmark, complied with the Danish Parliament's request to present her research on tax havens to the Parliament and to various Danish government agencies. Harrington was ultimately cleared of wrongdoing, but she ended up having to leave her job in Denmark to keep herself and her family safe. Dr. Jimmy Martínez-Correa, a Columbian economist working in Denmark, was also prosecuted for the same charges Harrington faced.

30. Ray 2019b.

31. Ray 2019c.

Chapter 9

1. https://twitter.com/Prof_Casanova/status/1021042634788401152.

2. https://threeminutethesis.uq.edu.au.

3. National Endowment for the Arts 2003, 55.

4. For more information about designing for color accessibility, see this blog post from the design experts at Tableau (Shaffer 2016).

5. Flaherty 2019d.

Chapter 10

1. https://twitter.com/RoxieBrookshire/status/1020865730286415872.

2. Berman 2011; Mettler 2014; Newfield 2011, 2016.

Chapter 11

1. https://twitter.com/Prof_WCByrd/status/1022099148944887808.

2. AAUP 2017; Kuo 2017.

3. AAUP 2018.

4. Full-time, non-tenure-track hires include postdocs, visiting assistant professors, lecturers, and research faculty who are "soft-funded" in that their salary comes from grants.

5. Kuo 2017.

6. Torpey 2018.

7. Basalla and Debelius 2007; Caterine 2020; Kelsky 2015.

8. Cottom 2018.

9. Some schools operate on a quarter system. In that case, teaching requirements might be listed differently (e.g., 2–2–1).

10. With a course "buyout," a faculty member can use grant money to pay the university for courses they would have otherwise taught and then use that time to conduct additional research instead.

11. Adjunct salaries vary widely across colleges and universities. However, recent news reports suggest that many institutions pay only three thousand dollars per course (Douglas-Gabriel 2019; Hall 2015; Harris 2019).

12. Cebula 2017; Childress 2019; Kezar, DePaola, and Scott 2019.

13. With my own job search, I was lucky to have a lot of flexibility. My partner was working from home at the time, in a nonacademic job, and while he would have preferred to stay close to family and friends, he was willing to go where I needed to go, provided I was willing and able to consider moving again in the future. Given those criteria, we decided I would apply to any job that was either (1) in a location where we would be interested in living long term or (2) had a low enough teaching load that I would have time to do enough research to have a shot at a different job down the line.

14. This section is relevant only if you're currently a postdoc or faculty member. If not, you can skip it until you get your first postdoc or academic job.

15. Forthcoming research is research that has been accepted for publication but has not yet appeared in print.

16. Invited talks indicate that other scholars are aware of your research and interested in hearing what you have to say. It's rare, though, for a grad student to be invited to give talks.

17. Braxton, Milem, and Sullivan 2000; Faust and Paulson 1998; Paulson 1999.

18. Bain 2004; Eng 2017; Honeycutt 2016.

19. Boring, Ottoboni, and Stark 2016; Goos and Salomons 2017; MacNell, Driscoll, and Hunt 2015.

20. Research shows that students give higher ratings to classes where they receive higher grades, regardless of the difficulty of the material (Boring, Ottoboni, and Stark 2016; Hornstein 2017; Stroebe 2016).

21. Halsey 2019a.

22. Burawoy 1998.

23. Hartshorn 2019.

24. Rucks-Ahidiana 2019c.

25. Halsey 2019b.

26. Smith 2016.

27. Foley 2018.

28. Aguilar 2018; Rowland and Szalinski 2016.

29. A recent audit study found that employers discriminate against mothers during the hiring process, evaluating them as less competent and less deserving of high salaries than fathers and childless women and men (Correll, Benard, and Paik 2007).

30. Granovetter 1977, 2018.

31. www.imaginephd.com.

32. https://myidp.sciencecareers.org.

33. www.usajobs.gov/Help/working-in-government/unique-hiring-paths /students.

34. www.opm.gov/policy-data-oversight/hiring-information/students-recent -graduates/#url=Overview.

35. www.opm.gov/policy-data-oversight/hiring-information/students-recent -graduates/#url=pmf.

36. www.whs.mil/careers.

37. www.nyfa.org/jobs?gclid=CjwKCAiA__HvBRACEiwAbViuUzmuqp -GGQoyUsWCdZxPgVtau7ZcACv_OG6fJTo7p_f5NuEh4DbV-BoCp_gQAvD_BwE.

38. https://onthinktanks.org/apply-to-an-internship.

39. www.bridgespan.org/jobs/nonprofit-jobs/nonprofit-job-board?gclid =CjwKCAiA__HvBRACEiwAbViuU6dVAJWBTRQF6BzSeSXIoPwJcFKEryXF -tAxMNZW7ovqnfoNZ3FiwBoCoYUQAvD_BwE.

40. www.nist.gov/iaao/academic-affairs-office/nist-professional-research -experience-program-prep.

41. www.nist.gov/iaao/academic-affairs-office/nist-nrc-postdoctoral-research -associateships-program.

42. www.neh.gov/about/human-resources/neh-internship-program.

43. www.smithsonianofi.com/tag/humanities.

44. www.pewresearch.org.

45. www.gallup.com/home.aspx.

46. www.icpsr.umich.edu/icpsrweb/sumprog.

47. https://strategicplan.duke.edu/initiatives/machine-learning-summer-school.

48. https://sph.umich.edu/bdsi.

49. https://voices.uchicago.edu/socscisummermethods.

50. www.sph.emory.edu/departments/gh/continuing-ed/index.html.

51. https://ecpr.eu/Events/EventDetails.aspx?EventID=131.

52. www.researchtalk.com/qrsi-2019.

53. www.maxwell.syr.edu/moynihan/cqrm/Institute_for_Qualitative_and _Multi-Method_Research.

54. https://careercenter.umich.edu/article/non-academic-job-search.

55. www.careereducation.columbia.edu/resources/non-academic-career-options -phds-humanities-and-social-sciences.

Chapter 12

1. https://twitter.com/DevonRGoss/status/1021176047272775680, https://twitter.com/DevonRGoss/status/1021176985748267008.

2. As I write this, I can hear my kids waking up from their Saturday afternoon naps. And I can feel myself hoping they'll wait just five minutes longer to start yelling for me because I want to finish this paragraph first. So yeah, I get it.

3. www.raulpacheco.org/resources/the-everything-notebook.

4. https://trello.com.

5. https://todoist.com.

6. Milkman and her colleagues found, in an experiment involving gym-goers, that people assigned to the "temptation bundling" groups made more frequent visits to the gym (Milkman, Minson, and Volpp 2014).

7. Lieberman 2019.

8. Abbasi and Alghamdi 2015; Flett, Blankstein, and Martin 1995; Sirois 2015, 2016.

9. Lieberman 2019.

10. MacBeth and Gumley 2012; Sirois 2014; Wohl, Pychyl, and Bennett 2010.

11. At the beginning of each class period, you can also remind students of the big objectives and explain how that day's lesson will build toward your larger goals. For example, when I teach, I start class by listing a series of questions students should be able to answer or skills they should be able to demonstrate by the end of that day's class.

12. National Endowment for the Arts 2003; Rose and Meyer 2002.

13. Some college students struggle with hunger and homelessness (Goldrick-Rab 2016). Others have to work long hours to make ends meet (Armstrong and Hamilton 2015; Ray 2017). Still others struggle to afford the kinds of basic tools (like books, cell phones, and computers) they need to feel connected and be successful in class (Gonzales, Calarco, and Lynch 2018; Ray 2017).

14. Embse et al. 2018.

15. Asnaani et al. 2010; Morgan et al. 2013.

16. Conley 2008; Reid and Moore 2008.

17. Fulton 2012; Ginsberg and Wlodkowski 2009; Sleeter 2012. In a recent *Chronicle of Higher Education* article, these end-of-class debriefs are described as a "new" innovation, based on techniques used by first responders (Supiano 2019). That said, and like many "innovations" in higher ed pedagogy, these debriefs have actually been common practice in K–12 education for a very long time (Cornelius 2013; Wylie, Lyon, and Goe 2009).

18. Calarco 2018; Jack 2019; Musto 2019; Streib 2011.

19. Brunsma, Embrick, and Shin 2017; Ellis 2001; Golde 1998; González 2006; Margolis and Romero 1998; Nettles 1990; Romero 1997; Zambrana et al. 2017.

20. Butner, Burley, and Marbley 2000; Williams et al. 2005.

21. Calarco 2018; Jack 2016; Ley and Hamilton 2008.

22. Madera, Hebl, and Martin 2009.

23. Bellas 1999; Matthew 2016; Rockquemore 2016c.

24. Gerber 2001; Lapworth 2004.

25. Marwell and Ames 1979.

26. Senior scholars and those from more privileged groups often feel more comfortable saying no when they're asked to do service work that won't directly benefit them in some way. If they can't say no, they're also more comfortable doing a less-than-stellar job. And so in many departments, universities, and disciplines, those scholars stop getting asked. Meanwhile, junior scholars and scholars from marginalized groups often feel compelled to say yes when asked to do service work, even when it won't have direct benefits for their careers (Bellas 1999; O'Meara 2016, 2018; Rucks-Ahidiana 2019b).

27. Rucks-Ahidiana 2019a.

28. Rucks-Ahidiana 2019a.

29. Sullivan 2014.

30. Thoits 2010.

31. Petriglieri 2019.

32. Collins 2019.

Conclusion

1. https://twitter.com/prabhbob/status/1021124290446585856.

2. Brunsma, Embrick, and Shin 2017; Ellis 2001; Golde 1998; González 2006; Margolis and Romero 1998; Nettles 1990; Romero 1997; Zambrana et al. 2017.

3. Brunsma, Embrick, and Shin 2017; Cohen and McConnell 2019; Ellis 2001; Paglis, Green, and Bauer 2006; Zambrana et al. 2017.

4. Margolis and Romero 1998.

5. Bellas 1999; June 2015; Matthew 2016; Rockquemore 2016c; Rucks-Ahidiana 2019b.

6. AFT 2010; Ceci and Williams 2011; Zambrana et al. 2015.

7. Margolis and Romero 1998.

8. https://college.indiana.edu/about/diversity-inclusion/ited-classrooms.html.

9. As research has shown, stated organizational commitments to diversity, equity, and inclusion are rarely enforced in practice (Ray 2019a).

10. Acker 2006; Ray 2019a. The culture of cruelty in academia effectively operates as its own hidden curriculum—what Margolis and Romero (1998, 11–12) call the "strong" hidden curriculum of grad school and of academia more generally. That strong hidden curriculum involves the "stigmatization, blaming the victim, cooling out, stereotyping, absence, silence, exclusion, and tracking" of scholars from

systematically marginalized groups as well as the lack of preparation more privileged scholars receive for working and learning in diverse settings.

11. Altbach, Gumport, and Berdahl 2011; Cohen and Kisker 2010.

12. Arguably, a shift in emphasis from quantity to quality in research could also help to address the "replication crisis" that many fields have experienced in recent years (Hubbard and Armstrong 1997; Resnick 2018; Shrout and Rodgers 2018; Yong 2018) and could help to reduce the pressures to falsify or exaggerate results.

13. Krause 2018; Sullivan 2014; Woo 2019.

14. Boring, Ottoboni, and Stark 2016; Eaton et al. 2020; Goos and Salomons 2017; Hornstein 2017; MacNell, Driscoll, and Hunt 2015.

REFERENCES

AAUP. 2017. *Trends in the Academic Labor Force, 1975–2015*. American Association of University Professors.

———. 2018. *Data Snapshot: Contingent Faculty in US Higher Ed*. American Association of University Professors.

Abbasi, Irum, and Nawal Alghamdi. 2015. "The Prevalence, Predictors, Causes, Treatment, and Implications of Procrastination Behaviors in General, Academic, and Work Setting." *International Journal of Psychological Studies* 7:59–66.

Acker, Joan. 2006. "Inequality Regimes: Gender, Class, and Race in Organizations." *Gender & Society* 20(4):441–64.

Addo, Fenaba R., Jason N. Houle, and Daniel Simon. 2016. "Young, Black, and (Still) in the Red: Parental Wealth, Race, and Student Loan Debt." *Race and Social Problems* 8(1):64–76.

AFT. 2010. *Promoting Racial and Ethnic Diversity in the Faculty: What Higher Education Unions Can Do*. American Federation of Teachers.

Aguilar, Stephen J. 2018. "Advice for Giving an Effective Job Presentation (Opinion)." *Inside Higher Ed*, January 10.

Altbach, Philip G., Patricia J. Gumport, and Robert O. Berdahl. 2011. *American Higher Education in the Twenty-First Century: Social, Political, and Economic Challenges*. Johns Hopkins University Press.

American Association for the Advancement of Science. 2019. "Retraction of the Research Article: 'Police Violence and the Health of Black Infants.'" *Science Advances* 5(12):eaba5491.

Anderson, Kathryn Freeman, and Jessie K. Finch. 2017. "The Role of Racial Microaggressions, Stress, and Acculturation in Understanding Latino Health Outcomes in the USA." *Race and Social Problems* 9(3):218–33.

Anderson, Nick. 2018. "Academia's #MeToo Moment: Women Accuse Professors of Sexual Misconduct." *Washington Post*, May 10.

Anyon, Jean. 1980. "Social Class and the Hidden Curriculum of Work." *Journal of Education* 162(1):11.

Armstrong, Elizabeth A., and Laura T. Hamilton. 2015. *Paying for the Party: How College Maintains Inequality*. Rev. ed. Harvard University Press.

ASA Task Force on Contingent Faculty Employment. 2019. *Contingent Faculty Employment in Sociology*. American Sociological Association.

Asnaani, Anu, J. Anthony Richey, Ruta Dimaite, Devon E. Hinton, and Stefan G. Hofmann. 2010. "A Cross-Ethnic Comparison of Lifetime Prevalence Rates of Anxiety Disorders." *Journal of Nervous and Mental Disease* 198(8):551–55.

Bain, Ken. 2004. *What the Best College Teachers Do*. Harvard University Press.

Balsam, Kimberly F., Yamile Molina, Blair Beadnell, Jane Simoni, and Karina Walters. 2011. "Measuring Multiple Minority Stress: The LGBT People of Color Microaggressions Scale." *Cultural Diversity and Ethnic Minority Psychology* 17(2):163–74.

Basalla, Susan, and Maggie Debelius. 2007. *"So What Are You Going to Do with That?" Finding Careers outside Academia.* 2nd ed. University of Chicago Press.

Basu, Kaustuv. 2012. "What Does a Post-tenure Review Really Mean?" *Inside Higher Ed*, March 2.

Beattie, Geoffrey, Doron Cohen, and Laura McGuire. 2013. "An Exploration of Possible Unconscious Ethnic Biases in Higher Education: The Role of Implicit Attitudes on Selection for University Posts." *Semiotica* 2013(197):171–201.

Belcher, Wendy Laura. 2019. *Writing Your Journal Article in Twelve Weeks, Second Edition: A Guide to Academic Publishing Success.* University of Chicago Press.

Bellas, Marcia L. 1999. "Emotional Labor in Academia: The Case of Professors." *ANNALS of the American Academy of Political and Social Science* 561(1):96–110.

Berger, Peter L., and Thomas Luckmann. 1967. *The Social Construction of Reality: A Treatise in the Sociology of Knowledge.* Anchor.

Bergman, Mindy E., Regina Day Langhout, Patrick A. Palmieri, Lilia M. Cortina, and Louise F. Fitzgerald. 2002. "The (Un)Reasonableness of Reporting: Antecedents and Consequences of Reporting Sexual Harassment." *Journal of Applied Psychology* 87(2):230–42.

Berman, Elizabeth Popp. 2011. *Creating the Market University: How Academic Science Became an Economic Engine.* Princeton University Press.

Berman, Elizabeth Popp, and Catherine Paradeise. 2016. *The University Under Pressure.* Emerald Insight.

Biernat, Monica, and Scott Eidelman. 2007. "Translating Subjective Language in Letters of Recommendation: The Case of the Sexist Professor." *European Journal of Social Psychology* 37(6):1149–75.

Bolker, Joan. 1998. *Writing Your Dissertation in Fifteen Minutes a Day: A Guide to Starting, Revising, and Finishing Your Doctoral Thesis.* Owl Books.

Boring, Anne, Kellie Ottoboni, and Philip Stark. 2016. "Student Evaluations of Teaching (Mostly) Do Not Measure Teaching Effectiveness." *ScienceOpen Research.* https://www.scienceopen.com/document_file/25ff22be-8a1b-4c97-9d88-084c8 d98187a/ScienceOpen/3507_XE6680747344554310733.pdf.

Brand, Jennie E., and Yu Xie. 2010. "Who Benefits Most from College? Evidence for Negative Selection in Heterogeneous Economic Returns to Higher Education." *American Sociological Review* 75(2):273–302.

Braxton, John M., Jeffrey F. Milem, and Anna Shaw Sullivan. 2000. "The Influence of Active Learning on the College Student Departure Process: Toward a Revision of Tinto's Theory." *Journal of Higher Education* 71(5):569–90.

Brown, M. Christopher, II, Guy L. Davis, and Shederick A. McClendon. 1999. "Mentoring Graduate Students of Color: Myths, Models, and Modes." *Peabody Journal of Education* 74(2):105–18.

Brown, Sarah. 2017. "Should Alice Goffman's Work Cost Her a Faculty Position?" *Chronicle of Higher Education*, April 26.

Browning, Beverly. 2007. *Perfect Phrases for Writing Grant Proposals*. McGraw-Hill Education.

Brunsma, David L., David G. Embrick, and Jean H. Shin. 2017. "Graduate Students of Color: Race, Racism, and Mentoring in the White Waters of Academia." *Sociology of Race and Ethnicity* 3(1):1–13.

Burawoy, Michael. 1998. "The Extended Case Method." *Sociological Theory* 16(1):4–33.

Burke, Lilah. 2019. "New Report Offers Analysis of Microcredential Completers." *Inside Higher Ed*, November 20.

Burris, Val. 2004. "The Academic Caste System: Prestige Hierarchies in PhD Exchange Networks." *American Sociological Review* 69(2):239–64.

Butner, Bonita K., Hansel Burley, and Aretha F. Marbley. 2000. "Coping with the Unexpected: Black Faculty at Predominately White Institutions." *Journal of Black Studies* 30(3):453–62.

Calarco, Jessica McCrory. 2011. "'I Need Help!' Social Class and Children's Help-Seeking in Elementary School." *American Sociological Review* 76(6):862–82.

———. 2014a. "Coached for the Classroom: Parents' Cultural Transmission and Children's Reproduction of Educational Inequalities." *American Sociological Review* 79(5):1015–37.

———. 2014b. "The Inconsistent Curriculum: Cultural Tool Kits and Student Interpretations of Ambiguous Expectations." *Social Psychology Quarterly* 77(2):185–209.

———. 2018. *Negotiating Opportunities: How the Middle Class Secures Advantages in School*. Oxford University Press.

———. 2019. "Cheating in College Admissions Plays Out on Several Different Levels." *Inside Higher Ed*, March 22.

Caren, Neal. 2013. "Academic Caste System 2013." *Scatterplot*, March 25. https://scatter.wordpress.com/2013/03/25/academic-caste-system-2013.

Caron, Christina. 2018. "A Black Yale Student Was Napping, and a White Student Called the Police." *New York Times*, May 9.

Caterine, Christopher. 2020. *Leaving Academia: A Practical Guide*. Princeton University Press.

Cebula, Geoff. 2017. *Adjunct*. Self-Published.

Ceci, Stephen J., and Wendy M. Williams. 2011. "Understanding Current Causes of Women's Underrepresentation in Science." *Proceedings of the National Academy of Sciences* 108(8):3157–62.

Chakravartty, Paula, Rachel Kuo, Victoria Grubbs, and Charlton McIlwain. 2018. "#CommunicationSoWhite." *Journal of Communication* 68(2):254–66.

Chamberlain, Lindsey Joyce, and Randy Hodson. 2010. "Toxic Work Environments: What Helps and What Hurts." *Sociological Perspectives* 53(4):455–77.

Childress, Herb. 2019. *The Adjunct Underclass: How America's Colleges Betrayed Their Faculty, Their Students, and Their Mission.* University of Chicago Press.

Cirillo, Francesco. 2006. *The Pomodoro Technique: The Acclaimed Time-Management System That Has Transformed How We Work.* Currency.

Clauset, Aaron, Samuel Arbesman, and Daniel B. Larremore. 2015. "Systematic Inequality and Hierarchy in Faculty Hiring Networks." *Science Advances* 1(1):e1400005.

Cobey, Kelly D., Manoj M. Lalu, Becky Skidmore, Nadera Ahmadzai, Agnes Grudniewicz, and David Moher. 2018. "What Is a Predatory Journal? A Scoping Review." *F1000Research* 7. https://dx.doi.org/10.12688%2Ff1000research.15256.2.

Cohen, Arthur M., and Carrie B. Kisker. 2010. *The Shaping of American Higher Education: Emergence and Growth of the Contemporary System.* John Wiley.

Cohen, Emma D., and Will R. McConnell. 2019. "Fear of Fraudulence: Graduate School Program Environments and the Impostor Phenomenon." *Sociological Quarterly* 60(3):457–78.

Collins, Caitlyn. 2019. *Making Motherhood Work: How Women Manage Careers and Caregiving.* Princeton University Press.

Collins, Randall. 1979. *The Credential Society: An Historical Sociology of Education and Stratification.* Columbia University Press.

Conley, David T. 2008. "Rethinking College Readiness." *New Directions for Higher Education* 2008(144):3–13.

Cornelius, Kyena E. 2013. "Formative Assessment Made Easy: Templates for Collecting Daily Data in Inclusive Classrooms." *Teaching Exceptional Children* 45(5):14–21.

Correll, Shelley J., Stephen Benard, and In Paik. 2007. "Getting a Job: Is There a Motherhood Penalty?" *American Journal of Sociology* 112(5):1297–1339.

Cottom, Tressie McMillan. 2018. *Lower Ed: The Troubling Rise of For-Profit Colleges in the New Economy.* New Press.

Cribb, Alan, and Sarah Bignold. 1999. "Towards the Reflexive Medical School: The Hidden Curriculum and Medical Education Research." *Studies in Higher Education* 24(2):195–209.

Crystal, David. 2015. *Making a Point: The Persnickety Story of English Punctuation.* St. Martin's.

Dancu, Elena, Michael Marinetto, Amber Pouliot, Margy Thomas, Karen St. Jean-Kufuor, and David Colquhoun. 2019. "Academics' Guilty Pleasures." *Times Higher Education*, June 6.

Davies, Huw Talfryn Oakley, Iain Kinloch Crombie, and Manouche Tavakoli. 1998. "When Can Odds Ratios Mislead?" *British Medical Journal* 316(7136):4.

Davis, Danielle Joy. 2007. "Access to Academe: The Importance of Mentoring to Black Students." *Negro Educational Review* 58(3/4):217–31.

Davis, Jeff. 2012. *The First Generation Student Experience: Implications for Campus Practice, and Strategies for Improving Persistence and Success.* Stylus.

Douglas-Gabriel, Danielle. 2019. "'It Keeps You Nice and Disposable': The Plight of Adjunct Professors." *Washington Post*, February 15.

Dua, Priya. 2007. "Feminist Mentoring and Female Graduate Student Success: Challenging Gender Inequality in Higher Education." *Sociology Compass* 1(2):594–612.

Duffy, Sean. 2019. "'Worker Power Is a Threat to the Way the University Is Run.'" *Jacobin Magazine*, June 4.

Dwyer, Rachel E. 2018. "Credit, Debt, and Inequality." *Annual Review of Sociology* 44(1):237–61.

Dyrbye, Liselotte N., David V. Power, F. Stanford Massie, Anne Eacker, William Harper, Matthew R. Thomas, Daniel W. Szydlo, Jeff A. Sloan, and Tait D. Shanafelt. 2010. "Factors Associated with Resilience to and Recovery from Burnout: A Prospective, Multi-institutional Study of US Medical Students." *Medical Education* 44(10):1016–26.

Eaton, Asia A., Jessica F. Saunders, Ryan K. Jacobson, and Keon West. 2020. "How Gender and Race Stereotypes Impact the Advancement of Scholars in STEM: Professors' Biased Evaluations of Physics and Biology Post-Doctoral Candidates." *Sex Roles* 82:127–41.

Editors. 2015. "How to Get Published in an Academic Journal: Top Tips from Editors." *Guardian*, January 3.

El Alam, Laura. 2019. "Coping with Microaggressions—A Guide for American Muslims." *About Islam*. https://aboutislam.net/family-life/your-society/coping-with-microaggressions-a-guide-for-american-muslims-allies.

Ellis, Evelynn M. 2001. "The Impact of Race and Gender on Graduate School Socialization, Satisfaction with Doctoral Study, and Commitment to Degree Completion." *Western Journal of Black Studies* 25(1):30–45.

Embse, Nathaniel von der, Dane Jester, Devlina Roy, and James Post. 2018. "Test Anxiety Effects, Predictors, and Correlates: A 30-Year Meta-analytic Review." *Journal of Affective Disorders* 227:483–93.

Eng, Norman. 2017. *Teaching College: The Ultimate Guide to Lecturing, Presenting, and Engaging Students*. Norman Eng.

Espeland, Wendy Nelson, and Michael Sauder. 2007. "Rankings and Reactivity: How Public Measures Recreate Social Worlds." *American Journal of Sociology* 113(1):1–40.

Evans, Teresa M., Lindsay Bira, Jazmin Beltran Gastelum, L. Todd Weiss, and Nathan L. Vanderford. 2018. "Evidence for a Mental Health Crisis in Graduate Education." *Nature Biotechnology* 36:282–84.

Faust, Jennifer L., and Donald R. Paulson. 1998. "Active Learning in the College Classroom." *Excellence in College Teaching* 9(2):3–24.

Fedynich, LaVonne. 2017. "The Grand Question: Do Entrance Examinations Determine Graduate Student Academic Success?" *Research in Higher Education Journal* 33. https://eric.ed.gov/?id=EJ1178436.

Ferguson, Christopher J., and Michael T. Brannick. 2012. "Publication Bias in Psychological Science: Prevalence, Methods for Identifying and Controlling, and Implications for the Use of Meta-analyses." *Psychological Methods* 17(1):120–28.

Fischer, Karin. 2017. "Trump's Travel Ban Leaves Students Stranded—and Colleges Scrambling to Help." *Chronicle of Higher Education*, January 29.

Fitzgerald, Louise F., Suzanne Swan, and Karla Fischer. 1995. "Why Didn't She Just Report Him? The Psychological and Legal Implications of Women's Responses to Sexual Harassment." *Journal of Social Issues* 51(1):117–38.

Flaherty, Colleen. 2014. "Research Shows Professors Work Long Hours and Spend Much of Day in Meetings." *Inside Higher Ed*, April 9.

———. 2017. "Recent Suicide by Professor Sparks Renewed Discussions about Access to Mental-Health Services for Faculty Members." *Inside Higher Ed*, April 21.

———. 2019a. "AAUP Study Finds Small Gains in Faculty Salaries, Offset by Inflation." *Inside Higher Ed*, April 10.

———. 2019b. "Controversial Tenure Denial at Harvard." *Inside Higher Ed*, December 4.

———. 2019c. "Graduate Student's Death at UW Madison Is a Devastating Cautionary Tale." *Inside Higher Ed*, November 4.

———. 2019d. "There's a Movement for Better Scientific Posters. But Are They Really Better?" *Inside Higher Ed*, June 24.

Flett, Gordon L., Kirk R. Blankstein, and Thomas R. Martin. 1995. "Procrastination, Negative Self-Evaluation, and Stress in Depression and Anxiety." In *Procrastination and Task Avoidance: Theory, Research, and Treatment, The Springer Series in Social Clinical Psychology*, edited by J. R. Ferrari, J. L. Johnson, and W. G. McCown, 137–67. Springer.

Foley, Nadirah. 2018. "Reconsidering the Use of 'Women and People of Color.'" *Scatterplot*, October 24. https://scatter.wordpress.com/2018/10/24/reconsidering-the-use-of-women-and-people-of-color.

Fountain, Henry. 2017. "Science Will Suffer under Trump's Travel Ban, Researchers Say." *New York Times*, January 30.

Franco, Annie, Neil Malhotra, and Gabor Simonovits. 2014. "Publication Bias in the Social Sciences: Unlocking the File Drawer." *Science* 345(6203):1502–5.

Fulton, Kathleen. 2012. "Upside Down and Inside Out: Flip Your Classroom to Improve Student Learning." *Learning & Leading with Technology* 39(8):12–17.

Garcia-Williams, Amanda G., Lauren Moffitt, and Nadine J. Kaslow. 2014. "Mental Health and Suicidal Behavior among Graduate Students." *Academic Psychiatry* 38(5):554–60.

Gardner, Susan K., and Karri A. Holley. 2011. "'Those Invisible Barriers Are Real': The Progression of First-Generation Students through Doctoral Education." *Equity & Excellence in Education* 44(1):77–92.

Garfield, Eugene. 2006. "The History and Meaning of the Journal Impact Factor." *JAMA* 295(1):90–93.

Gauchat, Gordon. 2012. "Politicization of Science in the Public Sphere: A Study of Public Trust in the United States, 1974 to 2010." *American Sociological Review* 77(2):167–87.

Gerber, Alan S., and Neil Malhotra. 2008. "Publication Bias in Empirical Sociological Research: Do Arbitrary Significance Levels Distort Published Results?" *Sociological Methods & Research* 37(1):3–30.

Gerber, Larry G. 2001. "'Inextricably Linked': Shared Governance and Academic Freedom." *Academe* 87(3):22–24.

———. 2014. *The Rise and Decline of Faculty Governance: Professionalization and the Modern American University.* Johns Hopkins University Press.

Gerin, William, Christine Kapelewski Kinkade, and Niki L. Page. 2017. *Writing the NIH Grant Proposal: A Step-by-Step Guide.* 3rd ed. SAGE.

Germano, William. 2013. *From Dissertation to Book.* 2nd ed. University of Chicago Press.

———. 2016. *Getting It Published: A Guide for Scholars and Anyone Else Serious about Serious Books.* 3rd ed. University of Chicago Press.

Ghaffarzadegan, Navid, Joshua Hawley, Richard Larson, and Yi Xue. 2015. "A Note on PhD Population Growth in Biomedical Sciences." *Systems Research and Behavioral Science* 32(3):402–5.

Gibson-Beverly, Gina, and Jonathan P. Schwartz. 2008. "Attachment, Entitlement, and the Impostor Phenomenon in Female Graduate Students." *Journal of College Counseling* 11(2):119–32.

Ginsberg, Margery B., and Raymond J. Wlodkowski. 2009. *Diversity and Motivation: Culturally Responsive Teaching in College.* John Wiley.

Ginther, Donna K., Shulamit Kahn, and Walter T. Schaffer. 2016. "Gender, Race/Ethnicity, and National Institutes of Health R01 Research Awards: Is There Evidence of a Double Bind for Women of Color?" *Academic Medicine* 91(8):1098–1107.

Ginther, Donna K., Walter T. Schaffer, Joshua Schnell, Beth Masimore, Faye Liu, Laurel L. Haak, and Raynard Kington. 2011. "Race, Ethnicity, and NIH Research Awards." *Science* 333(6045):1015–19.

Giroux, Henry A., and Anthony N. Penna. 1979. "Social Education in the Classroom: The Dynamics of the Hidden Curriculum." *Theory & Research in Social Education* 7(1):21–42.

Goffman, Alice. 2014. *On the Run: Fugitive Life in an American City.* University of Chicago Press.

Goffman, Erving. 1956. *Interaction Ritual: Essays in Face-to-Face Behavior.* Routledge.

———. (1961) 2017. *Asylums: Essays on the Social Situation of Mental Patients and Other Inmates.* Routledge.

Golash-Boza, Tanya. 2012a. "Five Steps to Making a Semester Plan for Academics." *Get a Life, PhD.* https://getalifephd.blogspot.com/2012/01/five-steps-to-making -semester-plan-for.html.

———. 2012b. "How Can an Academic Publish an Op/Ed?" *Get a Life, PhD.* http:// getalifephd.blogspot.com/2012/11/how-can-academic-publish-oped.html.

Golde, Chris M. 1998. "Beginning Graduate School: Explaining First-Year Doctoral Attrition." *New Directions for Higher Education* 1998(101):55–64.

Goldrick-Rab, Sara. 2016. *Paying the Price: College Costs, Financial Aid, and the Betrayal of the American Dream.* University of Chicago Press.

Gonzales, Amy L., Jessica McCrory Calarco, and Teresa Lynch. 2018. "Technology Problems and Student Achievement Gaps: A Validation and Extension of the Technology Maintenance Construct." *Communication Research.* doi:10.1177 /0093650218796366.

González, Juan Carlos. 2006. "Academic Socialization Experiences of Latina Doctoral Students: A Qualitative Understanding of Support Systems That Aid and Challenges That Hinder the Process." *Journal of Hispanic Higher Education* 5(4):347–65.

Goos, Maarten, and Anna Salomons. 2017. "Measuring Teaching Quality in Higher Education: Assessing Selection Bias in Course Evaluations." *Research in Higher Education* 58(4):341–64.

Grady, Christine. 2015. "Institutional Review Boards." *Chest* 148(5):1148–55.

Granovetter, Mark S. 1977. "The Strength of Weak Ties." In *Social Networks*, edited by S. Leinhardt, 347–67. Academic Press.

———. 2018. *Getting a Job: A Study of Contacts and Careers.* University of Chicago Press.

Grant, Linda, and Kathryn B. Ward. 1991. "Gender and Publishing in Sociology." *Gender & Society* 5(2):207–23.

Grant-Vallone, Elisa J., and Ellen A. Ensher. 2000. "Effects of Peer Mentoring on Types of Mentor Support, Program Satisfaction and Graduate Student Stress." *Journal of College Student Development* 41(6):637–42.

Green, Bernard Lee, Richard Maisiak, Ming Qi Wang, Marcia F. Britt, and Nonie Ebeling. 1997. "Participation in Health Education, Health Promotion, and Health Research by African Americans: Effects of the Tuskegee Syphilis Experiment." *Journal of Health Education* 28(4):196–201.

Griffin, Kimberly A., David Perez, Annie P. E. Holmes, and Claude E. Mayo. 2010. "Investing in the Future: The Importance of Faculty Mentoring in the Development of Students of Color in STEM." *New Directions for Institutional Research* 2010(148):95–103.

Hall, Donald E. 2005. "What to Do as an Endowed Chair." *Inside Higher Ed,* July 11. www.insidehighered.com/advice/2005/07/11/what-do-endowed-chair.

Hall, Joshua D., Anna B. O'Connell, and Jeanette G. Cook. 2017. "Predictors of Student Productivity in Biomedical Graduate School Applications." *PLOS ONE* 12(1):e0169121.

Hall, Lee. 2015. "I Am an Adjunct Professor Who Teaches Five Classes. I Earn Less Than a Pet-Sitter." *Guardian*, June 22.

Halsey, Samniqueka. 2019a. "Diversity Statements." *Twitter*. https://twitter.com /Samniqueka_H/status/1211723716998189056.

———. 2019b. "Minoritized." *Twitter*. https://twitter.com/Samniqueka_H/status /1211723816260517889.

Harrington, Brooke. 2019. "I Almost Lost My Career Because I Had the Wrong Passport." *New York Times*, December 3.

Harris, Adam. 2019. "The Death of an Adjunct." *Atlantic*, April 8.

Hartshorn, Ian M. 2019. "Diversity Statements." *Twitter*. https://twitter.com/imhart shorn/status/1166032098370523137.

Hollands, Fiona, and Aasiya Kazi. 2019. *Benefits and Costs of MOOC-Based Alternative Credentials*. Teachers College, Columbia University.

Honeycutt, Barbi. 2016. *Flipping the College Classroom: Practical Advice from Faculty*. Magna.

Hornstein, Henry A. 2017. "Student Evaluations of Teaching Are an Inadequate Assessment Tool for Evaluating Faculty Performance." Edited by H.F.E. Law. *Cogent Education* 4(1):1304016.

Houle, Jason N. 2014. "Disparities in Debt: Parents' Socioeconomic Resources and Young Adult Student Loan Debt." *Sociology of Education* 87(1):53–69.

House Committee on Education and the Workforce. 2014. *The Just-in-Time Professor: A Staff Report Summarizing e-Forum Responses on the Working Conditions of Contingent Faculty in Higher Education*. U.S. House of Representatives.

Hubbard, Raymond, and J. Scott Armstrong. 1997. "Publication Bias against Null Results." *Psychological Reports* 80(1):337–38.

Hyun, Jenny K., Brian C. Quinn, Temina Madon, and Steve Lustig. 2006. "Graduate Student Mental Health: Needs Assessment and Utilization of Counseling Services." *Journal of College Student Development* 47(3):247–66.

Isaac, Carol, Jocelyn Chertoff, Barbara Lee, and Molly Carnes. 2011. "Do Students' and Authors' Genders Affect Evaluations? A Linguistic Analysis of Medical Student Performance Evaluations." *Academic Medicine* 86(1):59–66.

Jack, Anthony Abraham. 2016. "(No) Harm in Asking: Class, Acquired Cultural Capital, and Academic Engagement at an Elite University." *Sociology of Education* 89(1):1–19.

———. 2019. *The Privileged Poor: How Elite Colleges Are Failing Disadvantaged Students*. Harvard University Press.

Jaschik, Scott. 2018. "Decision by Penn's Philosophy Department Renews Debate about GRE." *Inside Higher Ed*, September 17.

Johnson, David, and Lewis VanBrackle. 2012. "Linguistic Discrimination in Writing Assessment: How Raters React to African American 'Errors,' ESL Errors, and Standard English Errors on a State-Mandated Writing Exam." *Assessing Writing* 17(1):35–54.

Johnson, W. Brad, and Jennifer M. Huwe. 2002. "Toward a Typology of Mentorship Dysfunction in Graduate School." *Psychotherapy: Theory, Research, Practice, Training* 39(1):44–55.

June, Audrey Williams. 2015. "The Invisible Labor of Minority Professors." *Chronicle of Higher Education*, November 8.

———. 2018. "What Factors Hold Back the Careers of Women and Faculty of Color? Columbia U. Went Looking for Answers." *Chronicle of Higher Education*, October 18.

Karsh, Ellen, and Arlen Sue Fox. 2019. *The Only Grant-Writing Book You'll Ever Need.* 5th ed. Basic Books.

Kelsky, Karen. 2015. *The Professor Is In: The Essential Guide to Turning Your Ph.D. into a Job.* Three Rivers Press.

Kennelly, Ivy, Joya Misra, and Marina Karides. 1999. "The Historical Context of Gender, Race, & Class in the Academic Labor Market." *Race, Gender & Class* 6(3):125–55.

Kezar, Adrianna, Tom DePaola, and Daniel T. Scott. 2019. *The Gig Academy: Mapping Labor in the Neoliberal University.* Johns Hopkins University Press.

King, Molly M., Carl T. Bergstrom, Shelley J. Correll, Jennifer Jacquet, and Jevin D. West. 2017. "Men Set Their Own Cites High: Gender and Self-Citation across Fields and over Time." *Socius* 3. doi:10.1177/2378023117738903.

Konnikova, Maria. 2015. "How a Gay-Marriage Study Went Wrong." *New Yorker*, May 22.

Krause, Grace. 2018. "We Must Confront the Culture of Overwork to Tackle Academia's Mental Health Crisis." *Times Higher Education*, June 14.

Kuo, Maggie. 2017. "New Data Offer the Latest Look at Ph.D. Training and Employment Trends." *Science*, December 8. www.sciencemag.org/careers/2017/12/new-data-offer-latest-look-phd-training-and-employment-trends.

Lapworth, Susan. 2004. "Arresting Decline in Shared Governance: Towards a Flexible Model for Academic Participation." *Higher Education Quarterly* 58(4):299–314.

Lareau, Annette. 2000. *Home Advantage: Social Class and Parental Intervention in Elementary Education.* Rowman & Littlefield.

———. 2011. *Unequal Childhoods.* University of California Press.

Leahey, Erin. 2007. "Not by Productivity Alone: How Visibility and Specialization Contribute to Academic Earnings." *American Sociological Review* 72(4):533–61.

Lederman, Doug. 2016. "Ph.D. Recipients Increase in Number, Job Prospects Vary, New U.S. Data Show." *Inside Higher Ed*, December 9.

Lee, Elizabeth M., and Rory Kramer. 2013. "Out with the Old, In with the New? Habitus and Social Mobility at Selective Colleges." *Sociology of Education* 86(1):18–35.

Lehmann, Wolfgang. 2014. "Habitus Transformation and Hidden Injuries: Successful Working-Class University Students." *Sociology of Education* 87(1):1–15.

Levecque, Katia, Frederik Anseel, Alain De Beuckelaer, Johan Van der Heyden, and Lydia Gisle. 2017. "Work Organization and Mental Health Problems in PhD Students." *Research Policy* 46(4):868–79.

Ley, Timothy J., and Barton H. Hamilton. 2008. "The Gender Gap in NIH Grant Applications." *Science* 322(5907):1472–74.

Li, Ping, and Karen Marrongelle. 2012. *Having Success with NSF: A Practical Guide.* Wiley-Blackwell.

Lieberman, Charlotte. 2019. "Why You Procrastinate (It Has Nothing to Do with Self-Control)." *New York Times*, March 25.

Lincoln, Anne E., Stephanie Pincus, Janet Bandows Koster, and Phoebe S. Leboy. 2012. "The Matilda Effect in Science: Awards and Prizes in the US, 1990s and 2000s." *Social Studies of Science* 42(2):307–20.

Luker, Kristin. 2010. *Salsa Dancing into the Social Sciences: Research in an Age of Info-Glut.* Harvard University Press.

Lundine, Jamie, Ivy Lynn Bourgeault, Jocalyn Clark, and Dina Balabanova. 2018. "The Gendered System of Academic Publishing." *Lancet* 391(10132):1754–56.

Lunsford, Laura G. 2014. "Mentors, Tormentors, and No Mentors: Mentoring Scientists." *International Journal of Mentoring and Coaching in Education* 3(1):4–17.

Lunsford, Laura G., Vicki Baker, Kimberly A. Griffin, and W. Brad Johnson. 2013. "Mentoring: A Typology of Costs for Higher Education Faculty." *Mentoring & Tutoring: Partnership in Learning* 21(2):126–49.

Ma, Timmy, Karen E. Wood, Di Xu, Patrick Guidotti, Alessandra Pantano, and Natalia L. Komarova. 2018. "Admission Predictors for Success in a Mathematics Graduate Program." *ArXiv:1803.00595 [Math].*

MacBeth, Angus, and Andrew Gumley. 2012. "Exploring Compassion: A Meta-analysis of the Association between Self-Compassion and Psychopathology." *Clinical Psychology Review* 32(6):545–52.

MacNell, Lillian, Adam Driscoll, and Andrea N. Hunt. 2015. "What's in a Name: Exposing Gender Bias in Student Ratings of Teaching." *Innovative Higher Education* 40(4):291–303.

Madera, Juan M., Michelle R. Hebl, and Randi C. Martin. 2009. "Gender and Letters of Recommendation for Academia: Agentic and Communal Differences." *Journal of Applied Psychology* 94(6):1591–99.

Mankiw, N. G. 2019. "Reflections of a Textbook Author." https://scholar.harvard.edu/mankiw/publications/reflections-textbook-author.

Margolis, Eric. 2002. *The Hidden Curriculum in Higher Education.* Routledge.

Margolis, Eric, and Mary Romero. 1998. "'The Department Is Very Male, Very White, Very Old, and Very Conservative': The Functioning of the Hidden Curriculum in Graduate Sociology Departments." *Harvard Educational Review* 68(1):1–33.

Marsh, David. 2013. *For Who the Bell Tolls*. Guardian Faber.

Martin, Karin A. 1998. "Becoming a Gendered Body: Practices of Preschools." *American Sociological Review* 63(4):494–511.

Marwell, Gerald, and Ruth E. Ames. 1979. "Experiments on the Provision of Public Goods. I. Resources, Interest, Group Size, and the Free-Rider Problem." *American Journal of Sociology* 84(6):1335–60.

Mason, Mary Ann. 2009. "Role Models and Mentors." *Chronicle of Higher Education*, March 25.

Matthew, Patricia A. 2016. "What Is Faculty Diversity Worth to a University?" *Atlantic*, November 23.

McCloskey, Deirdre. 1999. *Economical Writing*. Waveland.

McCormick, Alexander C., and Chun-Mei Zhao. 2005. "Rethinking and Reframing the Carnegie Classification." *Change* 37(5):50–57.

McGregor, Loretta Neal, Damon E. Gee, and K. Elizabeth Posey. 2008. "I Feel Like a Fraud and It Depresses Me: The Relation between the Imposter Phenomenon and Depression." *Social Behavior and Personality* 36(1):43–48.

McKenzie, Lindsay. 2019. "A New Kind of 'Big Deal' for Elsevier and Carnegie Mellon University." *Inside Higher Ed*, November 22.

McWhorter, John. 2017. *Talking Back, Talking Black: Truths about America's Lingua Franca*. Bellevue Literary Press.

Medina, Jennifer, Katie Benner, and Kate Taylor. 2019. "Actresses, Business Leaders and Other Wealthy Parents Charged in U.S. College Entry Fraud." *New York Times*, March 12.

Merritt, Deborah Jones. 2000. "Scholarly Influence in a Diverse Legal Academy: Race, Sex, and Citation Counts." *Journal of Legal Studies* 29(S1):345–68.

Mettler, Suzanne. 2014. *Degrees of Inequality: How the Politics of Higher Education Sabotaged the American Dream*. Basic Books.

Milkman, Katherine L., Julia A. Minson, and Kevin G. M. Volpp. 2014. "Holding the Hunger Games Hostage at the Gym: An Evaluation of Temptation Bundling." *Management Science* 60(2):283–99.

Moneta-Koehler, Liane, Abigail M. Brown, Kimberly A. Petrie, Brent J. Evans, and Roger Chalkley. 2017. "The Limitations of the GRE in Predicting Success in Biomedical Graduate School." *PLOS ONE* 12(1):e0166742.

Moon, Margaret R. 2009. "The History and Role of Institutional Review Boards: A Useful Tension." *AMA Journal of Ethics* 11(4):311–16.

Morgan, Paul L., Jeremy Staff, Marianne M. Hillemeier, George Farkas, and Steven Maczuga. 2013. "Racial and Ethnic Disparities in ADHD Diagnosis from Kindergarten to Eighth Grade." *Pediatrics* 132(1):85–93.

Moss-Racusin, C. A., J. F. Dovidio, V. L. Brescoll, M. J. Graham, and J. Handelsman. 2012. "Science Faculty's Subtle Gender Biases Favor Male Students." *Proceedings of the National Academy of Sciences* 109(41):16474–79.

Musto, Michela. 2019. "Brilliant or Bad: The Gendered Social Construction of Exceptionalism in Early Adolescence." *American Sociological Review* 84(3):369–93.

Nadal, Kevin L., Katie E. Griffin, Yinglee Wong, Sahran Hamit, and Morgan Rasmus. 2014. "The Impact of Racial Microaggressions on Mental Health: Counseling Implications for Clients of Color." *Journal of Counseling & Development* 92(1):57–66.

National Academies of Sciences, Engineering, and Medicine. 2018. *Sexual Harassment of Women: Climate, Culture, and Consequences in Academic Sciences, Engineering, and Medicine*. National Academies Press.

———. 2019. *Reproducibility and Replicability in Science*. National Academies Press.

National Endowment for the Arts. 2003. *Design for Accessibility: A Cultural Administrator's Handbook*. National Assembly of State Arts Agencies.

National Institute of Allergy and Infectious Diseases. 2018. "When and How to Contact a Program Officer." www.niaid.nih.gov/grants-contracts/when-and-how -contact-program-officer.

National Science Foundation. 2018. *Doctorate Recipients from U.S. Universities 2018*. National Center for Science and Engineering Statistics. https://ncses.nsf.gov /pubs/nsf20301/.

Nature. 2020. "Editorial Criteria and Processes." www.nature.com/nature/for -authors/editorial-criteria-and-processes.

Nature Physics. 2007. "Elements of Style." 3(581). doi:10.1038/nphys724.

NCES. 2018. "The Condition of Education—Postsecondary Education— Postsecondary Students—Postbaccalaureate Enrollment—Indicator May (2018)." National Center for Education Statistics. https://nces.ed.gov/programs /coe/indicator_chb.asp.

Nettles, Michael T. 1990. "Success in Doctoral Programs: Experiences of Minority and White Students." *American Journal of Education* 98(4):494–522.

Neugeboren, Robert. 2005. *The Student's Guide to Writing Economics*. Routledge.

Newfield, Christopher. 2011. *Unmaking the Public University: The Forty-Year Assault on the Middle Class*. Repr. ed. Harvard University Press.

———. 2016. *The Great Mistake: How We Wrecked Public Universities and How We Can Fix Them*. Johns Hopkins University Press.

Okahana, Hironao, and Enyu Zhou. 2018. *Graduate Enrollment and Degrees: 2007 to 2017*. Council of Graduate Schools.

Oliver, Melvin, and Thomas M. Shapiro, eds. 2006. *Black Wealth / White Wealth: A New Perspective on Racial Inequality*. 2nd ed. Routledge.

Oliver, Pam. 2019. "Citing More Broadly." *Scatterplot*, December 6. https://scatter .wordpress.com/2019/12/06/citing-more-broadly.

O'Meara, Kerryann. 2016. "Whose Problem Is It? Gender Differences in Faculty Thinking about Campus Service." *Teachers College Record* 118(8):1–38.

———. 2018. "Ensuring Equity in Service Work." *Inside Higher Ed*, May 10.

Oswalt, Sara B., and Christina C. Riddock. 2007. "What to Do about Being Overwhelmed: Graduate Students, Stress and University Services." *College Student Affairs Journal* 27(1):24–44.

Owens, Deirdre Cooper. 2017. *Medical Bondage: Race, Gender, and the Origins of American Gynecology.* University of Georgia Press.

Ozlem, Sensoy, and Robin DiAngelo. 2017. "'We Are All for Diversity, but . . .': How Faculty Hiring Committees Reproduce Whiteness and Practical Suggestions for How They Can Change." *Harvard Educational Review* 87(4):557–80.

Pacheco-Vega, Raul. 2019. "Academic Writing (#AcWri)." www.raulpacheco.org /resources/academic-writing-acwri.

Paglis, Laura L., Stephen G. Green, and Talya N. Bauer. 2006. "Does Adviser Mentoring Add Value? A Longitudinal Study of Mentoring and Doctoral Student Outcomes." *Research in Higher Education* 47(4):451–76.

Parry, Marc. 2017. "Law Professor's New Book Puts Ethnography on Trial." *Chronicle of Higher Education*, December 15.

———. 2019. "Alice Goffman's First Book Made Her a Star. It Wasn't Enough to Get Her Tenure." *Chronicle of Higher Education*, June 6.

Paulson, Donald R. 1999. "Active Learning and Cooperative Learning in the Organic Chemistry Lecture Class." *Journal of Chemical Education* 76(8):1136.

Peach, Mark. 1994. "The Nonacademic Curriculum of the Japanese Preschool." *Childhood Education* 71(1):9–13.

Perry, Theresa, and Lisa D. Delpit. 1998. *The Real Ebonics Debate: Power, Language, and the Education of African-American Children.* Beacon.

Petriglieri, Jennifer. 2019. *Couples That Work: How Dual-Career Couples Can Thrive in Love and Work.* Harvard Business Press.

Pirtle, Whitney Laster. 2018. "Semester Plan Template." *TheSociologyPhDandMe*, August 19. https://thesociologyphdandme.wordpress.com/2018/08/19 /semester-plan-template.

Pomona College. 2019. "The Young Economist's Short Guide to Writing Economic Research." www.pomona.edu/administration/writing-center/student-resources /writing-humanities-and-social-sciences/young-economist%E2%80%99s-short -guide-writing-economic-research.

Posselt, Julie R. 2016. *Inside Graduate Admissions.* Harvard University Press.

Pugh, Allison J. 2011. "Distinction, Boundaries or Bridges? Children, Inequality and the Uses of Consumer Culture." *Poetics* 39(1):1–18.

Rank, Scott. 2015. *How to Finish Your Dissertation in Six Months, Even if You Don't Know What to Write.* Scholarpreneur.

Ray, Ranita. 2017. *The Making of a Teenage Service Class: Poverty and Mobility in an American City*. University of California Press.

Ray, Victor. 2019a. "A Theory of Racialized Organizations." *American Sociological Review* 84(1):26–53.

———. 2019b. "Academics Should Write for the Public for Political, Personal and Practical Reasons (Opinion)." *Conditionally Accepted*, May 17. www.insidehighered.com/advice/2019/05/17/academics-should-write-public-political-personal-and-practical-reasons-opinion.

———. 2019c. "Advice for Writing Effectively for the Public." *Conditionally Accepted*, July 12. www.insidehighered.com/advice/2019/07/12/advice-writing-effectively-public-opinion.

Reid, M. Jeanne, and James L. Moore. 2008. "College Readiness and Academic Preparation for Postsecondary Education: Oral Histories of First-Generation Urban College Students." *Urban Education* 43(2):240–61.

Reskin, Barbara F. 1993. "Sex Segregation in the Workplace." *Annual Review of Sociology* 19(1):241–70.

Resnick, Brian. 2018. "Social Science Replication Crisis: Studies in Top Journals Keep Failing to Replicate." *Vox*, August 27.

———. 2019. "The Costs of Academic Publishing Are Absurd. The University of California Is Fighting Back." *Vox*, March 1.

Resnick, Brian, and Julia Belluz. 2019. "Trump Might Help Free Science That's Locked behind Paywalls." *Vox*, December 19.

Rickford, John Russell, and Russell John Rickford. 2000. *Spoken Soul: The Story of Black English*. Wiley.

Rivera, Lauren A. 2011. "Ivies, Extracurriculars, and Exclusion: Elite Employers' Use of Educational Credentials." *Research in Social Stratification and Mobility* 29(1):71–90.

———. 2017. "When Two Bodies Are (Not) a Problem: Gender and Relationship Status Discrimination in Academic Hiring." *American Sociological Review* 82(6):1111–38.

Rockquemore, Kerry Ann. 2016a. "Advice to a White Professor about Mentoring Scholars of Color." *Inside Higher Ed*, February 17.

———. 2016b. "How to Be an Ally to Someone Experiencing Microaggressions." *Inside Higher Ed*, April 13.

———. 2016c. "How to Retain a Diverse Faculty." *Inside Higher Ed*, January 6.

Rojas, Fabio. 2011. *Grad Skool Rulz: Everything You Need to Know about Academia from Admissions to Tenure*. Fabio Rojas.

Romero, Mary. 1997. "Class-Based, Gendered and Racialized Institutions of Higher Education: Everyday Life of Academia from the View of Chicana Faculty." *Race, Gender & Class* 4(2):151–73.

Rose, David H., and Anne Meyer. 2002. *Teaching Every Student in the Digital Age: Universal Design for Learning*. Association for Supervision and Curriculum Development.

Rowland, Ashley, and Christina Szalinski. 2016. "Preparing Your Academic Chalk Talk." *ASCB*, May 13. www.ascb.org/careers/preparing-academic-chalk-talk.

Royal Historical Society. 2015. "ECH Publishing: Submitting to a Journal." https://royalhistsoc.org/submitting-to-a-journal/.

Rucks-Ahidiana, Zawadi. 2019a. "A Faculty Member Explains Why She Helps Students of Color Despite Warnings It Won't Help Her Get Tenure." *Inside Higher Ed*, July 19.

———. 2019b. "Nonwhite Faculty Face Significant Disadvantages on the Tenure Track." *Inside Higher Ed*, June 7.

———. 2019c. "Not relevant: Your non-white friends and romantic partners." *Twitter*. https://twitter.com/zra_research/status/1166041810545848320.

Schimel, Joshua. 2011. *Writing Science: How to Write Papers That Get Cited and Proposals That Get Funded*. Oxford University Press.

SciDevNet. 2008. "How Do I Write a Scientific Paper?—SciDev.Net." www.scidev.net/global/publishing/practical-guide/how-do-i-write-a-scientific-paper-.html.

Seamster, Louise, and Raphaël Charron-Chénier. 2017. "Predatory Inclusion and Education Debt: Rethinking the Racial Wealth Gap." *Social Currents* 4(3):199–207.

Senate Democrats. 2019. "Climate Committee to Hold Hearing on Dark Money and Climate Change." October 28. www.democrats.senate.gov/climate/hearings/climate-crisis-committee-to-hold-hearing-on-dark-money-and-climate-change.

Shaffer, Jeffrey. 2016. "5 Tips on Designing Colorblind-Friendly Visualizations." Tableau Software. www.tableau.com/about/blog/2016/4/examining-data-viz-rules-dont-use-red-green-together-53463.

Shrout, Patrick E., and Joseph L. Rodgers. 2018. "Psychology, Science, and Knowledge Construction: Broadening Perspectives from the Replication Crisis." *Annual Review of Psychology* 69(1):487–510.

Silvia, Paul J. 2019. *How to Write a Lot: A Practical Guide to Productive Academic Writing*. American Psychological Association.

Simmons, Joseph P., Leif D. Nelson, and Uri Simonsohn. 2011. "False-Positive Psychology: Undisclosed Flexibility in Data Collection and Analysis Allows Presenting Anything as Significant." *Psychological Science* 22(11):1359–66.

Sirois, Fuschia M. 2014. "Procrastination and Stress: Exploring the Role of Self-Compassion." *Self and Identity* 13(2):128–45.

———. 2015. "Is Procrastination a Vulnerability Factor for Hypertension and Cardiovascular Disease? Testing an Extension of the Procrastination-Health Model." *Journal of Behavioral Medicine* 38(3):578–89.

———. 2016. "Procrastination, Stress, and Chronic Health Conditions: A Temporal Perspective." In *Procrastination, Health, and Well-Being*, edited by F. M. Sirois and T. A. Pychyl, 67–92. Academic Press.

Sleeter, Christine E. 2012. "Confronting the Marginalization of Culturally Responsive Pedagogy." *Urban Education* 47(3):562–84.

Small, Mario Luis. 2017. *Someone to Talk To.* Oxford University Press.

Smith, I. E. 2016. "Minority vs. Minoritized." *Odyssey Online.* www.theodysseyonline.com/minority-vs-minoritize.

Smith, William A., Man Hung, and Jeremy D. Franklin. 2011. "Racial Battle Fatigue and the MisEducation of Black Men: Racial Microaggressions, Societal Problems, and Environmental Stress." *Journal of Negro Education* 80(1):63–82.

Sonnak, Carina, and Tony Towell. 2001. "The Impostor Phenomenon in British University Students: Relationships between Self-Esteem, Mental Health, Parental Rearing Style and Socioeconomic Status." *Personality and Individual Differences* 31(6):863–74.

Stivers, Abby, and Elizabeth Popp Berman. 2016. "Student Loans as a Pressure on U.S. Higher Education." In *The University under Pressure*, vol. 46. *Research in the Sociology of Organizations*, edited by Elizabeth Popp Berman and Catherine Paradeise, 129–60. Emerald.

Streib, Jessi. 2011. "Class Reproduction by Four Year Olds." *Qualitative Sociology* 34(2):337.

Stroebe, Wolfgang. 2016. "Why Good Teaching Evaluations May Reward Bad Teaching: On Grade Inflation and Other Unintended Consequences of Student Evaluations." *Perspectives on Psychological Science* 11(6):800–816.

Sue, Derald Wing, and Lisa Spanierman. 2020. *Microaggressions in Everyday Life.* 2nd ed. John Wiley.

Sullivan, Teresa A. 2014. "Greedy Institutions, Overwork, and Work-Life Balance." *Sociological Inquiry* 84(1):1–15.

Suneson, Grant. 2019. "College Endowment: Universities That Receive the Most Gifts, Funds." *USA Today*, March 28.

Supiano, Beckie. 2019. "This Professor Ends Class with a 'Hotwash,' a Technique Used by First Responders." *Chronicle of Higher Education*, July 25.

Teixeira, Pedro. 2016. "Two Continents Divided by the Same Trends? Reflections about Marketization, Competition, and Inequality in European Higher Education." In *The University under Pressure*, vol. 46. *Research in the Sociology of Organizations*, edited by Elizabeth Popp Berman and Catherine Paradeise, 489–508. Emerald.

Thoits, Peggy A. 2010. "Stress and Health: Major Findings and Policy Implications." *Journal of Health and Social Behavior* 51(1_suppl):S41–53.

Torpey, Elka. 2018. *Measuring the Value of Education: Career Outlook.* U.S. Bureau of Labor Statistics.

University of Wisconsin. 2019. "Planning and Writing a Grant Proposal: The Basics." *Writing Center.* https://writing.wisc.edu/handbook/assignments/grants-2.

U.S. News & World Report. 2019. "The Best Graduate Programs for Public Policy Analysis, Ranked." www.usnews.com/best-graduate-schools/top-public-affairs-schools/public-policy-analysis-rankings.

Van Cleve, Nicole Gonzalez. 2019. "Book Contracts: Lesson 1." *Twitter.* https://twitter
.com/nvancleve/status/1164546890215677953.

Van Noorden, Richard. 2013. "Open Access: The True Cost of Science Publishing."
Nature News 495(7442):426.

Villwock, Jennifer A., Lindsay B. Sobin, Lindsey A. Koester, and Tucker M. Harris.
2016. "Impostor Syndrome and Burnout among American Medical Students: A
Pilot Study." *International Journal of Medical Education* 7:364.

Waaijer, Cathelijn J. F., Christine Teelken, Paul F. Wouters, and Inge C. M. van der
Weijden. 2018. "Competition in Science: Links between Publication Pressure,
Grant Pressure and the Academic Job Market." *Higher Education Policy*
31(2):225–43.

Warren, John Robert. 2019. "How Much Do You Have to Publish to Get a Job in a
Top Sociology Department? Or to Get Tenure? Trends over a Generation."
Sociological Science 6:172–96.

Wilks, Scott E. 2008. "Resilience amid Academic Stress: The Moderating Impact of
Social Support among Social Work Students." *Advances in Social Work* 9(2):
106–25.

Williams, Meca R., Denise N. Brewley, R. Judith Reed, Dorothy Y. White, and
Rachel T. Davis-Haley. 2005. "Learning to Read Each Other: Black Female
Graduate Students Share Their Experiences at a White Research I Institution."
Urban Review 37(3):181–99.

Wohl, Michael J. A., Timothy A. Pychyl, and Shannon H. Bennett. 2010. "I Forgive
Myself, Now I Can Study: How Self-Forgiveness for Procrastinating Can Reduce
Future Procrastination." *Personality and Individual Differences* 48(7):803–8.

Woo, Erin. 2019. "'A Toxic Culture of Overwork': Inside the Graduate Student
Mental Health Crisis." *Stanford Daily*, March 13. www.stanforddaily.com/2019/03
/13/a-toxic-culture-of-overwork-inside-the-graduate-student-mental-health
-crisis.

Wren, David. 1999. "School Culture: Exploring the Hidden Curriculum." *Adolescence*
34(135):593–97.

Wylie, E. Caroline, Christine J. Lyon, and Laura Goe. 2009. "Teacher Professional
Development Focused on Formative Assessment: Changing Teachers, Changing
Schools." *ETS Research Report Series* 2009(1).

Yong, Ed. 2018. "Psychology's Replication Crisis Is Running Out of Excuses." *Atlantic*,
November 19.

Zambrana, Ruth Enid, Brianne A. Dávila, Michelle M. Espino, Lisa M. Lapeyrouse,
R. Burciaga Valdez, and Denise A. Segura. 2017. "Mexican American Faculty in
Research Universities: Can the Next Generation Beat the Odds?" *Sociology of
Race and Ethnicity* 3(4):458–73.

Zambrana, Ruth Enid, Rashawn Ray, Michelle M. Espino, Corinne Castro, Beth
Douthirt Cohen, and Jennifer Eliason. 2015. "'Don't Leave Us Behind': The

Importance of Mentoring for Underrepresented Minority Faculty." *American Educational Research Journal* 52(1):40–72.

Zhang, Olivia. 2019. "Trump Travel Ban Separates Students from Family." *Daily Illini,* April 30. https://dailyillini.com/features/2019/04/30/trump-travel-ban -separates-students-from-family.

Zhou, Larry. 2014. "Exclusive: Facebook Plans Event to Recruit Sociologists." *VentureBeat,* June 7. https://venturebeat.com/2014/06/07/exclusive-to-sell-ads-in -the-developing-world-facebook-is-hiring-sociologists.

INDEX

A NOTE ON THE TYPE

This book has been composed in Arno, an Old-style serif typeface in the classic Venetian tradition, designed by Robert Slimbach at Adobe.